# THE
# INSIDER'S
## COMPLETE GUIDE
### TO

# AP
# US HISTORY:
## THE
# ESSENTIAL
# CONTENT

LARRY KRIEGER

The Insider's Complete Guide To
AP US History:
The Essential Content

LARRY KRIEGER

ISBN: 978-0985291204

An INSIDER TEST PREP publication of Larry Prep LLC

Art Direction & Design by Station16 Creative (Station16 LLC)

For more Insider resources visit
www.InsiderTestPrep.com

# TABLE OF CONTENTS

# CHAPTER 11                                             57
## MAKING KEY COMPARISONS, 1492 - 1789

# CHAPTER 12                                             63
## THE FEDERALIST ERA, 1789 - 1800

# ABOUT THE AUTHOR

Larry Krieger earned a BA in history and an MAT in social studies education from the University of North Carolina at Chapel Hill. He also earned a MA in sociology at Wake Forest University.

Larry has taught urban, rural, and suburban students in a teaching career that began in 1970. During that time Larry prepared students for both the AP US History exam and the SAT II US History test. In 2004 and 2005 the College Board recognized Larry as one of America's most successful AP teachers.

Larry is the author of several US History, World History, and AP prep books that are used throughout the country. In addition, Larry is a renowned SAT teacher who is the author of The Essential 300 Words published by Insider Test Prep.

Larry is particularly proud of AP US History: The Essential Content. It contains a lifetime of key points, strategies, and tips that have helped almost all of his students score a 4 or 5 on the APUSH exam and above a 700 on the SAT II US History test.

# ACKNOWLEDGMENTS

Books do not write themselves. They require the help of a number of dedicated and creative people.

First and foremost, I would like to thank my wife Susan. Every chapter benefited from Susan's "close reads." I would also like to thank Jan Altman, Jacob Byrne, and Vinay Bhaskara for their invaluable advice and support. Special thanks to GauravJit "Raj" Singh who played an indispensable role in helping me create the series of Podcasts that accompany this book.

I would like to thank the creative team at Station16 in Atlanta for their hard work and dedication to producing a quality product. I would especially like to thank Annie Smith for her meticulous editing and fine eye for details.

# BOARD OF STUDENT ADVISORS

# PROLOGUE

Welcome to AP US History: The Essential Content. Our prep book is carefully designed to provide you with a focused, efficient, and thorough review of the key content you need to know to score a 4 or above on the APUSH exam and a 700 or above on the SAT II US History text. The Prologue begins by introducing you to the basic features of the APUSH exam and the SAT II US History test. We will then introduce you to the special approach and unique features that make AP US History: The Essential Content so distinctive.

# I. BASIC FEATURES OF THE APUSH EXAM

## THE MULTIPLE-CHOICE QUESTIONS

1. The APUSH exam begins with 80 multiple-choice questions. You are given 55 minutes to answer these questions. Each multiple-choice question is worth 1.125 points for a total of 90 points. These 90 points represent half of the 180 points on the APUSH exam.
2. The 80 multiple-choice questions are distributed into the following three broad chronological periods:

| | |
|---|---|
| · Pre-Columbian to 1789 | 20% or 16 questions |
| · 1790 to 1914 | 45% or 36 questions |
| · 1915 to Present | 35% or 28 questions |

3. The exam typically contains few if any questions before the founding of Jamestown in 1607. Recent tests have included one or two questions about important events and major demographic trends since the inauguration of President Reagan in 1981.
4. The 80 multiple-choice questions are distributed into the following four broad themes:

| | |
|---|---|
| · Political institutions, behavior, and public policy | 35% |
| · Social change, and cultural and intellectual developments | 40% |
| · Diplomacy and international relations | 15% |
| · Economic developments | 10% |

5. Beginning with the May 2011 exam, total scores on the multiple-choice section will be based on the number of correctly answered questions. Because the College Board will no longer deduct .25 points for each incorrect answer, be sure you answer all 80 multiple-choice questions!

# THE DOCUMENT–BASED ESSAY QUESTION (DBQ)

1. The DBQ is a special type of essay question. It asks you to interpret and use nine or ten brief primary source documents as part of your answer to a question on an important historic topic. The documents include excerpts from letters, speeches, diaries, party platforms, and Supreme Court decisions. The documents also often include maps, graphs, pictures, and political cartoons.

2. The DBQ begins with a mandatory 15-minute reading period. After reading the documents, deciding upon a thesis, and organizing your thoughts, you will have 45 minutes to write your essay.

3. The DBQ is scored on a 1-to-9 scale. Each point on this scale is worth 4.5 points. So a perfect score on the DBQ is worth 40.5 points. The DBQ is worth 22.5 percent of your total exam score.

4. Test readers expect you to incorporate outside information into your essay. An essay that relies solely upon the documents will probably not receive a score above a 4.

# THE FREE–RESPONSE ESSAY QUESTIONS

1. The APUSH exam allocates the final 70 minutes to free-response essay questions. The free-response questions are grouped into two sets. The first set contains two essay questions that focus on pre-Civil War topics. The second set contains two essay questions that focus on post-Civil War topics. You must select one question from each group.

2. The free-response essays are scored on a 1-to-9 scale. Each point is worth 2.75 points. So a perfect score on a free-response essay is worth 24.75 points. The two free-response essays are worth a combined total of 49.50 points or 27.5 percent of your total exam score.

3. The free-response questions deal with significant historical topics and themes. However, it is important to note that none of the four essay questions will deal exclusively with the period after 1980.

# THE APUSH SCALE

1. APUSH exams are scored on the following 1 to 5 scale:

| SCORE | QUALIFICATION |
| --- | --- |
| 5 | Extremely well qualified |
| 4 | Well qualified |
| 3 | Qualified |
| 2 | Possibly qualified |
| 1 | No recommendation |

Many colleges use APUSH scores to exempt students from introductory coursework. Each college's policy is different. However, most colleges require a minimum score of 3 or 4 to receive course credit.

Here is a summary of the 2011 APUSH results:

| SCORE | PERCENTAGE OF TEST-TAKERS |
|:-----:|:-------------------------:|
| 5 | 11.1% |
| 4 | 20.8% |
| 3 | 21.0% |
| 2 | 26.7% |
| 1 | 20.5% |

2. The APUSH scale varies with each exam. Here is the scale for the AP United States History 2006 Released Exam. Note that this scale has been adjusted to reflect that points are no longer subtracted for incorrect answers.

| SCORE RANGE | AP SCORE | MINIMUM % RIGHT |
|:-----------:|:--------:|:---------------:|
| 111 – 180 | 5 | 61.6% |
| 91 - 110 | 4 | 50.5% |
| 76 - 90 | 3 | 42.2% |
| 57 - 75 | 2 | 31.6% |
| 0 - 56 | 1 | 31.5% |

# II. BASIC FEATURES OF THE SAT II US HISTORY TEST

## QUESTIONS

1. The SAT II US History test consists of 90 multiple-choice questions. You are given 60 minutes to answer these questions.

2. The 90 multiple-choice questions are distributed into the following three broad chronological periods:

| | |
|---|---|
| · Pre-Columbian to 1789 | 20% or 18 questions |
| · 1790 – 1898 | 40% or 36 questions |
| · 1899 – Present | 40% or 36 questions |

3. The SAT II US History test typically contains one or two questions on topics before the founding of Jamestown in 1607 and three or four questions about important events and demographic trends since the inauguration of President Reagan in 1981.

4. The 90 multiple-choice questions are distributed into the following five broad thematic areas:

| | |
|---|---|
| · Political history | 31 – 35% |
| · Economic history | 13 – 17% |
| · Social history | 20 – 24% |
| · Intellectual and cultural history | 13 – 17% |
| · Foreign policy | 13 – 17% |

# SCORING

5. Each multiple-choice question is worth 1 point. So 90 is a perfect score.
6. The College Board still subtracts .25 points for each wrong answer. For example, if you correctly answer 66 questions and miss 24, your raw score will be 66 minus 6 or 60. No points are awarded for unanswered questions.
7. The *College Board's Official Study Guide for all SAT Subject Tests* includes a sample US History test. The scale on page 91 indicates that a raw score of 79 to 90 will translate into an 800. Here are several benchmark scores from this scale:

| RAW SCORE | SCALED SCORE |
|:---:|:---:|
| 90 | 800 |
| 85 | 800 |
| 80 | 800 |
| 75 | 770 |
| 70 | 730 |
| 65 | 700 |
| 60 | 670 |
| 55 | 650 |
| 50 | 620 |
| 45 | 600 |
| 40 | 570 |
| 35 | 540 |
| 30 | 520 |
| 25 | 490 |
| 20 | 460 |
| 15 | 440 |
| 10 | 410 |
| 5 | 390 |

This scale appears to be very generous. It is important to point out that many students are now reporting that recent tests use a much harsher scale.

# III. RETHINKING HOW TO PREPARE FOR THE APUSH EXAM AND THE SAT II US HISTORY TEST

## THE TRADITIONAL APPROACH

8. The College Board recommends that you prepare for the APUSH exam by taking a rigorous AP course, mastering the content in a college textbook, and reading a wide variety of primary source documents. Many AP prep books and websites urge students to prepare for the exam by studying "Giant AP Review Packets" featuring long lists of people, terms, and events. Some of the lists have well over 1,000 items!

9. The College Board recommends that you prepare for the SAT II US History text by taking a challenging class, studying hard, and learning as much of the classroom material as possible. This "classroom material" often includes long review packets that resemble the APUSH lists.

## A NEW LOOK AT THE TRADITIONAL APPROACH

1. The traditional approach assumes that the best way to prepare for the APUSH exam and the SAT II US History test is to master the content in your textbook by literally studying everything. Is this really the most effective way to prepare for these tests? Take another look at the AP Score Range chart on page XXV. It is very important to note that you can earn a 5 on the APUSH exam by correctly answering 61.6 percent of the questions. In order to be totally safe, let's push the level up to 66.67 or two-thirds correct. This means that if you correctly answer 53 of the 80 multiple-choice questions and average a 6 on your DBQ and free-response questions you will earn a 5! Amazingly, you can earn a 4 by correctly answering just 40 multiple-choice questions and scoring a 4 or 5 on your essays.

2. Now take another look at the SAT II US History scale on page XXVI. It is important to note that you can earn an 800 by correctly answering 80 or 88.8 percent of the 90 questions. You can earn a 700 by correctly answering just 72.2 percent of the questions!

3. This analysis convincingly reveals that you do NOT need to master your entire textbook to achieve high scores. But, if you don't study everything, what should you study? An exhaustive analysis of APUSH exams and SAT II US History tests reveals that the questions on both of these tests cluster around a common group of key topics. Better yet, these topical clusters are not a secret. They are clearly listed in the "Topic Outline" published in each annual edition of the College Board's United States History Course Description booklet. The Topic Outline contains 28 chronologically arranged topics and 135 subtopics. It is important to stress that every question on the APUSH exam and SAT II US History text is derived from the Topic Outline.

4. The Topic Outline is not an encyclopedic list of facts, people, terms, and events. The outline is in fact very selective. It ignores explorers, generals, specific places, foreign leaders, Watergate burglars, and dates. It also excludes most Indian tribes, battles, presidents, and Supreme Court cases. Instead, it stresses key terms, significant events,

African American history, women's history, demographic trends, and a select group of landmark acts of Congress and benchmark Supreme Court cases. This finding is equally true for both the APUSH exam and the SAT II US History test.

5. The DBQ and free-response essay topics are also derived from the Topic Outline. For example, the Topic Outline subpoint on "The Role of African Americans in the Civil War" generated the 2009 Form B DBQ on this topic. Similarly, the Topic Outline subpoint on the "creation of a national market economy" generated a 2008 free-response essay question on this subject.

# IV. A BOLD NEW BOOK

## A NEW SELECTIVE APPROACH

1. The traditional approach of preparing for the APUSH exam and the SAT II US History test by studying a giant list of historic information is clearly inefficient and unnecessary.

2. Insider Test Prep advocates a new selective approach that incorporates the following two key principles:
   - Ignore topics that rarely if ever generate questions.
   - Focus on topical clusters that generate the overwhelming majority of the questions.

3. Here's an example of how our selective approach works. Many students attempt to memorize 60 or more Supreme Court cases and famous trials. In reality, only about 20 Supreme Court cases and famous trials generate 95 percent of the questions on this topic. But what about the other 5 percent?
   - First and foremost, you don't need to know these miscellaneous cases to score a 4 or 5 on the APUSH exam or a 700+ on the SAT II US History test. Never forget that you only need to correctly answer two-thirds of the APUSH questions to score a 5 and 72 percent of the SAT II US History questions to score a 700.
   - Second, trying to study for randomly tested items will force you to memorize a very long list of Supreme Court cases. This is clearly a waste of valuable study time.

## UNIQUE FEATURES OF AP US HISTORY: THE ESSENTIAL CONTENT

*AP US History: The Essential Content* is based upon Insider Test Prep's selective approach to studying for both the APUSH exam and the SAT II US History test. Here is a brief summary our book's unique features:

### 1. UNIQUE CHRONOLOGICAL CHAPTERS
- *AP US History: The Essential Content* contains 40 chronological chapters. We begin with a chapter on "Spain and the New World, 1492 - 1700 and conclude with a chapter on "Key Events and Demographic Trends,1981 - 2000.
- Each of our chronological chapters is based upon a key period of time or historic theme identified in the College Board's Topic Outline.

## 2. UNIQUE MAKING KEY COMPARISON CHAPTERS

- Recent APUSH exams have included a significant number of free-response questions asking students to make comparisons between events, peoples, colonies, geographic regions, and social movements.
- *AP US History: The Essential Content* contains 4 chapters that provide clear and succinct comparisons of 20 frequently tested topics. For example, Chapter 35 includes a comparison of the goals and programs of the Populists and the Progressives.

## 3. UNIQUE SELECTION OF TOPICS

- Each chapter is divided into a highly focused set of historical topics. These topics examine key events, issues, people, terms, quotes, and Supreme Court cases that have generated significant clusters of questions.
- Many of our topics focus special attention on the causes and consequences of key events. These topics use a unique organization structure that examines three questions: What happened? Why did the event happen? And why should you remember the event? For example, Topic 97 on the Seneca Falls Convention begins with a brief summary of what happened at the convention. The topic then explores the events that led Elizabeth Cady Stanton and Lucretia Mott to organize the Seneca Falls Convention. And finally, the topic concludes with a discussion of the consequences of this watershed meeting. This unique structure will prepare you for multiple-choice questions that typically ask you to identify what happened at an event, why it happened, and what were its consequences.
- Many topics also focus special attention on key quotes. Both the APUSH exam and the SAT II US History test include a number of multiple-choice questions that ask you to identify or analyze a quote. These questions are among the most missed items on these tests. We have addressed this problem by creating special topics that focus on the most frequently asked quotes. The topics place the quote in its historic setting and then explain its significance. For example, Topic 12 focuses on John Winthrop's famous "City Upon a Hill" sermon. The topic first identifies John Winthrop. It then explains that this famous quote expresses Winthrop's belief that the Puritan colonists had a special pact with God to build a model Christian society. The quote thus represents the first expression of American Exceptionalism.

## 4. UNIQUE SIDEBAR STUDY TIPS

- Our Insider Test Prep team has taught thousands of US History students. We have devoted countless hours preparing our students for the APUSH exam and the SAT II US History test. This experience has given us unique insights into how to prepare students for these tests.
- Many pages contain sidebar study tips. These tips often specifically tell you what to ignore and what to emphasize. For example, the tip on *Marbury v. Madison* recommends that you ignore the details of the case and focus on the definition of judicial review.

## 5. UNIQUE USE OF AP CENTRAL

- The College Board's AP Central website is a treasure trove of valuable information. The APUSH section contains all of the DBQ and free-response questions from 1999 to the present. But this is only the beginning of the treasures that can be discovered at this site. AP Central also provides a high, medium, and low sample essay for each DBQ and each free-response question. In addition, there are often very useful information sheets that provide detailed time lines and lists of key points.

- AP Central is indisputably an extremely valuable source of authoritative information. Nonetheless, AP prep books have almost totally ignored the site. But we didn't! *AP US History: The Essential Content* is the first prep book to carefully study and utilize the vast resources on AP Central. We have shared our findings in three ways:

- First, our tips include references to specific test questions and even to specific essays you should read and study.

- Second, we have used the AP Central information sheets to enrich our narrative with insights prized by the test readers.

- Third, we have used our study of the top sample essays to inform our discussion of how to write outstanding DBQ and free-response essays.

## 6. UNIQUE COLLECTION OF KEY TERMS

- Prep books and websites often feature lists containing hundreds of terms. The compilers of these lists solemnly tell you to learn each term on their list. Unfortunately, most of the terms on these prodigious lists have little or no chance of appearing on either the APUSH exam or the SAT II US History test.

- *AP US History: The Essential Content* takes a very different approach. We have identified 65 regularly tested key terms. The narrative in our chronological chapters carefully defines each of these terms. We devote special topics to particularly important terms such as mercantilism (Topic 22) and Transcendentalism (Topic 100). And finally, our Glossary provides concise definitions for each term.

## 7. UNIQUE USE OF SAT VOCABULARY

- A large number of the students who take the APUSH exam and the SAT II US History test also take the PSAT and the SAT. Needless to say, vocabulary words generate a significant number of answers on both of these tests. Having a rich descriptive vocabulary can be the difference between an average score and a high score.

- Insider Test Prep publishes a very popular vocabulary book entitled *The Essential 300 Words*. We have taken the vocabulary from this book and incorporated it into our ongoing narrative. This way you are simultaneously preparing for two College Board tests at the same time!

## 8. UNIQUE ANNOTATED DBQ AND FREE-RESPONSE ESSAYS

- Most prep books are content to offer well-meaning tips on how to write DBQ and free-response essays. These tips tell you what to do without demonstrating how to do it.

- *AP US History: The Essential Content* takes a very different approach. We have carefully read and analyzed over 250 sample essays published on AP Central. This study has yielded a number of important insights that can turn an average score into a high score. Our special chapters on the DBQ and free-response essays provide carefully annotated sample essays that teach you how to write a sophisticated thesis and support it with well-chosen historic examples.

## 9. UNIQUE COLLECTION OF PREMIUM PODCASTS

- AP US History: The Essential Content includes a supplemental set of 50 Podcasts. The Podcasts are identified by a special logo in the margin of designated pages. For an example, see page 9 for the logo for Bacon's Rebellion. See page 430 for a full list of all 50 Podcasts.
- The Podcasts can be found by going to our **InsiderTestPrep.com** website. Several Podcasts will also be posted on our Facebook page (**facebook.com/insidertestprep**).
- The Podcasts enable Mr. Krieger to be your personal teacher. Each 2 - 3 minute Podcast focuses on a key event, person, or Supreme Court case. Mr. Krieger explains why the topic is important and how it is used on the APUSH exam.

# V. A THREE TIERED STUDY PLAN

The APUSH exam and the SAT II US History test both require a well-organized study plan. *AP US History: The Essential Content* provides you with a carefully organized study plan that includes long-term, mid-term, and short-term review materials. Our three tiered approach will help guide and organize your preparation.

## LONG–TERM MATERIALS

1. Our 40 chronological chapters and 4 making comparisons chapters are designed to provide you with a complete and focused review of everything you need to know to achieve high scores on the APUSH exam and the SAT II US History test. All important material has been included and all unimportant material has been excluded.
2. Our DBQ and free-response chapters have been designed to provide you with a complete guide for how to write outstanding essays. Both chapters include annotated examples that explain key techniques.
3. We recommend that you begin studying our long-term materials 3 to 4 weeks before the test day.

## MID–TERM MATERIALS

1. Each of our 40 chronological chapters opens with a numbered list of Essential Points. This is not a random collection of information. The points have been carefully selected to cover key topics that generate significant clusters of questions.
2. We recommend that you begin reviewing our Essential Points about 7 to 10 days before the test date.

# SHORT–TERM MATERIALS

1. Our book contains a special short-term review section called "The Drive for Five!" This section contains 20 special Top 10 lists of key points you absolutely, positively have to know. For example, we have a concise list of the Top 10 African American leaders and the Top 10 Women Reformers.

2. The Drive for Five section concludes with a unique autobiographic essay that links events in my life to key topics tested on the APUSH exam. I hope this personal story will provide you with vivid examples that will help you see the intersection of biography and history.

3. *AP US History: The Essential Content* concludes with 100 practice multiple-choice questions. These questions are designed to give you an opportunity to apply your knowledge to realistic AP questions.

4. We recommend that you begin studying our short-term review materials about 3 days before the test date.

# GOOD LUCK!

I have taught US History students for over 30 years. This book contains a lifetime of key points, strategies, and tips. Almost all of my students have scored 4's and 5's on the APUSH exam and above a 700 on the SAT II US History test. You will too! I hope you enjoy using *AP US History: The Essential Content* as much as I enjoyed writing it. Good luck!

# CHAPTER 1
# SPAIN AND THE NEW WORLD
# 1492 – 1700

## ESSENTIAL POINTS

*agriculture*

1. Pre-Columbian peoples learned how to domesticate *Maize* corn but did not invent wheeled vehicles.

2. The ~~Iroquois~~ Confederacy constituted the most important and powerful Native American political alliance.

3. The Spanish defeated and overthrew Aztec and Inca rulers who led centralized governments.

*disease on Natives↓* ⊗

4. European diseases facilitated the Spanish conquest by causing a catastrophic decline in the Native American population.

5. The **COLUMBIAN EXCHANGE** refers to the exchange of plants and animals between Europe and the New World following Columbus's discovery of America in 1492.

*Columbian exchange
Europe ⇌ New World trade*

6. The Spanish exploited the Indians in New Mexico. Led by Popé, the Pueblo briefly drove the Spaniards out of New Mexico. *(12 yrs; till 1692)*

## TOPIC 1
# KEY POINTS ABOUT PRE-COLUMBIAN NATIVE AMERICANS

### 1. PRE-COLUMBIAN NATIVE AMERICANS
- domesticated maize, tomatoes, and potatoes
- created a mathematically based calendar *math & science ✓*
- constructed irrigation systems *agriculture ✓*
- built multi-family dwellings
- lived in cities inhabited by 100,000 or more people
- practiced a division of labor based upon gender
- did NOT develop wheeled vehicles *transportation*
- did NOT develop water wheels
- did NOT have a tradition of private property rights

### 2. NATIVE AMERICANS IN NORTH AMERICA
- Eastern Woodland tribes lived in village communities and had agricultural economies based upon the domestication of corn.
- The Iroquois Confederacy constituted the most important and powerful North American political alliance. The confederacy ended generations of tribal warfare and formed the most important North American political organization to confront the colonists. The Iroquois lived in permanent settlements.
- The Anasazis of the Southwest were a sedentary (living in one area, not migratory) agricultural people who build elaborate pueblos.
- Tribes in the Pacific Northwest relied on hunting and fishing for food.

## INSIDER TIP
SAT II tests often include a question about the achievements of Pre-Columbian Native Americans. In contrast, APUSH test writers typically limit their coverage of this topic to a question about the Iroquois Confederacy.

## TOPIC 2
# THE SPANISH CONQUEST

### 1. CHRISTOPHER COLUMBUS
- Hoped to discover new a new trade route to Asia.
- Set the pattern for future Spanish explorers and conquistadores. Columbus was very ethnocentric (believing in the superiority of one's own ethnic group)

and saw no reason to respect or learn about the cultures of the Native Americans he encountered. Instead, Columbus proposed to Christianize the indigenous (native) peoples, exploit their labor, and teach them to speak Spanish.

*{ Americanize natives*

## 2. THE CONQUISTADORES
- Hernan Cortes conquered the Aztecs.
- Francisco Pizarro conquered the Incas.
- Both Cortes and Pizarro defeated and overthrew rulers who led centralized governments.
- Advanced weapons, horses, ruthless tactics, and diseases enabled the conquistadores to topple the Aztec and Inca empires.

## 3. THE ROLE OF DISEASES
- Native Americans lacked resistance to European diseases such as smallpox, influenza, and measles.
- Old World diseases caused a catastrophic decline in the Native American population.

*{ Native Deaths Pop↓*

## 4. FOLLOWING THE COLLAPSE OF THE AZTEC EMPIRE, THE SPANISH RENAMED THE REGION NEW SPAIN.

## INSIDER TIP
Most APUSH texts focus on the Spanish while ignoring the Portuguese. It is important to remember that the Portuguese, led by Prince Henry the Navigator, were the first to conduct regular maritime expeditions in the South Atlantic.

# TOPIC 3
# KEY FACTS ABOUT NEW SPAIN

1. Spanish imperial objectives included enriching their national treasury, converting the native population to Christianity, enhancing Spanish prestige, and using New World precious metals to dominate Europe. The Spanish did NOT attempt to create New World markets for manufactured goods.
2. The Spanish discovered and mined rich deposits of gold and silver. For example, between 1500 and 1650 New World mines produced an estimated 16,000 tons of silver and 200 tons of gold.
3. The Spanish began the COLUMBIAN EXCHANGE of plants and animals between Europe and the New World. For example, the Spanish first introduced horses and gunpowder to the New World. At the same time, New

*trade*

## INSIDER TIP

Recent APUSH exams have placed increased emphasis upon the Spanish Southwest. The 2000 exam included a free-response question asking students to analyze the cultural and economic responses of the Spanish to the Indians of North America. The 2003B exam included a free-response question asking students to discuss how the Pueblo Revolt (1680) reflected social tensions in the Spanish Southwest. And the 2008 exam included a free-response question asking students to describe the relationship between American Indians and European colonists in the Spanish Southwest.

World crops such as corn, potatoes, and tomatoes enriched the European diet and lengthened average lifespans.

4. Spanish rulers were autocratic monarchs determined to maintain tight personal control over their American possessions. Spanish rulers rewarded local officials by granting them villages and control over native labor. Known as the ENCOMIENDA system, this practice cruelly exploited Indian laborers. The Spanish missionary Bartolome de Las Casas branded the encomienda system, "a moral pestilence invented by Satan."

5. The Catholic Church sent missionaries to convert the native populations. Both the Spanish church and royal government approved intermarriage between the colonists and native peoples. Because of the frequency of intermarriage, the people of New Spain demonstrated greater tolerance of racial differences than the English settlers in North America.

6. By the middle of the 16th century, the Spanish built flourishing cities and towns and totally dominated millions of Native Americans. It is interesting to note that the Spanish founded universities in Mexico City and Peru in 1551, eighty-five years before the Puritans founded Harvard.

7. The Spanish were the first to colonize Florida. They built a fortress at St. Augustine in 1565 to protect the sea-lanes to the Caribbean.

## TOPIC 4
# THE SPANISH SOUTHWEST

1. The Spanish reluctantly concluded that the rich deposits of gold and silver found in Mexico and Peru did not exist north of the Rio Grande River.

2. As the Spanish slowly expanded northward they established permanent settlements in what is now New Mexico. By 1630, 3,000 Spaniards lived in New Mexico.

3. The Spanish used religion as an effective instrument to exercise colonial control. Franciscan missionaries established Catholic missions where they imposed Catholicism on the Native population.

4. The Spanish used the encomienda system to exploit the Pueblos and other Native American peoples.

5. The Franciscan friars and Spanish political officials forced the Pueblos to pay tribute, work on encomiendas, and convert to Christianity.

- In 1680, a charismatic (dynamic) Pueblo leader named Popé organized a widespread rebellion known as the Pueblo Revolt.

- The Pueblo rebels killed over 400 Spanish settlers and destroyed all the Catholic churches.

- The Spanish regained control over New Mexico in 1692. They then worked to create a mixed Indian and Spanish culture that continued to be dominated by Spanish officials responsible to the king.

PODCAST 1.1
THE PUEBLO REVOLT, 1680

**CHAPTER 2**
# THE CHESAPEAKE COLONIES, 1607 – 1754

## ESSENTIAL POINTS

1. Jamestown was founded by a **JOINT-STOCK** company for the purpose of making a profit.

2. Chesapeake Bay tobacco planters initially used indentured servants imported from England.

3. Bacon's Rebellion exposed tensions between poor former indentured servants and the wealthy tidewater gentry. It formed a key link in the chain of events that led planters to replace indentured servants with slaves imported from Africa.

4. A combination of geographic, economic, and social factors enabled slavery to take root and grow in the Southern colonies. A small but powerful group of wealthy planters dominated Southern society.

5. The Stono Rebellion was the first major slave rebellion in the South. The slaves hoped to reach Spanish-controlled Florida where they would be granted their freedom.

*Bacon's Reb. involved indentured servants; not slaves → led to slavery*

## TOPIC 5
# KEY FACTS ABOUT THE CHESAPEAKE COLONIES

## INSIDER TIP

APUSH exams now include a number of questions about the economic role of key colonial crops. Do not neglect the role played by rice and indigo. Colonists in South Carolina benefited from the knowledge of Africans about the cultivation of rice. By the mid-18th century, rice was the most important crop in South Carolina. Highly prized as a blue dye, indigo produced one-third of South Carolina's exports prior to the Revolutionary War. It is important to note that indigo was less labor intensive than tobacco and rice.

1. Founding overseas colonies required unprecedented (without prior example) amounts of capital. English merchants formed JOINT-STOCK companies to maximize profits and minimize risks. In a joint-stock company investors share the profits and losses in proportion to the amount they invest.
2. Virginia was financed by a joint-stock company for the express purpose of making a profit. *looked only after profit*
3. Religion played a minor role in the founding of Virginia.
4. During its first decade, the Jamestown settlement experienced a very high mortality rate.
5. The scarcity of women and the high rate of men's mortality strengthened the socioeconomic status of women in the Chesapeake colonies.
6. Virginia's House of Burgesses was the first representative legislative assembly in British North America.
7. Lord Baltimore founded Maryland as a refuge for his fellow Roman Catholics. The primary purpose of the Act of Religious Toleration (1649) was to protect Catholics in Maryland from religious persecution by the Protestants.

## TOPIC 6
# THE IMPORTANCE OF TOBACCO

1. Tobacco enabled the Chesapeake Bay colonies to become economically viable (possible, feasible).
2. The profitable cultivation of tobacco created a demand for a large and inexpensive labor force.
3. Chesapeake Bay planters initially used indentured servants imported from England.
4. The planters began to replace the indentured servants with slave labor imported from Africa in the late 1600s.
5. Tobacco was the most valuable cash crop produced in the Southern colonies until the invention of the cotton gin in 1793.

## TOPIC 7
# INDENTURED SERVANTS

1. Between 1607 and 1676 indentured servants comprised the chief source of agricultural labor in the Chesapeake colonies of Virginia and Maryland.
2. The system of indentured labor gave English workers an opportunity to improve their lives in America.
3. Planters used the HEADRIGHT SYSTEM to attract more settlers to Virginia. Under this system, planters received 50 acres for each person (or head) they brought to the colony.
4. Indentured servants faced difficult conditions. They could have their labor bought, willed, and attached for debt. Women serving as indentured servants had to remain unmarried until they completed their indenture.

## TOPIC 8
# BACON'S REBELLION, 1676

### 1. WHAT HAPPENED?
- Led by Nathaniel Bacon, land hungry freemen in Virginia rebelled against the arbitrary rule of Governor Berkeley.
- Bacon's discontented followers challenged Berkeley's power and burned down Jamestown.
- Bacon's sudden death (from dysentery) enabled Berkeley to crush the now leaderless rebels.

### 2. WHAT CAUSED BACON'S REBELLION?
- Small farmers (often called yeomen) opposed Governor Berkeley's policy of favoring wealthy planters and protecting Indian tribes engaged in the lucrative (profitable) fur trade.
- Yeomen farmers were frustrated by falling tobacco prices, rising taxes, and dwindling opportunities to purchase fertile land near navigable rivers.

### 3. WHY SHOULD YOU REMEMBER BACON'S REBELLION?
- Bacon's Rebellion exposed tensions between poor former indentured servants and the wealthy tidewater gentry.

PODCAST 2.1
BACON'S REBELLION

- Bacon's Rebellion persuaded planters to replace troublesome indentured servants with slaves imported from Africa. It thus formed a key link in the chain of events that led planters to begin what a later generation would call the South's "peculiar institution."

# TOPIC 9
# THE GROWTH OF SLAVERY IN THE SOUTHERN COLONIES

## 1. GEOGRAPHIC FACTORS

- Fertile land, a warm climate, and a long growing season enabled planters to grow tobacco, rice, and indigo as cash crops.
- Numerous navigable rivers provided convenient routes for transporting goods to ports such as Norfolk, Charleston, and Savannah.

## 2. ECONOMIC FACTORS

- Tobacco and other cash crops required a large supply of inexpensive labor. The spread of tobacco cultivation beyond the Chesapeake colonies created additional demand for slave labor.
- As the English Civil War ended and economic conditions improved, the number of people willing to become indentured servants sharply declined.
- Indentured servants proved to be both unreliable and rebellious. Following Bacon's Rebellion (1676), planters began to replace indentured servants with imported African slaves.

## 3. SOCIAL FACTORS

- By the early 1700s, slavery was legally established in all of the colonies. By the mid 1700s, slaves comprised about 40 percent of the South's population.
- A small but powerful group of wealthy planters dominated Southern society.
- Although the majority of white families in the South did not own slaves, they did aspire to become slave owners.
- Impoverished (very poor) whites felt superior to black slaves thus providing further support for the slave system.

## INSIDER TIP
The development of the slave system marked a watershed (critical, fateful) event in colonial history. Both the 2011 and the 2001 APUSH exams included free-response questions asking students to evaluate the role played by geographic, economic, and social factors in the origins and development of slavery in Britain's North American colonies. For a particularly good essay on this topic go to AP Central and see Essay AAA Question 2 on the 2001 exam. The essay illustrates the characteristic features of a Level 9 free-response answer

- Few seventeenth and early eighteenth century white colonists questioned human bondage as morally unacceptable.

## TOPIC 10
# THE STONO REBELLION, 1739

### 1. WHAT HAPPENED?
- The Stono Rebellion took place near the Stono River in South Carolina.
- The rebellion began when about 20 enslaved Africans killed two storekeepers and seized a supply of guns and ammunition. The rebels gathered new recruits and burned seven plantations killing 22 – 25 whites.
- The local militia finally suppressed the rebellion following a battle in which 20 whites and 44 slaves were killed.

### 2. WHAT CAUSED THE STONO REBELLION?
- Slaves comprised the majority of South Carolina's population.
- The slaves hoped to reach Spanish-controlled Florida where they would be granted their freedom.

### 3. WHY SHOULD YOU REMEMBER THE STONO REBELLION?
- The South Carolina legislature enacted strict laws prohibiting slaves from assembling in groups, earning money, and learning to read.
- The rebellion highlighted the growing tensions in colonial society between slaves and their owners.

PODCAST 2.2
THE STONO
REBELLION, 1739

# CHAPTER 3
# THE NEW ENGLAND COLONIES, 1620 – 1754

## ESSENTIAL POINTS

1. The Puritans did not settle in New England to make a profit. They were Calvinists who believed in a close relationship between church and state.

2. John Winthrop's "City Upon a Hill" sermon expressed his belief that the Puritans had a special pact with God to build a model Christian society.

3. Unlike the early Chesapeake colonies, the Puritans migrated in families and thus did not have a shortage of women. The Puritans had a longer life expectancy that did the Chesapeake colonists.

4. Roger Williams and Anne Hutchinson challenged the religious authority of the Puritan leaders. Williams advocated religious toleration and the complete separation of church and state. Hutchinson questioned the subordinate role of women and denied that only the clergy could interpret scripture.

5. The **HALFWAY COVENANT** responded to the decline of religious zeal among second generation Puritans by easing requirements for church membership.

INSIDER TIP
Don't expect to see multiple-choice questions about the *Mayflower*, Plymouth Rock, Squanto, or the first Thanksgiving. Instead focus on the significance of the Mayflower Compact as a first step toward self-government.

PODCAST 3.1
JOHN WINTHROP'S "CITY UPON A HILL" SERMON

## TOPIC 11
# KEY FACTS ABOUT THE PILGRIMS

1. The Pilgrims were Separatists who wanted to sever all ties with the Church of England.
2. The Pilgrims arrived in America without a royal charter. To ensure an orderly government, 41 men signed an agreement known as the Mayflower Compact pledging to "combine ourselves together into a civil body politick." Their decision to make political decisions based upon the will of the people established an important precedent (example) for self-government in the British colonies.

## TOPIC 12
# KEY QUOTE – JOHN WINTHROP'S "CITY UPON A HILL" SERMON

### 1. THE SETTING
- The Puritans were Protestants who wanted to reform or "purify" the Church of England.
- In 1630, John Winthrop led a fleet of 11 ships and 700 Puritans destined to found the Massachusetts Bay Colony in New England.
- While on board the flagship *Arabella*, Winthrop preached a sermon describing his expectations for the new Puritan colony.

### 2. THE QUOTE
- "For we must consider that we shall be as a city upon a hill, the eyes of all people are upon us. So that if we shall deal falsely with our God in this work we shall have undertaken, and so cause Him to withdraw His present help from us, we shall be made a story and a by-word through the world."

### 3. SIGNIFICANCE
- The sermon expresses Winthrop's belief that the Puritan colonists had a special pact with God to build a model Christian society.
- Winthrop's new Christian "city upon a hill" would serve as a beacon of righteousness that would inspire reforms in England.

- Winthrop's sermon is often cited as the first example of **AMERICAN EXCEPTIONALISM**, the belief that America has a mission to be a beacon of democratic reform.
- President Reagan often used the image of a "shining city" to express his ideal of an America "God-blessed and teeming with people of all kinds living in harmony and peace."

## TOPIC 13
# PURITAN BELIEFS AND VALUES

1. The Puritans were Calvinists who believed that men and women are by nature sinful. By God's grace a few people called the "elect" will be saved. Because God is all-knowing, He has known from the beginning of time the identity of these lucky souls. This doctrine is called **PREDESTINATION.**
2. Like other Protestants, the Puritans yearned to directly approach God. They therefore renounced the elaborate rituals of the Church of England and argued that a hierarchy of Church officials was unnecessary. Each Puritan congregation was a self-governing church with membership limited to "visible saints" who could demonstrate receipt of the gift of God's grace.
3. The Puritans believed in the Protestant work ethic. They taught their children that "idle hands are the devil's workshop."

## TOPIC 14
# KEY FACTS ABOUT PURITAN SOCIETY

1. Unlike the early Chesapeake settlers, the Puritans migrated to America in families.
2. The Puritans lived in compact villages clustered around a community meetinghouse where they met to discuss local issues.
3. The Puritans established a patriarchal society in which women and children played a subordinate role to men.
4. The Puritans valued education as a means to read and understand the Bible. They required each community of

### INSIDER TIP
Both APUSH and SAT II test writers frequently ask students to identify Winthrop's famous "city upon a hill" quote. In addition, it was the first document in a 2010 DBQ devoted to the influence of Puritan ideas and values. It is important to remember that Winthrop's sermon expresses his conviction that the Puritans had a mission to create a model Christian community.

## INSIDER TIP
Both SAT II and APUSH exams frequently ask students to identify a diagram of a typical New England town. New England colonists lived in compact communities clustered around a meeting house where people met to worship and to conduct community business.

50 or more families to provide a teacher of reading and writing. Harvard College was founded to train ministers.

5. The devout (devoted to religion; pious) Puritans embraced a more rigorous faith than the Chesapeake settlers. The typical Puritan community was characterized by a close relationship between church and state.

6. Puritan leaders enforced a strict code of moral conduct. For example, communities in colonial New England banned the theatre.

# TOPIC 15
# RELIGIOUS CONFORMITY, DISSENT, AND TOLERATION

## 1. RELIGIOUS CONFORMITY
- The church occupied a central position in Puritan society. Convinced that they were undertaking God's work, the Puritans emphasized religious conformity.
- Although the Puritans came to America for religious freedom, they did not tolerate dissent.

## 2. ROGER WILLIAMS
- Roger Williams challenged the religious authority of Puritan leaders by arguing for the complete separation of church and state. Declaring that, "Forced worship stinks in God's nostrils," Williams called for freedom from coercion (the use of force, pressure, and threats) in matters of faith.
- Banished from Massachusetts, Williams fled to Rhode Island where he founded a new colony based upon freedom of religion.

## 3. ANNE HUTCHINSON
- Like Williams, Anne Hutchinson advocated unorthodox (unconventional) religious views that challenged the authority of Puritan magistrates.
- Claiming to have had revelations from God, Hutchinson questioned established religious doctrines and the role of women in Puritan society. Outraged by Hutchinson's claim to have had direct divine inspiration, Governor Winthrop fulminated (a thunderous verbal attack): "We do not mean to discourse with those of your sex." In 1638,

Massachusetts authorities banished Hutchinson to Rhode Island. Hutchinson later moved to Long Island where she was killed by Indians.

### 4. RELIGIOUS TOLERATION
- The Puritans were unable to stamp out religious dissent.
- Ironically, religious intolerance in Massachusetts promoted religious tolerance in Rhode Island.

## TOPIC 16
# THE HALFWAY COVENANT

1. The first generation of Puritans were dedicated to building a model community based upon a strict moral code. Their churches only accepted persons who could demonstrate that they were among God's "elect."
2. As the Puritan communities became increasingly prosperous, the original Puritan mission became less important to second and third generation settlers. As a result, fewer adults could provide testimony of their own "election."
3. The **HALFWAY COVENANT** was designed to respond to the decline of religious zeal among second generation Puritans. It eased the requirement for church membership by allowing the baptism of children of parents who could not provide testimony of their own "election."

## TOPIC 17
# RELATIONS WITH THE INDIANS

1. The Puritan settlers did not settle in an uninhabited wilderness. As many as 100,000 Indians lived in New England.
2. In the beginning the coastal Indians taught the Puritan settlers how to plant corn. They also exchanged furs for various trinkets and manufactured goods.
3. Smallpox epidemics soon decimated the Indian population. For example, by 1675 the population of southern New England tribes fell from 65,000 people to just 10,000.
4. Surviving leaders quickly realized that the English settlers intended to "deprive us of the privilege of our land and

## INSIDER TIP
Roger Williams and Anne Hutchinson both played an important role in fostering the early growth of religious toleration. Although Williams is the more important historic figure, Hutchinson has actually generated more APUSH and SAT II multiple-choice questions.

drive us to our utter ruin." Many New England Indians were determined to defend their way of life from the relentless growth of white settlement. Led by Chief Metacom (also known as King Philip), the Indians attacked and burned settlements across Massachusetts. Although they suffered great losses, the colonists killed Metacom and defeated his followers.

# CHAPTER 4
# THE MIDDLE ATLANTIC COLONIES, 1664 - 1754

## ESSENTIAL POINTS

1. The Dutch founded New Netherland to expand their commercial network.
2. Pennsylvania was founded by William Penn as a refuge for Quakers. Quakers advocated religious toleration, supported a greater role for women in public worship, refused to bear arms, and denounced slavery.
3. Pennsylvania was the best advertised of all the American colonies. Its policies of religious toleration and peaceful relations with the Indians attracted a variety of ethnic and religious groups.

## TOPIC 18
# GEOGRAPHIC CHARACTERISTICS

1. The Middle Atlantic colonies enjoyed moderate winters, fertile soil, fine harbors, and a longer growing season than the New England colonies.
2. The Hudson, Delaware, and Susquehanna rivers enabled early settlers to tap into the lucrative (profitable) interior fur trade.

## TOPIC 19
# THE DUTCH AND NEW NETHERLAND

1. The Dutch West Indian Company founded the colony of New Netherland in 1664 in order to develop a commercial network in the New World.
2. Like the French, the Dutch did not found agricultural settlements. Instead, they traded furs with the Native Americans. As a result, the Dutch avoided conflict with Native Americans.
3. New Netherland was a rich prize located between New England to the north and the other English colonies farther south. Its capital, New Amsterdam, had one of the finest harbors on the eastern coast of North America.
4. In 1664, King Charles II of England sent a fleet of warships to force New Netherland's governor, Peter Stuyvesant, to surrender. Unprepared for a fight with the superior English force, Stuyvesant reluctantly surrendered without firing a shot. Both the town of New Amsterdam and the colony of New Netherland were renamed New York after the king's brother, James Duke of York.

## TOPIC 20
# WILLIAM PENN AND PENNSYLVANIA

### 1. KEY FACTS ABOUT THE QUAKERS
- Quakers were a group of religious dissenters who appeared in England in the mid-1600s.

- Quakers believed that every person had an inner light and needed only to live by it to be saved. Since every person had an inner light, all people were equal.
- Quakers were pacifists who refused to bear arms.
- Quakers advocated religious toleration, supported a greater role for women in public worship, and opposed the institution of slavery.
- Quakers did NOT refuse to pay taxes and did NOT practice clerical celibacy.

## 2. WILLIAM PENN

- William Penn was a wellborn son of a prominent British admiral.
- Penn embraced Quaker teachings when he was just sixteen years old.
- Penn secured a large grant of fertile New World land as payment for a monetary debt the crown owed his deceased father.
- The king named the area Pennsylvania ("Penn's Woodland") after William's father.

## 3. PENN'S "HOLY EXPERIMENT"

- Penn founded Pennsylvania as a "Holy Experiment" that would serve as a refuge for Quakers.
- Founded for religious toleration, Pennsylvania did not have an established church.
- Penn established amicable (friendly) relations with the local Indian tribes. He paid them for their land and protected them from unscrupulous (unprincipled) speculators and dishonest merchants.
- Penn launched an aggressive advertising campaign to encourage people to move to his colony. He published pamphlets in several languages promising settlers fertile land, low taxes, religious freedom, and a representative assembly.
- Penn's advertising campaign worked. Pennsylvania's policy of religious toleration and its economic prosperity attracted a diverse mix of ethnic and religious groups. By 1700, only Virginia and Massachusetts had a larger population than Pennsylvania. Philadelphia quickly became a prosperous port that rivaled Boston and New York City.

## INSIDER TIP

Most APUSH exams and SAT II tests have at least one multiple-choice questions devoted to the Middle Atlantic colonies. Be sure that you can identify William Penn and the characteristic features of colonial Pennsylvania.

**CHAPTER 5**

# KEY ASPECTS OF COLONIAL LIFE AND THOUGHT, 1730 – 1776

## ESSENTIAL POINTS

1. The **GREAT AWAKENING** was a wave of religious revivals and mass conversions that began in New England and then swept across all of the colonies during the 1740s.

2. The Great Awakening weakened the authority of established "Old Light" Puritan ministers, created divisions within both the Congregational and the Presbyterian churches, and encouraged missionary work among Native Americans and African slaves.

3. **MERCANTILISM** was a British economic policy designed to achieve a favorable balance of trade by purchasing raw materials from the American colonies and then selling them manufactured goods. Mercantilism was thus intended to increase Britain's wealth by making the colonial economies dependent upon their mother country.

4. The Navigation Acts were intended to implement Britain's mercantilist economic philosophy.

5. A married woman in colonial America had no legal identity apart from her husband. She typically lost control of her property when she married. However, single women and widows did have the legal right to own property.

6. Benjamin Franklin, Anne Bradstreet, and Phillis Wheatley are three key colonial authors. Franklin is best known for publishing *Poor Richard's Almanack* and writing an autobiographical account of his rise from poverty and obscurity to fame and affluence. Bradstreet is best remembered as a poet who was the first colonial woman to be published. Wheatley is best remembered as America's first notable African American poet.

# TOPIC 21
# THE GREAT AWAKENING

## INSIDER TIP
The Great Awakening has generated a significant number of multiple-choice questions. Most questions focus on the consequences of the Great Awakening. It is important to remember that the Great Awakening promoted religious pluralism and thus religious toleration.

## PODCAST 5.1
THE GREAT AWAKENING

## 1. WHAT HAPPENED?
- A wave of religious revivals began in New England in the mid-1730s.
- The revival swept across all of the colonies during the 1740s.

## 2. WHAT CAUSED THE GREAT AWAKENING?
- As the colonies prospered more and more people became pre-occupied with earning and spending money. By the 1730s, many ministers worried about a growing sense of religious decline.
- "Old Light" Puritan ministers continued to deliver long intellectual sermons emphasizing elaborate theological doctrines.
- Jonathan Edwards provided the initial spark for the Great Awakening by delivering emotional sermons warning sinners to repent. His most famous sermon, "Sinners in the Hands of an Angry God," painted a vivid picture of the torments of hell and the certainty of God's justice.
- George Whitefield spread the "New Light" fervor as he preached emotional sermons to huge crowds of enthralled (fascinated) listeners. Gripped by fear of divine justice, audiences from Georgia to New England promised to repent and accept Christ.
- "New Light" ministers stressed that individuals could attain salvation only by first experiencing a "new birth" – a sudden, emotional moment of conversion and salvation.

## 3. WHY SHOULD YOU REMEMBER THE GREAT AWAKENING?
- The Great Awakening undermined the authority of established churches and led to a decline in the power of traditional "Old Light" Puritan ministers.
- The Great Awakening split the Presbyterian and Congregational churches into "New Light" factions that supported the Great Awakening and "Old Light" factions that opposed it.
- The Great Awakening fragmented American Protestants thus promoting religious pluralism and toleration since no

single denomination could impose its dogma on the other sects.

- The Great Awakening encouraged missionary work among Native Americans and African slaves.
- The Great Awakening promoted the growing popularity of itinerant (wandering) ministers.
- The Great Awakening led to an increase in the number of women in church congregations.
- The Great Awakening led to the founding of "New Light" colleges such as Princeton, Rutgers, Dartmouth, Brown, and Columbia.

# TOPIC 22
# MERCANTILISM

1. Like other European nations, the British adopted MERCANTILISM as their economic policy.
2. Mercantilists argued that a country acquired wealth and thus power by having a favorable balance of trade.
3. Mercantilists believed that colonies existed to supply raw materials to their mother country and to purchase manufactured goods from their mother country.
4. Parliament passed a series of Navigation Acts to implement its mercantilist philosophy. The Navigation laws regulated colonial shipping by enumerating (listing) colonial products that could be shipped only to England and by requiring that all commerce flowing to and from the colonies be routed through English ports in British or colonial vessels.
5. Mercantilism impeded the growth of colonial manufacturing.
6. The Navigation laws were not rigorously enforced prior to 1763. During this period of "salutary neglect," enterprising colonial merchants successfully evaded burdensome mercantilist regulations.

## INSIDER TIP
It is important to remember that mercantile policies intentionally subordinated the colonial economy to Great Britain's economic interests.

## PODCAST 5.2
MERCANTILISM

## TOPIC 23
# WOMEN IN COLONIAL AMERICA

1. A married woman had no legal identity apart from her husband. For example, a woman generally lost control of her property when she married.
2. During the 18th century single women in the British North American colonies had the legal right to own property. However, they could not vote, hold political office, serve on juries or become ministers.
3. Women comprised a majority in many New England church congregations.

## TOPIC 24
# KEY COLONIAL AUTHORS

## 1. BENJAMIN FRANKLIN (1706 – 1790)
- Benjamin Franklin was a renowned polymath (person of great and diversified learning) whose varied achievements included founding an academy that became the University of Pennsylvania, conducting experiments with electricity, and publishing popular books.
- When he was just 27, Franklin published *Poor Richard's Almanack*. It featured a popular mixture of weather forecasts, practical household advice, and common sense maxims (wise sayings) on success and happiness.
- As old age approached, Franklin began writing an autobiography addressed to his son William. A self-made individual, Franklin proudly noted that he "emerged from the poverty and obscurity in which I was born and bred, to a state of affluence and some degree of reputation in the world."

## 2. ANNE BRADSTREET (1612 – 1672)
- Anne Bradstreet was the first published American poet and the first women to be published in colonial America.

## 3. PHILLIS WHEATLY (1753 – 1784)
- Phillis Wheatly was the first notable African American poet. She holds the distinction of being the first African American woman whose writing was published.

# CHAPTER 6
# THE ROAD TO REVOLUTION, 1754 – 1775

## ESSENTIAL POINTS

1. New France included Canada, the entire Mississippi River Valley, and Louisiana. This vast region was thinly populated by fur traders who established lucrative and cooperative relations with the Native American tribes.

2. Franklin's Albany Plan failed to achieve greater colonial unity because the colonies refused to give up their local autonomy.

3. The Peace of Paris of 1763 ended French power in North America by giving Britain title to Canada, Spanish Florida, and all of the French lands east of the Mississippi River.

4. The Proclamation of 1763 attempted to avoid conflict between colonists and trans-Appalachian Indians by forbidding settlers from crossing the crest of the Appalachian Mountains.

5. The Stamp Act was intended to raise revenue to support British troops stationed in America. The colonial boycott of British goods forced Parliament to repeal the Stamp Act.

6. The Stamp Act and the Coercive Acts intensified the colonists' commitment to republican values. **REPUBLICANISM** is the belief that government should be based on the consent of the governed.

## INSIDER TIP

SAT II and APUSH exams rarely include a multiple-choice question devoted to New France. However, APUSH free-response questions often ask students to compare New France with the Spanish Southwest and Puritan New England. For examples see free-response Question 2 on the 2011B exam and free-response Question 2 on the 2012B exam.

**TOPIC 25**
# NEW FRANCE

1. The first French explorers tried and failed to find a northwest passage to Asia.
2. New France included Canada, the entire Mississippi River Valley, and Louisiana. The French thus confined the British to territory east of the Appalachians.
3. The French government provided little economic incentive for its citizens to settle in New France. Although New France did include permanent settlements at Montreal and Quebec, its vast lands were sparsely populated.
4. French settlers were predominately single men who quickly developed a lucrative fur trade with the Native American tribes.
5. The French fur traders developed a cooperative relationship with the Native American tribes. Unlike the British settlers they did not build plantations and farms on lands claimed by Native Americans. Instead, they built widely dispersed trading posts on lands that were not claimed by Native American tribes.
6. Jesuit priests made a concerted effort to convert Native Americans to Catholicism. Unlike the Spanish, the Jesuits did not require Native American converts to move to missions.

**TOPIC 26**
# THE ALBANY PLAN OF UNION, 1754

1. Benjamin Franklin recognized the need for greater colonial cooperation. His Albany Plan called for a united colonial defense against French and Native American threats to frontier settlements. It proposed the formation of a Grand Council of elected delegates to oversee common defense, western expansion, and Indian relations.
2. Franklin's famous "Join, or Die" cartoon dramatically illustrated the need for greater colonial unity.
3. The Albany Plan failed because the colonial assemblies did not want to give up their autonomy (independence). At the same time, the British government feared that colonial unity would undermine their authority.

**TOPIC 27**
# THE FRENCH AND INDIAN WAR, 1754 – 1763

## 1. WHAT HAPPENED?
- The French and Indian War culminated the long struggle between Great Britain and France for control of the North American continent.
- France lost because its absolute government impeded the development of New France by imposing burdensome economic and immigration restrictions.
- Great Britain won because its colonies were far more populous than those of New France. In 1754, Britain's mainland colonies contained 1.2 million people compared to just 75,000 inhabitants of New France.
- During the French and Indian War, the Algonquian supported the French and the Iroquois supported the British.

## 2. WHAT CAUSED THE FRENCH AND INDIAN WAR?
- The French and Indian War began as a struggle for control of the upper Ohio River valley.
- The French and Indian War was part of a wider struggle between Great Britain and France known in Europe as the Seven Years' War.

## 3. WHY SHOULD YOU REMEMBER THE FRENCH AND INDIAN WAR?
- Great Britain emerged as the world's foremost naval power.
- The Peace of Paris of 1763 ended French power in North America. Britain took title to Canada, Spanish Florida, and all the French lands east of the Mississippi River.
- The French and Indian War left Britain with a large debt. As a result, British leaders planned to impose revenue taxes on their American colonies.
- The French and Indian War awakened the colonists' sense of separate identity.

PODCAST 6.1
THE CONSEQUENCES OF THE FRENCH AND INDIAN WAR

## INSIDER TIP

SAT II tests often ask students to identify the Proclamation Line of 1763 on a map of eastern America. The line is easy to spot since it runs along the crest of the Appalachian Mountains.

## TOPIC 28
# THE PROCLAMATION OF 1763

1. Now that the French threat had been removed, **American fur traders and land speculators** looked forward to exploiting the vast new lands west of the Appalachian Mountains.
2. While the colonists wanted to expand into the new territories, the British wanted to prevent land-hungry settlers from provoking hostilities with the Indians. The Proclamation of 1763 forbade settlers from crossing the crest of the Appalachian Mountains.
3. Hardy settlers soon **defied the prohibition** as they pushed over the Appalachian ridges into Kentucky and Tennessee.

## TOPIC 29
# THE STAMP ACT CRISIS, 1765

## 1. WHAT HAPPENED?

- Britain's national debt doubled as a result of the French and Indian War. In addition, Britain needed to raise funds to support 10,000 troops stationed in North America for defense against Indian troubles and a possible resurgence (revival) of French agitation.
- George Grenville, the new first minister and First Lord of the Treasury, persuaded Parliament that the prosperous and lightly taxed colonists did not pay their fair share of imperial expenses.
- Parliament passed the Stamp Act on February 13, 1765. It required colonists to affix stamps to over 50 items including newspapers, legal documents, almanacs, college diplomas, and playing cards.
- Led by the Sons and Daughters of Liberty, outraged colonists used the threat of violence to "persuade" almost every stamp agent to resign.
- The Stamp Act Congress rejected Parliament's right to tax the colonists and called for a boycott of British goods.
- The boycott proved to be a success. British merchants hurt by the loss of trade persuaded Parliament to repeal the Stamp Act. However, Parliament also passed the

Declaratory Act reaffirming (reasserting) its right to "make laws and statues … to bind the colonies … in all cases whatsoever."

## 2. WHAT CAUSED THE STAMP ACT CRISIS?

- The Stamp Act marked the end of Britain's policy of salutary neglect.
- The Stamp Act directly affected lawyers, newspaper publishers, merchants, and planters. These articulate and influential colonists denounced (spoke against) the Stamp Act.
- The Stamp Act provoked a contentious (argumentative) debate over Parliament's constitutional right to tax its American colonies.
- The British argued that Parliament was based upon a system of "virtual representation" that represented the interests of all Englishmen, including the colonists. For example, a member of Parliament from London represented the interests of Great Britain and the entire empire. As a result, Philadelphia had as much representation in Parliament as London.
- The colonists adamantly (unyielding) rejected "virtual representation." They argued that as Englishmen they could only be taxed by their own elected representatives. The principle of "no taxation without representation" was a cherished right of British subjects. Giving up this privilege would lead to tyranny.

## 3. WHY SHOULD YOU REMEMBER THE STAMP ACT CRISIS?

- The Stamp Act crisis marked the first major event that provoked colonial resistance to British rule.
- The Stamp Act crisis intensified the colonist's commitment to republican values. REPUBLICANISM is the belief that government should be based on the consent of the governed. Republican values inspired the Virginia Resolves and Patrick Henry's famous "Give me liberty or give me death" speech.

## INSIDER TIP

The Stamp Act crisis has generated a significant number of multiple-choice questions. It is important to remember that Parliament passed the Stamp Act to raise revenue and rescinded it because of the colonial boycott.

## TOPIC 30
# THE BOSTON MASSACRE, 1770

1. British authorities viewed Boston as a hotbed of discontent.
2. London dispatched troops to Boston to protect nervous Customs Commissioners. Tension between the townspeople and the crimson-coated regulars soon escalated.
3. On the night of March 5, 1770 a rowdy group of hecklers taunted a squad of British soldiers outside the Boston Customs house. A provoked soldier fired into the crowd and when the smoke cleared, five townspeople lay on the ground dead or dying.
4. Led by Samuel Adams, enraged patriots promptly branded the incident the "Boston Massacre." Paul Revere's highly partisan (very biased) engraving of the Boston Massacre further inflamed colonial opinion against the British.

## INSIDER TIP
Recent APUSH exams have included multiple-choice questions about the Coercive Acts. It is important to remember that the colonists viewed the Coercive Acts as the beginning of a movement to give Parliament greater control over colonial government.

## TOPIC 31.
# THE COERCIVE ACTS, 1774

1. On December 16, 1773 a group of Boston patriots disguised as Mohawk Indians boarded three British ships and threw 342 chests of tea into the harbor.
2. The Boston Tea Party infuriated British authorities. Parliament promptly passed the Coercive Acts to punish Boston for the wanton destruction of private property.
3. Known in America as the Intolerable Acts, the legislation closed the port of Boston, sharply curtailed (reduced) town meetings, and authorized the army to quarter troops wherever they were needed.
4. Parliament's attempt to limit political autonomy (independence) in Massachusetts seemed to confirm the colonist's fear that Britain intended to restrict each colony's right to self-government.
5. The British strategy of isolating Boston failed. In September 1774, fifty-five elected representatives met in Philadelphia to reach a unified colonial response to the Coercive Acts. The First Continental Congress called for a complete boycott of British goods and urged the colonies to organize militia for defensive purposes.

**TOPIC 32**
# THE SECOND CONTINENTAL CONGRESS, 1775

1. The Second Continental Congress began its deliberations in Philadelphia on May 10, 1775. As tensions mounted and fighting spread, it assumed more of the functions of a de facto American government.
2. The Second Continental Congress issued the "Declaration of Causes of Taking up Arms." This document declared that the colonists could either submit to tyranny or choose armed resistance.
3. The Second Continental Congress authorized an army and appointed George Washington its Commander-in-Chief. As events unfolded, Washington demonstrated a rare combination of soldier and statesman.

**CHAPTER 7**
# THE AMERICAN REVOLUTION, 1776 – 1783

## ESSENTIAL POINTS

1. Parliament passed taxes to raise revenue and enacted regulations to tighten control over the North American colonies. However, these measures intensified the colonists' resistance to British rule and their commitment to republican values.

2. Thomas Paine's pamphlet *Common Sense* urged Americans to reject British sovereignty and create an independent nation based upon republican principles.

3. The Declaration of Independence accused George III of tyranny and used the philosophy of natural rights to justify the colonists' right to declare their independence from Great Britain.

4. The American victory at Saratoga convinced France to negotiate a treaty of alliance with America.

5. The French monarchy was not sympathetic with America's republican ideals. Instead, France was motivated by a desire to avenge its humiliating loss to Great Britain in the Seven Years' War.

6. America won the Revolutionary War because of a combination of French military and financial support, a successful defensive military strategy, and a populace committed to republican ideals.

7. The Treaty of Paris of 1783 officially recognized American independence. The treaty recognized American sovereignty over territories extending from the Mississippi River on the west, to the Great Lakes on the north, and to Spanish Florida on the south.

# TOPIC 33 ·
# THE REVOLUTIONARY MINDSET

## INSIDER TIP

Could the British have done anything to mitigate the growing tensions with their North American colonies? Many historians point out that the king could have offered to give the colonies representatives in Parliament. This shrewd move would have negated the colonial argument that the king was an unjust tyrant while also ending the rallying cry of "No taxation without representation."

## 1. THE IMPACT OF BRITISH TAXES AND REGULATIONS

- Parliament passed the Stamp Act, the Townshend Acts, and the Tea Act to raise revenue to help pay for imperial expenses. Instead, these tax laws raised questions about Parliament's right to tax the colonists.
- Parliament passed the Proclamation of 1763, the Quartering Act of 1765 and the Coercive Acts to tighten its control over the increasingly rebellious colonists. Instead, these regulatory acts intensified the colonists' resistance to British rule and their commitment to republican values.

## 2. REPUBLICAN VALUES

- A belief in republican values inspired the American revolutionaries who defied British authority. REPUBLICANISM is the belief that government should be based upon the consent of the governed.
- Republican values took root early in the American experience. For example, New England town meetings and sessions of the Virginia House of Burgesses provided colonial leaders with valuable experience in the art of self-government. As they developed the habits of self-government, colonial leaders developed a firm sense of their rights.
- As resistance to British taxes and regulations intensified, colonial leaders became more and more convinced that a republic is preferable to a monarchy because it would establish a small, limited government that is responsible to the people. The colonists wanted to replace the hereditary British aristocracy with American leaders elected for their superior talent, wisdom, and integrity.
- The Stamp Act Congress and the First and Second Continental Congresses further underscored the colonists' commitment to republican values and determination to assert and defend their rights.

## TOPIC 34
### *COMMON SENSE, 1776*

1. As 1776 opened, popular sentiment vacillated (wavered) between calls for independence and loyalty to the crown. In January, Thomas Paine published a pamphlet called *Common Sense*. Within three months more than 150,000 copies of the pamphlet circulated throughout the colonies.
2. Paine rejected monarchy as a form of government. He attacked George III as a "royal brute" and a "hardened Pharaoh" who callously (without feeling) permitted his troops to "slaughter" innocent colonists.
3. Paine urged Americans to reject British sovereignty and create an independent nation based upon the republican principle that government should be responsible to the will of the people.

## TOPIC 35
# THOMAS JEFFERSON AND THE DECLARATION OF INDEPENDENCE, 1776

1. Thomas Jefferson was a leading thinker in the American Enlightenment. The Enlightenment was an 18th century philosophical movement which emphasized that reason could be used to improve the human condition.
2. Like other members of the educated elite in western Europe and America, Jefferson embraced Deism. Deists thought of God as a cosmic watchmaker who created the universe and then let it run according to natural laws.
3. Jefferson believed that natural laws regulate both the universe and human society. These natural laws could be discovered by human reason. For example, the discovery of laws of government would improve society and make progress and human happiness inevitable.
4. Jefferson opened the Declaration of Independence with a concise and compelling statement of principles and "self-evident" truths.

## INSIDER TIP
It is easy to allow Deism to slip off your APUSH radar screen. Don't let that happen. APUSH exams often include a multiple-choice question asking you to pick out the salient (essential) characteristic of DEISM. Keep in mind that Deists believe that God created the world and then allows it to operate through laws of nature that can be discovered by human reason.

5. Inspired by John Locke's philosophy of natural rights, Jefferson asserted that governments derive "their just powers from the consent of the governed." The governed are entitled to "alter or abolish" their ties to a government that denies them their "unalienable rights" to "life, liberty, and the pursuit of happiness."

6. Jefferson did not base his argument on the narrow "rights of Englishmen." Instead, he left a lasting impact on the conscience of the world by appealing to universal "laws of Nature and Nature's God."

7. The Declaration also contained a list of specific grievances against King George III. The King's lengthy record of "repeated injuries and usurpations" forced the "good people of these colonies" to declare their independence from Great Britain.

8. The Declaration of Independence did not call for the abolition of the slave trade. The reality of slavery thus belied (contradicted) Jefferson's eloquent statement of republican ideals.

## INSIDER TIP

The Revolutionary War is filled with famous battles such as Bunker Hill and Washington's surprise attack on the Hessians at Trenton. All of these battles can be safely skipped. Instead, make sure that you know that the American victory at Saratoga led to the French alliance.

## TOPIC 36
# THE BATTLE OF SARATOGA, 1777

1. During the first 18 months of the war, Washington's demoralized troops lost New York City and Philadelphia and then suffered through a bitter winter camped at Valley Forge.

2. In July 1777 a British force led by General John Burgoyne began a campaign designed to isolate New England from the Middle Atlantic colonies and thus cut the United States in two.

3. American forces led by Horatio Gates and Benedict Arnold thwarted the British plan by forcing Burgoyne to surrender 5,500 men at the Battle of Saratoga.

4. The Battle of Saratoga marked a crucial turning point in the Revolutionary War. The victory revived the colonial cause and helped convince France to declare war on Great Britain and openly support the American cause.

## TOPIC 37
# THE FRENCH ALLIANCE

### 1. WHAT HAPPENED?
- On February 6, 1778 France signed a **treaty** formally recognizing the United States.
- The Franco-American alliance provided the United States with crucial diplomatic, financial, and military support.

PODCAST 7.1
THE FRENCH ALLIANCE

### 2. WHAT CAUSED THE FRENCH ALLIANCE?
- France was an absolute monarchy that was not sympathetic to republican values. Instead, France was motivated by a desire to regain its prestige in Europe by avenging its humiliating loss to Great Britain in the Seven Years' War.
- Fearful of an American defeat, the French initially followed a cautious approach toward the rebellious colonies. They surreptitiously (secretly) provided vital military supplies including badly needed ammunition and fire arms.
- The skillful diplomacy of Benjamin Franklin captivated the court at Versailles and helped persuade the French to support the American cause.
- The American victory at Saratoga convinced French leaders that America had the resolve to defeat Great Britain.

### 3. WHAT SHOULD YOU REMEMBER ABOUT THE FRENCH ALLIANCE?
- The French alliance prevented any chance of an Anglo-American reconciliation.
- French military and financial aid played a decisive role in enabling America to win the Revolutionary War. For example, American forces received vital French help during the Battle of Yorktown.

## TOPIC 38
# REASONS WHY AMERICA WON THE REVOLUTIONARY WAR

### 1. MILITARY REASONS
- British commanders underestimated the fighting ability of American soldiers. They also failed to implement a coordinated military strategy.
- America's vast size enabled its commanders to fight a defensive war trading space for time.
- Led by George Washington, America's military commanders proved to be resourceful and resilient (able to bounce back from adversity).

### 2. DIPLOMATIC REASONS
- The British government was confused, inept, and divided. For example, prominent Whigs such as Edmund Burke and William Pitt sympathized with the American cause.
- The French alliance provided indispensible military, financial, and diplomatic support.

### 3. POLITICAL REASONS
- The dispute with Great Britain over economic policies soon exposed irreconcilable political differences.
- America lacked a monarchy or a hereditary aristocracy. Instead of fighting for the crown, American soldiers fought for republican ideals. John Adams later noted that, "The Revolution was effected before the war commenced. The Revolution was in the minds and hearts of the people."

**TOPIC 39**
# THE TREATY OF PARIS OF 1783

1. The Franco-American alliance influenced Great Britain to offer generous peace terms.
2. The treaty recognized the independence of the United States.
3. The treaty recognized American sovereignty over territories extending from the Mississippi River on the west, to the Great Lakes on the north, and to Spanish Florida on the south.
4. America pledged to compensate Loyalists whose lands had been confiscated by state governments.

# CHAPTER 8
# THE ARTICLES OF CONFEDERATION, 1777 – 1787

## ESSENTIAL POINTS

1. The Northwest Ordinance established an orderly procedure for territories to become new states. It banned slavery from the Northwest Territory thus becoming the first national law to prohibit the expansion of slavery.

2. The Articles of Confederation created a weak central government consisting of a unicameral Congress elected by state legislatures. Congress lacked the power to levy taxes or to regulate interstate commerce.

3. Shays' Rebellion convinced key leaders that the United States needed a stronger national government.

## TOPIC 40
# KEY FACTS ABOUT THE ARTICLES OF CONFEDERATION

1. A CONFEDERATION is a type of government with a loose union among sovereign states. The central government in a confederation is weak while the member states retain most of their sovereign powers. For example, the modern United Nations is a confederation of sovereign nations.

2. The United States began as a confederation of sovereign states under the Article of Confederation. The Articles of Confederation established "a firm league of friendship" with a deliberately weak central government.

3. The drafters of the Articles of Confederation created a weak central government for three reasons. First, they feared a strong centralized authority that was too remote from the people. Americans were wary of giving their new government powers they had just denied to Parliament. Second, they feared that big states such as Virginia, Massachusetts, and Pennsylvania would dominate the government. And finally, they believed that a representative republican government would only work in small communities with common interests.

4. The Articles created a central government consisting of a unicameral (one branch) Congress elected by state legislatures. Each state, regardless of size, had just one vote in Congress.

## TOPIC 41
# ACCOMPLISHMENTS OF THE ARTICLES OF CONFEDERATION

## 1. THE REVOLUTIONARY WAR
- The Confederate government successfully waged and won the Revolutionary War.
- The Confederate government successfully negotiated a mutual defense treaty with France.
- The Confederate government successfully negotiated the Treaty of Paris ending the Revolutionary War on favorable terms to the United States.

## 2. THE LAND ORDINANCE OF 1785

- Established uniform procedures for surveying western lands into townships and sections.
- Provided for the sale of public lands in the West at $1/acre with a 640-acre minimum.
- Reserved one section in each township to support public schools. This marked the first instance of federal aid to education.

## 3. THE NORTHWEST ORDINANCE OF 1787

- Established an orderly procedure for territories to become states equal to the original thirteen states.
- Banned slavery from the Northwest Territory thus becoming the first national law to prohibit the expansion of slavery.
- The Northwest Ordinance did NOT provide free land for settlers.

## INSIDER TIP

The Northwest Ordinance has generated a significant number of multiple-choice questions on both the APUSH exam and the SAT II test. Be sure that you know its provisions.

## TOPIC 42
# WEAKNESSES AND FAILURES OF THE ARTICLES OF CONFEDERATION

1. Congress lacked the power to levy taxes. The inability to raise revenue made it very difficult to pay off the Revolutionary War debt.
2. Congress lacked the power to regulate interstate or foreign commerce. It failed to restore exports of rice, indigo, and tobacco to Britain while allowing the British to flood the states with manufactured goods. These ineffective policies produced a huge balance of trade deficit.
3. The government lacked an executive branch to enforce national policy and provide national leadership.
4. The government lacked a national judiciary to resolve disputes between states.
5. Congress issued an inflated currency and failed to halt paper money abuses in Rhode Island and other states.
6. The Articles of Confederation lacked the flexibility needed to make necessary changes. Amendments required a unanimous vote of all thirteen states.

*[handwritten notes:]* • required unanimous voting to change • no way to resolve disputes btw states • trade deficit • no enforcement (shay's) • inflation & money abuses

## INSIDER TIP

Question 2 on the 2003 APUSH exam asked students to evaluate how effectively the Articles of Confederation government dealt with the problems confronting the new nation. See Essay I for a sophisticated thesis that differentiates between the Articles successes in dealing with territorial expansion and its failures to address America's economic troubles

## INSIDER TIP

Don't confuse Shays'
Rebellion with Bacon's
Rebellion. Shays'
Rebellion occurred after
the Revolutionary War
and contributed to calls
for a stronger national
government. Bacon's
Rebellion occurred in
17th century Virginia
and contributed to calls
to import African slaves
to work in the tobacco
fields.

## PODCAST 8.1
SHAYS' REBELLION

**TOPIC 43**
# SHAYS' REBELLION, 1787

*•Annapolis convention (failed) →*

## 1. WHAT HAPPENED? *made Congress revise Articles*

- Frustrated Massachusetts farmers were losing their farms because they could not repay their debts to eastern creditors in hard currency.
- The desperate farmers demanded that the state legislature halt farm foreclosures, lower property taxes, issue paper money, and end imprisonment for debt.
- Led by Captain Daniel Shays, armed farmers closed a courthouse where creditors were suing to foreclose farm mortgages.
- Wealthy Bostonians raised an army that quickly crushed the "rebellion."

## 2. WHAT CAUSED SHAYS' REBELLION?

- Shays' Rebellion reflected the tensions between impoverished (very poor) farmers and the wealthy merchants who dominated the Massachusetts legislature.

## 3. WHY SHOULD YOU REMEMBER SHAYS' REBELLION?

- Just before Shays' Rebellion five states sent delegates to Annapolis to discuss trade problems among the states. Although the Annapolis Convention failed to resolve the commercial problems, it did call upon Congress to summon a convention to revise the Articles of Confederation.
- Shays' Rebellion frightened many conservatives who feared a breakdown of law and order.
- The "great commotion" in Massachusetts convinced George Washington, James Madison and other key leaders that the United States needed a stronger national government.

# CHAPTER 9
# THE CONSTITUTION

## ESSENTIAL POINTS

1. The Framers opposed political parties seeing them as vehicles of ambition and selfish interests.
2. The Constitution submitted to the states in 1787 included an electoral college, a bicameral legislature, three branches of government, and a system of checks and balances.
3. The Constitution submitted to the states in 1787 did NOT contain a Bill of Rights or provisions for universal manhood suffrage, political parties, or the direct election of Senators.
4. Under the terms of the Three-Fifths Compromise each slave counted as three-fifths of a person for purpose of determining a states' level of taxation and representation.
5. Abigail Adams wrote a famous letter to her husband, John Adams, urging him to "remember the Ladies" by granting them greater political and legal rights. Adams' letter demonstrates that there were colonial women who wanted a greater voice in political affairs.

## TOPIC 44
# KEY PRINCIPLES OF THE CONSTITUTION

1. The Framers believed that they needed to write a new constitution in order to achieve their goal of forming "a more perfect Union."
2. The Framers believed that governments should be limited and that power should be divided into separate legislative, executive, and judicial branches.
3. The Framers believed that widespread ownership of property is a necessary foundation of representative government.
4. The Framers opposed political parties seeing them as vehicles of ambition and selfish interests that would threaten the existence of representative government.
5. James Madison believed that a large republic would curb factionalism. He reasoned that "in an expanding Republic, so many different groups and viewpoints would be included in the Congress that tyranny by the majority would be impossible."

## TOPIC 45
# KEY PROVISIONS THAT WERE IN THE CONSTITUTION SUBMITTED TO THE STATES IN 1787

1. A series of compromises that created a government acceptable to large and small states, as well as to free and slave states.
2. A bicameral or two-house Congress based upon the Great Compromise between large and small states. According to this compromise representation in the House of Representatives would be apportioned on the basis of population while each state would be allotted two seats in the Senate.
3. A Congress with the authority to levy taxes, declare war, and regulate interstate commerce.

4. An executive branch led by a President. The President would be required to deliver an annual State of the Union message.

5. An Electoral College designed to safeguard the presidency from direct popular election. The Framers believed this would insulate the presidency from the threat of "excessive democracy."

6. An independent judiciary branch with federal judges appointed by the President and confirmed by the Senate. As a result, the judiciary branch would be insulated from popular control.

7. A federal system of government in which power is divided between a central government and state governments.

8. A "necessary and proper" clause also known as the elastic clause. It gives Congress the power to make laws necessary for carrying out its enumerated powers. The elastic clause contradicted states' rights.

9. A system of checks and balances that included the following:
   - The President can veto an act of Congress.
   - Congress can override a presidential veto by a two-thirds vote in each house.
   - The President negotiates treaties that must be ratified by the Senate.

## TOPIC 46
# KEY PROVISIONS THAT WERE NOT IN THE CONSTITUTION SUBMITTED TO THE STATES IN 1787

## 1. UNIVERSAL MANHOOD SUFFRAGE
- Each state set requirements for who could vote. Universal manhood became a reality for white males during the 1830s.

## 2. THE DIRECT ELECTION OF SENATORS.
- Senators were not directly elected by the people until the passage of the 17th Amendment in 1913.

### 3. THE TWO-TERM LIMIT FOR A PRESIDENT.

- Presidents were not limited to two terms until the passage of the 22nd Amendment in 1951.

### 4. POLITICAL PARTIES

- Political parties are not mentioned in the Constitution. In fact, the Framers opposed political parties as divisive vehicles for self-interest and personal ambition. Political parties first emerged during the Washington administration in response to Hamilton's controversial economic program.

### 5. A PRESIDENTIAL CABINET

- As the nation's chief executive, the president does have the power to appoint top-ranking officials. Washington appointed a cabinet of four people to advise and assist him in his duties. The president's cabinet currently includes 14 executive departments and the attorney general.

### 6. A BILL OF RIGHTS

- During the ratification debate the Federalists promised to add a Bill of Rights to the Constitution. They kept their word. The First Congress ratified ten amendments collectively known as the Bill of Rights. They became part of the Constitution when ratified by the states in 1791.

## INSIDER TIP

SAT II tests often include a multiple-choice question asking students to identify a provision that was NOT in the Constitution as submitted to the states in 1787. Be sure to study the list of provisions highlighted in Topic 46.

## TOPIC 47
# THE CONSTITUTION AND SLAVERY

1. As the Framers met in Philadelphia a "First Emancipation" was already being implemented in the North. At that time, northern states had eliminated or were gradually eliminating slavery. In addition, the Confederation Congress had already excluded slavery from the Northwest Territory. As a result, slavery was becoming a distinctive southern institution.

2. Although the words "slave" and "slavery" did not appear in the original Constitution, it nonetheless guaranteed the legality of slavery in every state. This contradicted the assertion in the Declaration of Independence that "all men are created equal."

3. The Three-Fifths Compromise resolved a dispute between the slave states and the free states. Under the terms of this

compromise each slave counted as three-fifths of a person for purpose of determining a state's level of taxation and representation. This increased the congressional representation of the slave states and gave them a greater voice in the Electoral College.

4. The Constitution contained a provision requiring all states to return runaways to their masters.

5. Congress could not end the importation of slaves until 1808.

## TOPIC 48
# KEY QUOTE – ABIGAIL ADAMS' "REMEMBER THE LADIES" LETTER TO JOHN ADAMS

### 1. THE SETTING
- Married women had no legal identity apart from their husbands.
- Women could not vote, hold a political office, or serve on a jury.
- Abigail Adams was a well-educated woman who was an early proponent (supporter) of women's rights.

### 2. THE QUOTE
- "In the new Code of Laws which I suppose it will be necessary for you to make, I desire you would remember the Ladies, and be more generous and favorable to them than your ancestors. Do not put such unlimited power into the hands of Husbands."

### 3. SIGNIFICANCE
- Abigail Adams urges her husband, John Adams, to advocate greater rights for women.
- The quote shows that there were colonial women who sought to benefit from republican ideals of equality and individual rights by asking for a greater political voice.

## PODCAST 9.1
ABIGAIL ADAMS

# CHAPTER 10
# THE RATIFICATION DEBATE

## ESSENTIAL POINTS

1. The Anti-Federalists favored a weak national government and strong state governments. They argued that the proposed Constitution gave too much power to the executive and legislative branches. Anti-Federalists also maintained that a republic would not work in a large nation with diverse interests.

2. The Federalists favored a federal system in which power would be shared between state and federal governments. They argued that the proposed system of separation of powers and checks and balances would make it difficult for any special interest to dominate the government. Federalists maintained that the proposed Constitution would work in a large republic because the federal system would fragment power thus curbing the threat posed by wealthy minorities and impetuous (rash, impulsive) majorities.

3. The *Federalist Papers* were written by Madison, Hamilton, and Jay to support ratification of the Constitution. Madison argued in *Federalist No. 10* that political factions are undesirable but inevitable.

4. The Federalists pledged to add a Bill of Rights to protect the rights of individuals and the states.

## INSIDER TIP

The Federalists drew support from large landowners, wealthy merchants, and professionals. The Anti-Federalists drew support from small farmers and rural areas.

## TOPIC 49
# KEY ANTI-FEDERALIST ARGUMENTS

1. The proposed Constitution will create a powerful central government that will threaten individual liberties. Anti-Federalists favored a weak national government and strong state governments.
2. The proposed Constitution gives too much power to the President and the Senate. Both are too removed from the people since the President is chosen by the Electoral College and senators are chosen by state legislatures. The Senate will become an aristocratic body that will thwart the will of the more democratic House of Representatives.
3. The proposed Constitution will not work in a large nation with diverse interests. A republic works best in a small nation with a homogenous population.
4. The proposed Constitution does not contain a Bill of Rights listing individual liberties that cannot be violated by the central government.

## TOPIC 50
# KEY FEDERALIST ARGUMENTS

1. The proposed Constitution creates a federal system in which power is shared between state and federal governments. The powers of the national government are limited to issues affecting the entire country. All other powers are reserved to the states.
2. The proposed Constitution allows the majority to express its will while at the same time protecting minority rights. For example, the separation of powers and the use of checks and balances make it difficult for any special interest to dominate the government.
3. The proposed Constitution will work in a large republic. It will fragment political power and thus curb the threat posed by both the wealthy minority and the non-wealthy majority.
4. The proposed Constitution will create a federal government with enough power to preserve domestic tranquility by quickly responding to disturbances such as Shays' Rebellion.

## TOPIC 51
# THE *FEDERALIST PAPERS*

1. The *Federalist Papers* are a collection of newspaper editorials written by James Madison, Alexander Hamilton, and John Jay to support ratification of the Constitution of 1787.
2. The *Federalist Papers* challenged conventional political wisdom when they asserted that a large republic offered the best protection of minority rights.
3. In *Federalist No. 10*, Madison argued that political factions are undesirable but inevitable. He believed that a large republic with three branches of government would disperse power and thus curb factionalism.

## TOPIC 52
# THE BILL OF RIGHTS

1. The Constitution as originally written, contained a number of specific rights and restrictions on government authority. For example, the new government could not grant titles of nobility or require a religious oath for holding a federal office.
2. When Anti-Federalists objected to the absence of a bill of rights, the Federalists pledged that the First Congress would draw up a list of safeguards to protect the rights of individuals and states.
3. The First Amendment guarantees freedom of speech, freedom of press, and freedom of religion.
4. The Fourth Amendment guards against unreasonable searches and seizures.
5. The Sixth Amendment guarantees defendants the right to a speedy trial.

## INSIDER TIP

Most political scientists now agree that the *Federalist Papers* did not achieve their goal of influencing delegates in New York to ratify the Constitution. However, the *Federalist Papers* are considered a definitive explanation of the theoretical underpinnings of the Constitution.

## PODCAST 10.1
THE *FEDERALIST PAPERS*

# CHAPTER 11
# MAKING KEY COMPARISONS, 1492 – 1789

## ESSENTIAL POINTS

1. Recent APUSH exams have included a significant number of free-response questions asking students to make comparisons between events, peoples, colonies, geographic regions, and social movements. These comparison essays require substantial relevant information and an effective analysis of similarities and differences. This chapter is the first of four chapters designed to provide you with a clear and succinct comparison of frequently tested topics.

**TOPIC 53**

# COMPARING NATIVE AMERICANS AND NORTH AMERICAN COLONISTS

## 1. SIMILARITIES
- Both lived in village communities
- Both had strong spiritual beliefs
- Both practiced a division of labor based upon gender
- Both had economies based predominately upon agriculture

## 2. DIFFERENCES
- Native Americans believed that land could be used but not privately owned. In contrast, the North American colonists believed that land could be divided and owned by private individuals.
- Native Americans did not possess advanced weapons. In contrast, the North American colonists were equipped with guns, cannons, warships, and horses.
- Native Americans often lived in matrilineal societies in which property passed though the maternal line on the death of the mother. For example, the Iroquois had a matrilineal system in which women held property and hereditary leadership passed through their line. In contrast, the North American colonists lived in strict patrilineal societies in which property and hereditary leadership passed through the paternal line.

**TOPIC 54**

# COMPARING VIRGINIA AND MASSACHUSETTS

## 1. VIRGINIA
- Founded by a joint-stock company to make a profit
- Settled by males who experienced a high mortality rate
- Developed an agricultural economy based upon tobacco as a cash crop
- Utilized a labor system based upon indentured servants from England and then slaves from Africa

- Lived on widely dispersed plantations and small farms
- Founded as England's first royal colony
- Dominated by an elite group of tidewater gentry

## 2. MASSACHUSETTS
- Founded by Pilgrims and Puritans seeking religious freedom
- Settled by families who experienced a high birth rate and a high average age
- Developed a diversified economy based upon shipbuilding, fishing, and a leading role in the triangular trade.
- Utilized a labor system based upon independent farmers, craftsmen, and merchants
- Lived in tightly knit communities centered around a meeting house
- Forced to become a royal colony in 1691
- Dominated by an elite group of Puritan ministers and wealthy merchants

# TOPIC 55
# COMPARING NEW SPAIN AND NEW FRANCE

## 1. NEW SPAIN
- Explored by sea captains looking for a short route to Asia
- Conquered by conquistadores who toppled the centralized Aztec and Inca empires
- Included the Spanish Southwest, Mexico, Central America, and Peru
- Exploited by royal officials who mined Mexican and Peruvian gold and silver and shipped the mineral wealth to Spain
- Dominated by Spanish officials and priests who Christianized the native peoples and forced them to live and work on encomiendas
- Imposed Spanish culture, language, and religion on a mixed Indian and Spanish population

## 2. NEW FRANCE
- Explored by sea captains looking for a northwest passage to Asia
- Settled by traders and trappers who developed a lucrative fur trade with the Indian tribes
- Included Canada, the entire Mississippi River Valley, and Louisiana
- Christianized by Jesuit priests who did not require Native American converts to move to missions
- Populated primarily by male trappers who lived and worked in widely scattered trading posts
- Characterized by generally cooperative relations with the Native American tribes

# TOPIC 56
# COMPARING THE FEDERALISTS AND THE ANTI-FEDERALISTS

## 1. THE ANTI-FEDERALISTS
- Included small farmers, shopkeepers, and laborers
- Favored strong state governments and a weak national government
- Called for a Bill of Rights to protect individual liberties

## 2. THE FEDERALISTS
- Included large landowners, wealthy merchants, and professionals
- Favored a strong central government and weak state governments
- Promised to add a Bill of Rights specifically protecting individual liberties

**TOPIC 57**

# COMPARING BACON'S REBELLION AND SHAYS' REBELLION

## 1. BACON'S REBELLION, 1676

- Sparked by the anger of land-hungry former indentured servants who opposed Governor Berkeley's arbitrary rule and policies that protected Indian tribes and favored wealthy tidewater planters
- Exposed tensions in Virginia between poor former indentured servants and the wealthy and entrenched tidewater gentry
- Convinced planters to replace troublesome indentured servants with slaves imported from Africa

## 2. SHAYS' REBELLION, 1787

- Sparked by the anger of frustrated Massachusetts farmers who were losing their property because they could not repay their debts to Boston creditors in hard currency
- Exposed tensions in Massachusetts between struggling farmers and the wealthy bankers and merchants who dominated the Massachusetts legislature
- Convinced George Washington, James Madison, and other leaders that the United States needed a stronger national government to protect property owners and creditors

**CHAPTER 12**
# THE FEDERALIST ERA, 1789 – 1800

## ESSENTIAL POINTS

1. Hamilton's financial policies were designed to give the propertied interests a stake in the success of the new government. His plan included creating national bank, enacting a protective tariff, expanding manufacturing, and assuming the debts incurred by states during the Revolutionary War.

2. Jefferson opposed Hamilton's loose interpretation of the necessary and proper clause to justify creating a national bank. Jefferson advocated a strict interpretation arguing that what the Constitution does not permit, it forbids.

3. Shays' Rebellion demonstrated the weakness of the Articles of the Confederation. The Whiskey Rebellion demonstrated the strength of the executive branch created by the Constitution.

4. Washington's Farewell Address urged future leaders to avoid forming permanent alliances with foreign nations.

5. The Federalist Party supported Hamilton's economic policies and pro-British foreign policy. The Democratic-Republicans opposed the national bank and supported France over Great Britain.

6. The Quasi-War with France sparked public outrage that enabled the Federalists to pass a series of laws known as the Alien and Sedition Acts. These acts were intended to intimidate and punish the Democratic-Republicans.

7. The Virginia and Kentucky Resolutions formulated a **STATES' RIGHTS** doctrine asserting that the Constitution arose as a compact among sovereign states that retained the power to challenge and if necessary nullify federal laws.

## TOPIC 58
# HAMILTON'S FINANCIAL PROGRAM

### 1. GOALS
- To strengthen national finances and promote economic growth.
- To give the propertied and financial classes a stake in the success of the new government.
- To move the country away from its reliance on agriculture and toward an economy based on commerce and manufacturing.

### 2. COMPONENTS
- To fund the federal debt at face value and with current holders of government bonds.
- To assume state debts incurred during the Revolution.
- To adopt an excise tax on liquor to aid in raising revenue to fund the nation's debts.
- To impose tariffs on imported goods to raise revenue and to protect America's new industries.
- To charter a national bank that would provide a stable currency and source of capital for loans to fund the development of business and commerce.

## TOPIC 59
# THE NATIONAL BANK DEBATE

### 1. IS A NATIONAL BANK CONSTITUTIONAL?
- Congress passed the bank bill over Madison's objections. Before signing the bill into law, Washington asked Jefferson and Hamilton to compose written opinions on the constitutionality of the bank bill.
- Washington's request sparked America's first debate on constitutional interpretation. Should there be a strict or a broad interpretation of the Constitution?

### 2. JEFFERSON'S ARGUMENTS
- Jefferson admitted that a bank would be a convenient aid to Congress in regulating the currency and collecting taxes.
- However, Jefferson forcefully argued that a national bank was not absolutely necessary. The Constitution did

not specifically authorize Congress to create a national bank. Jefferson argued that what the Constitution does not permit, it forbids. He concluded that the states, not Congress, had the power to charter banks. "To take a single step beyond the boundaries thus specially drawn around the powers of Congress," Jefferson wrote, "is to take possession of a boundless field of power, no longer susceptible of any definition."

### 3. HAMILTON'S ARGUMENTS

- Hamilton argued that the Constitution specifically empowered Congress to collect taxes and regulate trade. A national bank would be more than a convenience; it would be a necessary institution for carrying out these powers.
- Hamilton believed that the necessary and proper clause gave Congress the implied power to charter a national bank. He argued that what the Constitution does not forbid, it permits. "If the end," Hamilton emphasized, "be clearly comprehended within any of the specified powers, collecting taxes and regulating currency, and if the measures have an obvious relation to that end, and is not forbidden by any particular provision of the Constitution, it may safely be deemed to come within the compass of the mutual authority."

### 4. WASHINGTON'S DECISION

- Hamilton's arguments prevailed and Washington signed the bank bill into law thus chartering the First National Bank of the United States.
- Hamilton's "loose construction" theory of the Constitution set an important precedent for the expansion of federal power.

## TOPIC 60
# THE WHISKEY REBELLION, 1794

PODCAST 12.1
THE WHISKEY
REBELLION

1. Hamilton's excise tax on liquor provoked resistance and evasion among frontier farmers.
2. Outraged farmers in western Pennsylvania tar and feathered federal tax collectors, stopped court proceedings, and blew up the stills of those who paid the tax.

## INSIDER TIP

The Whiskey Rebellion was a component in free-response questions on both the 2003B and 2007 APUSH exams. See Essay 2A (Question 2) on the 2007 exam for a very good comparison of Shays' Rebellion and the Whiskey Rebellion. It is important to remember that Washington's show of force set a precedent for using federal power to enforce laws passed by Congress.

3. Encouraged by Hamilton, Washington called out 12,900 militia-men to suppress the Whiskey Rebellion.

4. It is interesting to compare Shays' Rebellion and the Whiskey Rebellion. Both involved backcountry farmers whose protests tested the strength of new governments. Shays' Rebellion demonstrated the weakness of the Articles of Confederation and the need for a stronger national government. The suppression of the Whiskey Rebellion demonstrated the strength of the new federal government. Washington's prompt use of force showed that it was no longer acceptable to challenge unpopular laws with the type of revolutionary tactics used during the Stamp Act crisis.

# TOPIC 61
# FOREIGN AFFAIRS UNDER WASHINGTON

## 1. WASHINGTON'S NEUTRALITY PROCLAMATION, 1793

- The French Revolution soon led to a prolonged war between Great Britain and France that did not end until Napoleon's final defeat at Waterloo in 1815.
- Under the terms of the Franco-American alliance of 1778, the United States was a French ally, bound to defend her possessions in the West Indies. Washington resisted pressure from supporters of both France and Great Britain. On April 22, 1793 he issued a Neutrality Proclamation declaring the United States "friendly and impartial toward the belligerent powers:" As America's chief diplomat, Washington did not require the consent of either Congress or his cabinet to issue the Neutrality Proclamation.

## 2. JAY'S TREATY, 1794

- A number of issues strained relations between the United States and Great Britain. The British still refused to evacuate forts in the Northwest Territory. In addition, British naval commanders seized neutral ships trading with the French West Indies. This policy led to the seizure of some 250 American merchant ships.

- Determined to **avoid war with Great Britain**, Washington sent **Chief Justice John Jay to London** with orders to negotiate a treaty resolving the issues dividing the two countries. Jay brought back a treaty in which the **British promised to evacuate the Northwest forts and pay damages** for seized American ships. However, they refused to renounce their right to make future seizures. Jay also agreed that the **United States** would **pay the debts** owed to British merchants on pre-Revolution accounts.

- Jay's Treaty had a number of **important diplomatic consequences**. It kept the peace with Great Britain, strained relations with France and induced Spain to agree to a surprisingly favorable treaty. The Spanish feared that Jay's Treaty foreshadowed (indicate that something will happen) an Anglo-American alliance. They therefore signed **Pinckney's Treaty of 1795** granting the United States free navigation of the Mississippi River and the right to deposit goods at New Orleans.

- Jay's Treaty also had significant **domestic consequences**. Led by **Jefferson**, southern planters vehemently (passionately) opposed the treaty. They protested that it forced them to pay the lion's share of pre-Revolutionary debts while New England merchants collected damages from their seized ships. The ratification fight over Jay's Treaty played a **key role** in exacerbating (worsening) the increasingly bitter disputes between Hamilton's Federalist supporters and Jefferson's Democratic-Republican supporters.

# 3. WASHINGTON'S FAREWELL ADDRESS, 1796

- In his famous **Farewell Address** to the nation in 1796, Washington urged future American leaders to **avoid forming permanent alliances** with foreign nations.

- Washington's Farewell Address had a significant impact upon American foreign policy. For example, following World War I Republican congressmen used Washington's views to justify their refusal to support the League of Nations. During the 1930s, many congressional leaders used Washington's Farewell Address to justify a policy of isolationism to avoid becoming entangled in European conflicts.

## INSIDER TIP

Don't ignore Washington's Farewell Address. It has generated a significant number of multiple-choice questions. Be sure you know that Washington's admonition (earnest warning) influenced American foreign policy following World War I.

**TOPIC 62**
# THE EMERGENCE OF POLITICAL PARTIES

## 1. ORIGINS
- Political parties are not mentioned in the Constitution. Led by James Madison, the Framers opposed political parties as sources of corruption and vehicles for self-interest and personal ambition.
- During the Washington administration political parties began to coalesce (form, unite) around the economic policies and political philosophies of Alexander Hamilton and Thomas Jefferson.
- The Federalist party supported Hamilton's programs while opponents led by Jefferson formed the Democratic-Republican party.
- The question of how America should respond to the French Revolution further deepened the division between Federalists who supported Great Britain and Democratic-Republicans who sympathized with France.

## 2. FEDERALISTS
- Led by Alexander Hamilton and John Adams
- Drew support from New England and eastern port cities
- Favored a strong central government and a loose interpretation of the Constitution
- Supported the national bank and protective tariffs
- Favored commercial interests
- Favored the British over the French

## 3. DEMOCRATIC–REPUBLICANS
- Led by Thomas Jefferson and James Madison
- Drew support from the South and frontier farmers
- Favored a weak central government and a strict interpretation of the Constitution
- Opposed the national bank and protective tariffs
- Favored agricultural interests
- Favored the French over the British

## TOPIC 63
# THE ALIEN AND SEDITION ACTS

1. Adams inherited an **undeclared Quasi-War with France**. By mid-1797, French corsairs had **plundered** some 300 American merchant ships. Congress responded by suspending commerce with France, creating the Navy Department, enlarging the army, and renouncing (disavowing) the Franco-American alliance of 1778.

2. Adams resisted enormous pressure to **declare war** on France. He defied Hamilton and other war hawks by sending new envoys to France. Now led by Napoleon Bonaparte, the French preferred to avoid war with the United States and concentrate on their conflict with Great Britain.

3. The Federalists took advantage of the anti-French furor to pass a series of laws known as the Alien and Sedition Acts. These acts were intended to punish the Democratic-Republicans.

   - The Naturalization Act raised the residency requirement for U.S. citizenship from 5 to 14 years. Outraged Democratic-Republicans insisted that the act's real purpose was to prevent immigrants from voting for their party.

   - The Alien Acts authorized the president to deport dangerous aliens.

   - The Sedition Act made it illegal to speak, write, or print any statements about the president that would bring him "into contempt or disrepute."

PODCAST 12.2
THE ALIEN AND SEDITION ACTS

INSIDER TIP
Be sure that you know that the **Quasi-War** led to an **anti-French furor** that **prompted** the Federalist controlled Congress to pass the Alien and Sedition Acts.

## TOPIC 64
# THE KENTUCKY AND VIRGINIA RESOLUTIONS

1. The Federalists controlled all three branches of the federal government in 1798. Jefferson and Madison believed that the Alien and Sedition Acts embodied a threat to individual liberties caused by unchecked Federalist power.

2. Jefferson and Madison anonymously wrote a series of resolutions that were approved by the Kentucky and Virginia legislatures. They denounced the Alien and

## INSIDER TIP

The Virginia and
Kentucky Resolutions
were a response to the
Alien and Sedition Acts.
The Resolutions received
little support from the
other states. However,
they set an important
precedent for later
states' rights advocates

Sedition Acts as "alarming infractions" of constitutional
rights. The resolutions formulated a STATES' RIGHTS
doctrine asserting that the Constitution arose as a compact
among sovereign states. The states therefore retained the
power to challenge and if necessary nullify federal laws.

3. The immediate dispute over the Alien and Sedition
Acts faded when the laws expired in 1801. However, the
Kentucky and Virginia Resolutions advanced arguments
that John C. Calhoun adopted during the nullification
crisis of the 1830s.

# CHAPTER 13
# JEFFERSON, MADISON, AND THE WAR OF 1812, 1800 – 1815

## ESSENTIAL POINTS

1. The election of 1800 has been called "a second revolution" because there was a peaceful transfer of power between the victorious Democratic-Republicans and the defeated Federalists.
2. Jeffersonian democracy emphasized the virtues of republican simplicity, an agrarian way of life, and a reduced federal government.
3. Although he was an outspoken supporter of a strict interpretation of the Constitution, Jefferson approved the Louisiana Purchase in order to acquire New Orleans and fulfill his vision of enabling America to become an agrarian republic.
4. Jefferson proved to be a pragmatic (practical) leader who used Hamilton's doctrine of implied powers to justify the Louisiana Purchase and the Embargo Act of 1807.
5. The War of 1812 intensified a spirit of nationalism, transformed Andrew Jackson into a national hero, and contributed to the downfall of the Federalist Party.

## TOPIC 65
# THE REVOLUTION OF 1800

## INSIDER TIP

It is important to remember that the Election of 1800 marked a vital peaceful transfer of political power. Jefferson's famous Inaugural Address urged political reconciliation and set forth the principles of what has come to be called Jeffersonian Democracy.

1. Thomas Jefferson and James Madison organized the Democratic-Republican party. Jefferson narrowly defeated John Adams in the election of 1800 thus ending the "Federalist Decade."
2. The election of 1800 marked a watershed (key turning point) in American political history. It is often called "the Revolution of 1800" because there was a peaceful transfer of political power between the victorious Democratic-Republicans and the defeated Federalists.
3. In his inaugural address, Jefferson stressed that the "essential principles" of American government were above party politics when he reminded his fellow countrymen, "We are all Republicans – we are all Federalists."

## TOPIC 66
# JEFFERSONIAN DEMOCRACY

1. Jefferson's electoral victory marked both a peaceful transfer of power and a transition to a new set of political ideals.
2. Jefferson promised to practice republican simplicity. He carefully avoided the formal ceremonies that characterized the Federalist administrations. For example, White House guests were encouraged to shake hands with the president, rather than bowing as had been the Federalist practice.
3. Republican simplicity meant more than just a new code of presidential etiquette. In his inaugural address, Jefferson promised "a wise and frugal government." Believing that the government governs best that governs least, Jefferson cut the budget, fired federal tax collectors, eliminated the tax on whiskey, and reduced both the army and the navy.
4. Jefferson wanted America to become an agrarian (farm-oriented) republic. He strongly believed that farmers were the backbone of American society because they were the nation's most productive and trustworthy citizens.
5. Jefferson believed that freedom of speech is essential in a republic. He urged Congress to repeal the Alien and Sedition Acts and pardoned those who had been convicted.

# TOPIC 67
# THE LOUISIANA PURCHASE

1. Westerners depended upon the Mississippi River to ship their goods to New Orleans where they were reloaded aboard ocean-going vessels for shipment to the East Coast or to foreign ports.
2. The Pinckney Treaty with Spain granted the United States the right of deposit at New Orleans. However, in 1802 the Spanish revoked this privilege. To make matters worse, Spain ceded Louisiana back to France.
3. Napoleon dreamed of restoring the French Empire in America. However, led by Toussaint L'Ouverture, slaves on the West Indian island of Santo Domingo successfully revolted against French rule. Napoleon then decided to abandon Santo Domingo and sell Louisiana to the United States for about $15 million.
4. Napoleon's offer to sell Louisiana presented Jefferson with a difficult dilemma. The Constitution did not expressly grant the President or Congress the power to acquire foreign territory. As an outspoken proponent (supporter) of a strict interpretation of the Constitution, how could Jefferson approve the purchase of Louisiana? Jefferson's advisors argued that his presidential power to make treaties gave him the implied power to purchase territory. Fearing that the capricious (fickle) Napoleon might change his mind, Jefferson relented and the Senate overwhelmingly approved the Louisiana Purchase.
5. The Louisiana Purchase doubled the size of the United States. Jefferson optimistically believed that the purchase would fulfill his vision of enabling America to become an agrarian republic that would become an Empire of Liberty.
6. Jefferson sponsored the Lewis and Clark expedition to explore the Louisiana Territory. The expedition accomplished the following goals:
   - It strengthened American claims to the Oregon territory.
   - It added to the knowledge about northwestern America.
   - It mapped and explored the Mississippi River and the Columbia River.

## INSIDER TIP

It is important to remember that Jefferson advocated a strict interpretation of the Constitution in his debates with Alexander Hamilton. However, Jefferson adopted a more flexible position as president. The Louisiana Purchase forced the now more pragmatic Jefferson to adopt a broad interpretation of presidential power. It is interesting to note that the Louisiana Purchase added more territory to the United States than the purchase of Alaska in 1867.

## PODCAST 13.1
THE LOUISIANA PURCHASE

## INSIDER TIP

The principle of judicial review is one of the most frequently tested items on APUSH exams and SAT II tests. You do not have to know the complex details of the case. Instead, make sure you know the definition of judicial review.

## PODCAST 13.2
*MARBURY v. MADISON*

### TOPIC 68
# JOHN MARSHALL AND *MARBURY V. MADISON*

1. As Chief Justice of the Supreme Court from 1801 to 1835, John Marshall issued a number of landmark decisions that strengthened the power of the federal government, upheld the supremacy of federal law over state legislatures, and promoted business enterprise.
2. Marshall established the principle of JUDICIAL REVIEW in the famous case of *Marybury v. Madison*. Judicial review gave the Supreme Court the authority to determine the constitutionality of congressional acts.

### TOPIC 69
# WAS THE "REVOLUTION OF 1800" REALLY A REVOLUTION?

1. Jefferson liked to describe his election as the "Revolution of 1800." The election of 1800 did mark a peaceful transfer of power. But to what extent did Jefferson redirect federal policies away from Hamiltonian principles?

### 2. ECONOMIC POLICY
- Although he opposed its creation, Jefferson accepted Hamilton's national bank as an essential convenience.
- Jefferson pleased frontier farmers by repealing the whiskey tax.
- Jefferson reduced federal spending by cutting the size of both the army and the navy.

### 3. DOMESTIC POLICY
- Jefferson favored a "strict" interpretation of the Constitution. However, he proved to be a flexible and pragmatic (practical) leader when he used Hamilton's doctrine of implied powers to justify the Louisiana Purchase.
- Unlike Hamilton, Jefferson believed that the public could be trusted to govern itself. He supported public education and the expansion of voting rights to more white, male citizens. Jefferson thus laid the foundation for the expansion of suffrage during the Jackson administration.

## 4. FOREIGN POLICY

- Although he was an ardent supporter of the French Revolution, Jefferson continued Washington's policy of remaining neutral and avoiding foreign wars.
- In 1807, Jefferson persuaded Congress to pass an Embargo Act which stopped all exports of American goods to Europe. Jefferson once again drew upon Hamilton's doctrine of implied powers by claiming that the government's power to regulate commerce could be used to justify imposing an embargo. Although the embargo failed to force the British to abandon their practice of impressing Americans into the royal navy, it did inflict economic hardship on American farmers and merchants.

## INSIDER TIP

The 2004B APUSH exam asked students to evaluate the "Revolution of 1800." See Question 2 Essay 2A for a sophisticated analysis of this issue. The essay received a 9.

## TOPIC 70
# THE WAR OF 1812

## 1. WHAT HAPPENED?

- The United States tried to avoid war with Great Britain and France by following a policy of neutrality.
- Angered by the British practice of impressing American seaman into the Royal Navy, a group of "War Hawks" in Congress demanded war. In June 1812, President Madison asked Congress to declare war against Great Britain.
- The war proved to be indecisive. The United States controlled the Great Lakes but failed to conquer Canada. The British burned Washington, D. C., but suffered a major defeat at the Battle of New Orleans. The American navy won a number of duels with British vessels.

## 2. WHAT CAUSED THE WAR OF 1812?

- The British practice of impressment violated American neutrality and insulted national pride.
- Led by Henry Clay, the War Hawks supported war to drive the British from Canada and to remove the Indian threat from the frontier.

## INSIDER TIP

Test writers rarely ask questions about the military campaigns of the War of 1812. Instead, focus your attention on the war's causes and consequences.

## 3. WHY SHOULD YOU REMEMBER THE WAR OF 1812?

- The Battle of New Orleans restored American pride and transformed Andrew Jackson into a national hero.
- The interruption of trade led to an increase in domestic manufacturing thus promoting industrialization.
- New England merchants strongly opposed the War of 1812. Leading Federalists met at the Hartford Convention and proposed a number of constitutional amendments designed to limit the power of the federal government. However, the Hartford Convention contributed to the demise (death) of the Federalist party by making its leaders appear to be disloyal.
- The War of 1812 intensified a spirit of nationalism. The war "federalized" Madison who now supported rechartering the national bank and increasing tariffs to protect the nation's "infant" industries from foreign competition.

**CHAPTER 14**
# THE ERA OF GOOD FEELINGS, 1816 – 1824

## ESSENTIAL POINTS

1. In antebellum America, the term **INTERNAL IMPROVEMENTS** referred to transportation projects. Henry Clay's American System was a program of protective tariffs and internal improvements designed to promote economic growth and national unity.

2. The Marshall Court continued to render landmark decisions that opposed states' rights and strengthened the power of the federal government. For example, in *McCullock v. Maryland* the Court declared the national bank constitutional and denied the right of a state to tax the legitimate activities of the federal government.

3. The Missouri Compromise temporarily delayed a political crisis over slavery by maintaining the sectional balance in the Senate by providing for the admission of Missouri as a slave state and Maine as a free state. The Missouri Compromise closed the remaining portions of the Louisiana Purchase north of 36°30' to slavery.

4. The Monroe Doctrine was a unilateral declaration of principles announcing that the republican governments in the Americas are different and separate from the political systems in Europe and that the American continents are no longer open to European colonization.

## INSIDER TIP

The 2002B exam included a DBQ asking students to evaluate the accuracy of the label, "The Era of Good Feelings." See Essay 1C for a convincing thesis that patriotism, economic growth, and political stability combined to produce an "Era of Good Feelings." Readers scored the essay a 9 because of its strong thesis, mastery of the documents, and skillful use of outside information.

## TOPIC 71
# JAMES MONROE AND THE SURGE OF NATIONALISM

1. The Republican candidate James Monroe overwhelmed his Federalist opponent in the 1816 presidential election. He was then reelected in 1824 without opposition. Monroe was the last president of the "Virginia dynasty" that began with Washington and included Jefferson and Madison. He was also the last president to wear a powdered wig and knee breeches.

2. Monroe's presidency began with a surge of nationalism and a spirit of harmony. Americans looked forward to enjoying the benefits of peace and prosperity. One Boston newspaper captured the optimistic spirit of the times when it proclaimed that Monroe's election marked the beginning of an "Era of Good Feelings."

## TOPIC 72
# THE AMERICAN SYSTEM

1. Henry Clay began his career as one of the leading War Hawks. Following the War of 1812, Clay became the foremost proponent (advocate) of a legislative program called the "American System."

2. In antebellum America, the term INTERNAL IMPROVEMENTS referred to transportation projects.

3. Clay's American System was designed to promote economic growth and national unity. It included the following four components:
   • A tariff that would protect American industries and raise revenue to fund internal improvements.
   • A national bank that would promote financial stability.
   • A network of federally funded roads and canals.
   • A vibrant economy with increased trade among the nation's different regions.

4. Clay's American System is similar to Alexander Hamilton's economic vision. Both programs favored a strong federal government that promoted commercial and economic growth.

## TOPIC 73
# JUDICIAL NATIONALISM

1. The Marshall Court continued to render landmark decisions that opposed states' rights and strengthened the power of the federal government.

2. *MCCULLOCH V. MARYLAND*
   - Declared the national bank constitutional.
   - Confirmed the right of Congress to utilize its implied powers.
   - Denied the right of a state to tax the legitimate activities of the federal government.

3. *GIBBONS V. OGDEN*
   - Declared that only Congress had the constitutional power to regulate interstate commerce.
   - Established the commerce clause as a key mechanism for the expansion of federal power.

4. *DARTMOUTH COLLEGE V. WOODWARD*
   - Ruled that a state cannot pass laws to impair a legal private contract.
   - Upheld the sanctity of private contracts against state encroachments.

### INSIDER TIP
Clay's American System has generated a significant number of multiple-choice questions. Be sure that you can identify the plan's goals and recognize its similarities with Hamilton's economic proposals. It is important to note that both Madison and Monroe vetoed spending federal funds on internal improvements.

## TOPIC 74
# THE MISSOURI COMPROMISE

1. When Washington took office the North and South were roughly equal in wealth and population. However, with each passing decade the North steadily outgained the South in population growth. As a result, by 1819 the free states in the North had 105 representatives in the House while the slave states in the South had just 81 representatives.

2. While the North controlled a solid majority in the House of Representatives, the Senate was evenly balanced between 11 free and 11 slave states.

3. In 1819, the territory of Missouri applied for statehood as a slave state. The northern controlled House of Representatives responded by passing the Tallmadge Amendment prohibiting the further introduction of

PODCAST 14.1
THE MISSOURI
COMPROMISE

slaves into Missouri and also providing for the gradual emancipation of slaves already in the territory. Although the Senate rejected the Tallmadge Amendment, the issue of extending slavery into the new territories ignited a passionate sectional debate. Outraged southerners believed that the Tallmadge Amendment threatened the future of the plantation system while also implying a moral attack on slavery and thus the southern way of life.

4. House Speaker Henry Clay promoted a compromise that included the following provisions:
   - Missouri would be admitted into the Union as a slave state.
   - Maine would be admitted into the Union as a free state.
   - Slavery would be prohibited in the remaining portions of the Louisiana Purchase north of latitude 36°30′.

5. The Missouri Compromise temporarily defused the political crisis over slavery. However, the Missouri Compromise debate foreshadowed the divisive intersectional debates over the expansion of slavery that resurfaced during the 1840s and 1850s. Thomas Jefferson sensed the future peril when he wrote, "This momentous question, like a fire bell in the night, awakened and filled me with terror."

## TOPIC 75
# THE MONROE DOCTRINE

1. The Napoleonic Wars accelerated Spain's decline as a great power. The weak Spanish government found it increasingly difficult to maintain control over its possessions in the Americas.

2. Secretary of State John Quincy Adams exploited Spain's weakness by negotiating the Adams-Onis Treaty. Under the terms of this agreement, Spain ceded Florida to the United States. In exchange, the United States abandoned claims to northern Mexico (Texas). In addition, the Adams-Onis Treaty defined the southwestern boundary of the Louisiana Purchase.

3. Spain's losses were not confined to Florida. Spain lost almost its entire New World empire between 1808 and 1822 as Chile, Peru, Columbia, and Mexico all successfully waged wars of liberation.

PODCAST 14.2
THE MONROE
DOCTRINE

4. Following the defeat of Napoleon the European powers suppressed revolutionary movements in Europe. Humiliated by the loss of its New World colonies, Spain turned to France for help. President Monroe and John Quincy Adams feared that France might use force to help Spain overthrow the new Latin American republics.

5. Monroe presented the American position on Latin America in a speech to Congress delivered on December 2, 1823. The speech included a unilateral declaration of the following key points:

- The republican governments in the Americas are different and separate from those in Europe.
- The American continent is no longer open to European colonization.
- The United States will regard European interference in the political affairs of independent New World nations as hostile behavior.
- The United States will not interfere in the internal affairs of European nations.

6. Monroe's statement received little attention at the time. The European powers refrained from interfering in the New World because of the power of British warships, not the eloquence of Monroe's words.

7. Monroe's principles were not forgotten. First called the Monroe Doctrine in 1852, they became the cornerstone of American foreign policy in the Western Hemisphere.

## INSIDER TIP

The Monroe Doctrine is one of the most frequently asked topics on APUSH exams and SAT II tests. Be sure that you know it was a unilateral declaration. It is also interesting to note that like Washington's Farewell Address the Monroe Doctrine made a distinction between the republican government in America and the monarchical governments in Europe.

**CHAPTER 15**

# THE AGE OF JACKSON, 1824 – 1840

## ESSENTIAL POINTS

1. Jackson's election marked the beginning of a new era in American political history. As the hero of the common man, he endorsed expanding the suffrage to include virtually all white men. The Jacksonians also created a more open political system by replacing legislative caucuses with a party nominating convention.

2. Calhoun's **DOCTRINE OF NULLIFICATION** used states' rights arguments first formulated in the Virginia and Kentucky Resolutions. In the Webster-Hayne debate, Daniel Webster denounced states' rights and eloquently defended the principle of national union.

3. Although the Supreme Court's decision in *Worcester v. Georgia* upheld the Cherokee Nation's legal right to their land, President Jackson refused to enforce the ruling. The Trial of Tears refers to the removal of Cherokee Indians from their ancestral lands to the Indian Territory in what is now Oklahoma.

4. Jackson vetoed the Second Bank of the United States denouncing it as a "monster" that benefited special interests. Without the bank's restraining policies, state-chartered "pet banks" expanded credit, flooded the country with paper currency, and promoted speculation in western lands.

5. Led by Henry Clay and Daniel Webster, Jackson's opponents formed the Whig Party. The Whigs favored protective tariffs, internal improvements, and a renewed national bank.

## TOPIC 76
# THE ELECTION OF 1824

1. The demise (death) of the Federalists left the Republican Party unchallenged at the national level. In February 1824 a small group of congressional Republicans attended a caucus where they selected William Crawford of Georgia as their party's presidential nominee. Critics led by Andrew Jackson challenged the caucus as elitist and undemocratic. The Tennessee state legislature promptly nominated Jackson while the Kentucky legislature nominated Henry Clay. And finally, a group of New England Republicans nominated John Quincy Adams.

2. Buoyed by his fame as a war hero, Jackson received far more popular and electoral votes than his three rivals. However, since Jackson did not receive a majority of the electoral votes the election went to the House of Representatives which voted by states.

3. As Speaker of the House, Clay occupied a unique position of power. Although he had been defeated, Clay could use his position to influence the choice of the next president. Clay despised Jackson as a "military chieftain" who was unfit for office. Although Clay was not personally close to Adams, the two men were both nationalists and strong proponents (supporters) of the American System. Clay's influence prevailed and Adams won the presidency.

4. Shortly after winning the House vote, Adams named Clay his new Secretary of State. Jackson's outraged supporters promptly accused Adams and Clay of a "corrupt bargain" that thwarted the will of the people by cheating Old Hickory out of the presidency.

5. Adams' political deal with Clay tarnished his presidency and energized Jackson's supporters. Although he possessed a brilliant intellect, Adams lacked personal charm and a common touch. In contrast, Jackson was hailed as a military hero and champion of the people. While acknowledging that "Adams can write," Old Hickory's followers proudly boasted that "Jackson can fight!" In the 1828 presidential election, Jackson swept the South and West and easily defeated Adams.

## TOPIC 77
# JACKSONIAN DEMOCRACY

1. Jackson's election marked the beginning of a new era in American political history. As the hero of the common man, Jackson vowed to include the voice of the people in the election process. The Jacksonians dramatically expanded the suffrage to include virtually all white men. In addition, Jackson created a more open political system by replacing legislative caucuses with a party nominating convention.

2. As a self-made soldier, politician, and planter, Jackson believed that the average American could quickly master most government jobs. "Every man is as good as his neighbor," Jackson confidently declared. Jackson enthusiastically supported a "spoils system" by rewarding loyal party workers with government jobs.

3. As the first president from the West, Jackson shared the frontier's distrust of the Eastern elite. He promised to represent the interests of the common man by attacking special privileges in American life.

## INSIDER TIP
Jackson's image as the champion of the common man was at odds with his status as a wealthy planter. Jackson resolved this contradiction by embodying the frontier values of rugged individualism and hostility toward privileged elites.

## TOPIC 78
# THE TARIFF OF ABOMINATIONS AND THE NULLIFICATION CRISIS

### 1. THE TARIFF OF ABOMINATIONS

- Tariffs traditionally raised revenue and protected American industry from European competitors. In 1828, Congress passed a protective tariff that set rates at record levels.
- Led by South Carolina, the Southern states branded the hated law the "Tariff of Abominations." Planters argued that while the industrial Northeast flourished, the South was forced to sell its cotton in a world market unprotected by tariffs and buy manufactured goods at exorbitant (outrageously high) prices.

## INSIDER TIP

Like the earlier Kentucky and Virginia Resolutions and the Hartford Convention, the Nullification Crisis underscored the ongoing controversy over the relationship between the federal government and the state governments. It is interesting to note that none of the other Southern states rose to defend South Carolina. Militants then turned from nullification and embraced the doctrine of secession as the best way to remedy their grievances.

## 2. JOHN C. CALHOUN AND THE DOCTRINE OF NULLIFICATION

- In 1828 Vice-President John C. Calhoun anonymously wrote the "South Carolina Exposition and Protest" to denounce the Tariff of Abominations.
- Calhoun argued that the Union was a compact formed by sovereign states. If a state believed that a federal law exceeded the delegated powers of Congress, the state could declare the law "null and void" within its own boundaries.
- Calhoun's DOCTRINE OF NULLIFICATION used states rights' arguments first formulated by Jefferson and Madison in the Kentucky and Virginia Resolutions. Calhoun did not advocate secession. Instead, he saw nullification as a viable option that would prevent disunion.

## 3. THE WEBSTER–HAYNE DEBATE, 1830

- In January 1830, Senator Robert Hayne of South Carolina, vigorously defended states' rights and Calhoun's doctrine of nullification in a Senate speech that attracted national attention.
- Hayne's speech triggered a national debate with Senator Daniel Webster of Massachusetts. Renowned as the nation's greatest orator, Webster argued that the Constitution was created by the people, not the states. The Supreme Court, not the states, had the power to decide the constitutionality of the a law. Webster denounced states' rights and concluded by thundering, "Liberty and Union, now and forever, one and inseparable!"

## 4. JACKSON AND THE FORCE BILL

- Inspired by Calhoun and Hayne, South Carolina refused to back down. The South Carolina legislature adopted an ordinance of nullification that repudiated the tariff acts of 1828 and 1832.
- Jackson angrily called nullification an "impractical absurdity" and warned South Carolina that "disunion by armed force is treason." He then called upon Congress to pass a "Force Bill" authorizing him to use the army to enforce federal laws in South Carolina.

- As tensions mounted, Henry Clay proposed a new compromise tariff that would gradually reduce duties over the next ten years. The compromise worked and South Carolina rescinded its nullification ordinance.

## TOPIC 79
# JACKSON AND THE INDIAN REMOVAL ACT

### 1. THE INDIAN REMOVAL ACT
- The approximately 125,000 Native Americans who lived east of the Mississippi were surrounded by white settlers who wanted the tribes resettled across the Mississippi.
- Congress responded by passing the Indian Removal Act providing for the exchange of Indian lands in the East for government lands in the newly established Indian Territory.

### 2. *WORCESTER V. GEORGIA*, 1832
- The Cherokees legally challenged President Jackson's removal order.
- In *Worcester v. Georgia* Chief Justice John Marshall upheld the Cherokee Nation's legal right to their land.
- The Supreme Court is dependent upon the President to enforce its decisions. As a famous Indian fighter, Jackson harbored a well-known animosity (dislike) toward Native Americans. Jackson responded to the *Worcester v. Georgia* decision by defiantly declaring, "John Marshall has made his decision, now let him enforce it."

### 3. THE TRAIL OF TEARS
- Jackson defied the Court's decision and pushed forward with his policy of removing the remaining eastern tribes west of the Mississippi.
- In 1838, the U.S. Army forcibly removed about 17,000 Cherokees from their ancestral lands and marched them on an 800-mile journey to the Indian Territory. About one-fourth of the Cherokees died from disease and exhaustion on what poignantly (sorrowfully) came to be known as the Trail of Tears.

## INSIDER TIP
Be sure that you can identify the Trail of Tears on a map. The trail begins in northern Georgia and ends in Indian Territory in what is now Oklahoma.

## PODCAST 15.1
THE TRAIL OF TEARS

## INSIDER TIP

The 2001 AP exam included a free-response question asking students to evaluate the extent to which the Jacksonian era lived up to its characterization as a period of the "common man." See Question 3, Essay II for a particularly impressive analysis of how Jackson's frontier image, support for universal suffrage for white males, and war against the National Bank all contributed to his reputation as a champion of the "common man."

## INSIDER TIP

Although the Whigs and Democrats differed on most issues they both endorsed the increased political participation of the "common man."

# TOPIC 80
# THE BANK WAR

1. The twenty-year charter of the Second Bank of the United States was scheduled to expire in 1836.
2. Jackson regarded the bank as a "monster" that concentrated special financial privileges in the hands of an aristocratic elite. In July 1832, Jackson vetoed a bill to re-charter the bank. In his veto message, Jackson denounced the bank as a vehicle used by "the rich and powerful to bend the acts of government to their selfish purposes."
3. Without the bank's restraining policies, state-chartered "pet banks" expanded credit, flooded the country with paper currency, and promoted rampant (widespread) speculation in western lands and transportation projects.
4. The demise (death) of the Second Bank of the United States contributed to a financial panic in 1837. The Panic of 1837 evolved into a lengthy economic slump as businesses failed and unemployment rose.

# TOPIC 81
# THE RISE OF THE WHIGS

1. The South Carolina nullification crisis, the Indian Removal Act and the battle over the national bank were all divisive issues that provoked contentious (very argumentative) national debates.
2. Political opponents led by Henry Clay and Daniel Webster hated Jackson and derisively called him "King Andrew I." Jackson's rivals left the Democratic Party and drew together into a newly formed Whig Party.
3. The Whigs favored protective tariffs, internal improvements, and a renewed national bank. Above all, they were united by their animosity (dislike) toward Jackson and his chosen successor Martin Van Buren.
4. In 1840 the Whigs nominated William Henry Harrison to oppose Van Buren. The Whigs emphasized Harrison's heroic military victories over Indians and blamed "Van Ruin" for the economic slump. Harrison's election marked a triumph of a new democratic style of running political campaigns.

Although Harrison's father was a prominent Virginia planter who signed the Declaration of Independence, the Whigs adopted the log cabin and hard cider as campaign symbols to connect with the common man. Many historians consider the "log cabin and hard cider" campaign of 1840 the first "modern" election because both parties actively campaigned among the voting masses.

**CHAPTER 16**

# THE TRANSPORTATION AND MARKET REVOLUTIONS, 1815 – 1860

## ESSENTIAL POINTS

1. Turnpikes, canals, steamboats, and railroads sparked a **MARKET REVOLUTION** that created a national economy.

2. The Erie Canal strengthened commercial ties between eastern manufacturing centers and western agricultural regions. It ignited the rapid growth of Buffalo, New York while helping transform New York City into America's greatest commercial center.

3. The transportation and market revolutions created commercial ties between the Northeast and the Midwest. However, the South failed to keep up with the pace of industrialization and urbanization in these two regions.

## INSIDER TIP

Recent APUSH exams and SAT II US History tests have included multiple-choice questions on the consequences of the Erie Canal. It is interesting to note that these tests have devoted very few questions to railroads in the antebellum period.

## PODCAST 16.1
### THE ERIE CANAL

### TOPIC 82
# THE TRANSPORTATION REVOLUTION

1. Canals, steamboats, and railroads revolutionized American economic and social life during the antebellum period between 1820 and 1860.
2. Key transportation developments
   - Turnpikes such as the National Road promoted trade and communication with the Old Northwest.
   - Steamboats carried bulky farm products such as wheat, corn, and flour far more cheaply than covered wagons. By the 1840s, steamboats opened the Ohio and Mississippi river valleys to two-way traffic.
   - Canals strengthened ties between eastern cities and western agricultural regions.
   - Railroads connected cities, encouraged settlement, and reduced the cost of transporting goods. The number of miles of railroad track soared from just 13 when the Baltimore and Ohio line opened in 1829 to 30,626 in 1860.

### TOPIC 83
# THE ERIE CANAL

1. Farmers and merchants in the Old Northwest lacked efficient and inexpensive access to the markets along the east coast. For example, farmers surrounding Pittsburgh were forced to use the Ohio and Mississippi rivers to send their products to New Orleans and from there to cities on the east coast.
2. The Erie Canal connected Albany on the Hudson River with Buffalo on Lake Erie. When it opened in 1825 the 363-mile-long waterway created an all-water route that cut travel time from New York City to Buffalo from 20 days to 6 and reduced the cost of moving a ton of freight between these two cities from $100.00 to $5.00.
3. The Erie Canal had a number of significant consequences:
   - It helped transform New York City into America's greatest commercial center.
   - It created commercial ties between the eastern manufacturing centers and western agricultural regions.
   - It inspired a mania for building canals that lasted throughout the 1830s.

## TOPIC 84
# THE MARKET REVOLUTION

*The Asians I was talking about. Right there, just came* →

1. During the Era of Good Feelings, most Americans bought goods from friends and neighbors in a local economy.
2. The new network of roads, canals, and rail lines enabled people to buy and sell goods with consumers in distant markets.
3. The term MARKET REVOLUTION in the antebellum period refers to the creation of a national economy that connected distant communities for the first time.
4. The creation of large lucrative (profitable) markets led to an American system of manufacturing that utilized machines with interchangeable parts to mass produce standardized low-cost goods.

## TOPIC 85
# IMPACT OF THE TRANSPORTATION AND MARKET REVOLUTIONS

## 1. IMPACT ON THE NORTHEAST
- Accelerated the rate of industrial growth.
- Prompted the construction of textile mills in New England.
- Created a close trade relationship between New England and the Old Northwest.
- Created a wealthy class of urban capitalists.

## 2. IMPACT ON THE MIDWEST
- Accelerated the migration of settlers into the Midwest.
- Transformed Chicago into an important rail-center and agricultural distributor to the West.
- Enabled Pittsburgh, Cincinnati, St. Louis, Cleveland, and Detroit to become thriving industrial and commercial centers.
- Increased the production of cash crops such as corn and wheat.
- Linked closely to the Northeast by canal and railroad networks.

## INSIDER TIP
Both the 2003 (Question 3) and the 2008 (Question 3) APUSH exams contained free-response questions on the impact of the transportation and market revolutions. See Essay I (2003) and Essay 3A (2008) for excellent responses that received 9's.

## 3. IMPACT ON THE SOUTH

- Failed to keep up with the pace of industrialization and urbanization in the Northeast and Midwest.
- Extended a plantation system based on cotton and slavery westward into Alabama and Mississippi.
- Remained an agricultural economy dominated by an elite group of wealthy planters.

# CHAPTER 17
# THE OLD SOUTH, 1815 – 1860

## ESSENTIAL POINTS

1. The invention of the cotton gin transformed cotton into America's most valuable cash crop. By 1860 a vast region extending from eastern North Carolina to the Mississippi River Valley produced over half of the world's supply of cotton.

2. As the South became committed to a one-crop cotton economy it also became committed to slavery. The presence of slavery discouraged manufacturing, slowed urban growth, and deterred European immigrants from moving to the South.

3. A small but powerful group of planters owned more than half of all the slaves and harvested most of the region's cotton and tobacco. The majority of white families in the antebellum South owned no slaves.

4. The westward spread of slavery into the Deep South uprooted countless families. Despite forced separations, slaves maintained strong kinship networks and a separate African American culture.

5. Southerners defended slavery as a "positive good" saying that the Bible condoned slavery and that blacks were an inferior people who required white guardianship.

## TOPIC 86
# THE COTTON KINGDOM

### 1. THE CHESAPEAKE REGION AND SLAVERY
- The Chesapeake Bay economy was originally built around using a labor force of indentured servants to work on tobacco plantations.
- Laws in early 17th century Virginia did not make a clear legal distinction between a slave and a servant. However, by the early 1700's, new "slave codes" made black people and their children the lifetime property (or "chattels") of white slave owners.
- Slavery faced an uncertain future in the Chesapeake region in 1790. The tobacco market had already experienced a slowdown before the Revolution and continued to decline in the post-war years. As slave labor became less necessary, Chesapeake planters began to switch to grain and livestock.

### 2. ELI WHITNEY AND THE COTTON GIN
- During the late 1700s a series of inventions revolutionized the textile industry in Great Britain. These advances created an insatiable (limitless) demand for raw cotton. Southern farmers could not meet the demand for raw cotton because of the difficulty of separating cotton fiber from its sticky seeds. It required a full day for a laborer to separate a pound of cotton by hand.
- In 1793, Eli Whitney invented a machine to perform this tedious chore. His cotton gin enabled slaves to separate fifty times as much cotton as could be done by hand. As a result of Whitney's invention, cotton production soared from 9,000 bales in 1791 to 987,000 in 1831 and 4 million in 1860. It is interesting to note that each bale contained 500 pounds of cotton.

### 3. KING COTTON
- Cotton quickly became America's most valuable cash crop. In 1840, cotton production accounted for more than half of the value of all American exports.
- The excessive cultivation of tobacco depleted the soil. As old fields in the Chesapeake states wore out ambitious

planters looked south and west for rich new farm lands. By 1860, a vast cotton belt stretched from eastern North Carolina to the Mississippi River Valley. This region produced over half of the world's supply of cotton. Proud southern planters confidently boasted that "Cotton is King."

## 4. THE IMPACT OF THE COTTON ECONOMY

- Cotton irrevocably (irreversibly) altered the South's attitude toward slavery. Prior to the invention of the cotton gin thoughtful southerners regarded slavery as a necessary evil that would gradually be phased out. However, as the South became committed to a one-crop cotton economy it also became committed to slavery. Of the 2.5 million slaves engaged in agriculture in 1850, 75 percent worked at cotton production.

- The presence of slavery discouraged immigrants from moving to the South. In 1860 just 4.4 percent of the southern population was foreign-born. Meanwhile, between 1844 and 1854 over 3 million European immigrants flooded into eastern seaports. The overwhelming majority of these immigrants came from Ireland and Germany.

- As the South devoted more and more resources to growing cotton, the region lagged behind the North in trade and manufacturing. Southern cotton was primarily exported in northern vessels. While northern factories produced manufactured goods at an ever increasing rate, southern farmers purchased finished goods under a credit system that kept them in debt.

- The South's commitment to growing cotton slowed urban growth. With the exception of New Orleans and Charleston, the South had few urban centers. Instead, most southerners lived on widely dispersed farms and plantations.

## INSIDER TIP

By 1860 there were 4 million black slaves in the South. At that time Southern planters had invested $2 billion of their capital into slaves.

## TOPIC 87
# WHITE SOCIETY IN THE OLD SOUTH

### 1. THE PLANTERS
- Planters comprised just 4 percent of the South's adult white male population. This small but powerful group owned more than half of all the slaves and harvested most of the cotton and tobacco.
- Planters were a wealthy elite who dominated southern economic and social life. The image of the paternalistic (fatherly) planter who lived in a white-columned mansion came to embody (represent) a distinctive southern way of life that valued tradition, honor, and genteel (refined) manners.

### 2. YEOMAN FARMERS
- The majority of white families in the antebellum South were independent yeoman farmers who owned few, if any, slaves.
- Although the South's numerical majority, yeoman farmers did not set the region's political and social tone. Instead, they deferred to the large planters since many aspired to become large landowners themselves.

### 3. POOR WHITES
- As many as 25 to 40 percent of southerners were unskilled laborers who owned no land and no slaves. These "poor whites" often lived in the backwoods where they scratched out a meager living doing odd jobs.
- Although they did not own slaves and frequently resented the aristocratic planters, poor whites nonetheless supported the South's biracial social structure. The existence of slavery enabled even the most impoverished (very poor) white to feel superior to black people. Poor whites, yeoman farmers, and planters all shared a sense of white supremacy that softened class distinctions.

## INSIDER TIP
It is very important to remember that three-quarters of white southern families owned no slaves. Both APUSH exams and SAT II US History tests contain multiple-choice questions on this important fact.

# TOPIC 88
# KEY FACTS ABOUT SLAVERY

1. The African slave trade was outlawed in 1808. However, as the cotton economy expanded so did the slave population. In the half century before the Civil War the number of slaves increased from 1.2 million to just under 4 million. Most of this increase was due to the natural population increase of American-born slaves.

2. The spread of cotton plantations into the Deep South precipitated (hastened) a major change in the movement and distribution of slavery. In 1790, planters in Virginia and Maryland owned 56 percent of all American slaves. During the 1800s, tobacco-depleted Chesapeake planters sold as many as 700,000 slaves to planters in a vast cotton belt that extended from western Georgia to eastern Texas. By 1860, just 15 percent of all slaves lived in Virginia and Maryland while over half lived in the Deep South. A majority of the blacks on the Deep South lived on large plantations with communities of 20 or more slaves.

3. The domestic slave trade uprooted countless families. Despite forced separations and harsh living conditions, slaves maintained strong kinship networks while creating a separate African American culture. Religion played a particularly important role. For example, spiritual songs enabled slaves to express their sorrows, joys, and hopes for a better life.

4. With the exception of the Nat Turner insurrection in 1831, vigilant planters successfully suppressed slave rebellions. Instead of rebelling, a majority of slaves did not rebel or run away. Slaves retaliated against their masters by slowing the pace of work, damaging equipment, and feigning illness.

5. All blacks were not slaves. By 1860, as many as 250,000 free blacks lived in the South. Many of these "free persons of color" were the descendants of men and women who had been freed by idealistic owners following the Revolutionary War. Others successfully purchased their freedom. Free blacks occupied a precarious position in southern society. For example, they were often subject to discriminatory laws that denied them property rights and forbade them from working in certain professions and testifying against whites in court.

## INSIDER TIP

Question 3 on the 2010B APUSH exam asked students to "compare and contrast the experiences of slaves on tobacco plantations in the early seventeenth-century Chesapeake region with that of slaves on nineteenth-century cotton plantation in the Deep South." The AP Central Information List for this question contains an especially detailed discussion on the growth, spread, and characteristics of slavery.

PODCAST 17.1
"THE PECULIAR
INSTITUTION"

**TOPIC 89**
# CHANGING ATTITUDES TOWARDS SLAVERY IN THE SOUTH

## 1. SLAVERY AS A "NECESSARY EVIL"
- During the late 1700s spokesmen for the South's "peculiar institution" apologized for slavery as a "necessary evil" inherited from the past.
- Leading southern statesmen such as Thomas Jefferson and James Monroe advocated a policy of gradually emancipating slaves while at the same time compensating their owners.

## 2. SLAVERY AS A "POSITIVE GOOD"
- During the early 1830s slaveholders in the South worked out a systematic proslavery argument to justify their "peculiar institution. " First expressed by John C. Calhoun, the "positive good" argument dominated southern thought until the Civil War.
- Proslavery advocates insisted that citations in the Bible condoned slavery. They also used "scientific" theories of their day to create a false image of blacks as inferior people who required paternal white guardianship. And finally, planters warned that abolition would ruin the South's economy and destroy its distinctive way of life.

# CHAPTER 18
# THE CRUSADE AGAINST SLAVERY, 1815 – 1860

## ESSENTIAL POINTS

1. The American Colonization Society was dedicated to returning freed slaves to Africa. The Society's gradual approach could not solve the rapidly growing problem of slavery.

2. William Lloyd Garrison founded *The Liberator* in 1831. Its first issue called for the immediate and uncompensated emancipation of all slaves. Garrison's uncompromising declaration marked the beginning of a radical movement to abolish slavery and transform American society.

3. Garrison also played a key role in founding the American Anti-Slavery Society. The Society's leaders were predominately religious middle-class men and women. The Society split into factions over the issues of women's rights and the necessity of taking organized political action to oppose slavery.

4. Frederick Douglass was America's foremost black abolitionist. His speeches and autobiography played an important role in persuading a growing number of Northerners that slavery was an evil institution that should be abolished.

## INSIDER TIP

Don't overlook the American Colonization Society. APUSH exams often include a multiple-choice question asking you to identify the Society's goal of returning freed slaves to Africa.

## PODCAST 18.1

WILLIAM LLOYD GARRISON

## TOPIC 90
# THE AMERICAN COLONIZATION SOCIETY

1. The American Colonization Society was founded in 1817 and soon became the dominant antislavery organization of the 1820s. The ACS advocated the gradual abolition of slavery combined with the goal of returning freed slaves to Africa.

2. Although Society members opposed slavery, many were openly racist. Leaders of the ACS did not believe that free blacks could be integrated into American society. For example Henry Clay argued that since an "unconquerable prejudice" would prevent free blacks from assimilating into white society it would be better for them to emigrate to Africa.

3. The ACS was instrumental in founding the colony of Liberia on the west coast of Africa. However, the Society's gradual approach could never resolve the problem of slavery. By 1860, the Society helped approximately 12,000 free blacks migrate to Liberia. At that time there were about 4 million slaves in the South.

## TOPIC 91
# KEY QUOTE – WILLIAM LLOYD GARRISON'S "I WILL BE HEARD" DECLARATION

### 1. THE SETTING

• William Lloyd Garrison began his career as a newspaper editor working with abolitionist Benjamin Lundy in Baltimore. Like Lundy, Garrison originally supported the American Colonization Society's gradual approach to ending slavery.

• Garrison soon became convinced that the ACS's gradual approach would never end the "peculiar institution." His contact with slavery in Baltimore transformed him into a radical abolitionist who believed that slavery was a cruel, brutal, and sinful institution that should be immediately abolished.

- As Garrison's views became more militant he resolved to move to Boston and begin his own antislavery newspaper. On January 1, 1831 the 26-year-old Garrison began to publish *The Liberator*.

## 2. THE QUOTES

- "Let Southern oppressors tremble …. I shall strenuously contend for immediate enfranchisement …. I will be as harsh as truth, and as uncompromising as justice …. I do not wish to think, or speak, or write with moderation – I will not excuse – I will not retreat a single inch – AND I WILL BE HEARD!"

## 3. SIGNIFICANCE

- *The Liberator* was actually a small newspaper with a low circulation. In its first year, the four-page weekly had only six subscribers. Its maximum circulation was never more than about 5,000.
- *The Liberator's* modest circulation belied (misrepresented) its significance. Garrison's uncompromising call for immediate and uncompensated emancipation marked the beginning of a radical movement to abolish slavery and transform American society. Unlike the American Colonization Society, Garrison believed that blacks and whites could live together as equals. *The Liberator* boldly called for biracial cooperation in the antislavery movement.
- Garrison and *The Liberator* also played a key role in founding the American Anti-Slavery Society. Organized in 1833, the Society grew rapidly across the North. Within just five years, it claimed to have 250,000 members and 1,350 local affiliates.

## INSIDER TIP

William Lloyd Garrison's dramatic call for the immediate and uncompensated emancipation of slaves has generated multiple-choice questions on most APUSH exams and SAT II tests.

# TOPIC 92
# THE ABOLITIONIST MOVEMENT SPLINTERS

1. The American Anti-Slavery Society was radical, uncompromising and intensely moralistic. Garrison forcefully argued that one did not ask sinners to gradually stop sinning. He believed that slavery was a sin and that slave owners were sinners who should repent and immediately free their bondspeople.

2. The leaders of the American Anti-Slavery Society were predominantly religious middle-class men and women. At first they were united by their unyielding opposition to slavery. However, in 1840 two divisive issues split the organization into rival factions.

- First, Garrison believed that the American Anti-Slavery Society should fully endorse women's rights. For example, he insisted that the Grimké sisters and other feminists had a right to play an important public role in the abolitionist movement. Moderate members disagreed, arguing that women's rights was a secondary issue that should not be allowed to distract the organization from its primary goal of abolishing slavery.

- Second, Garrison opposed political action arguing that the abolitionists should rely upon moral persuasion to promote change. The moderate pragmatic (practical) majority viewed Garrison as an impractical fanatic. The politically-minded abolitionists founded the Liberty Party in 1840 and backed the Free Soil Party in 1848.

## INSIDER TIP
Frederick Douglass is the first of a group of black leaders who regularly appear on multiple-choice questions on SAT II and APUSH tests. Be sure to remember that Frederick Douglass was America's foremost black abolitionist.

## TOPIC 93
# FREDERICK DOUGLASS

1. Frederick Douglass was America's foremost black abolitionist. Born a slave in Maryland, Douglass escaped from bondage in 1838 when he was just twenty-one.

2. Recruited by William Lloyd Garrison, Douglass became a lecturer for the American Anti-Slavery Society. Douglass was a gifted orator who enthralled (captivated) his audiences with his commanding personal presence and authentic stories about the horrors of slavery. For example, he told a spellbound audience in Massachusetts, "I appear before the immense assembly this evening as a thief and a robber. I stole this head, these limbs, this body from my master, and ran off with them."

3. Douglass was also a prolific (very productive) writer. In 1845 he published his *Narrative of the Life of Frederick Douglass* describing his life on a Maryland plantation, brutal fight with a slave driver, and dramatic escape to the North. In 1847, he founded the *North Star*, an influential antislavery newspaper for blacks.

4. Douglass's eloquent speeches and writings played an important role in persuading a growing number of Northerners that slavery was evil and that its further spread into the western lands should be halted.

persuade North to view slavery as bad

no westward expansn is slave state

**CHAPTER 19**
# WOMEN IN ANTEBELLUM AMERICA, 1789 – 1848

## ESSENTIAL POINTS

1. The idea of **REPUBLICAN MOTHERHOOD** began to emerge after the Revolutionary War. Its advocates suggested that women would be responsible for raising their children to be virtuous citizens of the new American republic.

2. The **CULT OF DOMESTICITY** idealized women in their roles as nurturing mothers and faithful wives.

3. The cult of domesticity created a cultural ideal that best applied to upper and middle-class white women. It ignored the harsh realities faced by women working in factories and on the frontier. Enslaved black women were completely excluded from any hope of participating in the cult of domesticity.

4. During the 1820s and 1830s the Lowell textile mills primarily employed young New England women. The Lowell experiment ended when the owners cut wages and began hiring Irish immigrants.

5. The Seneca Falls Convention was organized by Elizabeth Cady Stanton and Lucretia Mott. The Declaration of Sentiments began by declaring that "We hold these truths to be self-evident: that all men and women are created equal." The Seneca Falls Convention marked the beginning of the women's rights movement in the United States.

## TOPIC 94
# REPUBLICAN MOTHERHOOD

1. The new American republic promoted equality and social democracy. Women, however, were denied many basic rights. For example, they could not vote, hold political office, or serve on juries. In addition, married women were denied rights to own and manage property, to form contracts, and to exercise legal control over children. Given these restrictions, what should be the role for women in the new republic?

2. The idea of REPUBLICAN MOTHERHOOD began to emerge after the Revolutionary War. Its advocates stressed that the new American republic offered women the important role of raising their children to be virtuous and responsible citizens. By instructing their children, and especially their sons, in the principles of liberty, women played a key role in shaping America's moral and political character.

3. Catherine Beecher argued that republican motherhood gave women a unique opportunity to use their moral influence to shape America's political character: "The mother writes the character of the future man; the sister bends the fibres that hereafter are the forest tree; the wife sways the heart, whose energies may turn for good or for evil the destinies of a nation. Let the women of a country be virtuous and intelligent, and the men will certainly be the same."

## TOPIC 95
# CULT OF DOMESTICITY

1. Prior to the Industrial Revolution many men and women worked together as an economic unit on small family farms. However, as the Industrial Revolution gained momentum it encouraged a division of labor between home and work. While men held jobs in a competitive market economy, the home became the appropriate place or "sphere" for a woman.

## INSIDER TIP
The 2006 APUSH exam included a DBQ devoted to "the changing ideals of American womanhood" as expressed in the ideals of republican motherhood and the cult of domesticity. See Essay 1A for a particularly well-organized and insightful discussion that received a 9.

2. The CULT OF DOMESTICITY idealized women in their roles as wives and mothers. As a nurturing mother and faithful spouse, the wife created a home that was a "haven in a heartless world." The home thus became a refuge from the world rather than a productive economic unit.

3. The cult of domesticity created a cultural ideal that best applied to upper and middle-class white families that could afford to maintain separate spheres for their work life and for their home life. It is important to note that there was a wide gap between the ideals of the cult of domesticity and the harsh realities faced by women working in factories and on the frontier. In addition, enslaved black women were completely excluded from any hope of participating in the cult of domesticity.

4. Reformers such as Margaret Fuller recognized that the cult of domesticity relegated women to a separate domestic sphere that continued to deny them the basic rights of American citizenship.

## TOPIC 96
# WOMEN AND THE LOWELL EXPERIMENT

1. In 1790, Moses Brown built America's first textile mill in Pawtucket, Rhode Island. The pace of textile production, however, remained slow until the Embargo Act of 1807 and the War of 1812 stimulated domestic production.

2. In 1813, Francis Cabot Lowell and a group of investors known as the Boston Associates constructed a textile factory in Waltham, Massachusetts. The Waltham mill used both modern spinning machines and power looms to produce cheap cloth. Investors earned a 20 percent profit as sales soared from $3,000 in 1814 to $300,000 in 1823. The profitable commercial manufacture of textiles marked an important step in moving production from the home to the factory.

3. Inspired by the success of the Waltham mill, Francis Lowell built a model factory town at Lowell, Massachusetts 27 miles from Boston. Lowell built clean red-brick factory centers and dormitories designed to avoid the drab conditions

## INSIDER TIP

Both the SAT II and APUSH tests use pictures to illustrate the cult of domesticity and the lack of gender equality in the workplace. Pictures that illustrate the cult of domesticity typically show a middle or upper-class father benignly watching as his wife reads to his children. Pictures that illustrate the lack of gender equality depict rows of women workers supervised by a stern male supervisor.

## PODCAST 19.1
THE SENECA FALLS CONVENTION

in English mill towns. He hired young New England farm women to work in his mill. The girls worked 12 hours a day, 6 days a week. They lived together in boarding houses under the watchful eyes of older women who enforced mandatory church attendance and strict curfews.

4. The Lowell experiment worked well at first. By the early 1830s, young unmarried women from rural New England comprised the majority of workers in Massachusetts textile mills. However, the factory owners soon became more interested in profit than in the welfare of their employees. In 1834 and 1836 the owners cut wages without reducing working hours. The women responded by going out on strike and petitioning the Massachusetts state legislature to pass a law limiting the workday to 10 hours. Although this measure failed to pass, it convinced the owners that the female workers were too troublesome. Factory owners then turned to the impoverished (very poor) and compliant Irish immigrants who were then pouring into Massachusetts.

## TOPIC 97
# THE SENECA FALLS CONVENTION, 1848

### 1. WHAT HAPPENED?
- In 1848, Elizabeth Cady Stanton and Lucretia Mott organized the first convention in support of women's rights. The convention met for two days in Seneca Falls, New York. The delegates discussed "the social, civil, and religious condition and rights of women."
- The convention adjourned after two days and issued a "Declaration of Sentiments and Resolutions" modeled after the Declaration of Independence. The Declaration demanded greater rights for women.

### 2. WHAT CAUSED THE SENECA FALLS CONVENTION?
- During the 1830s and 1840s many women dedicated themselves to working for the abolition of slavery. Led by Elizabeth Cady Stanton and Lucretia Mott, a small but

determined group of feminists realized that they were also the victims of injustice. The abolition movement thus helped inspire a demand for equal rights for women.
- Stanton and Mott questioned the prevailing idea that women should be subordinate to men.

## 3. WHY SHOULD YOU REMEMBER THE SENECA FALLS CONVENTION?

- The Seneca Falls Convention marked the beginning of the women's rights movement in the United States.
- Written primarily by Elizabeth Cady Stanton, the Declaration of Sentiments opened by declaring, "We hold these truths to be self-evident: that all men and women are created equal." The document called for greater divorce and child custody rights, equal opportunities in education, the right to retain property after marriage, and the extension of suffrage to women. Taken together, these demands formed the agenda of the women's rights movement into the twentieth century. It is important to note that the Declaration of Sentiments did NOT call for equal pay for equal work or for greater access to birth control methods.

## INSIDER TIP

It is important to remember that middle-class women dominated the women's rights movement. Poor women did not have the time or resources to participate.

# CHAPTER 20
# RELIGION, REFORM, AND ROMANTICISM, 1815 – 1860

## ESSENTIAL POINTS

*abolish slavery*
*womens Rights*
*Temperance*

1. The **SECOND GREAT AWAKENING** was a wave of religious enthusiasm that swept across America during the early eighteenth century. It inspired reform movements to abolish slavery, promote women's rights, and restrict the sale of alcoholic beverages.

2. The Burned-Over District was an area in western New York where preachers such as Charles Grandison Finney delivered "hellfire and damnation" sermons calling upon their listeners to repent and perform good works.

*Ed.*
*Reform Tenter*

*Mental Hospitals*

3. Horace Mann was a leading educational reformer who promoted the public schools.

4. Dorothea Dix launched a crusade to create special hospitals for the mentally insane.

5. The **TRANSCENDENTALISTS** were a small but influential group of writers and thinkers who stressed the importance of human intuition, non-conformity, and the belief that truth could be found in nature. Ralph Waldo Emerson, Henry David Thoreau, and Margaret Fuller were the leading Transcendentalists.

6. Utopian communities such as Brook Farm were concrete expressions of the **PERFECTIONIST** vision of building a just society.

*American landscape*

7. Romantic artists and writers rebelled against Deism's reliance upon reason. Instead they emphasized nature, emotion, and spontaneous feelings. For example, Hudson River School artists painted landscapes that portrayed America's natural beauty.

**TOPIC 98**
# THE SECOND GREAT AWAKENING

PODCAST 20.1
THE SECOND GREAT
AWAKENING

INSIDER TIP
It is important to remember that Charles Grandison Finney was the foremost Second Great Awakening preacher. Recall that Jonathan Edwards and George Whitefield were the leading First Great Awakening preachers.

## 1. BACKGROUND
- As the eighteenth century ended, the religious fervor ignited by the First Great Awakening seemed to wane (decline).
- During the early 1800s, a new wave of religious enthusiasm called the **SECOND GREAT AWAKENING** swept across much of the country. The Second Great Awakening began on the western frontier and then quickly spread to the more densely populated East coast.

## 2. KEY CHARACTERISTICS
- The Puritans believed in a just but stern God. Second Great Awakening preachers replaced the hellfire-and-damnation Puritan God with a gentler divinity of love and grace.
- The Puritans believed that humanity was doomed by original sin and thus marked at birth for membership in either the small group of the "elect" or the much larger mass of the "damned." Second Great Awakening preachers instead emphasized humanity's inherent goodness and each individual's potential for self-improvement.
- The Puritans believed that God controlled the destiny of each human being. In contrast, Second Great Awakening preachers stressed that each individual was a "moral free agent" who could improve both himself and society. The Second Great Awakening inspired a belief in PERFECTIONISM – the faith in the human ability to consciously build a just society. This close link between religion and reform awakened many Americans to a variety of social and moral issues.

## 3. THE "BURNED–OVER DISTRICT"
- Intense religious revivals were especially widespread in central and western New York. This region became known as the "Burned-Over District" because of particularly fervent revivals that crisscrossed the region.
- Charles Grandison Finney emerged as the most popular and influential preacher from the Burned-Over District. Finney's emotional sermons stressed that each individual

could choose to achieve salvation by a combination of faith and good works.

- The Burned-Over District was the birthplace of the Church of Jesus Christ of Latter-day Saints, or the Mormons. The Mormons were originally led by their founder Joseph Smith.

# TOPIC 99
# REFORM MOVEMENTS

## 1. EDUCATIONAL REFORM

- Horace Mann was America's leading educational reformer. As Secretary of the newly created Massachusetts Board of Education, he wrote a series of annual reports that influenced education across America. Mann sponsored many reforms in Massachusetts including a longer school year, higher pay for teachers, and a larger public school system. As a result of his tireless work, Mann is often called the "Father of the Common School Movement."
- Emma Willard was an early advocate of women's education. She founded the Troy Female Seminary, America's first woman's school of higher education.
- America's public school children learned about literature from a series of graded textbooks called *McGuffey Readers*. Also called *Eclectic Readers*, the books included stories illustrating the virtues of patriotism, hard work, and honesty.
- The first half of the nineteenth century witnessed a dramatic increase in the number of newspapers from about 1,200 in 1833 to 3,000 in 1860. The proliferation (rapid increase) of newspapers promoted literacy and a well-informed public.

## 2. THE MENTALLY ILL

- Dorothea Dix launched a crusade to create special hospitals for the mentally ill. An indefatigable (tireless) champion of reform, Dix travelled more than 10,000 miles and visited almost every state.
- Dix and other reformers created the first generation of American mental asylums. By the 1850s there were special hospitals in 28 states.

## INSIDER TIP
Dorothea Dix is closely associated with the campaign to reform mental asylums. It is important to remember that she was NOT actively involved with feminist issues.

### 3. TEMPERANCE

- In the early 1800s America had over 14,000 distilleries producing 25 million gallons of alcoholic drink each year. By 1830, Americans drank 5 gallons of alcohol per capita.
- The TEMPERANCE MOVEMENT was a widespread campaign to convince Americans to drink less alcohol or to drink none at all. Founded in 1826, the American Society for the Promotion of Temperance soon boasted 5,000 state and local temperance groups. Their campaign against "Demon Rum" worked. By the mid-1840s Americans drank just 2 gallons of alcohol per capita.

## TOPIC 100
# TRANSCENDENTALISM

1. The Transcendentalists were a small group of writers and thinkers who lived in and around Boston. The leading Transcendentalists included Ralph Waldo Emerson, Henry David Thoreau, and Margaret Fuller. The Transcendentalists published a journal of literature, art, and ideas called *The Dial*. Margaret Fuller served as its first editor.
2. TRANSCENDENTALISM included the following key beliefs:
- The divinity of man: The Transcendentalists believed that God lived within each individual. Each person possessed an inner soul or spirit and thus a capacity to find spiritual truth.
- The value of human intuition: The Transcendentalists minimized logic and reason. They believed that human intuition transcended or rose above the limits of reason. Intuition enabled humans to discover and understand spiritual truths.
- Nonconformity and dissent: The Transcendentalists were fiercely and uncompromisingly individualistic. They repudiated (rejected) the "tyranny of the majority." "If a man does not keep pace with his companions," Thoreau wrote, "perhaps it is because he hears a different drummer."
- The importance of nature: The Transcendentalists believed that truth could be found in nature. Transcendentalists viewed communion with nature as a religious experience that enlightened their soul. For example, Thoreau turned

## INSIDER TIP

The Transcendentalists often held informal discussion meetings at their homes in Boston and Concord. It is important to note that Edgar Allen Poe did not attend these meetings since he was not a Transcendentalist.

away from the artificiality of "civilized" life and lived for two years in a cabin at the edge of Walden Pond near Concord. He strived to acquire self-knowledge by living close to nature.

# TOPIC 101
# UTOPIAN COMMUNITIES

1. Utopian communities were concrete social expressions of the Perfectionist vision of achieving a better life through conscious acts of will. Idealists founded over 100 utopian communities between 1800 and 1900. The movement reached its peak between 1830 and 1860.

2. The various utopian communities all shared the following common goals:
   - They rejected the competitive business practices of the market economy.
   - They tried to build an egalitarian (equal) social order by creating an economy based on shared wealth.
   - They regulated moral behavior in order for members to realize their full spiritual potential.
   - They organized their members into cooperative work and living units.

3. Brook Farm was the most celebrated utopian community. Founded at West Roxbury, Massachusetts in 1841, it enjoyed the support of Ralph Waldo Emerson, Margaret Fuller, and other leading Transcendentalists. Brook Farm's experiment in plain living and high thinking proved to be short-lived. The community disbanded following a devastating fire in 1846. Brook Farm nonetheless had a lasting impact upon its members. Years later, Nathaniel Hawthorne remembered, "our beautiful scheme of a noble and unselfish life, and how fair, in that first summer, appeared the prospect that it might endure for generations."

# TOPIC 102
# ROMANTIC ART AND LITERATURE

## 1. FROM DEISM TO ROMANTICISM

- Thomas Jefferson, Benjamin Franklin, and other leading late eighteenth century American intellectuals were all Deists. DEISM is the belief that God created the world but then allowed it to operate through the laws of nature. These natural laws could be discovered by human reason and expressed as mathematical formulas.
- During the 1820s and 1830s, artists and writers in Europe and America began to rebel against Deism's logical and well-ordered world. "Feeling is all!" became the guiding spirit of a new generation of Romantic painters and poets. Inspired by the Transcendentalists, the romantic movement in America emphasized nature, emotion, and spontaneous feelings.

## 2. THE HUDSON RIVER SCHOOL

- The Hudson River School was America's first native school of art. Its members concentrated on painting landscapes that portrayed America's natural beauty.
- Hudson River School artists typically painted large compositions which suggested America's unlimited opportunities and boundless future. For a famous example, see *The Oxbow* by Thomas Cole.

## 3. WALT WHITMAN

- Walt Whitman was America's leading Romantic poet.
- In *Leaves of Grass*, first published in 1855, Whitman rejected reason and celebrated his own feelings and emotions.

## INSIDER TIP

The Hudson River School has begun to make frequent appearances as a multiple-choice item on APUSH and SAT II tests. Be sure to remember that Hudson River School artists idealized landscapes.

**CHAPTER 21**

# IMMIGRATION IN ANTEBELLUM AMERICA, 1815 – 1860

## ESSENTIAL POINTS

1. During the 1840s and 1850s Ireland supplied the largest number of immigrants to the United States. Most Irish settled in the fast-growing cities along the Northeast coast. Irish immigrants avoided the South because they did not want to compete for jobs with slave laborers.

2. During the 1840s and 1850s Germany supplied the second largest number of immigrants to the United States. The Germans were a very diversified group that typically settled in rural areas of the Midwest.

3. The great wave of Irish and German immigrants sparked a **NATIVIST** or anti-foreign reaction among native-born Americans.

4. The Know-Nothings were America's first nativist political party. They directed their hostility toward Catholic immigrants from Ireland and Germany.

## INSIDER TIP

The 2011 (Question 4), 2009B (Question 3), and 2007B (Question 3) exams all included free-response questions that focused on immigration in antebellum America. An excellent Information List accompanies each of these three questions. Essay 3A on the 2007B exam received a 9.

## TOPIC 103
# KEY FACTS ABOUT IMMIGRATION IN ANTEBELLUM AMERICA

1. Immigration to America slowed dramatically during the four decades between the Revolutionary War and the War of 1812. The French Revolution and the prolonged war between Britain and France reduced immigration from Europe to a trickle.

2. The first great wave of nineteenth century immigration took place between 1820 and 1860. During this period, almost 5 million people immigrated to America. While many immigrants came from England and Scandinavia, over two-thirds of the total came from Ireland and Germany.

3. The overwhelming majority of the antebellum immigrants chose to settle in urban areas of the North and on Midwestern farms. Most immigrants avoided the South because they did not want to compete for jobs with slave laborers.

## TOPIC 104
# THE IRISH IMMIGRATION

### 1. WHAT HAPPENED?

- Between 1840 and 1860 almost 1.7 million men, women, and children left Ireland for America. By 1860, Irish-born immigrants comprised over 4 percent of the U.S. population.

- Most Irish immigrants settled in the fast-growing port cities along the Northeast coast. By 1860, Irish made up over one-third of the population of Boston and New York City.

### 2. WHAT CAUSED THE IRISH IMMIGRATION?

- Desperate living conditions in Ireland made mass immigration inevitable. Most rural Irish were impoverished (very poor) tenant farmers who subsisted (barely survived) on a diet that depended upon the potato.

- Beginning in 1845 a blight destroyed three successive potato crops. A million people died from starvation and disease while another 1.7 million immigrated to the United States.

## 3. WHY SHOULD YOU REMEMBER THE IRISH IMMIGRATION?

- The flood of Irish immigrants transformed Boston, New York City, and Philadelphia into densely populated centers that experienced high rates of poverty and crime.
- Most Irish immigrants were forced to work in the lowest-paying and most demanding unskilled jobs. Irish women found work as domestic servants while the men built roads, canals, and railroad beds. The percentage of Irish workers employed in the Lowell mills jumped from 8 percent in 1845 to 50 percent in 1860.
- The Irish played a key role in the growth of the Catholic Church in the United States. The number of Catholic churches in America increased from 700 in 1840 to over 2,500 in 1860.
- The wave of Irish immigration aroused intense anti-Catholic prejudice. Many native-born Protestants stereotyped the Irish as an ignorant and clannish people who would never assimilate into American life. Prejudiced employers posted "No Irish Need Apply" signs, while Protestant leaders complained that Irish-sponsored parochial schools would undermine support for public education.
- Irish voters supported the Democrats as the party of the "common man." Irish bosses soon played a key role in the formation of big city political machines.

## TOPIC 105
# THE GERMAN IMMIGRATION

1. Just over 1.5 million Germans immigrated to American between 1830 and 1860.
2. Unlike the Irish, the Germans typically settled in rural areas of the Midwest rather than in East coast cities.
3. The Germans were a very diversified group that included exiled political refugees and displaced farmers. Although the majority of Germans were Protestants, about one-third were Catholics and a significant number were Jewish. Because the Germans were such a heterogeneous (varied) group, they were difficult to stereotype. As a result, the Germans experienced less prejudice than did the Irish.

## INSIDER TIP
The Germans opposed the Whigs because of the party's commitment to temperance. It is interesting to note that German immigrants introduced kindergartens, beer halls, and the Christmas tree to American culture.

PODCAST 21.1
NATIVISM AND THE
KNOW-NOTHING
PARTY

INSIDER TIP
SAT II tests often include
a question based on
a quote from a Know-
Nothing political handbill
or party platform. The
authors of the quote are
easily identified as Know-
Nothing Party members
because of their bias
against Irish and German
immigrants.

## TOPIC 106
## NATIVISM AND THE KNOW-NOTHING PARTY

1. The great wave of Irish and German immigration sparked a NATIVIST or anti-foreign reaction among native-born Protestants.

2. Nativist leaders argued that Catholics posed a danger to America's republican institutions. They pointed to a statement by Pope Pius IX denouncing republican institutions because they relied upon the sovereignty of the people instead of the sovereignty of God. Nativists also argued that immigrants would work for low wages and therefore take jobs away from native workers.

3. During the early 1850s, nativists formed the American Party. The party began as a secret society, complete with special passwords and elaborate handshakes. When members were asked about their party, they were instructed to reply: "I know nothing!" As a result, the American Party was soon popularly called the Know-Nothing Party.

4. The Know-Nothing Party directed its hostility toward Catholic immigrants from Ireland and Germany. The party's platform demanded that immigrants and Catholics be excluded from public office claiming that they would corrupt the political process.

5. Know-Nothing candidates enjoyed initial success. The party captured over 40 congressional seats in the 1854 election. Its 1856 presidential candidate Millard Fillmore won 21 percent of the popular vote and 8 electoral votes. The Know-Nothing's success proved to be fleeting. The anti-Catholic fervor subsided as immigration declined and the country shifted its focus to the great national debate over the future of slavery.

**CHAPTER 22**
# TERRITORIAL EXPANSION, 1836 – 1848

## ESSENTIAL POINTS

1. Texas remained an independent republic for nine years before becoming a state. President Jackson resisted admitting Texas into the Union because he recognized that Americans were badly divided over the issue of adding another slave state.

2. Supporters of **MANIFEST DESTINY** believed that America was foreordained to extend its civilization across the North American continent. Opponents of manifest destiny included many Whigs and most New England abolitionists.

3. Henry David Thoreau and Abraham Lincoln both opposed the Mexican War. The war prompted Thoreau to write an essay urging civil disobedience as an appropriate response to an unjust conflict.

# TOPIC 107
# THE "LONE STAR REPUBLIC"

## 1. THE TEXAS REVOLUTION

- Texas belonged first to Spain and then, after 1821, to Mexico. The Mexican government opened Texas to settlers from the United States. The Anglo-Americans received generous land grants at low prices. In exchange they agreed to become Roman Catholics and citizens of Mexico. By 1830, there were about 30,000 people in Texas, ninety percent of whom were Anglo-Americans.
- Friction soon developed between the Mexican government and the Anglo-American settlers. Few converted to Catholicism or applied to become Mexican citizens.
- The rapid growth of the Anglo-American population of Texas alarmed Mexican officials. In 1830, the Mexican government announced that slaves could no longer be brought into any part of Mexico and that Americans could no longer settle in Texas. Faced with these restrictions, the Texans rebelled and declared their independence on March 2, 1836.
- The Texas Revolution lasted less than two months. After suffering defeats at the Alamo and Goliad, Texan forces led by Sam Houston destroyed the Mexican army at the Battle of San Jacinto on April 21, 1836.

## 2. THE ANNEXATION ISSUE

- Sam Houston, the hero of San Jacinto, was elected President of the newly founded Republic of Texas in October 1836. Houston and most Texans wanted to join the United States.
- Many Americans opposed admitting Texas into the Union. The Texas constitution allowed slavery. Northern antislavery Whigs opposed admitting another slave state into the Union. Other opponents of annexation warned that this action might provoke a war with Mexico.
- President Jackson resisted admitting Texas into the Union. He feared that a prolonged debate over the admission of a slave state would ignite a divisive campaign issue that could cost the Democrats the presidential election. As a result, Jackson postponed annexation and Texas remained an independent "Lone Star Republic."

## INSIDER TIP

Hollywood movies and television shows have glamorized Colonel Travis, Davy Crockett, and other heroes who fell at the Alamo. In contrast, APUSH test writers ignore the Alamo and instead focus their questions on why Jackson resisted the admission of Texas into the Union.

# TOPIC 108
# POLK AND MANIFEST DESTINY

## 1. THE EXPANSIONIST SPIRIT

- During the 1820s many Americans thought the boundaries of the United States would not go beyond the Rocky Mountains. However, the quest for land, opportunity, and adventure excited a new generation eager to explore and settle the western frontier. By 1860, over 4 million people lived west of the Mississippi River.
- John L. O' Sullivan, the editor of the Democratic Review, gave the nation's expansionist spirit a name when he coined (invented) the term MANIFEST DESTINY. O'Sullivan declared that America's right to expansion lay in "our manifest destiny to occupy and to possess the whole of the Continent which Providence has given us."
- O'Sullivan and other proponents (supporters) of Manifest Destiny believed that expansion was necessary to extend democratic institutions and the blessings of American agriculture and commerce to sparsely populated regions. America had a God-given destiny to extend its civilization across the continent and create a country that would serve as a shining example to the rest of the world.

## 2. POLK'S ELECTION

- The annexation of Texas and territorial expansion emerged as the key issues in the 1844 presidential campaign. The Whig Party nominee Henry Clay refused to support the annexation of Texas. In contrast, the Democrat candidate James K. Polk ran on a platform demanding the annexation of Texas and asserting America's right to all of Oregon.
- Polk won a narrow electoral victory. As an ardent expansionist he used manifest destiny as an argument to justify annexing Texas, claiming Oregon, purchasing California, and displacing Native American tribes.

## 3. TEXAS AND OREGON

- Following the election, Congress approved a resolution annexing Texas as the nation's 28th state. President Tyler signed the resolution three days before Polk took office.

## PODCAST 22.1
POLK AND MANIFEST DESTINY

## INSIDER TIP

It is interesting to note that both John Winthrop's "City Upon a Hill" sermon and O'Sullivan's manifest destiny essay assumed that America had divinely sanctioned support to create a model society.

- Acquiring Oregon proved to be more difficult than annexing Texas. Both the United States and Great Britain claimed the territory. The Democrat's campaign slogan "Fifty-four forty or fight" meant that the United States would go to war with Britain in order to obtain the entire Oregon territory. Despite his belligerent (warlike) campaign slogan, Polk proposed a compromise that would divide Oregon at the 49th parallel. The British accepted Polk's proposal thus averting a war with the United States.

# TOPIC 109
# THE MEXICAN WAR

## 1. THE OUTBREAK OF WAR
- While Polk avoided a war with Great Britain, the explosive Texas question remained to be settled with Mexico. Outraged by the annexation of Texas, Mexico broke off diplomatic relations with the United States.
- Polk exacerbated (worsened) tensions by supporting Texas' claim to the Rio Grande River as its southwestern boundary. The Mexican government denied this claim insisting that Texas went no farther than the Nueces River.
- On April 25, 1846 a large Mexican force crossed the Rio Grande and attacked a small American reconnaissance party. In the ensuing fight eleven Americans were killed and the rest wounded or captured. Polk promptly demanded that Congress declare war on Mexico, declaring that "Mexico has … shed American blood upon American soil." Congress agreed and approved a declaration of war on May 13, 1846.

## 2. OPPOSITION TO THE MEXICAN WAR
- New England abolitionists denounced the Mexican War as an unjust conflict designed to extend slavery into new territories. Henry David Thoreau refused to pay his state poll tax as a gesture of opposition. He then wrote a classic essay "Civil Disobedience" urging passive resistance to laws that require a citizen "to be an agent of injustice." Thoreau's essay later influenced Dr. King's philosophy of non-violent protest.

- Whig leaders also opposed the war with Mexico. Abraham Lincoln, then an obscure Whig congressman from Illinois, challenged Polk to identify the exact spot on American soil where American blood had been shed. Like other Whigs, Lincoln believed that Polk used the skirmish as a pretext (excuse) for declaring war so that he could claim new territories.

## 3. THE CONQUEST OF MEXICO

- Led by General Zachery Taylor, American forces won a series of victories in northeastern Mexico. Taylor became a national hero when he defeated a much larger Mexican army at the Battle of Buena Vista.
- Led by Colonel Stephen W. Kearny, American forces captured Santa Fe, New Mexico and then helped secure California.
- Led by General Winfield Scott, American forces landed at Vera Cruz and then battled their way to Mexico City. Scott entered and took control of the Mexican capital on September 14, 1847.

## 4. THE TREATY OF GUADALUPE HIDALGO

- Under the terms of this treaty Mexico lost about one-third of its territory. It ceded New Mexico and California to the United States and accepted the Rio Grande as the Texas border. It is important to remember that New Mexico actually included present-day Arizona, Nevada, and Utah, as well as parts of Colorado and Wyoming.
- The United States acquired more than 500,000 miles of new territory. In return the U.S. agreed to pay Mexico $15 million and pay all the claims American citizens had against the Mexican government.

## 5. THE WAR'S CONSEQUENCES

- The Mexican War gave combat experience to a group of junior officers that included Robert E. Lee and Ulysses S. Grant.
- The Mexican War transformed America into a continental nation that spanned from the Atlantic to the Pacific.
- The Mexican War added vast new territories thus igniting an increasingly bitter dispute about the extension of slavery. The Mexican War marked a key step in the road to disunion.

## INSIDER TIP

APUSH test writers have thus far focused more attention on the consequences of the Mexican War than its causes. Be sure you can identify the provisions of the Treaty of Guadalupe Hidalgo and explain how the war reflected the sectional interests of New Englanders and Southerners.

# CHAPTER 23
# THE ROAD TO DISUNION, 1846 – 1860

## ESSENTIAL POINTS

1. The Wilmot Proviso prohibited slavery in lands acquired from Mexico in the Mexican War. It was defeated in the Senate where the South remained strong. The Wilmot Proviso did not support popular sovereignty.

2. The Fugitive Slave Act was the most controversial part of the Compromise of 1850. It enraged abolitionists who refused to support it. This resistance infuriated Southerners who accused the North of acting in bad faith.

3. The Kansas-Nebraska Act heightened sectional tensions by repealing the Missouri Compromise and helping to spark the formation of the Republican Party.

4. The Supreme Court's decision in the Dred Scott case held that black people were not citizens of the United States. The ruling also struck down the Missouri Compromise of 1820.

5. The Republican Party platform accepted slavery where it existed but opposed the further expansion of slavery into the territories.

# TOPIC 110
# THE WILMOT PROVISO, 1846

## INSIDER TIP

Supporters of the Wilmot Proviso argued that slavery degraded free labor. They believed that "free soil" would guarantee liberty, free competition, and a worker's "right to rise."

## 1. WHAT HAPPENED?

- In August 1846, David Wilmot, a previously little-known Congressman from Pennsylvania, attached a rider to an appropriations bill barring slavery from any territory acquired as a result of the Mexican War.
- Supported in the North and opposed in the South, the Wilmot Proviso passed the House twice but was defeated in the Senate.

## 2. WHY DID WILMOT PROPOSE HIS PROVISO?

- Since the passage of the Missouri Compromise of 1820, both political parties attempted to suppress divisive questions about the status of slavery in the western territories.
- Wilmot defended his proviso as a necessary means of insuring the "rights of white freemen" to live and work in the new territories without the unfair burden of competing with slave labor.

## 3. WHY SHOULD YOU REMEMBER THE WILMOT PROVISO?

- The Wilmot Proviso became a rallying point for an antislavery coalition that formed the Free Soil Party. The Free Soilers became active participants in the 1848 election. They pledged to support "free soil, free speech, free labor, and free men."
- Apprehensive Southern leaders warned that the Wilmot Proviso marked the beginning of a long postponed attack on slavery. Determined to defend their "peculiar institution," they denounced any attempt to restrict the expansion of slavery.
- The Wilmot Proviso reawakened dormant sectional tensions over the expansion of slavery. It thus marked the beginning of a long series of increasingly acrimonious (very bitter) crises that dominated American politics until the outbreak of the Civil War in 1861.
- Supporters of the Wilmot Proviso argued that slavery degraded free labor. They believed that "free soil" would guarantee liberty, free competition, and a worker's "right to rise."

# TOPIC 111
# THE COMPROMISE OF 1850

1. The growing sectional differences between the North and the South over the extension of slavery touched off one of the most dramatic Senate debates in American history.
2. Henry Clay hoped to once again play his historic role of the "Great Compromiser." The now 73-year-old senator from Kentucky offered a package of resolutions designed to settle the outstanding issues and restore sectional harmony. Clay's proposals included the following key points:
   - The immediate admission of California as a free state.
   - The organization of territorial governments in Utah and New Mexico without an immediate decision as to whether they would be free or slave.
   - The abolition of the domestic slave trade in Washington, D.C.
   - The enactment of a stringent (very strict) new Fugitive Slave Act.
3. The debate over Clay's proposals featured dramatic speeches by Daniel Webster and John C. Calhoun. Webster's March 7 Speech implored Northern and Southern senators to find common ground "for the preservation of the Union."
4. After months of rancorous (bitter, showing deep-seated resentment) debate, Senator Stephen A. Douglas of Illinois successfully maneuvered Clay's proposals through the Senate as separate bills. It is interesting to note that Abraham Lincoln did not participate in the negotiations that resulted in the passage of the Compromise of 1850 since he was not a member of Congress.
5. The Compromise of 1850 seemed to defuse the crisis and establish an uneasy sectional peace. Americans now turned to what they hoped would be a bright future undisturbed by the issue of slavery in the territories. This hope, however, proved to be fleeting.

# TOPIC 112
# THE KANSAS–NEBRASKA ACT, 1854

## 1. HARRIET BEECHER STOWE AND *UNCLE TOM'S CABIN*

- The Compromise of 1850 temporarily settled the issue of slavery in the territories. However, the furor over the Fugitive Slave Act kept the issue of slavery alive.
- The Fugitive Slave Act appalled Harriet Beecher Stowe. A dedicated abolitionist, Stowe wrote *Uncle Tom's Cabin* to help her readers understand the cruelty of the slave system by vividly describing the fear and panic endured by slaves.
- First published in book form in 1852, *Uncle Tom's Cabin* sold 305,000 copies within a year. It soon became an international sensation selling over 2.5 million copies world wide.
- *Uncle Tom's Cabin* intensified antislavery sentiment in the North. At the same time, it aroused resentment in the South.

## 2. STEPHEN A. DOUGLAS AND POPULAR SOVEREIGNTY

- In January 1854, Senator Stephen A. Douglas of Illinois reopened the issue of slavery in the territories by proposing a bill that would organize two new territories, Kansas and Nebraska. Both territories were part of the Louisiana Territory where the Missouri Compromise banned slavery. In order to win Southern support, Douglas included an amendment specifically repealing the Missouri Compromise.
- Douglas' bill proposed that the people of Kansas and Nebraska be allowed to decide for themselves whether their states would be free or slave. Letting the settlers of a given territory have the sole right to decide whether or not slavery would be permitted within their borders was known as POPULAR SOVEREIGNTY.
- Congress finally passed Douglas' Kansas-Nebraska Act after a divisive debate that sharpened antagonism between the North and the South.

## 3. MOMENTOUS CONSEQUENCES

- The Kansas-Nebraska Act broke the uneasy truce between the North and the South. Indignant (outraged) Northerners denounced the act as a violation of the Missouri Compromise's "sacred pledge" to ban slavery north of the 36°30′ line.
- The Kansas-Nebraska Act placed Whigs opposed to slavery in a difficult position. As a result, it destroyed the Whig Party in the Deep South and contributed to the demise (downfall) of the party in the North.
- The Kansas-Nebraska Act galvanized (mobilized) a spontaneous outpouring of popular opposition in the North that led to the formation of the Republican Party.
- The furor over the Kansas-Nebraska Act even affected American foreign policy. The Pierce administration hoped to buy Cuba from Spain. American ministers meeting in Ostend, Belgium drew up a secret memorandum urging Pierce to invade Cuba if Spain refused to sell the island. When the so-called Ostend Manifesto became public it ignited a storm of opposition to what seemed like a plot to extend slavery. The public outcry forced Pierce to abandon his plan to obtain Cuba.

PODCAST 23.1
THE KANSAS-NEBRASKA ACT

## TOPIC 113
# THE RISE OF THE REPUBLICAN PARTY

1. The Democrats and Whigs formed a two-party system that dominated American politics from the 1830's to the early 1850's. The furor over the Kansas-Nebraska Act dealt the Whigs a fatal blow by leading to the formation of the Republican Party.
2. Kansas marked the first important test of popular sovereignty. Within a short time, "Bleeding Kansas" became a battleground between proslavery and antislavery settlers.
3. Kansas soon found itself with two governments. One supported slavery but rested upon a small minority of the population. The other government opposed slavery and represented the majority opinion in the embattled territory. The Democrats accepted the proslavery government and committed their party to the admission

## INSIDER TIP
Free-Response Question 3 on the 2009 APUSH exam asked students to analyze the factors that led to the emergence of the Republican Party. See Essay 3A for an outstanding response that received a 9.

of Kansas as a slave state. In contrast, the Republicans opposed the Kansas-Nebraska Act and supported the antislavery forces in Kansas.

4. The Whig Party completely disintegrated under the pressure of the violence in Kansas. As their party collapsed, Whigs joined the rapidly growing Republican Party. Antislavery Democrats and former Know-Nothings also joined the burgeoning (rapidly growing) Republican coalition.

5. The Republicans held their first national convention in 1856. The party nominated John C. Frémont for president and adopted a platform opposing slavery. The Democrats turned to James Buchanan of Pennsylvania and endorsed the Kansas-Nebraska Act. The 1856 election was quickly transformed into a sectional contest. Although Buchanan won the election, Frémont carried eleven free states. The results underscored the ominous sectionalization of politics in an increasingly polarized (divided) nation.

# TOPIC 114
# THE DRED SCOTT CASE, 1857

## 1. THE CASE
- Dred Scott was a slave who belonged to John Emerson, an army surgeon assigned to a post in Missouri. When the army transferred Emerson from the slave state of Missouri to the free state of Illinois he took Scott with him as a servant. The pair then moved to the Wisconsin Territory, an area where the Missouri Compromise expressly forbade slavery.
- When Emerson died, Scott returned to Missouri where he was placed under the authority of his former master's wife. Helped by abolitionists, Scott sued for his freedom. He contended that living in a free state and in a free territory made him a free man.

## 2. THE LEGAL QUESTIONS
- Did Dred Scott have a right to bring his case into the federal courts? Scott had that right only if he were a citizen of the United States.

- Did Dred Scott become a free man by living in a free state and in a free territory? If yes, this would limit slavery since most slave owners would not risk taking their human "property" into a free state.
- Did Congress have the authority to prohibit slavery in the territories? If not, then the Missouri Compromise restriction on slavery in the territories was unconstitutional.

## 3. THE DECISION

- Led by Chief Justice Roger B. Taney, the Supreme Court ruled that neither slaves nor free blacks were citizens in the political community created by the Constitution. Taney declared that slaves were "chattel property ... so far inferior that they have no rights which the white man is bound to respect." Since Dred Scott was not a citizen he was not entitled to sue in a federal court.
- The Court emphatically ruled that Scott did not become free by living in a free state or free territory.
- The Court ruled that as a constitutionally protected form of property, slaves could be taken into any state or territory. The Dred Scott decision therefore declared the Missouri Compromise to be unconstitutional. This marked the first time the Supreme Court struck down an act of Congress since the *Marbury v. Madison* decision in 1803.

## 4. THE CONSEQUENCES

- The Dred Scott decision repealed the Missouri Compromise thus establishing the principle that Congress could not limit the spread of slavery in the territories.
- The Dred Scott decision invalidated the Republican Party's platform pledge opposing the extension of slavery into the territories. Although this initially appeared to be a serious setback, Republicans redoubled their efforts to win the presidency. They promised that a victory would enable them to change the composition of the Southern dominated Supreme Court and reverse the Dred Scott decision.
- The Dred Scott decision played a key role in a series of debates between Stephen A. Douglas and his Republican rival Abraham Lincoln. During the debate in Freeport, Illinois, Lincoln asked Douglas if there was any way the people of a territory could keep slavery from their land before they were organized into a state. In what came to

## INSIDER TIP

The Dred Scott case is one of the most frequently tested Supreme Court cases. Both the APUSH exam and the SAT II test expect you to know that the Supreme Court ruled that black people were not citizens while also effectively repealing the Missouri Compromise.

be called the Freeport Doctrine, Douglas responded that the settlers could prevent slavery by refusing to pass a slave code defining a slave's legal status and the rights of an owner. The Freeport Doctrine outraged the South and cost Douglas political support he would need in the 1860 presidential election.

## TOPIC 115
# THE UNION IN PERIL

### 1. THE CONSEQUENCES OF JOHN BROWN'S RAID ON HARPER'S FERRY

- John Brown's doomed raid on Harper's Ferry in 1859 set off a wave of fear throughout the slaveholding South. As rumors of slave insurrections swept across the region, frightened Southerners suppressed all criticism of slavery. Proslavery Southerners incorrectly linked John Brown to the now-hated "Black Republican" Party.
- Although his raid was a military failure, John Brown became a martyr for the antislavery cause.
- John Brown's raid on Harper's Ferry intensified the sectional bitterness and left the nation on the brink of disunion.

### 2. THE ELECTION OF 1860

- The Democratic Party fragmented into two factions. Northern Democrats nominated Stephen A. Douglas on a platform promising congressional noninterference with slavery. Deep South Democrats nominated John C. Breckinridge on a platform calling for a national slave code that would protect slavery in the territories.
- The Republicans met in Chicago sensing that they had an excellent opportunity to defeat the now-divided Democrats. The Lincoln-Douglas debates transformed Abraham Lincoln into a nationally known figure. The Republicans nominated Lincoln on the third ballot.
- The Republican platform stated that slavery would continue to be protected in the states where it already existed. However, the Republican Party firmly opposed the expansion of slavery into the western territories.
- Lincoln won the election by carrying all 18 free states. He did not win a single state in the South.

## 3. THE FAILURE OF COMPROMISE

- Lincoln's victory precipitated (caused) the secession of South Carolina and six other states in the Deep South.
- In a final desperate effort to save the Union, Senator John Crittenden of Kentucky proposed to restore the boundary line between slave and free states established by the Missouri Compromise of 1820. The line would be extended to include the new territories in the West. Lincoln refused to support the Crittenden Compromise because it violated the Republican position against the further extension of slavery into the western territories.
- The heated atmosphere of distrust allowed intransigents (those who refuse to compromise) in both the North and South to oppose all efforts to achieve a compromise. The nation thus continued on an inexorable (can't be stopped) road to disunion and a bloody Civil War.

INSIDER TIP

Free-Response question 3 on the 2004 APUSH exam asked students to analyze the effectiveness of political compromise in reducing sectional tensions. See Essay 3C for an outstanding response that received a 9.

# CHAPTER 24
# THE CIVIL WAR, 1861 – 1865

## ESSENTIAL POINTS

1. Delaware, Maryland, Kentucky, and Missouri were all slaveholding Border States that remained in the Union.
2. The North enjoyed significant advantages in population, industrial capacity, and railroad mileage.
3. The South enjoyed the advantage of being led by an able group of military commanders who fought a defensive war on their own territory.
4. The Union victory at Antietam enabled President Lincoln to issue the Emancipation Proclamation. The victory persuaded Great Britain and France to remain neutral.
5. The Republican dominated Congress passed the Homestead Act and the Morrill Act. It also authorized the construction of a transcontinental railroad and the creation of a more uniform national banking system.
6. The Emancipation Proclamation only freed slaves living in states that had rebelled against the Union. It did not free slaves in the Border States.

Homestead: provided free 160 acres from Great Plains if someone lived on it and made something of it after 5 years.

Morrill: public lands get donated to states $ for colleges that teach agricultural and mech. arts.

## TOPIC 116
# TAKING SIDES

## 1. THE CONFEDERATE STATES OF AMERICA

- Most Southerners believed that the Republican victory posed an unacceptable threat to a way of life based upon slave labor. They assumed that the Western territories would become free states thus increasing the political imbalance in the Senate between free and slave states.
- Led by South Carolina, seven states in the Deep South seceded before Lincoln took office.
- The firing on Fort Sumter and Lincoln's call for troops forced the states in the Upper South to take sides. It is important to note that slaves were scarce and Union support was strong in eastern Tennessee, western Virginia, and western North Carolina. Nonetheless, Virginia, North Carolina, Tennessee, and Arkansas all seceded. The Confederate Congress meeting in Montgomery welcomed these states and moved its capital to Richmond, Virginia. The noted Civil War historian Bruce Catton underscored the significance of this move when he wrote that "American history has known few events more momentous than the secession of Virginia, which turned what started out to be a simple suppression of a rebellion into a four-year cataclysm."

## 2. THE BORDER STATES

- Delaware, Maryland, Kentucky, and Missouri were all slaveholding Border States that remained in the Union.
- Kentucky provided especially important industrial and agricultural resources that proved vital to the Union. Lincoln recognized Kentucky's strategic importance when he declared, "I hope to have God on my side, but I must have Kentucky."

**TOPIC 117**
# THE BALANCE OF POWER

## 1. NORTHERN ADVANTAGES
- The North enjoyed a significant population advantage. In 1861, the 23 states in the Union had a population of about 21 million. In contrast, the 11 Confederate states had just 9 million people, about one-third of whom were slaves.
- The North enjoyed an enormous advantage in industrial capacity. The Union produced over 90 percent of the nation's manufactured goods. In addition, the Union had far more wagons, ships, and miles of railroad track than the Confederacy.
- The North enjoyed a significant advantage in presidential leadership. Lincoln proved to be an inspiring leader and forceful commander-in-chief. He successfully held the Republican Party together despite its internal conflicts.

## 2. NORTHERN DISADVANTAGES
- When the war began, the North lacked an able group of military commanders. Lincoln had to frequently replace generals as he searched for commanders who could rival those of the South.
- When the war began, the North did not enjoy a consensus on its war aims. While Lincoln's announced goal was to preserve the Union, abolitionists argued that the Union should also fight to abolish slavery. Although most northern Democrats supported a war to save the Union, a vocal group of "Copperheads" called for peace by negotiation even if it risked the Union.

## 3. SOUTHERN ADVANTAGES
- The South enjoyed the advantage of fighting a defensive war on its own familiar territory. The South needed only to hold back the invading Union armies and wait for the North to tire of fighting a prolonged and costly war.
- The South enjoyed the advantage of a strong military tradition that produced an exceptional group of experienced commanders.
- The South enjoyed the initial advantage of believing that Great Britain would aid the Confederacy because its

## INSIDER TIP
SAT II tests often include a multiple-choice question on the strengths and weaknesses of the North and the South. Be sure to remember that Northern advantages did NOT include raw materials for textiles.

textile industry would grind to a halt without Southern cotton. However, this advantage proved to be illusory when "King Cotton diplomacy" failed.

## 4. SOUTHERN DISADVANTAGES
- The disparities (inequalities) in population, industrial capacity, and railroad mileage meant that the South could not sustain a prolonged war.
- Jefferson Davis proved to be an ineffective political and military leader. He frequently quarreled with his Cabinet and failed to implement a consistent military strategy.
- The Confederacy was founded on the principle of preserving states' rights. But a strong central government is needed to conduct an efficient war effort. Independent-minded Confederate governors often frustrated the Davis government's attempts to raise the money and troops it needed to fight the war.

# TOPIC 118
# KEY CIVIL WAR BATTLES

## 1. ANTIETAM
- Lee and his battle-tested troops crossed the Potomac River into Maryland. Lee's objectives included seizing the vital rail center at Harrisburg, Pennsylvania, isolating Washington from the rest of the North and convincing Britain and France to recognize the Confederacy.
- The two armies fought the bloodiest one-day battle of the war. The battle ended in a narrow Union victory forcing Lee to withdraw back across the Potomac into Virginia. Disappointed by McClellan's failure to pursue Lee and gain a decisive victory, Lincoln removed his popular but hesitant general from command of the Army of the Potomac.
- The Union victory at Antietam persuaded Great Britain and France to remain neutral.
- The Union victory at Antietam enabled Lincoln to issue the Emancipation Proclamation.

## 2. VICKSBURG
- Vicksburg was a seemingly impregnable fortress that commanded a key portion of the Mississippi River.

- Led by General Ulysses S. Grant, the Union forces captured Vicksburg following a long siege. The fall of Vicksburg gave the Union control of the Mississippi River thus splitting the Confederacy in half.

## 3. SHERMAN'S MARCH TO THE SEA

- Sherman captured Atlanta in September 1864. His victory helped boost Lincoln's sagging popularity thus enabling the President to defeat the Democratic candidate General McClellan in the November election.
- Sherman burned Atlanta on November 15, 1864. He then began his famous "March to the Sea." Determined to wage a total war on the people of Georgia, Sherman's army promptly made the Georgians "feel the hard hand of war." His soldiers burned homes, ruined crops, killed animals, and destroyed railroad tracks as they left a path of destruction 60 miles wide. Sherman arrived in Savannah in time to present the city to President Lincoln as a Christmas present.

# TOPIC 119
# KEY CONGRESSIONAL ACTIONS

INSIDER TIP

APUSH exams and SAT II US History tests contain very few questions on Civil War battles or generals. Do not expect to see questions on Gettysburg or the campaigns of Grant and Lee. Focus instead on knowing the significance of the Union victory at Antietam, the fall of Vicksburg, and Sherman's March to the Sea.

## 1. THE REPUBLICAN CONGRESS

- During the 1840s and 1850s, Southern congressmen consistently blocked tariff, railroad, banking, and land policies favored by the North and West.
- The secession of the Southern states enabled the Republicans to dominate Congress. They promptly passed a series of landmark acts with far-reaching social and economic consequences.

## 2. THE HOMESTEAD ACT, 1862

- Under the terms of the Homestead Act a settler twenty-one years old or older could acquire a free tract of 160 acres of surveyed public land. Title to the land went to the settler after five years of continuous residence.
- The Homestead Act opened the Great Plains to settlers. By 1935, 1.6 million homesteaders received 270 million acres of federal lands.

## INSIDER TIP

Expect to see more questions on Civil War legislation than on Civil War battles. It is important to remember that Congress did NOT pass legislation to abolish segregation, make high school education compulsory, or grant subsidies to encourage the export of manufactured goods.

### 3. THE MORRILL LAND GRANT ACT, 1862

- The Morrill Land Grant Act stipulated that public lands be donated to the states for the purpose of providing colleges to train students in agriculture and mechanical arts.
- Land-grant colleges played an important role in promoting agriculture, engineering, and veterinary medicine.

### 4. THE FIRST TRANSCONTINENTAL RAILROAD, 1862

- Prior to the Civil War, Southern congressmen strongly supported a transcontinental railroad that would link New Orleans with Los Angeles.
- Following the outbreak of the Civil War, Congress approved a transcontinental route connecting Omaha, Nebraska with Sacramento, California. The government provided the Central Pacific and Union Pacific companies with generous loans and extensive land grants.

### 5. THE NATIONAL BANKING ACT OF 1863

- Banking policies had been a source of contention (dispute) since the formation of the First National Bank in 1791. The rising cost of financing the Civil War highlighted the urgent need for a national currency and an orderly banking system.
- The National Banking Act of 1863 established a national banking system to provide a uniform national currency. No additional important changes were made in the nation's banking system until the Federal Reserve Act was passed in 1913.

# TOPIC 120
# AFRICAN AMERICANS AND THE CIVIL WAR

## 1. CONTRABAND

- The Civil War disrupted plantation life throughout the South. Soon thousands of escaped slaves sought refuge behind Union lines.
- CONTRABAND was the official term given to fugitive slaves who sought protection behind Union lines. The First Confiscation Act authorized Union troops to seize all property, including slaves, used on behalf of the Confederacy.

## 2. THE EMANCIPATION PROCLAMATION, 1863

- President Lincoln issued the Emancipation Proclamation on New Year's Day, 1863. The proclamation declared that all slaves in the areas "wherein the people … are this day in rebellion … are, and hence forward shall be free."
- It is important to understand that the Emancipation Proclamation only freed slaves living in states that had rebelled against the Union. It did not free slaves in the Border States such as Kentucky and Missouri. Slavery was not legally and completely abolished until the enactment of the Thirteenth Amendment in 1865.
- The Emancipation Proclamation strengthened the Union's moral cause. The Civil War was now widened into a crusade against slavery.
- With slavery doomed, public opinion in Britain and France swung decisively behind the Union cause. The Emancipation Proclamation thus ended any chance that the European powers would support the Confederacy.

## 3. BLACK SOLDIERS

- The Emancipation Proclamation permitted blacks to join the federal army. Frederick Douglas urged blacks to rally to the Union cause. "The iron gate of our prison," he told them, "stands half open."
- Approximately 180,000 African Americans served in the Union army. Although black soldiers fought with great valor, they were paid less than white soldiers of equal rank. More than 38,000 black soldiers lost their lives during the Civil War.

# CHAPTER 25
# MAKING KEY COMPARISONS, 1789 – 1865

## ESSENTIAL POINTS

1. Recent APUSH exams have included a significant number of free-response questions asking students to make comparisons between events, peoples, colonies, geographic regions, and social movements. These comparison essays require substantial relevant information and an effective analysis of similarities and differences. This chapter is the second of four chapters designed to provide you with a clear and succinct comparison of frequently tested topics.

# TOPIC 121
# COMPARING DEISM AND TRANSCENDENTALISM

## 1. DEISM

- Deism was a part of an 18th century European intellectual movement known as the Enlightenment.
- Deists thought of God as a cosmic watchmaker who created the universe and then let it operate according to unchanging natural laws.
- Deists believed that natural laws regulate both the universe and human society. These natural laws could be discovered by human reason. The discovery of laws of economics and government would improve society and make progress inevitable.
- Thomas Jefferson and Benjamin Franklin were the best known American Deists.

## 2. TRANSCENDENTALISM

- Transcendentalism was an American philosophical and literary movement that developed in the 1830s and 1840s in New England.
- Transcendentalists rejected Deism's reliance upon reason and its lack of emotion. Transcendentalists emphasized the use of human intuition to discover spiritual truths. They advocated living a simple life and celebrating personal emotion and imagination.
- Ralph Waldo Emerson, Henry David Thoreau, and Margaret Fuller were the leading Transcendentalist writers.
- Transcendentalists shared many similarities with Romantic artists and writers. For example, Hudson River School artists celebrated America's natural beauty while Romantic writers such as Walt Whitman rejected reason and discovered insight from their own feelings.

## TOPIC 122
# COMPARING THE FIRST GREAT AWAKENING AND THE SECOND GREAT AWAKENING

## 1. THE FIRST GREAT AWAKENING

- A wave of religious revivals that began in New England in the mid-1730s and then swept across all of the colonies during the 1740s.
- "New Light" ministers advocated an emotional approach to religious practice that undermined the authority of traditional "Old Light" ministers.
- Leading New Light ministers such as Jonathan Edwards and George Whitefield delivered emotional sermons warning sinners to repent.
- This new emotional approach fragmented American Protestants, thus creating religious pluralism and toleration since no single denomination could impose its will on the other sects.
- As the movement spread across the colonies, more and more women became active in their churches.

## 2. THE SECOND GREAT AWAKENING

- A wave of religious revivals that began on the western frontier in the early 1800s and then quickly spread to the more densely populated East coast.
- Leading Second Great Awakening preachers such as Charles Finney delivered inspiring sermons that advocated spiritual rebirth, individual self-improvement, and perfectionism.
- The emphasis upon individual self-improvement sparked a variety of movements to reform American society.
- The close link between religion and reform awakened America to the evils of slavery.
- Middle class women played an especially important role in the reform movements engendered (generated) by the Second Great Awakening.

# TOPIC 123
# COMPARING THE WHIGS AND THE DEMOCRATS

## 1. THE WHIGS

- The Whigs supported a strong federal government, a loose construction of the Constitution, the Second National Bank, Clay's American System, and social reform.
- The Whigs opposed Andrew Jackson, the spoils system, Indian removal, and the Mexican War.
- Henry Clay and Daniel Webster were the party's most prominent leaders.
- Supporters included small businessmen, professionals, manufacturers, and some Southern planters.
- The Whigs dissolved in the early 1850s because of sectional differences over the expansion of slavery into the western territories. The passage of the Kansas-Nebraska Act led to the party's final demise.

## 2. THE DEMOCRATS

- The Democrats supported states' rights, a strict construction of the Constitution, Indian removal, and western expansion.
- The Democrats opposed the Second National Bank and Clay's American System.
- Andrew Jackson and Martin Van Buren were the party's most prominent leaders.
- Supporters included Irish immigrants, poor farmers in the North and Midwest, small planters in the South, skilled and unskilled workers in cities and towns, and the "common man."
- The Democrats split into Northern and Southern factions in the election of 1860. The Democrats nonetheless emerged from the Civil War as a national party with a strong base in the "Solid South."

# TOPIC 124
# COMPARING TERRITORIAL EXPANSION UNDER JEFFERSON AND POLK

## 1. TERRITORIAL EXPANSION UNDER JEFFERSON

- Jefferson advocated a strict interpretation of the Constitution. However, he proved to be a flexible and pragmatic president.
- Jefferson agreed to the Louisiana Purchase in order to eliminate the French threat to the port of New Orleans and to fulfill his vision of enabling America to become an agrarian republic that would become an Empire of Liberty.
- The Louisiana Purchase doubled the size of the United States.
- The lands acquired in the Louisiana Purchase soon sparked a sectional dispute over the spread of slavery into the new western territories.

## 2. TERRITORIAL EXPANSION UNDER POLK

- Polk was an ardent expansionist who supported America's manifest destiny to extend its civilization across the continent. Manifest destiny can thus be seen as an extension of Jefferson's idea of an Empire of Liberty.
- Polk ran for president on a platform demanding the annexation of Texas and the right to acquire all of Oregon.
- Despite his campaign slogan "Fifty-four forty or fight," Polk agreed to a compromise settlement with Britain that divided Oregon at the 49th parallel.
- While Polk avoided conflict with Great Britain he deliberately provoked a war with Mexico. The United States won the Mexican War. Under the terms of the Treaty of Guadalupe Hidalgo the US acquired more than 500,000 square miles of territory including Texas, New Mexico, and California.
- The lands acquired from Mexico soon sparked an increasingly bitter sectional dispute over the spread of slavery into the western territories.

**TOPIC 125**

# COMPARING THE MISSOURI COMPROMISE AND THE COMPROMISE OF 1850

## 1. THE MISSOURI COMPROMISE

- In 1819, the North controlled a solid majority in the House of Representatives. However, the Senate was evenly divided between 11 free states and 11 slave states.
- In 1819, the territory of Missouri applied for statehood as a slave state. The issue of extending slavery into the new territories ignited a passionate sectional debate.
- House Speaker Henry Clay promoted a compromise that settled the dispute by admitting Missouri as a slave state and Maine as a free state. In addition, the Missouri Compromise prohibited slavery in the remaining portions of the Louisiana Territory north of latitude 36°30'.
- The Missouri Compromise temporarily defused the political crisis over slavery. It is important to note that the North initially perceived slavery as a political and economic threat and not as a moral issue.

## 2. THE COMPROMISE OF 1850

- In 1850, the North continued to control an overwhelming majority in the House of Representatives. However, the Senate remained evenly balanced with 15 free states and 15 slave states.
- In 1850, the territory of California applied for statehood as a free state. The issue of extending slavery into the western territories ignited a dramatic Senate debate.
- Senators Henry Clay and Stephen Douglas promoted a compromise that finally settled the dispute by admitting California as a free state, allowing for popular sovereignty in Utah and New Mexico, abolishing the domestic slave trade in Washington, D.C. and enacting a stringent Fugitive Slave Act.
- The Compromise of 1850 briefly defused the political crisis over slavery. It is important to note that for the first time the North began to perceive slavery as both an economic and a moral threat to free labor.

# CHAPTER 26
# RECONSTRUCTION, 1865 – 1877

## ESSENTIAL POINTS

1. The Black Codes enacted by Southern state legislatures were designed to limit the freedom of African Americans by depriving them of their civil rights.

2. The Fourteenth Amendment invalidated the Dred Scott decision. It also protected legislation guaranteeing civil rights to African Americans by requiring both federal and state governments to provide all citizens with equal protection of the law and due process.

3. The Radical Republican program of Reconstruction included military occupation of the South and the enactment of the Fourteenth and Fifteenth Amendments. Congress did not redistribute land to provide freedmen with "forty acres and a mule."

4. The House of Representatives impeached President Johnson because he obstructed enforcement of Reconstruction legislation enacted by Congress.

5. The Fifteenth Amendment provided suffrage for Black males while denying the vote to women.

6. **SHARECROPPING** became an important element in the South's agricultural economy. It left sharecroppers trapped in a cycle of debt and poverty.

7. The Compromise of 1877 ended Congressional Reconstruction by removing all federal troops from the South.

# TOPIC 126
# PRESIDENTIAL RECONSTRUCTION

## 1. LINCOLN'S TEN PERCENT PLAN

- Abraham Lincoln led the United States through a long and bloody Civil War. When the conflict finally ended, the problems of winning the war gave way to the even harder problems of restoring the Union.
- Lincoln suggested a basis for Reconstruction in a Proclamation of Amnesty and Reconstruction issued on December 8, 1863. His Ten Percent Plan proposed a generous settlement. Lincoln offered a full pardon (except for high-ranking Confederate leaders) to Southerners who pledged loyalty to the Union and to the Constitution. Southern states in which 10 percent of the 1860 electorate took such an oath and accepted emancipation would be restored to the Union.
- Lincoln concluded his Second Inaugural Address by promising "malice toward none, with charity for all." He pledged "to bind up the nation's wounds" and strive for "a just and lasting peace among ourselves and with all nations." We will never know if Lincoln could have fulfilled his inspiring pledge. Just over a month later, John Wilkes Booth assassinated Lincoln while he was watching a play at Ford's Theater in Washington.

## 2. JOHNSON'S PLAN

- Lincoln's tragic death placed the burden of reconstructing the South on the untested shoulders of his former Vice-President, Andrew Johnson.
- Johnson issued his own Reconstruction plan in May, 1865. Like Lincoln, Johnson offered amnesty to most Confederates who took an oath of loyalty to the Union. High official and wealthy planters had to apply for a presidential pardon. Whites in each Southern state could then elect delegates to a state convention. The convention had to repeal all secession laws, repudiate Confederate war debts, and ratify the Thirteenth Amendment abolishing slavery.

## INSIDER TIP

Do not become bogged down comparing and contrasting details of Lincoln's Reconstruction plan and Johnson's Reconstruction plan. Instead, focus on the Black Codes. These codes deprived Blacks of their basic civil rights. The Black Codes set off a chain of events that led Congress to pass the Fourteenth Amendment.

## 3. SOUTHERN INTRANSIGENCE

- All of the Southern states soon complied with Johnson's plan. Moderate Republicans hoped the restored governments would act responsibly and treat their former slaves fairly. That did not happen. Resentful and intransigent (unyielding) white Southerners called for a renewal of laws to control the freed black population.

- Newly elected state legislatures promptly enacted laws known as Black Codes to limit the freedmen's basic civil and economic rights. The codes circumscribed (limited) the socioeconomic opportunities open to black people. For example, the codes barred blacks from owning land, marrying whites, and carrying weapons. They were forced to return to farm labor under conditions reminiscent of slavery.

- The Black Codes underscored the difficulty of assimilating four million former slaves into Southern society. Racial tensions soon erupted into violent riots in Memphis and New Orleans. Mob violence in these cities claimed the lives of 80 African Americans and 5 whites. Rioters looted and burned hundreds of black homes, churches, and schools.

- The new Johnson state governments provided further evidence that the South remained unrepentant. When Congress reconvened in December 1865 a large number of former Confederate politicians and military officers were waiting to take seats in the House and Senate.

## PODCAST 26.1
THE BLACK CODES

# TOPIC 127
# RADICAL RECONSTRUCTION

## 1. CONGRESS VERSUS PRESIDENT JOHNSON

- The Republican-dominated Congress refused to admit the senators and representatives elected by the Southern states. Dismayed by the results of Johnson's lenient policies and eager to assert its own authority, Congress formed a Joint Committee on Reconstruction.

- The Committee recommended a Civil Rights Act to clarify the rights of freed slaves. The act stated that blacks were citizens who had the same civil rights as those enjoyed by whites. Congress passed the bill in March 1866.

- Johnson stunned Congress by vetoing the bill. He claimed it was an unwarranted extension of federal power that would "foment discord among the races."
- Johnson's veto galvanized (energized) the Republicans. They successfully overrode the presidential veto. This marked the first time Congress had prevailed over a veto of a major piece of legislation. It also marked the beginning of a two-year struggle between Congress and President Johnson that ended with an impeachment trial.

## 2. THE FOURTEENTH AMENDMENT

- The Republican majority in Congress feared that Johnson would not enforce the Civil Rights Act. They also worried that the courts would declare the law unconstitutional. These concerns prompted Congress to pass the Fourteenth Amendment to the Constitution in June 1866.
- The Fourteenth Amendment overturned the Dred Scott decision by declaring that "all persons born or naturalized in the United States … are citizens of the United States and of the State wherein they reside."
- The amendment also gave the federal government responsibility for guaranteeing equal rights under the law to all Americans. The amendment prohibited the states from depriving "any person of life, liberty, or property, without due process of law; nor deny to any person within its jurisdiction equal protection of the laws. "The Fourteenth Amendment intensified the struggle for power between President Johnson and Congress. Saying that blacks were unfit to receive "the coveted prize" of citizenship, Johnson urged state legislatures in the South to reject the amendment. He also vigorously campaigned for Congressional candidates who supported his policies. Johnson's strategy backfired. Outraged voters repudiated the President's policies by giving the Republicans a solid two-thirds majority in both houses of Congress.

## 3. THE RADICAL REPUBLICANS

- The victorious Republicans returned to Congress in an angry and determined mood. Led by Representative Thaddeus Stevens of Pennsylvania and Charles Sumner of Massachusetts, the Radicals now controlled Congress. They were resolved to punish the former Confederate states and protect the rights of black citizens.

- The Reconstruction Act of 1867 eliminated the state governments created by Johnson's plan. It divided the South into five military districts, each under the command of a Union general. In order to be readmitted into the Union, a state had to approve the Fourteenth Amendment and guarantee black suffrage.
- The growing rift between the Radical Republicans and the President deepened when Johnson vetoed the Reconstruction Act. Congress immediately overrode his veto.

## 4. THE IMPEACHMENT CRISIS

- Although he had been rejected by the electorate and humiliated by Congress, Johnson remained defiant. He undermined the Radical program by appointing generals who obstructed the implementation of the Reconstruction Act.
- Congress escalated the crisis by passing the Tenure of Office Act. It required Senate consent for the removal of any official whose appointment had required Senate confirmation. Convinced that the law was unconstitutional, Johnson fired Secretary of War Edwin Stanton, a leading Radical Republican ally.
- To no one's surprise, Johnson's provocative action prompted the Radicals to pass a resolution declaring that the President should be impeached. On February 24, 1868 the Republican-dominated House of Representatives impeached Johnson for "high crimes and misdemeanors in office," that included violating the Tenure of Office Act. After a tense trial, the Senate failed to convict Johnson by one vote.
- Although Johnson escaped conviction, the trial crippled his presidency. Ten months later, voters sent the Union war hero Ulysses S. Grant to the White House. The Republicans completed their overwhelming victory by retaining two-thirds majorities in both houses of Congress.

## INSIDER TIP

Congress ostensibly (apparently) impeached President Johnson for violating the Tenure of Office Act. In reality, the Radical Republicans opposed Johnson for obstructing Radical Reconstruction. Johnson's acquittal set a precedent that Presidents should not be impeached solely on political grounds.

INSIDER TIP
The Fifteenth Amendment has received increased attention on recent tests. Be sure that you know how women's rights activists responded to the amendment.

## TOPIC 128
# THE FIFTEENTH AMENDMENT

1. The Fifteenth Amendment marked the last of the three Reconstruction Amendments. Ratified on February 3, 1870, it forbade either the federal government or the states from denying citizens the right to vote on the basis of "race, color, or previous condition of servitude."

2. The Fifteenth Amendment enabled African American males to exercise political influence for the first time. Freedmen provided about 80 percent of Republican votes in the South. Over 600 blacks served as state legislators in the new state governments. In addition, voters elected 14 blacks to the House of Representatives and 2 to the Senate. Black voters supported the Republican Party by loyally casting votes that helped elect Grant in 1868 and 1872.

3. While African Americans celebrated the passage of the Fifteenth Amendment, leading women's rights activists felt outraged and abandoned. They angrily demanded to know why the suffrage was granted to ex-slaves but not to women. Julia Ward Howe and other leaders of the women's suffrage movement finally accepted that this was "the Negro's hour." However, both Susan B. Anthony and Elizabeth Cady Stanton actively opposed passage of the Fifteenth Amendment.

4. It is important to note that the South would soon find ways to circumvent (evade, get around) the amendment. For example, property qualifications, poll taxes, and literacy tests all denied blacks the vote without legally making skin color a determining factor.

## TOPIC 129
# FROM SLAVE TO SHARECROPPER

1. The Civil War brought freedom to the slaves. However, Reconstruction brought few freedmen the "40 acres and a mule" promised by zealous reformers. Many former slaves stayed on their old plantations because they could not afford to leave.

2. During the late 1860s, cotton planters and black freedmen entered a new labor system called **SHARECROPPING**. Under this system, black (and sometimes white) families exchanged their labor for the use of land, tools, and seed. The sharecropper typically gave the landowner half of the crop as payment for using his property.

3. In addition to being in debt to the landlord, sharecroppers had to borrow supplies from local storekeepers to feed and clothe their families. These merchants then took a lien or mortgage on the crops.

4. Sharecropping did not lead to economic independence. Unscrupulous (unprincipled) merchants often charged sharecroppers exorbitant (excessively high) prices and unfair interest rates. As a result, the freedmen became trapped in a seemingly endless cycle of debt and poverty.

## INSIDER TIP

Be sure to remember the phrase "endless cycle of debt and poverty." It can come in very handy if you have a free-response essay on Reconstruction and the plight of the sharecroppers.

# TOPIC 130
# THE COLLAPSE OF RECONSTRUCTION

## 1. THE KU KLUX KLAN

- Two centuries of slavery created deeply entrenched (firmly established) racial prejudices that could not be easily changed. Southerners bitterly resented governments imposed by Radical Republicans that repealed Black Codes and guaranteed voting and other civil rights to African Americans.

- White Southerners reserved their greatest scorn for **CARPETBAGGERS** and **SCALAWAGS**. Carpetbaggers were Northerners who supposedly packed their belongings into a carpetbag suitcase and then headed south to seek power and profit. The much despised Scalawags were Southerners who "betrayed" the South by supporting and then benefitting from Republican Reconstruction polices.

- The years immediately following the Civil War witnessed the proliferation (rapid spread) of white supremacist organizations. The Ku Klux Klan began in Tennessee in 1866 and then quickly spread across the South. Anonymous Klansmen dressed in white robes and pointed cowls used whippings, house-burnings, kidnappings, and lynchings to keep blacks "in their place."

- The Klan's reign of terror worked. Without the support of black voters, Republican governments fell across the South. By 1876, Democrats replaced Republicans in eight of the eleven former Confederate states. Only South Carolina, Louisiana, and Florida remained under Republican control.

## 2. THE EROSION OF NORTHERN INTEREST

- Radical Republicans had long been the driving force behind the program to restructure Southern society. Sympathy for the freedmen began to wane (fade) as these leaders died or left office. A new generation of "politicos" began to focus their attention on a series of issues that included Western expansion, Indian wars, tariffs, and railroad construction.
- President Grant showed little enthusiasm for Reconstruction. His administration soon became distracted by scandals and charges of corruption. In addition, a business panic followed by a crippling economic depression further undermined public support for Reconstruction.

## 3. THE COMPROMISE OF 1877

- Disillusioned voters looked to the 1876 presidential election for a a return to honest government. The Republicans nominated Rutherford B. Hayes, an Ohio governor untarnished by the scandals of the Grant administration. The Democrats countered by nominating Samuel Tilden, a New York governor who earned a reputation as a reformer by battling Boss Tweed.
- Tilden won a convincing victory in the popular vote and 184 of the 185 votes needed for election. However, both parties claimed 19 disputed electoral votes in Florida, Louisiana, South Carolina, and one in Oregon.
- Congress created an electoral commission to determine which candidate would receive the disputed electoral votes. As tensions mounted, Democrats and Republican leaders reached an agreement known as the Compromise of 1877. The Democrats agreed to support Hayes. In return, Hayes and the Republicans agreed to withdraw all federal troops from the South, appoint at least one Southerner to a cabinet post, and support internal improvements in the South.
- The Compromise of 1877 ended Reconstruction. The Republican governments in Louisiana and South Carolina quickly collapsed as Southern Democrats proclaimed a return to "home rule" and white supremacy.

## INSIDER TIP

It is important to note that Reconstruction failed to establish durable political equality for African Americans. However, the three Reconstruction amendments did recognize that black Americans had civil rights. A future generation of black leaders could thus demand that these constitutional rights be enforced since they had already been legally established.

# CHAPTER 27
# THE NEW SOUTH, 1877 – 1900

## ESSENTIAL POINTS

1. Led by Henry Grady, New South advocates supported developing an industrial base in the South.
2. Redeemer-led governments successfully used literacy tests and poll taxes to evade the Fifteenth Amendment and disfranchise black voters.
3. The Supreme Court decision in *Plessy v. Ferguson* upheld Jim Crow segregation by approving "separate but equal" facilities for African Americans.
4. Ida B. Wells was an early civil rights pioneer and an outspoken opponent of lynching in the South.
5. Booker T. Washington encouraged African Americans to avoid political agitation and pursue vocational education to promote economic progress. W.E.B. Du Bois opposed Washington's program of accommodation. He favored a program of "ceaseless agitation" to obtain full economic, social, and political equality.

# TOPIC 131
# ECONOMIC GROWTH

## 1. HENRY GRADY'S VISION OF A "NEW SOUTH"

- Cotton plantations and slavery dominated the Old South's economy. As a result, the region had few cities and little manufacturing.
- Henry Grady, editor of the *Atlanta Constitution*, called for a "New South" that would be home to thriving cities, bustling factories, and rewarding business opportunities. Grady inspired a new generation of Southern leaders who strived to fulfill his vision by building a more diversified Southern economy.

## 2. THE BEGINNING OF A NEW INDUSTRIAL BASE

- New South enthusiasts began by promoting the textile industry. During the antebellum years, planters shipped cotton to textile factories in New England and Great Britain. Investors recognized that the South's ready supply of cheap labor, low taxes, and proximity (closeness) to cotton fields created ideal conditions for building a profitable textile industry. Mills soon flourished in small towns across the Piedmont region of North Carolina, South Carolina, and Georgia. The number of cotton mills in the South quickly doubled from 161 in 1880 to 400 in 1900.
- Tobacco had long played an important role in the South's history and economy. Still the region's second most important cash crop, tobacco helped launch one of the South's great industrial success stories. James Buchanan Duke took over his father's small but successful tobacco company in the early 1880s. In 1885, Duke acquired a license to use the first automated cigarette making machine. Duke's shrewd investment soon paid spectacular dividends. Within twenty years, Duke's American Tobacco Company produced 80 percent of the cigarettes manufactured in the United States.
- Iron ore mines near Birmingham, Alabama helped fuel the South's third great industrial success story. Founded in 1871, Birmingham quickly became a major industrial

*Piedmont ↳ textile industry*

*James Buchanan ↳ Duke's American Tobacco Company*

*Birmingham, Alabama ↳ railroad of "Pittsburg of the South"*

center and railroad hub. The city's thriving iron and steel mills led proud boosters to call their city "The Pittsburgh of the South."

## 3. THE LIMITS OF DEVELOPMENT

- Despite important progress, Grady's dream of a diversified Southern economy remained elusive (hard to reach). The South's economic future continued to be closely tied to cotton. The crop depleted the soil, used an inefficient sharecropping system, and tied the entire region's economy to unpredictable and often falling cotton prices.
- Although there were pockets of industrial development, the South remained overwhelmingly agricultural. In 1900, two-thirds of all Southern men still earned their living in farming. At that time, the average income in the South was only 40 percent of that in the North.
- Sharecropping encouraged a cycle of debt that tied tenant farmers to the land. The system offered little hope for economic improvement to impoverished Black or white farmers.

## INSIDER TIP

The 2008 APUSH exam included a free-response question asking students to evaluate the successes and limitations of the New South. See Question 4 for a particularly comprehensive Information List that provides key facts on economic development, politics, and race relations in the New South.

## TOPIC 132
# THE DISFRANCHISEMENT OF BLACK VOTERS

1. The end of Reconstruction left political control in the South in the hands of white Democratic Party leaders known collectively as "Redeemers." Their supporters referred to these postwar leaders as Redeemers because they "redeemed" or saved the South from Republican rule.

2. The Redeemers included merchants, financiers, and politicians who promoted economic growth based upon industrialization and railroad expansion. At the same time, they cut taxes and reduced state spending. As a result, the Redeemers reversed the gains in public education made during the years of Republican rule.

3. The Redeemers were committed to economic development and to white supremacy. Poor whites did not see impoverished blacks as fellow victims of economic forces they could not control. Instead, they supported the Redeemers policy of disfranchising African American voters.

## INSIDER TIP

Louisiana enacted the first grandfather clause in 1898. The law established literacy and property qualifications for voters. However, it exempted the sons and grandsons of those eligible to vote before 1867, the year the Fifteenth Amendment went into effect. The Supreme Court declared grandfather clauses unconstitutional in 1915.

## PODCAST 27.1

*PLESSY V. FERGUSON*

4. The Fifteenth Amendment prohibited states from denying anyone the right to vote because of race. Redeemer governments used literacy tests and poll taxes to evade the amendment. For example, literacy tests required voters to read and explain the Constitution in a way that satisfied voting registration officials. Needless to say, the white registrars rarely passed black voters. Poll taxes ranged from $1.00 in Georgia to $3.00 in Florida. Voters who skipped an election found that the tax accumulated from one election to the next.

5. These tactics worked. During the 1890s the number of black voters plummeted. For example, in 1896, 130,000 blacks were registered to vote in Louisiana. Just four years later the number plunged to just 5,320. By the early 1900s, African Americans had effectively lost their political rights in the South.

## TOPIC 133
# *PLESSY V. FERGUSON,* 1896

### 1. WHAT HAPPENED?

- In 1890, the Louisiana General Assembly enacted a Separate Car Law requiring railroads in the state to provide "equal but separate accommodations for the white and colored races."
- Outraged African Americans in New Orleans formed a Citizens' Committee to challenge the segregation law. On June 7, 1892, Homer Plessy, a young dark-skinned Creole who was one-eighth black, tested the statute by taking a first class seat in a train car reserved for whites. When the conductor asked Plessy to move to the Negro car he refused and was arrested.
- Judge John H. Ferguson of New Orleans ruled against Plessy's plea that the law violated the equal protection clause of the Fourteenth Amendment. When the Louisiana Supreme Court upheld Ferguson's decision, the Citizens' Committee appealed the case to the United States Supreme Court.
- The Supreme Court handed down its decision on May 18, 1896. The Court ruled against Plessy by a 7 to 1 vote.

The Court's decision upheld segregation by approving "separate but equal" railroad facilities for African Americans.

- In his famous dissenting opinion, Justice John Marshall Harlan argued that the Louisiana law created "a badge of servitude" that violated the equal protection clause of the Fourteenth Amendment.

## 2. WHAT FACTORS CONTRIBUTED TO THE SUPREME COURT'S DECISION?

- Following the Civil War, Southern states enacted Black Codes to limit the legal and social rights of African Americans. These codes played an important role in prompting Congress to pass the Fourteenth Amendment to protect the civil rights of African Americans.

- The Civil Rights Act of 1875 guaranteed blacks "full and equal enjoyment" of public facilities. However, the Supreme Court began handing down a series of decisions that limited federal protection of African Americans and opened the door to racial segregation. For example, the 1883 *Civil Rights Cases* ruled that the Fourteenth Amendment only applies to state actions and could not be used to regulate the behavior of private individuals or private organizations. This set a legal precedent that would be used in *Plessy v. Ferguson*.

- The Supreme Court does not reach decisions in a political and social vacuum. By the 1890s, more and more white Southerners rejected the idea of racial equality. The crash of 1893 and the ensuing economic depression further sharpened racial tensions. The Court's decision in *Plessy v. Ferguson* reflected the ongoing trend toward enacting Jim Crow segregation laws.

## 3. WHY SHOULD YOU REMEMBER *PLESSY V. FERGUSON*?

- *Plessy v. Ferguson* allowed Jim Crow segregation laws to spread across the South. Within a few years, state and local statutes required segregated schools, restaurants, and hotels. Ubiquitous (everywhere) signs saying "White only" or "Colored" appeared on restroom doors, above water fountains, and inside stores.

INSIDER TIP

*Plessy v. Ferguson* is a landmark Supreme Court case that has generated a large number of multiple-choice questions. Be sure that you know that the case sanctioned "separate but equal" facilities but was later reversed by Brown v. *Board of Education of Topeka*.

- *Plessy v. Ferguson* sanctioned (approved) a **pattern** of court-supported segregation that lasted about **60 years**. Segregated schools used separate facilities that were rarely equal. The Supreme Court finally reversed itself and overturned *Plessy v. Ferguson* when it ruled in *Brown v. Board of Education of Topeka* that segregated schools are inherently unequal.

## TOPIC 134
# LYNCHING IN THE SOUTH

1. Jim Crow laws, poll taxes, and literacy tests were all forms of legalized racial discrimination. White racists also used public lynchings to terrorize blacks and enforce white supremacy. Lynching is the practice of executing a person without a legal trial. During the peak years from 1889 to 1909, more than 1,700 African Americans were lynched in the South.

2. A number of motives combined to cause the outburst of lynchings in the South. For many perpetrators, lynching was a way of enforcing segregation by punishing perceived violations of Jim Crow customs. It was also a way to dissuade blacks from voting and intimidate successful African Americans whose economic progress threatened white ideas about black inferiority.

3. Resisting the wave of lynching required great courage. Ida B. Wells, an elementary school teacher and journalist, was galvanized to take action when a white mob in Memphis lynched three of her friends. Wells believed that the victims' "crime" was successfully competing with a white-owned grocery store. Outraged by the crime, Wells began a lifelong crusade against lynching. She attempted to educate the public by publishing articles, writing books, and organizing black women's clubs. After a particularly horrifying lynching of a black postmaster in South Carolina, Wells spent five weeks in Washington, D.C. in a futile effort to persuade the federal government to intervene.

## INSIDER TIP
Recent APUSH exams and SAT II US History tests have begun to give Ida B. Wells the attention she deserves. Although Wells is best known for her opposition to lynching, she was also an outspoken champion of women's suffrage and one of the founders of the National Association for the Advancement of Colored People (NAACP).

## TOPIC 135
# KEY QUOTE – BOOKER T. WASHINGTON'S "SEPARATE AS THE FINGERS" SPEECH

## 1. THE SETTING

- Booker T. Washington was a former slave who attended the Hampton Institute, a school in Virginia that stressed industrial education. Washington later founded a similar school, the Tuskegee Institute, in Alabama.
- Washington became a leading spokesman for industrial education. He believed that blacks were poor because they had few skills. With a practical vocational education black people would be able to improve their lives by learning useful trades.
- In 1895, the organizers of an international exhibition in Atlanta invited Washington to speak to a predominately white audience at the opening ceremonies of their exposition. Although the organizers worried that "public sentiment was not prepared for such an advanced step," they decided that inviting a black speaker would demonstrate racial progress in the New South.

## 2. THE QUOTE

- "In all things that are purely social we can be as separate as the fingers, yet one as the hand in all things essential to material progress … The wisest among my race understand that the agitation of questions of social equality is the extremist folly, and that progress in the enjoyment of all the privileges that will come to us must be the result of severe and constant struggle rather than of artificial forcing."

## 3. IMPORTANCE

- Finding a place in Southern society for African Americans was one of the most pressing issues facing the New South. Washington's conciliatory (soothing) message that African Americans and whites could lead socially separate lives while working together for economic progress pleased his listeners. He avoided the defiant stand taken by abolitionist leaders such as William Lloyd Garrison and

## INSIDER TIP
Be sure that you can compare and contrast the different strategies advocated by Booker T. Washington and W.E.B. Du Bois. This topic generated a DBQ in 1989 and has been the subject of numerous recent multiple-choice questions.

Frederick Douglass. Instead, he encouraged blacks to accept segregation, seek economic opportunities, and avoid political agitation. Washington urged Southern employers to reject troublesome European immigrants and hire loyal black workers who would be "the most patient, faithful, law-abiding, and unresentful people that the world has seen."

- Proponents (supporters) of the New South praised Washington's message of accommodation and self-help. In a short time, the speech catapulted Washington into the position of being the nation's acknowledged spokesperson for African Americans. As a result, he gained access to wealthy northern philanthropists who generously supported the Tuskegee Institute and other industrial education projects in the South.

- Younger, educated blacks led by W.E.B. Du Bois strongly criticized Washington's commitment to gradual progress. Du Bois derisively (scornfully) called Washington's speech "the Atlanta Compromise" and instead advocated an alternate program of "ceaseless agitation" to challenge Jim Crow segregation and demand full economic, social, and political equality.

# CHAPTER 28
# THE WEST, 1865 – 1900

## ESSENTIAL POINTS

1. A diverse group of miners, cattlemen, and farmers settled the West in the decades following the Civil War. It is important to note that Irish and Chinese workers helped build the transcontinental railroads and that black pioneers called **EXODUSTERS** settled in Kansas.

2. Helen Hunt Jackson's book *A Century of Dishonor* documented the wrongs inflicted on Native Americans by broken treaties and corrupt government practices. Jackson bitterly declared that every page of American history contains misdeeds perpetrated on Native Americans.

3. The Dawes Act forced Native Americans to give up tribal lands and become self-supporting farmers. Rather than respect tribal cultures the act attempted to assimilate Native Americans into the mainstream of American culture.

4. According to Turner's famous thesis, the frontier experience had a profound effect on the American character by promoting individualism and democracy.

## TOPIC 136
# KEY FACTS ABOUT THE WEST

### 1. THE TRANSCONTINENTAL RAILROADS

- Railroad workers and company officials celebrated the completion of the first transcontinental railroad on May 10, 1869 at Promontory Point, Utah. By 1900, four additional transcontinental railroads crisscrossed the West. Irish and Chinese workers played an important role in these vast construction projects.
- The transcontinental railroads enabled diverse groups of miners, cattlemen, and farmers to settle in the West.
- The transcontinental railroads also enabled hunters to nearly exterminate the herds of buffalo that roamed the Great Plains. This indiscriminate slaughter dealt a catastrophic blow to the culture of the Plains Indians.

### 2. THE MINERS' FRONTIER

- Discoveries of gold and silver sparked a frenetic rush of prospectors to mines scattered across the Rocky and Sierra Mountains. For example, the Comstock Lode near Virginia City, Utah yielded deposits of gold and silver worth more than 300 million dollars.
- Mining camps included a diverse group of white, black, American Indian, Mexican, and Chinese miners.

### 3. THE COWBOYS' FRONTIER

- During the twenty years after the Civil War, cowboys herded cattle on long drives from Texas to "cow towns" in Kansas. For example, the Chisholm Trail was used to drive cattle from San Antonio, Texas to a railhead in Abilene, Kansas.
- During the peak years of the 1870s, as many as 40,000 cowboys roamed the Great Plains. About one-third of the cowboys were Mexicans and African Americans.
- The era of long drives ended by the late 1880s. Open-range cattle ranching became less profitable as beef prices fell. In addition, many ranchers lost half or more of their herds because of unusually cold winters that struck the Great Plains in 1886 and 1887.

## INSIDER TIP

Do not expect to see APUSH questions about the Gunfight at the O.K. Corral or famous outlaws such as the James Gang. Instead, make sure that you can identify the Chisholm Trail and the Exodusters.

## 4. THE FARMER'S FRONTIER

- Great Plains agriculture posed new challenges for farmers eager to take advantage of the Homestead Act. Blizzards, fires, and swarms of locusts swept across the arid and treeless prairies. Farmers used to living in log cabins had to learn how to build sod homes. A series of new tools including mechanical reapers, wind-driven water pumps, iron plows, and barbed-wire fences enabled determined farmers to overcome natural obstacles and build successful homesteads.

- In the late 1870s about 25,000 black pioneers called EXODUSTERS left the South to start new lives in Kansas. By 1890, over 500,000 blacks lived west of the Mississippi River.

# TOPIC 137
# THE DEFEAT AND TRANSFORMATION OF THE PLAINS INDIANS

## 1. THREATS TO NATIVE AMERICAN CULTURE

- About 250,000 Native Americans lived on the Great Plains in the early 1860s. They relied upon the buffalo herds for food, clothing, and shelter.

- The construction of the transcontinental railroads, the slaughter of the buffalo, the spread of epidemic diseases, and the destructive effects of constant warfare all caused a decline in Native American population.

## 2. *A CENTURY OF DISHONOR*  1881

- Helen Hunt Jackson was an outspoken and prolific (very productive) writer who championed the cause of Native Americans. Jackson published A Century of Dishonor in 1881. Her book documented the misdeeds of corrupt Indian agents, duplicitous (untruthful) government officials, and land-hungry settlers who encroached (violated, overran) onto tribal reservations. Jackson castigated (sharply criticized) the US government for its role in "a tale of wrongs and oppressions… that is too monstrous to be believed."

## INSIDER TIP

Do not expect to see multiple-choice questions asking you to identify Chief Sitting Bull and General Custer. Instead make sure you can identify Helen Hunt Jackson and summarize the provisions and goals of the Dawes Act.

## PODCAST 28.1
### THE DAWES ACT

- Like many other well-meaning reformers, Jackson supported policies designed to bring Native Americans into the mainstream of American life. *A Century of Dishonor* played a key role in mobilizing public support for the Dawes Act.

### 3. THE DAWES ACT, 1887

- The Dawes Act divided tribal lands into individual homesteads of 160 acres, which were then distributed to the head of each Indian family.
- The Dawes Act tried to "civilize" Native Americans by turning them into self-supporting farmers. Although well-intentioned, the policy failed to work. The Plains Indians were nomadic warriors and hunters who were unprepared for a culture based upon private property and settled agriculture.
- Prior to the Dawes Act, Indian tribes controlled 150 million acres of land. By the time the Indian Reorganization Act was passed in 1934, the Plains Indians lost almost two-thirds of their land.

### 4. THE GHOST DANCE AND THE WOUNDED KNEE MASSACRE, 1890

- The slaughter of the buffalo caused an irrevocable disruption of Plains Indian culture. Inspired by visions of a Paiute prophet named Wovoka, many desperate Native Americans performed a ritual Ghost Dance they believed would hasten the return of the buffalo and the departure of the white settlers.
- Suspicious government agents wanted to suppress performances of the Ghost Dance. Fearing that the Indians intended to go on the warpath, the army dispatched troops to reservations in the Pine Ridge area of present-day South Dakota.
- Tensions mounted when the army assumed that Sioux wearing Ghost Dance shirts were preparing to revolt. When a Sioux fired a single shot at the troops, the soldiers returned fire with repeating rifles. As many as 300 men, women, and children died in what came to be called the Wounded Knee Massacre.

# TOPIC 138
# TURNER'S FRONTIER THESIS

1. After studying the 1890 population count the Superintendent of the U.S. Census issued a statement declaring that the western frontier had closed. The finding surprised and intrigued Frederick Jackson Turner, a young professor of history at the University of Wisconsin. He concluded that the close of the frontier symbolized the end of a great historic movement.

2. In a paper entitled, "The Significance of the Frontier in American History," Turner wrote that the frontier experience profoundly shaped the American character. For three centuries land-hungry settlers had been forced by trial and error to create a new way of life. According to Turner, the frontier promoted democracy and encouraged individualism. It produced a unique combination of traits that included resilience (the ability to bounce back from adversity), restlessness, and self-reliance, together with an optimistic faith in democratic institutions. The western frontier also promoted opportunity by providing an open society where rigid class lines did not block social mobility.

3. It is important to note that Turner did not state that the frontier was the sole force shaping the American character. He acknowledged the importance of religious freedom, sectionalism, and industrialization. However, he continued to insist that the frontier experience left an indelible (lasting) impression on the American character.

## INSIDER TIP
The Turner Thesis is often used in quote-based multiple-choice questions. Here is a typical quote from Turner's famous essay: "From the beginning of the settlement of America, the frontier regions have exercised a steady influence toward democracy… American democracy is fundamentally the outcome of the experience of the American people in dealing with the West."

# CHAPTER 29
# BIG BUSINESS AND LABOR UNIONS, 1865 – 1900

## ESSENTIAL POINTS

1. Led by John D. Rockefeller and Andrew Carnegie, American industrialists used horizontal and vertical integration to create huge consolidated business organizations. **HORIZONTAL INTEGRATION** is the process by which one company gains control over other firms that produce the same product. **VERTICAL INTEGRATION** is the process by which a single company owns and controls all phases of production.

2. **SOCIAL DARWINISM** is the belief that the "laws" of biological evolution also apply to human society. Social Darwinists promoted competition and rugged individualism and opposed government intervention in the free market.

3. In his essay "The Gospel of Wealth," Andrew Carnegie argued that the wealthy have a responsibility to use their fortunes for the benefit of their communities.

4. The Knights of Labor attempted to organize all workers into a union committed to idealistic social goals. In contrast, the AFL attempted to organize skilled craftsmen into a union committed to "bread and butter issues."

5. Wage cuts precipitated (caused) the Great Railroad, Homestead, and Pullman strikes. The federal government used force to crush all three strikes.

**TOPIC 139**
# KEY CHARACTERISTICS OF THE NEW INDUSTRIAL ERA

## 1. NATURAL AND HUMAN RESOURCES

- The United States was blessed with abundant supplies of coal, iron, petroleum, and timber. For example, the Mesabi Range in Minnesota contained the world's largest deposits of iron ore.
- Labor was both plentiful and inexpensive. A huge pool of unskilled American workers included many women and children. In addition, waves of European immigrants provided a seemingly inexhaustible supply of low-wage laborers.

## 2. GOVERNMENT SUPPORT

- Nineteenth century federal and state governments were committed to the concept of private property and limited regulation of business activity.
- While the federal government was reluctant to regulate business, it did enact high protective tariffs to shield companies from foreign competition.
- A group of ambitious and sometimes ruthless entrepreneurs took advantage of this stable business environment to build a number of enormously profitable corporations.

## 3. THE GOLDEN AGE OF RAILROADS

- America's railroad network increased from 35,000 miles in 1865 to 193,000 miles in 1900. Railroad construction stimulated industrial growth by consuming vast quantities of iron, steel, coal, and lumber.
- The railroads played a key role in creating an interconnected national transportation and communication network.

## 4. HORIZONTAL AND VERTICAL INTEGRATION

- Railroads, steel companies, and oil refineries all faced intense competition from ambitious rivals. During the 1880s and 1890s, corporate executives used horizontal and vertical integration to create huge consolidated organizations.

- HORIZONTAL INTEGRATION is the process by which one company gains control over other firms that produce the same product. Horizontal integration was primarily a response to economic competition. For example, John D. Rockefeller believed that his competitors reduced profits by flooding the market with too much refined oil. He used horizontal integration to take over twenty-two of his twenty-six competitors. As a result, Standard Oil controlled almost 95 percent of the oil refining in America.
- VERTICAL INTEGRATION is the process by which a single company owns and controls the entire productive process from the unearthing of raw materials to the manufacture and sale of finished products. Vertical integration was primarily motivated by a desire to control raw materials. For example, Andrew Carnegie used vertical integration when he bought the mines that produced iron ore and the ships and railroad lines that carried the ore to his steel plants near Pittsburgh.

## 5. EDISON AND THE BUSINESS OF INVENTION

- Thomas Edison was one of the most prolific (productive) inventors in American history. His list of inventions included the first phonograph and the first commercially successful incandescent light bulb.
- Edison established his famous "invention laboratory" at Menlo Park, New Jersey. It was the prototype (model) for the modern research laboratory.

## 6. THE WORLD'S COLUMBIAN EXPOSITION OF 1893

- Held in Chicago, the World's Columbian Exposition celebrated the 400th anniversary of Columbus' discovery of America.
- The fair was more than a tribute to Columbus. It also celebrated Chicago's dynamic growth and America's amazing technological progress.

INSIDER TIP

Be sure you understand the difference between horizontal and vertical integration. Both concepts have generated a significant number of multiple-choice questions. Be sure to remember that vertical integration was motivated by a desire to control raw materials.

# TOPIC 140
## SOCIAL DARWINISM

## INSIDER TIP

APUSH and SAT II test writers often use a quote-based multiple-choice question to test your ability to identify sentiments characteristic of Social Darwinist thought. If the quote contains the phrase "survival of the fittest," you can be sure Social Darwinism is the answer.

1. Between 1869 and 1899 the value of American manufactures increased by 600 percent. America's booming economy produced unprecedented (without previous example) personal fortunes. The new millionaires filled their mansions with fine furniture and precious works of art. By 1900, the richest 2 percent of American households owned over one-third of the nation's physical wealth.

2. SOCIAL DARWINISM was a set of beliefs that both explained and justified how a small group of business and industrial leaders could accumulate such great wealth. Social Darwinists applied Charles Darwin's theory that plants and animals are engaged in a constant "struggle for existence" to society. According to Social Darwinists, individuals and corporations are also engaged in a ruthless struggle for profit in which only the fit survive and succeed.

3. Wealthy "captains of industry" such as Rockefeller and Carnegie used the "law of competition" to explain their wealth and praise the free market economic system that made it possible. In an often quoted statement, Rockefeller explained that, "The growth of a large business corporation is merely the survival of the fittest … The American Beauty rose can be produced in the splendor and fragrance which bring cheer to its beholder only by sacrificing the early buds which grow up around it. This is not an evil tendency in business. It is merely the working out of a law of nature and a law of God."

4. Social Darwinism explained that wealth is a reward for hard work and talent while poverty is a punishment for laziness and bad judgment. Governments must therefore avoid the temptation to regulate economic activities by supporting wage increases and social welfare programs. These policies are doomed to fail because they interfere with the natural workings of a free market.

## TOPIC 141
# ANDREW CARNEGIE AND THE GOSPEL OF WEALTH

1. Andrew Carnegie was an ardent supporter of Social Darwinism. He believed that disparities (inequalities) in wealth were inevitable in a free economic system. However, he also believed that great wealth brought great responsibilities.
2. In his 1889 "The Gospel of Wealth" essay, Carnegie warned that men who died wealthy would pass away "unwept, unhonored, and unsung." The public would justly condemn these men because, "The man who dies thus rich dies disgraced." Instead of squandering (wasting) their money on passing fantasies, men of wealth have a duty to regard their surplus fortunes as a trust to be administered for the benefit of the community. Carnegie encouraged philanthropists (benefactors) to support public libraries, universities, museums, and other "ladders upon which the aspiring can rise."
3. Carnegie practiced what he preached. After selling his huge steel and iron holdings to J.P. Morgan for $500 million, Carnegie devoted the rest of his life to promoting the public good. His munificent (very generous) grants supported parks, hospitals, concert halls, and especially public libraries.

## INSIDER TIP

SAT II and APUSH test writers often use the following quote by Andrew Carnegie to test your knowledge of the Gospel of Wealth: "This, then, is held to be the duty of the man of wealth: to consider all surplus revenues which come to him simply as trust funds…the man of wealth thus becoming the mere agent and trustee for his poorer brethren."

## TOPIC 142
# LABOR UNIONS

### 1. WAGE AND WORKING CONDITIONS

- Owners enjoyed enormous profits while their workers earned meager (inadequate) salaries. For example, Marshall Field, the founder of a Chicago-based chain of department stores, earned $600.00 an hour while his shopgirls survived on a salary of just $3.00 to $5.00 a week. In 1900, a male industrial worker earned an average of $597.00 a year while his female counterpart earned an average of only $314.00 a year.

- Factory laborers typically worked ten-hour days, six days a week. Hours were even longer in steel mills where workers put in 12-hour shifts for $1.25 a day.
- America's poorly paid workers were also unprotected by safety regulations. American industry had the highest accident rate in the world. Health hazards abounded in factories, mines, and railroad yards. In 1890, railroad accidents injured one railroader for every 30 employed workers.

## 2. THE KNIGHTS OF LABOR

- The Knights of Labor was founded in 1869. It attempted to unify all working men and women into a national union under the motto, "An injury to one is the concern of all." With the exception of lawyers, bankers, and saloon keepers, the Knights accepted anyone who worked for wages including women and African Americans.
- The Knights denounced "wage-slavery" and were dedicated to achieving a "cooperative commonwealth" of independent workers. The Knights hoped to achieve this idealistic goal by encouraging workers to combine their wages so that they could collectively purchase mines, factories, and stores.
- The Knights' open-membership and a few successful strikes contributed to a period of rapid growth in the 1880s. Membership rolls swelled from 42,000 in 1882 to over 700,000 in 1886.
- The Knights began to lose strength when newspapers unjustly blamed them for causing the Haymarket Square riot. As a result of this misrepresentation, the public erroneously (wrongly) linked the Knights with violent anarchists who opposed all forms of government. The economic depression following the Panic of 1893 ended the union's importance.

## 3. SAMUEL GOMPERS AND THE AFL

- As the Knights of Labor declined in national importance, the American Federation of Labor (AFL) began to grow. Founded in 1886, the AFL was an alliance of skilled workers in craft unions. Unlike the Knights of Labor, the AFL did not welcome unskilled workers, women, or racial minorities.
- Led for 37 years by Samuel Gompers, the AFL opposed political activity not directly related to the union. Instead,

Gompers advocated using collective bargaining and, if necessary, strikes to win concrete "bread and butter" goals such as higher wages, shorter hours, and better working conditions.

- Membership in the AFL grew steadily as it replaced the Knights of Labor as America's most powerful labor union. By 1904, the AFL had 1.7 million members and Gompers was recognized as a national spokesman for American laborers. It is interesting to note that the AFL's traditional goals attracted support from late 19th century middle-class reformers.

## 4. THE INDUSTRIAL WORKERS OF THE WORLD

- The AFL's commitment to craft unionism excluded many workers. Like the Knights of Labor, the Industrial Workers of the World (IWW or Wobblies) was intended to be "One Big Union" that would unite all skilled and unskilled workers.
- While the AFL pursued "bread and butter" issues, the IWW was founded on what one of its early leaders called "the irrepressible conflict between the capitalist class and the working class." The IWW advocated a socialist economic system in which the government would own the basic industries and natural resources.
- The Wobblies never attracted more than 150,000 members. Branded as dangerous radicals and agitators, they faded from the national scene by the end of World War I.

INSIDER TIP
The 2009 APUSH exam contained a free-response question on the successes and limitations of labor unions in the period between 1875 and 1925. See the Question 4 Fact Sheet for a detailed discussion of the programs, strategies, and achievements of the Knights of Labor, AFL, and IWW.

## TOPIC 143
# LABOR STRIKES AND UNREST

## 1. THE GREAT RAILROAD STRIKE OF 1877

- The Panic of 1873 triggered a severe depression that bankrupted 47,000 firms and drove wholesale prices down by 30 percent. As orders for industrial goods fell, railroad lines in the East began a series of pay cuts. On July 16, 1877 railroad workers spontaneously walked off their jobs to protest a second wage cut buy the Baltimore & Ohio Railroad. Walkouts and sympathy demonstrations quickly formed as the strike spread from Maryland to California.

PODCAST 29.1
THE GREAT RAILROAD
STRIKE OF 1877

INSIDER TIP

Labor unions organized
the strike at the
McCormick reaper
factory to demand an
eight-hour work day
in Chicago and across
the United States. At
that time, most workers
labored ten to twelve
hours a day, often for six
days a week.

- The Great Railroad Strike of 1877 was the first major interstate strike in American history. As the strike rippled across the country it paralyzed rail service. Looters and rioters destroyed millions of dollars of property. State militia and federal troops called out by President Hays finally crushed the strikes. Over 100 workers died before the troops finally restored order.

- The Great Railroad Strike of 1877 signaled the beginning of a period of strikes and violent confrontations between labor and management. Between 1880 and 1900 over 23,000 strikes, the most in the industrial world, shook America and hardened relations between unions and owners.

## 2. THE HAYMARKET SQUARE RIOT, 1886

- On May 4, 1886 nearly 1,500 working people gathered at Chicago's Haymarket Square to protest violent police actions the previous day at a strike at the McCormick reaper factory. As about 180 policemen tried to disperse the crowd an unidentified person hurled a bomb into the police ranks. The explosion killed seven officers and injured sixty-seven other people. The police fired wildly into the crowd killing four people and wounding over 100 others.

- Although no one knew who threw the bomb, outraged and frightened Americans blamed anarchists. Supported by an alarmed public, employers compiled blacklists of strikers and used private security firms to break strikes.

## 3. THE HOMESTEAD STRIKE, 1892

- The Amalgamated Association of Iron and Steel Workers was the largest craft union in the AFL. The union's history of friendly relations with Andrew Carnegie's company abruptly changed in 1892 when Henry Clay Frick became president of the Homestead plant outside Pittsburgh. Frick was determined to replace expensive skilled workers with new labor-saving machinery. He reduced the number of workers and slashed salaries by nearly 20 percent in a deliberate attempt to break the union.

- When the Amalgamated called for a strike, Frick closed the Homestead plant and hired 300 union-busting Pinkerton detectives to protect nonunion workers. Enraged strikers fired at barges carrying Pinkertons to the plant. Three detectives and ten workers died before the Pinkertons finally surrendered.

- The workers' victory proved to be short-lived. The governor of Pennsylvania ordered the state's entire contingent of 8,000 National Guard troops to Homestead to protect the plant. The strike finally ended four months later leaving the Amalgamated Association broken and defeated. The Homestead Strike underscored the government's determination to protect property rights and maintain law and order. The strike ushered in a decade of violent strikes that set back the industrial union movement for forty years.

## 4. THE PULLMAN STRIKE, 1894

- The Pullman Strike was one of the most serious labor strikes of the late nineteenth century. It began as a dispute between the Pullman Palace Car Company and its 3,000 employees. Following the Panic of 1893, the Pullman company cut the wages of its workers by about 25 percent. However, the company did not reduce the rent or prices it charged workers in company-run stores at the "model" town of Pullman just outside of Chicago.

- As tensions mounted and negotiations failed, many workers joined the American Railway Union led by Eugene Debs. Fearing that they they had no alternative, desperate Pullman workers walked off their jobs. The American Railway Union then staged a nationwide boycott of Pullman cars. Because most railroad companies used Pullman cars, rail traffic ground to a halt in Chicago and across twenty-seven states and territories.

- President Cleveland had no sympathy for the striking workers. He called out federal troops to break the strike on the grounds that it obstructed delivery of the U.S. mail. The Pullman strike once again demonstrated that the federal government would actively intervene to crush strikes and protect management. The strike left Debs disillusioned and embittered. Within a few years, he became a key leader of the Socialist Party of America.

## INSIDER TIP

Recent APUSH exams have begun to focus more attention on the Great Railroad Strike of 1877. Be sure that you know that the strike followed a series of wage cuts, crippled railroad service, and marked America's first national strike.

# CHAPTER 30
# URBAN AMERICA, 1865 – 1900

## ESSENTIAL POINTS

1. The industrial revolution dramatically changed the appearance and size of American cities. Electric trolley cars promoted the growth of the central business district while enabling employees to commute to work from a new ring of suburbs.

2. The new immigrants came from southern and eastern Europe and settled in large cities in the northeast and midwest.

3. Urban political machines provided some welfare for poor immigrants in exchange for their votes. Thomas Nast's political cartoons helped expose and destroy Boss Tweed.

4. Nativist agitation in California led to the passage of the Chinese Exclusion Act prohibiting the immigration of Chinese workers into the United States.

5. Jacob Riis, Jane Addams, and Walter Rauschenbusch were noteworthy urban reformers. Riis used photographs to expose the poverty and despair in New York City's Lower East Side. Addams used Hull House to inspire a national settlement house movement. Rauschenbusch used the Social Gospel to motivate churches and ministers to take an active role in helping the poor.

6. Horatio Alger and D.W. Griffith played an important role in shaping American popular culture. Alger wrote novels that expressed the idea of the self-made man. Griffith directed movies that used innovative film techniques. His epic film *The Birth of a Nation* glorified the Ku Klux Klan.

7. The Ashcan School of Art is best known for realistic portraits of urban life in New York City.

## TOPIC 144
# URBAN GROWTH

## 1. THE OLD AGRARIAN DREAM
- Thomas Jefferson wanted America to become a nation of independent farmers. The Louisiana Purchase seemed to fulfill Jefferson's vision of enabling America to become an agrarian republic. During the pre-Civil War period the sturdy settler building a log cabin embodied the agrarian dream.
- The closing of the frontier in 1890 symbolized the end of a historic era in American history. As the western frontier experience drew to an end a new urban frontier began to emerge.

## 2. THE NEW URBAN REALITY
- Between 1870 and 1900 urban centers assumed a dominant role in American life and culture. Just after the Civil War only one in six Americans lived in a city. By 1900 one in three Americans made their homes in cities. By 1920 a majority of the population lived in urban areas.
- A large number of the new urban dwellers came from small towns and rural areas. New mechanical farm equipment pushed many workers off the land. Still others wanted to exchange the drudgery of farm life for the excitement of living in cities. Electricity, indoor plumbing, telephones, and department stores all combined to make cities an irresistible magnet that promised an exciting new life.

## 3. INDUSTRY AND URBAN GROWTH
- Before the Civil War, factories were dependent upon water for their power. As a result, they were usually built in towns near swift rivers and waterfalls. However, in the late nineteenth century, factories increasingly used steam and then electrical power. Factory owners could now build their plants near growing centers of population.
- During the post-Civil War period transportation centers became booming industrial cities. Meat-packing plants in Chicago, flour mills in Minneapolis, and oil refiners in Cleveland all offered jobs for unskilled workers.

## 4. THE IMPACT OF THE ELECTRIC TROLLEY CAR

- New forms of transportation had a profound effect on urban life. In 1888 Richmond, Virginia successfully tested the first electric trolley system. Within two years 200 other cities opened trolley lines. By 1900, 30,000 cars carried passengers on 15,000 miles of track.

- The new electric street cars encouraged the growth of the central business district. They also promoted the physical expansion of cities. For the first time, employees could commute to work from a new ring of streetcar suburbs. It is important to note that these suburbs marked the beginning of a process of segregating urban residents by class, race, and ethnicity.

## INSIDER TIP

SAT II and APUSH exams often include questions on such pivotal forms of transportation as the transcontinental railroads and the automobile. As a result, it is easy to let the electric trolley car drop off of your radar screen. Don't let that happen. It is important to remember that the electric trolley car encouraged the growth of the central business district and enabled employees to commute into the city from a new ring of streetcar suburbs.

# TOPIC 145
# THE NEW IMMIGRANTS

## 1. A NEW WAVE OF IMMIGRATION

- Before the 1880s most immigrants to the United States came from countries in northern and western Europe. However, the last two decades of the nineteenth century witnessed a massive wave of immigrants from southern and eastern Europe. The overwhelming majority of these "new" immigrants came from Italy, Poland, Austro-Hungary, and Russia.

- Europe's new industrial economy replaced the older agricultural way of life uprooting millions of people. Most of the immigrants from Italy and southern Europe were pushed out by unemployment and crushing poverty. Jewish immigrants from Poland and Russia also wanted to escape from widespread persecution. Almost all of these uprooted people viewed America as a land of freedom and opportunity.

## 2. A HARD NEW LIFE

- The overwhelming majority of the new immigrants settled in large cities in the northeast and midwest. They quickly faced a grim reality that tested their optimistic faith in America as the "land of opportunity." Many immigrants lived in crowded tenements and worked 12-hour days

## PODCAST 30.1
### THE NEW IMMIGRANTS

in grimy factories, dangerous coal mines, and dreary garment-making sweatshops. One Italian saying expressed the sense of disillusionment felt by many immigrants: "I came to America because I heard the streets were paved with gold. When I got here, I found out three things: First, the streets weren't paved with gold; second, they weren't paved at all; and third, I was expected to pave them."

- The bewildered immigrants often congregated into urban enclaves. The "Little Italys," "Little Hungarys" and other ethnic neighborhoods provided close-knit communities where the new immigrants could speak their native language and practice their religious faith.

## 3. IMMIGRANTS AND POLITICAL MACHINES

- Most immigrants were politically inexperienced. America's federal system with its local, state, and national governments seemed complex and overwhelming. As a result, many immigrants became clients of big city political machines. The boss and his ward leaders provided poor immigrants with some welfare in exchange for their votes. "If a family is burned out," explained one candid (open and honest) machine boss, "I don't ask whether they are Republicans or Democrats. I just get quarters for them, bring clothes for them if their clothes were burned up, and fix them up till they get things runnin' again. Who can tell how many votes these fires bring me?" The political machines provided the new immigrants with a rudimentary (early stage) form of welfare. At the same time, venal (corrupt) bosses often engaged in illegal schemes that cost their cities millions of dollars. New York City, for example, fell under the control of a group of corrupt politicians known as the "Tweed Ring" after their leader "Boss" William Marcy Tweed. Boss Tweed and his cronies stole as much as $200 million from the public treasury.

- Tweed's reign of unbridled greed and theft finally came to an end from an unlikely source. Thomas Nast exposed Tweed's fraudulent practices in a series of political cartoons that mercilessly portrayed the boss as the leader of a group of thieves and scoundrels. When asked why he considered Nast such a threat, Tweed replied that while immigrant voters did not know how to read, they could "look at the damn pictures."

## 4. NATIVIST REACTION

- The wave of Irish and German immigrants in the 1840s sparked a NATIVIST or anti-foreign reaction among native-born Protestants. The wave of new immigrants at the end of the nineteenth century provoked a similar nativist response.
- The new immigrants spoke different languages, practiced different religions, and worked for low wages. Alarmed nativists accused the new immigrants of being a threat to their jobs and way of life. Francis A. Walker, president of Massachusetts Institute of Technology, summarized nativist resentment when he pronounced the newcomers "beaten men from beaten races; representing the worst failures in the struggle for existence."

## 5. THE CHINESE EXCLUSION ACT, 1882

- Nativist resentment of immigrants was not limited to eastern and midwestern cities. Chinese immigrants were the largest non-European group in California. Most of California's 75,000 Chinese residents lived in sections of cities called "Chinatowns." Working class Californians bitterly complained that Chinese laborers provided unfair competition because they worked for low wages.
- Proponents (advocates) of immigration restriction demanded that Congress enact a law restricting Chinese immigration. Congress responded to this intense pressure by passing the Chinese Exclusion Act of 1882. The law suspended immigration of all Chinese laborers for ten years. Congress renewed the law in 1892 and then made it permanent in 1902. The Chinese Exclusion Act marked the first law enacted to exclude a specific ethnic or racial group from immigrating to the United States.

**TOPIC 146**
# URBAN REFORMERS AND THE SOCIAL GOSPEL

## PODCAST 30.2
JACOB RIIS and
JANE ADDAMS

## 1. JACOB RIIS AND *HOW THE OTHER HALF LIVES*

- Immigrant families packed into rows of squalid (filthy and wretched) tenement buildings. Landlords often squeezed a family into one airless room. A single square mile in New York City's Lower East Side contained 334,000 people, making it the most densely populated place in the world.
- Jacob Riis was a journalist and photographer who exposed the poverty and despair of the Lower East Side. His book *How the Other Half Lives* (1890) included particularly poignant photographs of destitute (very poor) families struggling to survive against overwhelming odds. Riis was not content to simply document the wretched conditions in New York's disease-ridden tenements. He hoped that his photographs would shock a complacent public into calling for reforms. Riis's concern for the plight of the poor was not in vain. New York City tore down some of the worst slums and replaced them with new parks and playgrounds.

## 2. JANE ADDAMS AND THE SETTLEMENT HOUSE MOVEMENT

- Jane Addams, like Jacob Riis, chose to devote her life to bettering the condition of the urban poor. In 1889 Addams rented Hull House, an old mansion in one of Chicago's poorest immigrant neighborhoods. Addams began by providing day nurseries for working mothers and offering adult-education classes for immigrants who wanted to learn English. As Hull House became more successful Addams opened a reading room and installed showers in the basement. At its peak, Hull House expanded to a dozen buildings that served 2,000 people a week.
- Hull House served as a model for other settlement houses. Idealistic middle-class women took the lead in founding over 400 settlement houses in cities across America.

### 3. WALTER RAUSCHENBUSCH AND THE SOCIAL GOSPEL

- Walter Rauschenbusch, a Baptist theologian, was deeply stirred by the plight of his parishioners in the "Hell's Kitchen" section of New York City. Convinced that something had to be done, he advocated that the Christian principles of love and justice should be applied to the nation's pressing urban problems.

- Rauschenbusch's religious philosophy became known as the **SOCIAL GOSPEL**. Supporters of the Social Gospel believed that America's churches had a moral responsibility to take the lead in actively confronting social problems and helping the poor.

INSIDER TIP

Carnegie's Gospel of Wealth and Rauschenbusch's Social Gospel are easily confused. Remember, Carnegie believed that the rich have a duty to serve their communities. Rauschenbusch believed that Christian ministers and their churches must play an active role in helping the unfortunate.

## TOPIC 147
# POPULAR CULTURE

### 1. NEW FORMS OF POPULAR CULTURE

- The last two decades of the nineteenth century witnessed the birth and growing popularity of a number of new forms of popular culture. While many of these activities were short-lived, sports generated major businesses that have endured to the present day.

- Professional team sports first became popular during the last quarter of the nineteenth century. Baseball began its reign as the national pastime when eight teams formed the National League in 1876. The American League followed in 1901. The two rival leagues held the first World Series in 1903.

### 2. HORATIO ALGER AND THE SELF–MADE MAN

- Horatio Alger was America's most popular author of juvenile fiction. Alger was a prolific (very productive) writer who published over 100 novels which together sold more than 20 million copies. Each novel tells a formulaic (standard) story of how an impoverished (very poor) young boy became successful through hard work, honesty, perseverance, and luck.

- Alger's name soon became synonymous with finding fame and fortune through "luck and pluck." Indeed, Alger

## INSIDER TIP

A number of APUSH and SAT II multiple-choice questions have asked students to equate Horatio Alger's novels with the ideal of the self-made man. In addition, Horatio Alger appeared in 1979, 1987, and 1994 free-response questions asking students to evaluate the reality and influence of the ideal of the self-made man during the late nineteenth century.

believed that his novels owed their success to stories that brought to life "inspiring examples of what energy, ambition, and honest purpose may achieve."

- Historians believe that Alger's books are more than just didactic (instructive) adventure stories for young readers. His novels were written as America made the difficult transition from an agrarian to an industrial society. Alger's stories reassured Americans that the poor but determined "self-made man" could still achieve success in an economy increasingly dominated by huge corporations.

## 3. D. W. GRIFFITH AND *THE BIRTH OF A NATION*

- In late 1903 American audiences shrieked with shock and delight as they watched a movie called *The Great Train Robbery*. The popularity of *The Great Train Robbery* helped launch a new American industry that played a significant role in shaping popular culture. By 1916 some 25 million people a day spent anywhere from a nickel to a quarter to laugh at the zany antics of Charlie Chaplin and to fall in love with the charms of "America's Sweetheart" Mary Pickford. By 1915 movies had become America's fifth largest industry and Hollywood had become the center of movie production.

- D.W. Griffith quickly established himself as Hollywood's most innovative and controversial director. Griffith's epic movie *The Birth of a Nation* was Hollywood's first blockbuster film and the highest grossing movie of the silent film era. Although *The Birth of a Nation* was a triumph of cinematic art, it is best remembered for its glorified depiction of the rise of the Ku Klux Klan after the Civil War. Griffith's movie helped inspire the resurgence of the Ku Klux Klan in the 1920s.

# TOPIC 148
# REALISTIC ART AND LITERATURE

## 1. A NEW REALISM

- Romanticism dominated American art and literature during most of the nineteenth century. However, the twin forces of industrialization and urbanization created harsh new social realities that conflicted with Romanticism's emphasis upon nature. A talented group of American artists and authors rejected Romanticism turning instead to Realism's hard-edged portraits of urban life.
- Realism's artists and authors focused on the facets of the modern world they could personally experience. Idealized landscapes and sentimental love stories seemed out of touch with America's raw and raucous (loud and jarring) cities.

## 2. THE ASHCAN SCHOOL OF ART

- Ashcan artists wanted above all to connect with the crowds and congestion in New York City. They relished being part of the city's vibrant and unruly life. Ashcan artists typically portrayed working class taverns, bleak tenements, and dark alleys. For a famous example of Ashcan art see *Cliff Dwellers* by George Bellows.
- Ashcan artists prided themselves on being young and urban. The 1913 Armory Show in New York City exposed American artists for the first time to Europe's revolutionary Cubist and Modern artists. After touring the exhibit, Stuart Davis, a leading Ashcan artist, called the show "the greatest single experience … in all my work." The Armory Show marked a watershed (pivotal) event that had a lasting impact upon American art.

## 3. REALISM IN LITERATURE

- Talented authors also rejected Romanticism. They strived to create a more authentic or realistic portrayal of American life by using regional dialects and describing "true" relationships between people.
- Stephen Crane and Theodore Dreiser were two of America's foremost Realist authors. Crane captured the impact of poverty in *Maggie: A Girl of the Streets* (1893). Dreiser's novel *Sister Carrie* (1900) described the story of a young Wisconsin farm girl who moved to Chicago to pursue a new life.

## INSIDER TIP

You will not need to know the names of specific Ashcan artists. However, you should know that Ashcan artists often portrayed urban tenements, taverns, and alleys. SAT II tests often expect students to know that the Armory Show first exposed American artists to Europe's revolutionary Cubist artists.

# CHAPTER 31
# THE POPULIST REVOLT, 1880 – 1896

## ESSENTIAL POINTS

1. During the last quarter of the nineteenth century, new machinery and fertilizers enabled American farmers to increase the number of acres under cultivation.
2. As the supply of crops increased, farm prices decreased. Angry farmers blamed their distress on discriminatory freight rates charged by the railroads.
3. The wave of agrarian discontent gave birth to the People's or Populist Party. The Populist platform demanded government control of the railroads, free coinage of silver, and the direct election of United States senators.
4. Silverites believed that the free coinage of silver would increase the supply of money and end the economic depression.
5. The election of 1896 led to the collapse of the Populist Party and a new period of Republican Party dominance.

# TOPIC 149
# AGRARIAN ANGER

## 1. CAUSES OF AGRARIAN ANGER

- American farmers seemed to have much to be proud of. Between 1870 and 1900 the population of the United States doubled to just over 76 million people. New machines and fertilizers enabled American farmers to increase the number of acres under cultivation. As a result, farmers were able to dramatically expand production and feed the nation's soaring population.

- However, the law of supply and demand worked against the farmers. The more wheat, corn, and cotton they produced the lower prices fell. For example, the price of a bushel of wheat plummeted from $1.19 in 1881 to just .49 cents in 1894. Cotton that sold for 15.1 cents a pound in 1870 commanded only 5.8 cents a pound in 1894.

- Angry and desperate farmers blamed the railroads for many of their problems. Railroads made large-scale agriculture possible by transporting corn, wheat, and cattle to cities and then shipping heavy machinery and supplies to the farms. Most farmers were thus completely dependent upon the railroads. Farmers bitterly complained that the railroads used their monopoly to charge unfair rates. For example, the Burlington line charged its customers west of the Missouri four times what they charged customers east of the river.

- Farmers had to borrow heavily to build houses and buy land and equipment. Following the Civil War, America experienced a prolonged period of deflation which meant that both prices and the money supply were falling. As a result, a farmer had to pay back loans with dollars that had doubled in value since he borrowed them.

## 2. THE GRANGER MOVEMENT

- Many farmers endured a lonely existence on widely separated farms. The Granger movement began as a social and educational organization in response to the farmers' isolation. As local Grange chapters spread across the southern and western farm belts, membership rolls reached 1.5 million people by 1874.

- The Grange soon became more than an organization to end the loneliness of farm life. The Grange founded cooperatives through which they sold their crops and bought supplies as a group. They even tried to manufacture farm machinery. At the same time the Grange began to fight the railroads. Several states passed "Granger laws" regulating railroad freight rates.
- The Granges' early success proved to be short-lived. Many of the cooperatives failed because of mismanagement. Meanwhile, the railroads successfully challenged the state regulations in federal courts. By 1890, the Supreme Court ruled that states could not regulate railroads engaged in interstate commerce. These setbacks led to the decline of the Grange after 1876.

## 3. THE FARMERS' ALLIANCE

- The farmers still had much too complain about. As the Grange lost members a new organization known as the Farmers' Alliance grew in size and importance. Founded in Texas in the mid-1870s, the National Farmers' Alliance quickly spread through the South and Plains' states. By 1891, the Alliance movement boasted over 1.5 million members. A separate Alliance for black farmers had another quarter-million members.
- The Alliance movement sponsored an ambitious program of economic and political reforms. As a "grand army of reform" it welcomed women members. Many women embraced this opportunity and assumed key leadership roles.

INSIDER TIP
The 2003B APUSH exam included a free-response question asking students to "analyze the ways in which farmers and industrial workers responded to industrialization." See Question 4, Essay I for an excellent response that received a 9.

# TOPIC 150
# THE POPULIST PARTY

## 1. THE BIRTH OF THE POPULIST PARTY

- America's increasingly militant farmers believed that they had good reasons to organize a third party. Once praised as the backbone of American democracy, the farmers now saw themselves as victims of an unjust system that penalized them with low crop prices and predatory railroad rates while rewarding Wall Street financiers with extravagant profits. A Populist leader Mary Ellen Lease captured the farmers' militant mood when she advised them "to raise less corn and more hell."

- The wave of agrarian discontent gave birth to the **People's or Populist Party.** Alliance leaders discussed plans for a third party at conventions held in Cincinnati in May 1891 and St. Louis in February 1892. Finally in July 1892, 1,300 exhilarated (filled with high spirits) delegates met in Omaha, Nebraska to formulate a platform and nominate a candidate for the fall presidential election.

- The Populist platform emphatically demanded government control of the railroads. It also called for the free and unlimited coinage of silver. Populist leaders believed that free silver would increase the money supply and therefore spur inflation. And finally, the Populist platform endorsed the eight-hour work day, a graduated income tax, and the direct election of senators by voters instead of state legislatures.

- The Populists nominated former congressman and Union general James B. Weaver of Iowa to run for president. Weaver received just over one million votes, more than any previous third-party candidate. In addition, the Populists elected ten congressmen, five senators, and almost fifteen hundred members to different state legislatures. Buoyed by their success, the Populists eagerly looked forward to the 1896 presidential election.

## 2. THE DEPRESSION OF 1893

- **Grover Cleveland** began his second term as President on March 4, 1893. Just two months later a panic on Wall Street touched off a severe economic depression. A worried advisor warned Cleveland, "We are on the eve of a very dark night." His gloomy prediction proved to be accurate. In 1893 over 15,000 businesses and 600 banks closed. By the following year, one-fifth of the nation's workers had lost their jobs.

- An Ohio Populist named James S. Coxey urged the federal government to launch a $500 million road-building program to provide unemployed workers with desperately needed jobs. When Congress ignored his proposal, Coxey led a ragtag army of unemployed workers on a protest march to Washington. When "Coxey's army" finally reached the U.S. Capitol armed police arrested Coxey for walking on the lawn. He was fined $5.00 and sentenced to 20 days in jail. It is interesting to note that Coxey died in 1951 having lived long enough to see his ideas for public works projects enacted during the New Deal.

## 3. THE POPULISTS AND FREE SILVER

- Unemployed workers and debt-ridden farmers called for an immediate solution to end the depression. Populist leaders believed that the depression underscored the urgent need for the free coinage of silver.
- The Populists believed that there was a direct relationship between the amount of money in circulation and the level of economic activity. Strict adherence to the gold standard reduced the supply of money in circulation and thus limited economic activity. This policy benefited bankers and creditors while punishing debtors. The free and unlimited coinage of silver would bring back prosperity by putting more money in circulation and thus increasing business activity. One Populist summed up the case for free silver by explaining that, "It means the reopening of closed factories, the relighting of fires in darkened furnaces; it means hope instead of despair; comfort in place of suffering; life instead of death."
- Populist leaders believed that free silver offered a compelling solution to the depression. With the 1896 election fast approaching, Populists prepared for a climatic battle with the Republicans and Democrats that many believed would determine the nation's future for generations to come.

## INSIDER TIP

Be sure that you can identify the Omaha Platform. It included a number of reforms that were later incorporated into the Progressive agenda.

# TOPIC 151
# THE ELECTION OF 1896

## PODCAST 31.1
THE ELECTION OF 1896

## 1. THE CANDIDATES

- The Republicans correctly sensed that the depression weakened Cleveland and the Democrats. They confidently nominated William McKinley, the affable and well-liked governor of Ohio. The Republican platform supported tariffs and forthrightly (openly and honestly) stated that "the existing gold standard must be maintained."

- Pro-silver delegates controlled the Democratic convention in Chicago. The Silverites promptly repudiated Cleveland and wrote a platform demanding the free coinage of silver. The Democrats now had an issue but still lacked a candidate. That changed when William Jennings Bryan, a 36 year-old former congressman from Nebraska, addressed the convention. Bryan reminded the pro-silver delegates that, "We have petitioned and our petitions have been scorned!" Bryan thundered defiance as he reached his free silver conclusion: "You shall not press down upon the brow of labor this crown of thorns. You shall not crucify mankind upon a cross of gold!" Bryan's "Cross of Gold" speech galvanized (electrified) the cheering delegates. The next day euphoric (deliriously happy) delegates wearing silver badges and waving silver banners nominated Bryan for President.
- The Democrat's decision to nominate a pro-silver candidate presented the Populists with a difficult choice. Nominating their own candidate would divide the silver vote and ensure McKinley's election. Endorsing Bryan would mean giving up their identity as a separate party. After much debate, the Populists chose to support Bryan.

## 2. THE CAMPAIGN

- Bryan ignored tradition and launched a whirlwind campaign that crisscrossed the country. The "Boy Orator" conveyed boundless energy and an almost evangelical (missionary) enthusiasm as he delivered over 600 speeches extolling (praising) the benefits of free silver.
- While Bryan campaigned across the country, McKinley stayed home in Canton, Ohio and ran a "front porch" campaign adroitly (skillfully) managed by his close friend Mark Hanna. Friendly railroads provided reduced fares enabling over 750,000 people to visit Canton and hear McKinley earnestly promise "good work, good wages, and good money." Hanna's strategy cleverly allowed McKinley to maintain an image of decorum and dignity. The president of a New England woman's club approvingly noted, "He does not talk wildly, and his appearance is that of a President."

## 3. THE RESULTS

- McKinley's well-financed campaign overwhelmed Bryan. McKinley won the popular vote by 7.1 million to 6.5 million and the electoral vote by 271 to 176. The South and much of the thinly populated West supported Bryan. McKinley captured all of the Northeast and the upper Midwest, including the crucial swing states of Ohio and Illinois.

- As expected, industrialists and the middle class solidly endorsed McKinley. However, McKinley surprised Bryan by also winning a majority of votes from urban workers. Despite the pro-labor planks in their platform, the Democrats were unable to build a rural-urban coalition. Bryan's obsession with the silver issue diverted attention from labor's traditional focus on wages, hours, and working conditions. Many labor leaders feared that free silver would inflate the value of the dollar and thus shrink the real value of their wages. Industrial workers also approved the Republican support for high tariffs. They believed tariffs would protect American industries and thus save working-class jobs.

## 4. THE CONSEQUENCES

- The election of 1896 led to the swift collapse of the Populist Party. The silver issue melted away as gold strikes in South African, the Yukon, and Alaska enlarged the money supply and reversed the deflationary spiral. In addition, crop failures in Europe led to an increase in American grain exports. As commodity prices rose, farmers entered a period of renewed prosperity that lasted until the end of World War I.

- The return of prosperity did not end the spirit of reform. A new generation of Progressive reformers successfully fought for many of the Populist reforms.

- The election of 1896 began a generation of almost unbroken Republican dominance that lasted until the election of Franklin Roosevelt in 1932.

INSIDER TIP

Frank Baum's *The Wonderful Wizard of Oz* was originally written as a political allegory of free silver and the plight of American farmers. In this interpretation, the Scarecrow represents farmers, the Tin Woodman represents industrial workers, and the Cowardly Lion represents William Jennings Bryan. It is interesting to note that in Baum's book Dorothy wore silver slippers, not the ruby slippers used in the 1939 Hollywood film.

# CHAPTER 32
# THE PROGRESSIVE ERA, 1900 – 1917

## ESSENTIAL POINTS

1. Progressives rejected laissez-faire government policies. They had an optimistic faith in the ability of government to address a broad range of social problems.

2. Muckrakers were journalists who exposed corruption and social problems through investigative reporting. Upton Sinclair's *The Jungle* and the enactment of the Meat Inspection Act illustrate the relationship between muckraking and reform legislation.

3. During the Progressive Era women reformers campaigned to eliminate alcohol abuse, pass a constitutional amendment giving women the right to vote, and improve working conditions for women and children.

4. The initiative, recall, referendum, and direct primary were all measures designed to enable voters to have greater control over the political process.

5. During his administration Teddy Roosevelt arbitrated a labor dispute, launched antitrust action against the Northern Securities Company, secured passage of the Hepburn Act to regulate railroads, and added millions of acres to the system of national parks.

6. Woodrow Wilson successfully implemented his New Freedom program by reducing tariffs, creating the Federal Reserve system, and strengthening antitrust laws.

7. Progressive Era reformers devoted little attention to the plight of African Americans. However, the era did witness the formation of the NAACP and the emergence of W.E.B. Du Bois as an influential black leader.

## TOPIC 152
# THE PROGRESSIVE SPIRIT

## 1. FROM POPULISM TO PROGRESSIVISM

- The Populists focused their attention on the problems faced by farmers. They sought federal relief for the distress caused by high tariffs, discriminating railroad rates, and a deflationary gold standard.
- After the collapse of the Populist Party the reform spirit shifted to the cities where a new generation of middle and upper-middle class reformers focused on a broad range of problems caused by industrialization and urbanization. The term PROGRESSIVISM embraced a widespread, many faceted effort to build a more democratic and just society. The Progressive Era is usually dated from 1900 to America's entry into World War I in 1917.

## 2. KEY ELEMENTS OF THE PROGRESSIVE SPIRIT

- Both the Populists and the Progressives rejected laissez-faire government policies. Instead, they wanted government to play an active role in public life. The Progressives believed that complex social problems required a broad range of government responses. "The real heart of the movement," declared one Progressive reformer, was "to use the government as an agency of human welfare."
- Progressives were often college graduates who believed that modern cities were too complex to be left in the hands of corrupt party bosses. They prized social scientific knowledge and had confidence in the use of experts to efficiently manage public affairs. This "gospel of efficiency" was inspired by the principles of "scientific management" developed by Frederick W. Taylor. TAYLORISM used time-and-motion studies to eliminate wasted movements, reduce costs, and promote efficiency. Progressives believed that Taylor's approach could be used to streamline municipal governments.
- Progressives were idealists who rejected the main tenets (beliefs) of Social Darwinism. They believed that conflict and competition would not inevitably improve society.

Instead, they optimistically believed that informed citizens could create a just society that would reduce poverty, regulate corporations, protect the environment, and elect honest leaders.

## 3. THE MUCKRAKERS

- During the early 1900s popular magazines such as *Collier's* and *McClure's* began to hire writers to expose corrupt practices in business and politics. Known as **MUCKRAKERS**, these investigative reporters expressed the new spirit of Progressive reform by uncovering social wrongs.

- Muckraking magazines published more than 2,000 investigative reports between 1903 and 1912. Ida Tarbell wrote a devastating expose' of the ruthless practices John D. Rockefeller used to eliminate competitors and build the Standard Oil Company into the "Mother of Trusts." Lincoln Steffens documented the corrupt alliance between big business and urban bosses in a series of articles in *McClure's* titled "The Shame of the Cities." David Graham Phillips published an essay in *Cosmopolitan* entitled "The Treason of the Senate," which charged that most United States senators were puppets controlled by the railroads and trusts.

- The muckraking reports of Tarbell, Steffens, Phillips, and others enabled the Progressive spirit to reach a wide national audience. They helped mobilize public opinion to demand and support needed reforms.

## INSIDER TIP

Taylorism or "scientific management" has generated a number of difficult SAT II questions. SAT II test writers often use the following lines from an industrial brochure to illustrate Taylorism's focus on time management: "I hear the whistle. I must hurry. It is time to go into the shop…I work until the whistle blows to quit."

## TOPIC 153
# WOMEN AND PROGRESSIVE REFORM

## 1. THE "NEW WOMAN"

- When the Progressive Era began most women lived in states where they could neither vote nor hold public office. There were very few female lawyers, physicians, engineers, or scientists. The majority of women who did work outside the home were young and unmarried domestic servants and garment workers. Teaching, nursing, and library work were widely regarded as "helping" professions best filled by women.

- Despite (or because of) these obstacles a new generation of college-educated women played a prominent role in the Progressive movement. Settlement houses often founded by activist women pressed federal, state, and local politicians for better working and living conditions in urban areas. At the same time, women's clubs waged effective campaigns for temperance and the right to vote. The boldest of the "new women" declared their right to live independent lives and enjoy legal equality with men.

## 2. *MULLER v. OREGON*, 1908

- In 1903 Oregon enacted a law barring women in factories and laundries from working more than ten hours a day. Backed by local business groups, a laundry owner named Curt Muller challenged the law.
- Led by Florence Kelly, the National Consumers' League worked to promote protective legislation for women and children. Kelly hired Louis D. Brandeis, a noted reform lawyer, to defend the Oregon law before the United States Supreme Court.
- In a celebrated brief Brandeis used sociological data to document his argument that long working hours take a toll on women's health and role as mothers. Brandeis therefore concluded that women need special protective legislation.
- The Supreme Court agreed unanimously with Brandeis and upheld the Oregon law. This victory opened the door for a wave of other special laws protecting women and children. Brandeis' use of sociological data rather than legal precedents would later play a key role in influencing how the Supreme Court reached its ruling in the *Brown v. Board of Education of Topeka* decision overturning the "separate but equal" doctrine in public schools.
- Not all women welcomed the Court's decision in *Muller v. Oregon*. Feminists led by Charlotte Perkins Gilman rejected the Court's reasoning that women need legal protection because of their physical frailty and role as future mothers. Gilman, Margaret Sanger, and other early feminists supported a single standard of behavior for men and women. Several feminists joined the birth-control movement led by Sanger.

## 3. WOMEN AND THE WORKPLACE

- During the late 19th and early 20th centuries, the majority of female workers employed outside the home were young and unmarried.
- Women were most likely to work outside their homes as domestic servants, garment workers, and teachers. Women were least likely to work as lawyers and physicians.

## 4. THE TEMPERANCE MOVEMENT

- Woman played a leading role in the temperance movement to outlaw the sale of alcoholic beverages. The Women's Christian Temperance Movement (WCTU) boasted nearly 1 million members making it the largest organization of women in the world. The WCTU convinced many women that they had a moral duty to eliminate alcohol abuse and thus strengthen the stability of American families.
- As the crusade against alcohol gathered momentum more and more states outlawed saloons. In 1918, Congress passed the Eighteenth Amendment outlawing the manufacture, sale, and transportation of intoxicating liquors.

## 5. WOMAN SUFFRAGE

- When the Progressive Era began the law denied criminals, lunatics, idiots, and women the right to vote. Beginning with the Seneca Falls Convention in 1848 a determined group of women fought a long and at times frustrating battle for female suffrage. By 1900, only four western states allowed women to vote.
- The Progressive movement sharpened the nation's social conscience and motivated a new generation of suffragists. Led by Carrie Chapman Catt and Alice Paul, women organized rallies, signed petitions, and demonstrated in public marches. Their campaign of mounting pressure finally became irresistible. On June 4, 1919, Congress passed the Nineteenth Amendment stating that no citizen could be denied the right to vote, "on account of sex." The amendment received final state ratification fourteen months later. *The Kansas City Star* underscored the historic importance of this amendment when it proclaimed that woman suffrage "is a victory for democracy and the principle of equality upon which the nation is founded."

## INSIDER TIP

The 2010 APUSH exam included a free-response question on "the roles that women played in Progressive Era reform." See the Question 4 Fact Sheet for a detailed summary on the role Progressive women played in politics, social conditions, and working conditions.

## TOPIC 154
# PROGRESSIVE POLITICAL REFORMS

## 1. A NEW WAVE OF POLITICAL REFORMS
- Lincoln Steffens and other muckrakers documented how alliances between bosses and special interests corrupted city and state governments across the country. These conditions appalled Progressive reformers who believed local governments should be responsive to the public will.
- Progressive reformers had confidence in the ability of experts to devise rational solutions to complex urban problems. During the Progressive Era they launched a widespread political movement to replace "entrenched interests" with reform leaders committed to promoting the public good.

## 2. URBAN POLITICAL REFORM
- During the 1890s and early 1900s a new generation of reform mayors ousted machine bosses and began the process of cleaning up their cities.
- Progressive reformers believed that city governments should be run like a business. Many cities adopted either the commission system or the city manager plan to achieve this goal. First adopted in Galveston, Texas, the commission system placed authority in the hands of a board composed of five professional administrators who each ran one of the city's major departments. The more widely adopted city manager plan gave executive power to a professional administrator who ran the government in accordance with policies set by the elected council and mayor.

## 3. STATE POLITICAL REFORM
- Many states enacted measures designed to enable voters to have greater control over the political system.
- The direct primary allows the people to choose candidates for office instead of politicians or nominating conventions.
- The initiative allows voters to bypass state legislatures by signing a petition to place a proposed statute or constitutional amendment directly on the ballot.
- The referendum forces legislatures to return proposed laws to the voters who then approve or reject the proposals.

- The recall allows voters to remove an elected official from office before the completion of his or her term.

## 4. NATIONAL REFORM

- The Sixteenth Amendment gave Congress the power to lay and collect income taxes. Prior to the amendment tariffs and land sales constituted the government's primary source of income.
- The Seventeenth Amendment provided that United States senators would be elected by a popular vote within each state. Senators had previously been elected by the state legislatures.
- The Eighteenth Amendment forbade the sale or manufacture of intoxicating liquors.
- The Nineteenth Amendment granted women the right to vote.

## INSIDER TIP

The four Progressive Era constitutional amendments have generated a number of multiple-choice questions. It is also important to know that the Progressive Era amendments did not include measures banning poll taxes or limiting the president to two terms in office.

## TOPIC 155
# THEODORE ROOSEVELT AND THE SQUARE DEAL

## 1. A NEW DYNAMIC PRESIDENT

- An assassin's bullet took President McKinley's life just six months after his second inauguration. At age 42, Theodore Roosevelt became the youngest President in American history.
- Roosevelt quickly became a major voice in the Progressive movement. Like other Progressives, TR believed that government should be used to solve the nation's pressing problems. The dynamic force of his personality revitalized the presidency and established the White House as the focal point of American life.

## 2. THE ANTHRACITE COAL STRIKE, 1902

- On May 12, 1902, 147,000 members of the United Mine Workers (UMW) struck coal mines across Pennsylvania and West Virginia. They demanded official recognition of their union, a reduction in daily hours from ten to nine, and a 20 percent increase in their average annual salary of $560.00. The mine owners refused to negotiate thus precipitating (causing) a long and bitter strike.

- History and precedent seemed to be on the owner's side. Just eight years before, the railroad workers struck the Pullman Palace Car Company. Led by President Cleveland, the federal government supported management by using federal troops to break the strike.
- As the nation faced the prospect of enduring a winter without heat, TR invited both management and labor to the White House. When the owners refused to negotiate, TR threatened to order the Army to seize and operate the coal mines. Stunned by Roosevelt's unprecedented threat, the owners reluctantly accepted federal arbitration.
- The Anthracite Coal Strike marked the first time that a President had successfully intervened in a labor dispute as an impartial arbiter. The settlement established TR's reputation as a fearless champion of the working class. TR later wrote that his purpose was "to see to it that every man has a square deal."

## 3. TR AND THE TRUSTS

- Roosevelt's commitment to using the power of the federal government to protect the public interest can also be seen in his approach to trusts. A TRUST was a large business combination formed by merging several smaller companies under the control of a single governing board. By 1901, giant trusts dominated the American economy. Like the Populists before them, Progressives complained that trusts restrained trade, fixed prices, and posed a threat to free markets.
- Roosevelt made a distinction between "good trusts" and "bad trusts." Good trusts were efficient and responsible manufacturers of needed goods and services. In contrast, bad trusts unscrupulously (unprincipled) exploited the public and consumers. TR was determined to use the power of the federal government to regulate good trusts and breakup bad trusts.
- The Sherman Antitrust Act of 1890 forbade unreasonable combinations "in restraint of trade or commerce." The law, however, had been applied more vigorously to curb labor unions than to breakup trusts.
- In 1902, TR used his executive power to order the attorney general to breakup the Northern Securities Company, a giant trust that monopolized rail traffic in the Northwest.

Two years later, the Supreme Court upheld the antitrust suit and dissolved the company. This victory established TR's reputation as a "trust-buster."

- TR continued to strengthen federal regulation of the railroads. Created in 1887, the Interstate Commerce Commission (ICC) had the power to investigate and expose unfair rates and practices among interstate rail carriers. Although creation of the ICC established a precedent for federal regulation of business and industry the commission accomplished very little. TR was determined to revitalize the agency. In 1906, Congress passed the Hepburn Railway Act empowering the ICC to set maximum shipping rates. The act marked a significant expansion of the federal government's regulatory powers over business.

## 4. CONSUMER PROTECTION

- Upton Sinclair's muckraking novel *The Jungle* (1906) dealt with conditions in the Chicago meatpacking industry. Sinclair included a particularly graphic account of the filthy conditions in the packing houses: "There would be meat stored in great piles in rooms; and the water from leaky roofs would drip over it, and thousands of rats would race about on it."

- *The Jungle* illustrates the relationship between muckraking and reform legislation during the Progressive Era. When federal agents confirmed Sinclair's charges an indignant (outraged) public demanded action. Congress promptly passed the Meat Inspection Act and the Pure Food and Drug Act. These laws set strict new Federal standards for food and drugs destined for interstate commerce.

## 5. CONSERVATION

- TR used the White House's "bully pulpit" to educate the public about the need to halt the destruction of America's natural resources.

- TR believed in the managed development of natural resources. He opposed both rapacious (reckless and greedy) commercial interests and "romantic" preservationists.

- TR approved five new national parks and added fifty federal wildlife refuges. He also signed executive orders protecting millions of acres of forest land.

# TOPIC 156
# WILSON AND THE NEW FREEDOM

## 1. THE ELECTION OF 1912

- TR expected that his hand-picked successor William Howard Taft would continue his progressive reforms. However, Taft was an inept (unskilled) politician who soon alienated Roosevelt's Progressive supporters. When the Republican convention renominated Taft, Roosevelt formed the new Progressive or Bull Moose Party.
- Sensing an opportunity to defeat the divided Republicans, the Democrats nominated New Jersey's popular reform governor Woodrow Wilson. The 1912 election turned into a contest between two contrasting legislative programs – TR's New Nationalism and Wilson's New Freedom. The New Nationalism insisted that America needed a strong federal government to regulate large corporations. In contrast, the New Freedom insisted that the federal government needed stronger antitrust laws to breakup large corporations into smaller more competitive units.
- Wilson won the election with just 42 percent of the popular vote. However, he did win an overwhelming victory in the electoral college with 435 votes to TR's 88 and Taft's 8. Wilson thus became only the second Democrat to win the White House since the Civil War.

## 2. "THE TRIPLE WALL OF PRIVILEGE"

- Once in office, Wilson launched a vigorous legislative offensive against what he called "the triple wall of privilege": the tariff, the banks, and the trusts.
- Roosevelt failed to address the issue of tariff reform. In contrast, Wilson called a special session of Congress to reduce tariffs. Prodded by the President, Congress lowered tariff rates by 8 percent. Congress made up for the lost revenue by using its authority under the recently ratified Sixteenth Amendment to enact a modest tax on incomes.
- Wilson next turned to reform of the nation's banking system. The landmark Federal Reserve Act of 1913 established a system of twelve district banks coordinated by a Federal Reserve Board appointed by the President.

The "Fed" had the power to raise and lower interest rates and issue paper money. These financial tools enabled the Federal Reserve Board to control both credit and the supply of money.

- Buoyed by his tariff and banking reforms Wilson focused on the final wall of privilege – the trusts. The Clayton Antitrust Act of 1914 strengthened the Sherman Antitrust Act by prohibiting price discrimination and forbidding interlocking directorates between large companies. It is important to note that the Clayton Antitrust Act specifically exempted labor unions from antitrust prosecution.

## INSIDER TIP
APUSH and SAT II tests ignore Taft and devote surprisingly little attention to Wilson's domestic achievements. Questions on Wilson focus on the provisions of the Federal Reserve Act and the Clayton Antitrust Act.

# TOPIC 157
# AFRICAN AMERICANS AND PROGRESSIVE REFORM

## 1. WIDESPREAD RACIAL DISCRIMINATION
- By the beginning of the twentieth century, Southern states successfully enacted laws which effectively disfranchised most black voters. Progressive reform legislation was least concerned with fighting racial discrimination. President Taft reflected the depth of white prejudice when he applauded Southern laws as necessary to "prevent entirely the possibility of domination by …an ignorant electorate."
- Faced with overwhelming white resistance, Booker T. Washington urged blacks to work for economic self-improvement and to avoid political agitation.

## 2. W.E.B. DU BOIS
- W.E.B. Du Bois emerged as Washington's most prominent black critic. In his book *The Souls of Black Folk* (1903), Du Bois repudiated Washington's accomodationist philosophy and instead called for full political, economic, and social equality for African Americans. Du Bois urged a "talented tenth" of educated blacks to spearhead the fight for equal rights.
- In 1905 Du Bois and a small group of black activists formed the Niagara Movement to oppose Jim Crow laws.

## PODCAST 32.1
**W.E.B. Du BOIS**

## INSIDER TIP
It is important to remember that Progressive reformers did not fight for the passage of Civil Rights laws. The NAACP therefore adopted a strategy of using the courts to strike down Jim Crow laws.

# 3. THE NATIONAL ASSOCIATION FOR THE ADVANCEMENT OF COLORED PEOPLE, 1909

- The Niagara Movement failed to generate either financial or public support. Du Bois now recognized that biracial cooperation was essential to achieving racial progress.
- In 1908 over fifty blacks were killed or injured in a bloody race riot in Springfield, Illinois. The riot in Lincoln's hometown shocked white Progressives. The following year Du Bois and a number of prominent white and black reformers founded the National Association for the Advancement of Colored People (NAACP). The founding of the NAACP marked the first major attempt since Reconstruction to make black rights the focus of a national reform effort.
- The NAACP was committed to a strategy of using lawsuits in the federal courts as its chief weapon against segregation. The organization achieved a noteworthy success in 1915 when the Supreme Court struck down a grandfather clause in an Oklahoma law. The statute had denied the vote to any citizen whose ancestors had not been enfranchised in 1860.
- While NAACP lawyers filed lawsuits against Jim Crow segregation, Du Bois wrote articles for an NAACP journal called *The Crisis*. Du Bois criticized racist films such as *The Birth of a Nation* while calling for equal rights and black pride.

# CHAPTER 33
# EXPANSION AND EMPIRE, 1890 – 1908

## ESSENTIAL POINTS

1. The United States undertook an expansionist foreign policy to locate new markets for surplus products, to compete with European nations for colonies, and to spread the blessings of American civilization to Latin America and the Pacific.

2. American expansion during the late nineteenth century differed from manifest destiny during the 1840s. The new expansion sought to extend American civilization to overseas territories.

3. Secretary of State John Hay called the Spanish-American War a "splendid little war" because the United States won quick victories in Cuba and the Philippines with minimal casualties.

4. The Treaty of Paris ceded Puerto Rico and Guam to the United States. Spain recognized Cuban independence and agreed to cede the Philippine Islands to the United States for $20 million.

5. Acquisition of the Philippine Islands ignited a controversial debate. The Anti-Imperialist League argued that annexation would violate America's long-standing commitment to human freedom. Expansionists countered by arguing that the Philippines would provide a strategic base for trade with China. President McKinley stressed America's duty to educate and "uplift" the Filipinos.

6. The Open Door policy was intended to support American trading opportunities in China.

7. The Roosevelt Corollary was a unilateral declaration proclaiming a policing role for the United States in Central America and the Caribbean. It was first applied to the Dominican Republic.

# TOPIC 158
# THE ROOTS OF EXPANSION

## 1. A DRAMATIC CHANGE
- In 1890 the United States still played a minor role in the game of global power politics. With the exception of its Revolutionary War alliance with France, America carefully followed Washington's admonition (earnest warning) to avoid entangling foreign alliances. For most of the nineteenth century America had been a continental republic focused on settling the western frontier and building democratic institutions.
- In less than a decade America became an imperial republic with interests in the Caribbean, Latin America, and the Pacific. The speed of this change astonished President McKinley. The proud but perhaps a bit perplexed President correctly noted that "in a few short months we have become a world power."

## 2. THE QUEST FOR NEW MARKETS AND RAW MATERIALS
- The total value of goods and services produced by America's farms and factories quadrupled between 1870 and 1900. This burst of productivity transformed America into the world's foremost industrial power.
- As an ever growing stream of sewing machines, reapers, textiles, and household goods poured out of the nation's factories, business leaders worried that they were producing more products than Americans could buy. Many corporate executives looked to Latin America, Asia, and the Pacific for new markets and new sources of raw materials.
- The deep depression from 1893 to 1897 exerted a powerful influence on American political leaders. Fearing renewed labor unrest, they linked economic growth and social stability to their quest for foreign markets and raw materials.

### 3. ALFRED MAHAN AND NEW STRATEGIC THINKING

- In 1890 Captain Alfred T. Mahan published *The Influence of Sea Power upon History*. Mahan argued that sea power is the key to commercial prosperity and national greatness. He forcefully argued that the United States must no longer view the Atlantic and Pacific as protective barriers. Instead, these oceans were best understood as commercial highways that could only be controlled by a powerful navy.
- Theodore Roosevelt, Henry Cabot Lodge, and other influential leaders championed Mahan's recommendations. As a result, his views on sea power soon became the cornerstone of American strategic thinking.

### 4. THE IDEOLOGY OF EXPANSION

- Social Darwinists believed that Darwin's theory of the survival of the fittest could be applied to the rise and fall of nations. During the late nineteenth century strong European powers led by England, France, and Germany began to dominate weak nations in Africa and Asia. Proponents (supporters) of expansion warned that the United States had to play a more aggressive role in world affairs. If the U.S. failed to accept this challenge, it risked falling behind its rivals in the global race for markets and natural resources.
- Americans also believed in the inherent superiority of their political and economic systems. During most of the nineteenth century, America fulfilled its manifest destiny by spreading its civilization from the Atlantic to the Pacific. Now America had a responsibility to bring the benefits of its civilization to less advanced peoples in Latin America and Asia.

## INSIDER TIP
Mahan, Lodge, TR, and other expansionists favored building a strong navy, constructing the Panama Canal, acquiring fueling stations in the Pacific, and exercising a dominant role in the Caribbean.

## TOPIC 159
# THE SPANISH–AMERICAN WAR

### 1. WHAT HAPPENED?

- Congress declared war on Spain on April 25, 1898. The "splendid little war" lasted just 114 days.
- The United States suffered minimal casualties as it quickly defeated the Spanish forces in the Philippines and Cuba.

- The war produced two military heroes. Commodore Dewey led the U.S. Navy's mighty Asiatic Squadron to a decisive victory over the Spanish fleet at the Battle of Manila Bay. Grateful consumers nicknamed a chewing gum "Dewey's Chewies" to honor their hero. Lieutenant-Colonel Theodore Roosevelt led a volunteer regiment called the "Rough Riders" in a dramatic charge up San Juan Hill. Grateful voters in New York promptly elected TR governor of their state.

## 2. WHAT CAUSED THE SPANISH–AMERICAN WAR?

- Cuban rebels waged a guerilla war against Spanish rule. The Spanish commander Valeriano Weyler herded Cubans into detention centers in a brutal attempt to suppress the rebellion.
- William Randolph Hearst's *New York Journal* and Joseph Pulitzer's *New York World* were locked in a furious circulation war for readers. Both papers published daily stories about the atrocities committed by "Butcher" Weyler. Known as "yellow journalism," these sensational and often lurid (deliberately shocking) stories sparked widespread public indignation (outrage) against Spain.
- The 7,000-ton *U.S.S. Maine*, the navy's newest battleship, arrived in Havanna Harbor on January 25, 1898 on what was called a visit of "friendly courtesy." Three weeks later a deafening explosion tore through the vessel sinking the ship and killing over 260 sailors. Although the cause of the blast was never fully determined the press and most Americans blamed the Spanish. A *New York Journal* headline screamed "Whole Country Thrills with War Fever."
- Popular passion against Spain now became a major factor in the march to war. President McKinley faced mounting pressure from an outraged public and from belligerent (warlike) leaders of his own party such as Theodore Roosevelt and Henry Cabot Lodge. Faced with the imminent prospect of war, the Spanish yielded to almost every American demand. Like John Adams in the Quasi-War with France, McKinley could have defied public opinion and avoided war. However, McKinley decided that the political risk of ignoring an aroused public was too high.

## 3. WHY SHOULD YOU REMEMBER THE SPANISH–AMERICAN WAR?

- The war marked the end of Spain's once powerful New World empire.
- The war marked the emergence of the United States as a world power.
- The Treaty of Paris ceded Puerto Rico and Guam to the United States. Spain recognized Cuban independence and agreed to cede the Philippine Islands to the United States for $20 million. This marked the first time that the United States acquired overseas territory.
- The war gave McKinley a pretext (excuse) to annex Hawaii in July 1898.

# TOPIC 160
# AMERICAN INVOLVEMENT IN THE PHILIPPINES AND CUBA

## 1. THE DEBATE OVER THE PHILIPPINES

- The provision in the Treaty of Paris ceding the Philippines to the United States aroused a powerful anti-imperialist movement to block ratification of the treaty. The Anti-Imperialist League pointed out the inconsistency of liberating Cuba and annexing the Philippines. They also insisted that annexation would violate America's long-standing commitment to human freedom and rule by the "consent of the governed."
- Expansionists countered by arguing that the Philippines would provide a strategic base from which the United States could trade with China. While acknowledging that the Philippines offered lucrative (profitable) commercial opportunities, President McKinley stressed America's duty "to educate the Filipinos, and uplift and civilize and Christianize them." Although McKinley's argument ignored the fact that most Filipinos were already Christians, his views prevailed. After a heated debate, the Senate approved the Treaty of Paris with just one vote to spare.

## 2. THE PHILIPPINE INSURRECTION

- Most Americans were unaware that Filipino patriots had been fighting a war for independence since 1896. Filipinos hoped the United States would assist them in expelling the Spaniards and establishing an independent Philippine state.
- Despite strong evidence that Filipinos wanted independence, the McKinley administration decided that they were not ready for self-government. Led by Emilio Aguinaldo, the Filipinos resisted American control of their country.
- The Philippine Insurrection, called the War for Independence by Filipinos, foreshadowed the guerrilla wars fought in the twentieth century. As the scale of fighting rose, both sides committed atrocities. Mark Twain bitterly noted that, "We have pacified some thousands of the islanders and buried them; destroyed their fields; burned their villages, and turned their widows and orphans out-of-doors." After three years of fighting, America's overwhelming military power finally crushed the rebels.
- The Philippine Insurrection cost the lives of more than 4,000 American soldiers and between 16,000 and 20,000 Filipino rebels. Disease and starvation may have claimed the lives of as many as 200,000 civilians.
- In 1916 Congress passed the Jones Act formally committing the United States to eventually granting the Philippines independence. The Filipinos finally gained their full independence on July 4, 1946.

## 3. CUBA AND THE PLATT AMENDMENT

- Congress attached the Teller Amendment to its resolution declaring war on Spain. The Teller Amendment guaranteed American respect for Cuba's sovereignty as an independent nation.
- The United States surprised many skeptics (doubters) by keeping its promise not to annex Cuba. However, in 1901 Congress made the withdrawal of US troops contingent upon Cuba's acceptance of the Platt Amendment. This amendment prohibited Cuba from making any foreign treaties that might "impair" its independence or involve it in a public debt that it could not pay. The amendment also gave the United States the right to maintain a naval station

## INSIDER TIP

Do not overlook the Philippine Insurrection. Make sure that you can identify Emilio Aguinaldo. He has a much better chance of being on your test than either Commodore Dewey or the Rough Riders.

at Guantanamo Bay on the southeast corner of Cuba. The Platt Amendment was incorporated into the Cuban constitution and provided the grounds for American intervention four times in the early 1900s.

# TOPIC 161
# THE OPEN DOOR POLICY

1. Many American business leaders blamed industrial overproduction for the economic slump and social unrest during the 1890s. They looked to China's "illimitable markets" to spur American economic growth. America's victory in the Spanish-American War gave it possession of strategic coaling stations in Wake, Guam, and the Philippines. As a result, American commercial ships could now reach the fabled Chinese market.

2. Great Britain dominated trade with China for most of the nineteenth century. However, during the 1880s and 1890s Germany, France, Russia, and Japan all began carving out their own spheres of influence in an ever-weakening China. Each foreign power controlled trade, tariffs, harbor duties, and railroad charges within its own sphere of influence.

3. Secretary of State John Hay became increasingly worried that the European powers and Japan would restrict American trading opportunities in China. On September 6, 1899 he dispatched a series of notes to Great Britain, Germany, Russia, France, Italy, and Japan asking the governments of these six nations to agree to respect the rights and privileges of other nations within its sphere of influence. In short, no nation would discriminate against other nations.

4. Hay's Open Door policy was designed to protect American commercial interests in China. The European powers and Japan neither accepted nor rejected Hay's Open Door Notes. Although America's Open Door policy had no legal standing, Hays boldly announced that all of the powers had agreed, and their consent was therefore "final and definitive."

## INSIDER TIP
Most APUSH exams contain a multiple-choice question on the Open Door policy. Do not become bogged down in the details of Chinese history. Just remember that the Open Door protected American trading opportunities in China.

## TOPIC 162
# BIG STICK DIPLOMACY

### 1. "SPEAK SOFTLY AND CARRY A BIG STICK"

- Theodore Roosevelt was keenly aware that America's victory in the Spanish-American War gave it a new role in world affairs. In his Inaugural Address, TR proudly reminded Americans of their new responsibilities: "We have become a great nation, forced by the fact of its greatness into relations with the other nations of the earth, and we must behave as beseems a people with such responsibilities." Roosevelt believed that "civilized and orderly" nations such as the United States and Great Britain had a duty to police the world and maintain order. To do that, he said that the United States should, in the words of a West African proverb, "Speak softly and carry a big stick."

### 2. THE PANAMA CANAL

- Roosevelt and other expansionists focused on the pressing need to build a canal through Central America. The much-publicized voyage of the battleship *Oregon* dramatically illustrated the need for a canal. When the *Maine* blew up, seventy-one days passed before the *Oregon* could reach Cuba because it had to sail from San Francisco around the tip of South America. Expansionists persuasively argued that the *Oregon's* 12,000 mile voyage would have been 8,000 miles shorter had there been a canal across Central America.
- After much debate Congress approved a canal through the Isthmus of Panama. At that time Panama was a province of Columbia. The United States offered to pay Columbia ten million dollars for the right to dig a canal across the isthmus. But the Columbian Senate refused to ratify the treaty and held out for more money. Encouraged and supported by Roosevelt, Panama revolted against Columbia and declared itself an independent nation. Roosevelt promptly recognized Panama. He signed a treaty with the new nation which guaranteed its independence and also gave the United States a lease on a ten-mile-wide canal zone.

- Construction of the Panama Canal began in 1904. A workforce of about 30,000 laborers completed the 51-mile-long "Big Ditch" in just ten years. When it opened in 1914, the Panama Canal gave the United States a commanding position in the Western Hemisphere.

# 3. THE ROOSEVELT COROLLARY

- The construction of the Panama Canal made the security of the Caribbean a vital American interest. Roosevelt became concerned when the Dominican Republic borrowed more money from its European creditors than it could pay back. Roosevelt worried that financial instability in the Dominican Republic would lead to European intervention.
- Roosevelt responded to the crisis in the Dominican Republic by proclaiming the Roosevelt Corollary to the Monroe Doctrine. The Monroe Doctrine stated America's opposition to European intervention in Latin America. Roosevelt updated the Monroe Doctrine by declaring that "flagrant cases of wrongdoing" in Central America and the Caribbean "may force the United States to exercise an international police power." The Roosevelt Corollary, like the Monroe Doctrine, was a unilateral declaration motivated by American national interest. It changed the Monroe Doctrine from a statement against the intervention of European powers in the affairs of the Western Hemisphere to a justification of the unrestricted American right to regulate Caribbean affairs. Roosevelt backed up his words with prompt action. Citing the Roosevelt Corollary, American personnel supervised the Dominican customs office to assure the payment of debts to European creditors.

PODCAST 33.1
THE ROOSEVELT COROLLARY

INSIDER TIP
The Roosevelt Corollary is one of the most frequently tested items on both the APUSH exam and the SAT II test. Be sure that you know that it was a unilateral declaration that proclaimed a policing role for the United States in Caribbean affairs. It was first applied in the Dominican Republic.

# CHAPTER 34
# WOODROW WILSON AND WORLD WAR I, 1909 – 1919

## ESSENTIAL POINTS

1. President Wilson rejected both Roosevelt's big stick diplomacy and Taft's dollar diplomacy. He believed that the United States should practice moral diplomacy by promoting democratic values and moral progress.

2. Wilson attempted to keep America out of World War I while at the same time insisting on American neutral rights on the high seas. Germany's resumption of unrestricted submarine warfare forced Wilson to ask Congress for a declaration of war.

3. The Selective Service, Espionage, and Sedition acts all illustrate the trend toward increasing government control during World War I.

4. The Great Migration of African Americans from the South to the industrial cities in the North began during World War I.

5. The Fourteen Points declared general principles of international conduct and made specific recommendations for adjusting postwar boundaries based upon the principle of self-determination. The fourteenth and most famous point called for "a general association of nations" later called the League of Nations.

6. Opponents of the League argued that it would limit American sovereignty and involve the United States in entangling foreign alliances. Wilson hardened Senate opposition by refusing to compromise with Senator Lodge and the Reservationists.

## TOPIC 163
# WILSON AND LATIN AMERICA

## 1. WILSON AND MORAL DIPLOMACY

- When Woodrow Wilson became President in 1913 he focused his attention on implementing his New Freedom program of domestic reforms. He revised the tariff, reformed the banking system, and signed the Clayton Antitrust Act. Although Wilson was an expert on domestic issues, he had little experience in foreign affairs. "It would be an irony of fate," Wilson wryly (with a dry sense of humor) observed, "if my administration had to deal chiefly with foreign affairs."

- Wilson rejected both TR's policy of big stick diplomacy and Taft's policy of dollar diplomacy. Instead, he believed that his foreign policy should be guided by moral principles and not power and money. Wilson believed that the United States should practice moral diplomacy by promoting democratic values and moral progress.

- Wilson's stubborn adherence to his moral view of international politics inspired many people in America and throughout the world. However, getting things done often required practicing the art of compromise. Wilson's idealistic moral diplomacy would soon be tested by the hard realities of international politics.

## 2. THE CARIBBEAN

- Roosevelt relied upon the power of the United States Navy to enforce big stick diplomacy in the Caribbean. In contrast, Taft relied upon dollar diplomacy or the use of American money to influence Caribbean nations. For example, the Taft administration encouraged American bankers to take charge of the finances in debt-ridden Nicaragua.

- Wilson found it difficult to practice his moral ideals in the Caribbean. Despite his objections to using military force, Wilson sent marines to Haiti, the Dominican Republic, and Nicaragua to protect American financial interests in these countries.

## 3. MEXICO

- Events in Mexico also tested Wilson's commitment to moral diplomacy. In 1911 Francisco Madero overthrew Mexico's dictator Porfirio Diaz. Madero promised to institute a series of domestic reforms. However, in 1913 he was overthrown and murdered by a general named Victoriano Huerta. The new Mexican leader represented everything Wilson despised. "I am going to teach the South American republics to elect good men," Wilson vowed.

- The crisis in Mexico continued when Venustiano Carranza overthrew Huerta in 1914. Wilson welcomed the change but was dismayed when Carranza refused to accept American advice. For a time, Wilson supported Francisco "Pancho" Villa, a bandit who opposed both Huerta and Carranza.

- In October 1915, Wilson changed his mind and recognized the Carranza government. Feeling betrayed, Villa stopped a train in Northern Mexico and killed 17 US citizens. Two months later, Villa and his men burned Columbus, New Mexico and killed 17 more Americans. Outraged by these events, Wilson ordered a force of 11,000 men commanded by General John J. Pershing to invade Mexico and capture Villa. Pershing failed to apprehend the elusive (hard to catch) Villa and his invasion alienated the Carranza government.

## INSIDER TIP

Don't worry about the succession of Mexican leaders. Instead, remember that Pancho Villa actually invaded the United States and eluded an army sent to apprehend him.

# TOPIC 164
# THE ROAD TO WORLD WAR I

## 1. "NEUTRAL IN FACT AS WELL AS NAME"

- The nations of Europe enjoyed an extended period of prosperity and progress in the century following the defeat of Napoleon in 1815. But an arms race between Germany and Great Britain, competition for colonies in Africa, and the formation of rival alliances created an atmosphere of tension and suspicion. The assassination of Archduke Francis Ferdinand on June 28, 1914 set in motion an inexorable (can't be stopped) chain of events that led to the outbreak of World War I less than six weeks later. German forces overran Belgium and soon threatened France.

- The explosive events in Europe stunned Wilson. He was now forced to shift his focus from the New Freedom and relations with Mexico to how the United States would respond to the war in Europe. On August 19, 1917 Wilson announced that "the United States must be neutral in fact as well as name."

## 2. AMERICAN TIES TO BRITAIN AND FRANCE

- America had stronger cultural and political ties with Britain and France than with Germany. Most Americans viewed Germany as a militaristic country ruled by an autocratic (dictatorial, despotic) ruler. British propaganda skillfully reinforced this image by depicting the Germans as ruthless barbarians who committed unspeakable atrocities against the defenseless people of Belgium.
- Strong commercial ties also connected the United States with Britain and France. In 1916, the US sold $275 million worth of goods to Britain and France and only $29 million worth of goods to Germany. During this time American investors loaned $2.3 billion to the Allies and just $27 million to the Germans.

## 3. FREEDOM OF THE SEAS AND GERMAN NAVAL POLICY

- As a neutral nation, the United States could legally trade with all belligerent (warring) nations involved in World War I. Enforcing America's neutral rights proved to be difficult. The British fleet established a blockade that prevented countries from trading with Germany. The Germans retaliated by using their new U-boats or submarines to sink without warning all enemy merchant ships found approaching Great Britain.
- After sinking the British passenger liner the *Lusitania* and the French steamer the *Sussex*, the Germans issued the *Sussex* Pledge promising not to attack merchant vessels without warning. Wilson sternly warned Germany that a violation of this pledge would risk war with the United States.
- On January 31, 1917 Germany announced that it would resume unrestricted submarine warfare. The Germans understood that this action would bring the United States into the war. However, they gambled that they could defeat France and Great Britain before America could mobilize and train an army large enough to thwart their offensive along the Western Front.

## 4. "THE WORLD MUST BE MADE SAFE FOR DEMOCRACY"

- Events now pushed the United States to the brink of war. In early February 1917, Wilson broke diplomatic relations with Germany. Less than a month later British officials released a decoded message from German Foreign Secretary Arthur Zimmerman to the German ambassador in Mexico. The ambassador was instructed to offer Mexico an alliance with Germany. In return, Mexico would receive German support to recover Texas, New Mexico, and Arizona.
- The Zimmerman Telegram and the sinking of several unarmed American ships compelled Wilson to ask a special session of Congress for a declaration of war against Germany. Wilson told Congress that the United States "had no selfish ends to serve" by entering the war. "The world," Wilson insisted, "must be made safe for democracy."

## INSIDER TIP

Do not spend time memorizing the names of ships sunk by German U-boats. Instead, remember that the United States entered World War I as a direct result of Germany's resumption of submarine warfare.

# TOPIC 165
# KEY HOME FRONT DEVELOPMENTS

## 1. THE SELECTIVE SERVICE ACT

- The United States Army had a grand total of just 208,034 men when Congress declared war on Germany.
- The Selective Service Act of 1917 quickly remedied this lack of manpower by requiring all men aged twenty-one to thirty to register for military service. By the end of the war the armed services enlisted 3.7 million men about half of whom reached Europe.

## 2. THE COMMITTEE ON PUBLIC INFORMATION

- President Wilson recognized that the American public had to be mobilized to support a war against an enemy that did not present a direct threat to the nation's homeland.
- Wilson issued an executive order creating a Committee on Public Information. Led by George Creel, the Committee worked to convince the public that America was fighting a righteous war for freedom and democracy. An army of 75,000 Four-Minute Men gave speeches urging citizens to buy Liberty Bonds and conserve fuel and food. Meanwhile, propaganda films and posters portrayed the Germans as barbaric enemies of freedom.

INSIDER TIP
The Great Migration has generated a number of multiple-choice questions. Be sure that you know that the wartime demand for labor attracted African Americans to industrial cities in the North.

### 3. CIVIL LIBERTIES

- The Committee on Public Information's propaganda campaign promoted a national mood of suspicion and distrust. On Wilson's request, Congress passed the Espionage and Sedition Acts to outlaw criticism of government leaders and war policies.
- Ironically, while the United States embarked on a crusade to "make the world safe for democracy," these two acts stifled dissent and encouraged intolerance.

### 4. THE GREAT MIGRATION

- World War I created a labor shortage by moving about four million men from the nation's farms and factories to the armed services.
- The wartime demand for industrial workers encouraged over 400,000 southern blacks to move to northern industrial cities. Known as the Great Migration, this mass movement opened new opportunities for African Americans while also exacerbating (worsening) racial tensions in many northern cities.

## TOPIC 166
# THE FOURTEEN POINTS

1. On January 8, 1918 Woodrow Wilson announced a peace program known as the Fourteen Points. The first five points called for general principles of international conduct that included open diplomacy, freedom of the seas, removal of trade barriers, reduction of armaments, and impartial mediation of colonial claims. The next eight points contained specific recommendations for adjusting postwar boundaries based upon the principle of self-determination for the population involved. Wilson's fourteenth and most famous point called for "a general association of nations" that would protect "great and small states alike." That association or League of Nations would keep the peace by encouraging its members to solve problems by negotiation.

2. The Fourteen Points offered generous peace terms to the defeated Central Powers. When the German government surrendered in November 1918 it was assured that the peace conference would be based upon the Fourteen Points.

PODCAST 34.1
THE GREAT MIGRATION

3. The Fourteen Points articulated the hopes of people for a just settlement that would ensure a lasting peace. Wilson received thunderous ovations when he arrived in Paris to negotiate the Treaty of Versailles. However, the Fourteen Points raised expectations that would be very difficult to achieve. The French premier George Clemenceau reflected the cynical attitude of many European leaders when he scornfully observed, "God gave us the Ten Commandments, and we broke them. Wilson gives us the Fourteen Points. We shall see."

# TOPIC 167
# THE FIGHT FOR THE LEAGUE

## 1. A FLAWED TREATY

- The peace conference opened in Paris on January 18, 1919. Woodrow Wilson personally headed the American delegation. It is important to note that Wilson made the mistake of not asking any Senators or Republican politicians to join the delegation. This proved to be a serious error in judgment because the Senate would have to ratify the peace treaty he proposed and because the Republicans had won control of both houses of Congress in 1918.

- Wilson soon faced the grim realities of European power politics. Both Great Britain and France wanted to make Germany pay for the terrible suffering their people endured in the war. Although Wilson argued for the principles of his Fourteen Points, the final treaty reflected the Allies vindictive (vengeful) attitude toward Germany. The Treaty of Versailles forced Germany to give up 13 percent of its territory and all of its colonies. In addition, the treaty compelled Germany to accept full blame for starting the war and to pay reparations later set at $33 billion.

- Wilson recognized that the Treaty of Versailles was too punitive. However, he signed it in exchange for Allied support for the League of Nations. The League represented Wilson's hopes for the postwar world. He was convinced that the League would rectify (correct) problems in the Treaty of Versailles and that its provisions for collective security would ensure international peace.

## INSIDER TIP
A number of multiple-choice questions ask you to identify a point that was NOT part of the Fourteen Points. The Fourteen Points did NOT include the International Monetary Fund, secret alliances, recognition of the Soviet Union, or a call for a global currency.

## INSIDER TIP

Remember, that opponents of the League argued that the organization's commitment to collective security violated America's traditional policy of avoiding entangling alliances.

## 2. SENATE OPPOSITION

- When Wilson returned to the United States he faced a tough fight to win Senate approval for the Treaty of Versailles. The 96 Senators divided into three groups. First, the Internationalists who supported the treaty without reservations. Second, the Irreconcilables who opposed the treaty in any form. And finally, a large group of Reservationists who were willing to accept the treaty with changes that would clarify or limit the League's authority over American actions.
- The Reservationists were led by Henry Cabot Lodge, the Senate Majority Leader and Wilson's bitter political enemy. Lodge objected to the collective security provision in the League covenant obligating member nations to take joint action to protect nations from "external aggression." Lodge argued that this provision would limit American sovereignty and undermine the power of Congress in foreign affairs. He preferred America's long-standing policy of avoiding entangling foreign alliances.

## 3. REJECTION AND DEFEAT

- Wilson denounced his critics by saying that they were myopic (shortsighted) "pygmies" who failed to see that membership in the League would give the United States "leadership in the world." Wilson's refusal to compromise with Lodge and the Reservationists hardened Senate opposition to the treaty.
- Frustrated by the Senate debate, Wilson elected to take his case to the American people. He left Washington on September 4, 1919. Wilson traveled 8,000 miles and made 37 speeches in 29 cities. Three weeks into the grueling trip Wilson collapsed from exhaustion. A few days later he suffered a severe stroke that partly paralyzed his left side. For weeks he could not sit up or even sign his name. He was so ill that only his doctors, his wife, and his closest aides were allowed to see him.
- The Senate never approved the Treaty of Versailles and the United States never joined the League of Nations. Wilson left office a beaten and embittered man.

**CHAPTER 35**

# MAKING KEY COMPARISONS, 1866 – 1919

## ESSENTIAL POINTS

1. Recent APUSH exams have included a significant number of free-response questions asking students to make comparisons between events, peoples, colonies, geographic regions, and social movements. These comparison essays require substantial relevant information and an effective analysis of similarities and differences. This chapter is the third of four chapters designed to provide you with a clear and succinct comparison of frequently tested topics.

**TOPIC 168**
# COMPARING BOOKER T. WASHINGTON AND W.E.B. DU BOIS

## 1. BOOKER T. WASHINGTON
- Believed that white racism was a consequence of slavery.
- Advocated black economic self-help. Washington called upon African Americans to master trades. He believed that economic progress would earn white respect and gradually end racism.
- Supported accommodation to white society. In his Atlanta Compromise Speech Washington offered a conciliatory approach that was welcomed by his white audience: "In all things purely social we can be as separate as the fingers, yet one as the hand in all things essential to mutual progress."
- Supported vocational education. Washington helped found Tuskegee Institute in Alabama to provide industrial education for African American students.
- Opposed public political agitation to challenge Jim Crow segregation. Washington recognized that African Americans faced a wall of discrimination that could only be overcome by gradual and patient progress. Washington believed that political rights would follow economic success.

## 2. W.E.B. DU BOIS
- Believed white racism was the cause of slavery and the primary reason why African Americans were forced into a subordinate position in American society.
- Advocated the intellectual development of a "talented tenth" of the African American population. The talented tenth would become a vanguard of influential leaders who would fight for social change.
- Supported legal action to oppose Jim Crow segregation. Du Bois helped found the National Association for the Advancement of Colored People. The NAACP adopted a strategy of using lawsuits in federal courts to fight Jim Crow segregation.
- Opposed Booker T. Washington's policy of gradualism and accommodation. In *The Souls of Black Folk*, Du Bois called

upon African Americans to "insist continually, in season and out of season, that voting is necessary to modern manhood, that color discrimination is barbarism, and that black boys need education as well as white boys."

- Believed that economic success would only be possible if African Americans first won political rights. Du Bois therefore advocated a strategy of "ceaseless agitation" and litigation to achieve equal rights.

## TOPIC 169
# COMPARING THE KNIGHTS OF LABOR AND THE AMERICAN FEDERATION OF LABOR

## 1. THE KNIGHTS OF LABOR
- Founded in 1869 and led by Terrance V. Powderly.
- Attempted to unify all working men and women into a national union under the motto, "An injury to one is the concern of all."
- Experienced a period of rapid growth in the 1880s as membership rolls swelled from 42,000 in 1882 to over 700,000 in 1886.
- Called for an end to trusts, restrictions on child labor, a graduated income tax, an eight-hour day, and equal pay for equal work for both sexes.
- Wanted to eliminate conflict between labor and management. The Knights were idealists who hoped to create a cooperative society in which workers collectively purchased mines, factories, and stores.
- Blamed for the Haymarket Square riot in 1886. Membership plummeted as the Knights were unfairly and erroneously linked with violent anarchists.

## 2. THE AMERICAN FEDERATION OF LABOR
- Founded in 1886 and led by Samuel Gompers.
- Organized as an alliance of skilled workers in craft unions. The AFL did not welcome unskilled workers, women, or racial minorities.
- Advocated using collective bargaining and, if necessary, strikes to win concrete "bread and butter" goals such

as higher wages, shorter hours, and better working conditions.

- Experienced a period of rapid growth as the AFL replaced the Knights of Labor as America's most powerful labor union. By 1904, the AFL had 1.7 million members and Gompers was recognized as a national spokesperson for American laborers.

## TOPIC 170
# COMPARING MANIFEST DESTINY AND IMPERIALISM

### 1. MANIFEST DESTINY

- The phrase "Manifest Destiny" is associated with the territorial expansion of the United States from 1812 to 1860. During this time, the United States expanded to the Pacific Ocean.
- John O'Sullivan coined the term Manifest Destiny in 1845. An influential journalist and proponent of Jacksonian democracy, O'Sullivan believed that the United States had a right to claim the entire Oregon Territory. O'Sullivan argued that America's claim to these lands "is by the right of our Manifest Destiny to overspread and to possess the whole of the continent which Providence has given us for the development of the great experiment of liberty and federated self-government entrusted to us."
- Manifest Destiny assumes that from its earliest beginnings America embarked upon a special experiment in freedom and democracy. The United States thus had a divinely sanctioned mission to spread its democratic institutions across the continent.
- President Polk and other leaders used Manifest Destiny to justify the annexation of Texas and the Mexican War.
- Whigs criticized Manifest Destiny as an excuse for justifying the war with Mexico. New England abolitionists forcefully argued that the slogan "extending the area of freedom" really meant extending the institution of slavery.

## 2. IMPERIALISM

- Between 1865 and 1897 America was a continental republic focused on Reconstruction, industrial development, and settling the West.
- Imperialism is the policy of extending a nation's power through military conquest, economic domination, or annexation. Imperialism gained support in the United States in the late 1890s.
- Advocates of imperialism argued that the United States had to play a more aggressive role in world affairs. They pointed out that American industry needed new foreign markets and sources of raw materials in order to expand.
- Unlike Manifest Destiny, imperialism included the idea of moral improvement by bringing the blessings of civilization to less technologically advanced peoples. Often called "the White Man's Burden," this idea justified a new national mission to "elevate backward peoples."
- The Anti-Imperialism League opposed the annexation of the Philippines. League members argued that imperialism violated America's long-established commitment to the principles of self-determination and anti-colonialism.
- Like the Whigs before them, the anti-imperialists opposed a policy they felt betrayed America's democratic institutions.

# TOPIC 171
# COMPARING THE GOSPEL OF WEALTH AND THE SOCIAL GOSPEL

## 1. THE GOSPEL OF WEALTH

- Promoted by Andrew Carnegie in an essay published in 1889.
- Carnegie believed that great wealth brought great responsibility. He argued that the rich have a duty to serve society by supporting what Carnegie called "ladders upon which the aspiring can rise."
- Over his lifetime, Carnegie donated more than $350 million to support libraries, schools, peace initiatives, and the arts.

## 2. THE SOCIAL GOSPEL
- Promoted by Walter Rauschenbusch and Washington Gladden.
- A reform movement based on the belief that Christian principles of love and justice should be applied to the nation's pressing urban problems.
- Supporters of the Social Gospel believed that America's churches had a moral responsibility to take the lead in actively confronting social problems and helping the poor.

## TOPIC 172
# COMPARING THE POPULISTS AND THE PROGRESSIVES

## 1. THE POPULISTS
- Populists were predominately angry farmers living in the Midwest and South.
- Populists focused their attention on problems faced by farmers. Militant farmers believed they were being unfairly exploited by discriminatory railroad rates, high protective tariffs, and a deflationary monetary policy based on the gold standard.
- The Populist Party challenged America's traditional two-party system. The party platform called for free coinage of silver, government control of the railroads, and the direct election of United States senators.
- Racism prevented poor white and black farmers from working together to improve their standard of living.
- The defeat of William Jennings Bryan in the 1896 presidential election led to the collapse of the Populist Party and a new period of Republican dominance.

## 2. THE PROGRESSIVES
- Progressives were predominately well educated middle and upper-middle class reformers living in urban areas.
- Progressives focused on a broad range of problems caused by industrialization, urbanization, and immigration.
- Progressives wanted government to play an active role in solving social problems and improving the quality of American life.

- Progressives supported a **wide range of reforms** including women's suffrage, temperance, a graduated income tax, and the popular election of United States senators.
- Progressives devoted little attention to the plight of African Americans.
- Progressives challenged America's two-party system by joining Theodore Roosevelt's short-lived Bull Moose Party. The Bull Moose Party split the Republican vote and led to the election of Woodrow Wilson.
- The Progressives achieved many of their goals. The Progressive spirit began to rapidly decline when America entered World War I.

# CHAPTER 36
# THE NEW ERA, 1919 – 1929

## ESSENTIAL POINTS

1. Henry Ford's use of the moving assembly line enabled the Ford Motor Company to mass produce affordable cars which average Americans could afford to buy.

2. The automobile, radio, and motion picture all contributed to the rise of American mass culture in the 1920s. Movies were the most popular form of mass entertainment during this decade.

3. Flappers provided the most visible model of the new American woman. They challenged traditional norms of feminine appearance and moral behavior.

4. F. Scott Fitzgerald, Sinclair Lewis, and other **LOST GENERATION** authors challenged middle-class conformity and materialism.

5. The Red Scare, Sacco and Vanzetti case, Scopes trial, National Origins Act, and reemergence of the Ku Klux Klan all illustrate aspects of the widespread intolerance and nativism of the 1920s.

6. The Harlem Renaissance was a literary and artistic movement that flourished in the 1920s. **HARLEM RENAISSANCE** writers expressed pride in their African American culture.

7. Marcus Garvey was a black leader who founded the Universal Negro Improvement Association to promote black pride and African nationalism. Unlike W.E.B. Du Bois, Garvey advocated black separatism.

8. Warren Harding, Calvin Coolidge, and Herbert Hoover were Republican presidents who reconfirmed the partnership between business and government. Secretary of Treasury Andrew Mellon reduced taxes for the wealthy, raised tariffs on imports, and ignored antitrust regulations.

## TOPIC 173
# THE ROARING TWENTIES

## 1. MASS PRODUCTION

- The 1920s witnessed the mass production of a new generation of affordable consumer products. Labor-saving devices such as refrigerators, washing machines, electric irons, and vacuum cleaners made household chores easier thus creating time to enjoy leisure activities.

- The mass production of automobiles had the greatest impact upon American society. When automobiles first appeared in the late 1890s they seemed to be a luxury toy for the rich. However, a gifted self-taught engineer named Henry Ford audaciously (boldly) vowed "to democratize the automobile. When I'm through," Ford predicted, "everybody will be able to afford one."

- Ford fulfilled his prediction by applying the principles of assembly line production to the manufacture of automobiles. In the first automobile factories cars remained in one place while a number of skilled mechanics built the vehicle from the ground up. In contrast, on Ford's new assembly line the car moved from one worker to the next. Each worker performed the same operation on each passing car. The assembly line enabled Ford to reduce the time it took to build a car from 12.5 hours of work to just 1.5 hours of work. By 1925 the Ford Motor Company produced a new car every ten seconds. The price for a Model T fell from $850 in 1908 to $290 in 1924.

- The mass production of automobiles had far-reaching consequences for American economic and cultural life. Surging car sales stimulated the growth of companies that produced steel, rubber tires, glass, and gasoline. Spurred by the Federal Highway Act of 1916 a network of new roads crisscrossed the nation. Within just a few years the automobile transformed America from a land of isolated farms and small towns into a mobile nation on wheels.

## 2. MASS CONSUMPTION

- A growing advertising industry fueled interest in the new consumer products. Advertisements glorified consumption and celebrated an enticing (tempting) lifestyle based upon the possession of material objects. By 1929, advertising accounted for 3 percent of the nation's gross national product.
- Companies used advertisements to promote a new array of purchasing techniques. Instead of waiting until they could afford a product, consumers could now use installment plans to "buy now and pay later." As a result, the old values of thrift and saving gave way to a new culture that emphasized spending and consumption.

## 3. MASS CULTURE

- The automobile provided a convenient form of personal transportation. At the same time, radio and motion pictures publicized the new lifestyle of urban America and promoted the rise of a homogenized mass culture.
- On November 2, 1920 radio station KDKA in Pittsburgh announced the news that the Republican candidate Warren Harding won a landslide victory over his Democratic rival James Cox. The broadcast signaled the birth of a new industry. Just seven years later, millions of Americans anxiously listened to breathless accounts of Charles Lindbergh's solo flight across the Atlantic. As the radio mania swept across the country, families could now gather around their sets and listen to the same programs, laugh at the same jokes, sing the same songs, and of course hear the same advertisements.
- Silent films first appeared in the early 1900s. However, the modern American motion picture industry began with the release of D.W. Griffith's *The Birth of a Nation* in 1915. Soon feature-length films turned Greta Garbo, Charlie Chaplin, and Rudolph Valentino into celebrities. In 1927 enthralled (fascinated) fans watched and listened to the first "talkie," *The Jazz Singer*. Silent films quickly vanished and by 1930 motion pictures became the nation's most popular form of entertainment.

## INSIDER TIP

The 2006B APUSH exam included a free-response question asking students to discuss how advertising, entertainment, and mass produced goods shaped American culture in the 1920s. See Essay 5A for a particularly thoughtful discussion that received a 9.

**TOPIC 174**
# POSTWAR DISILLUSIONMENT AND REBELLION

## 1. A NEW MOOD

- The immense human suffering and economic destruction caused by World War I dealt a shattering blow to the comforting belief that progress was inevitable. John F. Carter expressed the pervasive (widespread) postwar mood of disillusionment when he wrote in the *Atlantic Monthly*: "I would like to observe that the older generation had certainly pretty well ruined this world before passing it on to us. They gave us this Thing, knocked to pieces, leaky, red-hot, threatening to blow up; and then they are surprised that we don't accept it with the same enthusiasm with which they received it."
- New inventions and greater leisure time made a new kind of individual freedom possible. A rebellious generation of young adults challenged traditional values while a critical group of writers questioned the conformity and materialism they saw in American society.

## 2. THE NEW WOMAN

- The new independent spirit expressed itself in the changes postwar women were making in their lives. Although most women still followed traditional paths of marriage and family, a growing number of young, well-educated women began choosing a different lifestyle. Influenced by feminists, women wanted greater freedom in their lives. They argued that wives should be equal partners with their husbands and supported Margaret Sanger's campaign for birth control. A vanguard (advance group) of college-educated women sought new careers in medicine, law, and science.
- Young women called flappers provided the most visible and shocking model of the new American woman. Flappers challenged conventional (established) norms of feminine appearance by wearing short skirts, heavy makeup, and close-cut bobbed hair. They further jolted the traditional guardians of morality by enjoying carefree dances such as the Charleston, listening to the lively, loose beat of jazz, and attending parties that featured drinking, smoking, and petting.

### 3. THE LOST GENERATION OF WRITERS

- A group of novelists also found much to criticize in America's new mass culture. These writers have often been called the LOST GENERATION because they were disillusioned with American Society and often moved to Paris.
- F. Scott Fitzgerald and Sinclair Lewis were the best-known Lost Generation authors. Lewis lampooned (satirized, ridiculed) middle-class conformity and materialism in *Main Street, Babbitt* and other novels. George F. Babbitt was a gung-ho real-estate broker who lived in the fictional Midwestern city of Zenith. Babbitt represents most of what appalled Lewis about America. He was a superficial (shallow) person with no ideas of his own and very little awareness of the world outside Zenith. Babbitt parroted Republican positions on issues and prized material objects as symbols of his success.

## TOPIC 175
# INTOLERANCE AND NATIVISM

### 1. THE RED SCARE AND PALMER RAIDS

- In November 1917 Bolsheviks led by Vladimir Lenin seized power in Russia and promptly created a communist dictatorship. The revolutionary upheaval in Russia alarmed many Americans who believed that communist sympathizers and other radicals were secretly planning to undermine the United States government.
- The fear of subversives escalated in late April 1918 when the post office intercepted 38 packages containing bombs addressed to prominent citizens. A wave of labor strikes and race riots further intensified public anxiety adding to calls for action. Anyone who appeared different or foreign was branded "un-American" and therefore a "Red."
- The Red Scare, or nationwide fear of aliens, forced Attorney General Mitchell Palmer to act. Although no more than one-tenth of one percent of adult Americans actually belonged to the domestic communist movement, Palmer launched a massive roundup of foreign-born radicals.

## INSIDER TIP

Although Flappers are flamboyant and thus easy to remember, they don't generate too many SAT II or APUSH multiple-choice questions. In contrast, Margaret Sanger's campaign for birth control and the Lost Generation's protest against American materialism and conformity do generate a significant number of questions. It is important to remember that many Lost Generation writers moved to Paris.

- On January 2, 1920, agents of the Department of Justice arrested over 4,000 people in a dozen cities across America. The Palmer Raids violated civil liberties by breaking into homes and union offices without arrest warrants. Although most of those arrested were released, the Department of Justice deported about 500 aliens without hearings or trials.
- The Palmer Raids marked the end of the Red Scare. However, they did not mark the end of the postwar drive for "one hundred percent Americanism." The defenders of traditional values both resented and resisted the changes sweeping across America. The conflict between the "old" insular (provincial) rural America and the "new" more cosmopolitan (sophisticated) urban America expressed itself itself in two famous legal cases and a resurgence (revival) of nativism.

## 2. THE SACCO AND VANZETTI CASE

- The most celebrated criminal trial of the 1920s involved two Italian-born anarchists, Nicola Sacco and Bartolomo Vanzetti. The two men were arrested for a payroll robbery and murder.
- The evidence against Sacco and Vanzetti was inconclusive. Many were convinced that the two men were victims of prejudice against radicals and recent immigrants. After seven years of litigation Sacco and Vanzetti died in the electric chair. Their execution sparked protests around the world.

## 3. THE SCOPES TRIAL

- In January 1925 the state of Tennessee passed the Butler Act forbidding the teaching of evolution in the public schools. The act expressed the alarm felt by many fundamentalist Christians who opposed Darwin's theory of evolution because it challenged a literal interpretation of the Bible.
- John T. Scopes, a Tennessee high school science teacher, accepted the American Civil Liberties Union offer to test the constitutionality of the Butler Act. Clarence Darrow, a well-known champion of civil liberties agreed to defend Scopes. William Jennings Bryan, a three-time Democratic presidential candidate and well-known religious fundamentalist, represented the state.

- The Scopes Trial ostensibly (on the surface) tested the legality of teaching the theory of evolution in Tennessee's public schools. However, for a national and international audience the case illustrated a cultural conflict between fundamentalism represented by Bryan and modernism represented by Darrow.
- In the end the court found Scopes guilty and fined him $100.00. The Tennessee Supreme Court overruled the fine on a technicality while upholding the Butler Act. Bryan died five days after the trial from a heart condition probably aggravated by Darrow's grueling and sarcastic cross-examination.

## 4. IMMIGRATION RESTRICTION

- The Sacco and Vanzetti case highlighted the public's fear of recent immigrants. A new postwar wave of arrivals from Southern and Eastern Europe sparked a nationwide movement to limit immigration from these regions.
- Congress responded to the nativist push for restrictive measures by passing the National Origins Act of 1924. The law limited annual immigration to 2 percent of a country's population in the United States at the time of the 1890 census. Since the new immigration began in 1890 the quotas favored immigration for Northern and Western Europe while sharply curtailing (cutting) the flow of newcomers from Southern and Eastern Europe.

## 5. THE RISE AND FALL OF THE KU KLUX KLAN

- The original Ku Klux Klan terrorized newly freed blacks in the post-Civil War South before dying out in the 1870s. The post-World War I mood of distrust and intolerance fueled a revival of the KKK. The new Klan was hostile toward immigrants, Catholics, Jews, and African Americans. It favored immigration restriction and white supremacy.
- By the mid-1920s membership in the Klan swelled to as many as 4 million people. However, passage of the National Origins Act removed the Klan's most popular issue. Divided by recurring leadership quarrels, the Klan once again became a marginal group on the periphery (fringe) of American society.

## INSIDER TIP

The 1920s are usually remembered as a decade dominated by fads, Fords, and celebrities such as Babe Ruth, Rudolph Valentino, and Charles Lindbergh. This is not how College Board test writers remember the decade. Most APUSH and SAT II tests include a multiple-choice question designed to test your knowledge of how intolerance and nativism shaped life in the 1920s.

## TOPIC 176
# AFRICAN AMERICANS IN THE 1920S

### 1. THE GREAT MIGRATION CONTINUES
- The Great Migration of African Americans from the rural South to industrial cities in the North and Midwest began during World War I. Attracted by the promise of jobs and the possibility of escaping Jim Crow segregation over 400,000 African Americans left the South between 1910 and 1920.
- The Great Migration continued during the 1920s. By 1930, another 600,000 blacks moved to cities in the North.

### 2. THE HARLEM RENAISSANCE
- Harlem soon emerged as a vibrant center of African American culture. During the 1920s a new generation of black writers and artists created an outpouring of literary and artistic works known as the HARLEM RENAISSANCE.
- Langston Hughes, Claude McKay, Jean Toomer, James Weldon Johnson, and Zora Neal Hurston formed the core group of Harlem Renaissance writers. Taken together their poems, novels, and essays comprised a distinctive African American literature.

### 3. MARCUS GARVEY
- The Harlem Renaissance writers had little immediate impact upon the majority of African Americans. In contrast, Marcus Garvey emerged as one of the earliest and most influential black-nationalist leaders in the twentieth century.
- Garvey organized the Universal Negro Improvement Association (UNIA) to increase racial pride and promote black nationalism. Unlike W.E.B. Du Bois, Garvey championed black separatism.
- Garvey's meteoric (sudden and rapid) rise captured the imagination of black people in America, the Caribbean, and Africa. Within a short time Garvey was one of most famous black spokesmen in the world.
- Garvey's fame and influence did not last long. In 1919 he founded a steamship company, the Black Star Line, to promote trade between New York, Africa, and the West Indies. Garvey proved to be a poor businessman. The

PODCAST 36.1
MARCUS GARVEY

steamship line collapsed in 1921 costing investors over $750,000. Irregularities in fund-raising led to Garvey's arrest and conviction for mail fraud. President Coolidge commuted Garvey's sentence and he was deported to his native Jamaica.

## TOPIC 177
# THE REPUBLICAN ASCENDANCY

### 1. HARDING AND THE "RETURN TO NORMALCY"

- In 1920 voters overwhelmingly elected Warren Harding President of the United States. Harding was a small-town Ohio politician who rose though the Republican ranks to become a U.S. Senator. Voters forgave Harding for never giving an important speech or for never proposing an important law. Instead, he was a handsome man who looked "presidential" and promised the country a "return to normalcy." The American public welcomed an end to Wilson's idealistic crusades and a return to simpler times.
- Harding's economic policies reconfirmed the partnership between business and government. His Secretary of Treasury Andrew Mellon reduced the tax rates for the wealthy, raised tariffs, and ignored antitrust regulations.
- Although Harding was personally honest, his relaxed leadership enabled venal (dishonest) appointees to profit from corrupt activities. For example, Albert Fall, the Secretary of the Interior, illegally leased the Teapot Dome oil reserves in Wyoming to the Mammoth Oil Company of Harry F. Sinclair. In return, Sinclair "lent" Fall nearly $300,000 in cash. Visibly troubled by this and other scandals rocking his administration, Harding suffered a sudden heart attack and died on August 2, 1923.

### 2. "SILENT CAL"

- Vice-President Calvin Coolidge succeeded Harding. The new President was a former governor of Massachusetts who became a national figure by suppressing a Boston police strike in 1919. As Vice-President, Coolidge was untouched by the scandals that tarnished (discredited) the

## INSIDER TIP
The Harlem Renaissance and Marcus Garvey are two of the most tested topics from the 1920s. Be sure that you know that Marcus Garvey promoted black pride, black separatism, and black nationalism. He is considered a forerunner of the black power movement in the 1960s.

## INSIDER TIP
The presidencies of Harding and Coolidge have generated several political cartoons. Be alert for cartoons depicting the Harding scandals and a group of wealthy Coolidge business supporters.

Harding administration. A man of few words, Coolidge deserved his popular nickname "Silent Cal."

- Coolidge moved quickly to remove everyone involved in the Teapot Dome scandal. After winning the 1924 election Coolidge asserted that, "The business of America is business." He retained Mellon as Secretary of Treasury and supported his conservative economic policies.
- The popular Coolidge could have easily won the Republican nomination for a second full term. However, the taciturn (sparring of words) President unexpectedly announced, "I do not choose to run."

## 3. HERBERT HOOVER
- The Republicans turned to Secretary of Commerce Herbert Hoover to be their party's standard bearer in the 1928 presidential election. Hoover was widely respected as a generous humanitarian and a skilled administrator.
- Hoover decisively defeated the Democratic candidate Al Smith of New York. Hoover's landslide victory seemed to confirm the public's endorsement of the Republican New Era of peace and prosperity. Hoover confidently predicted, "We in America are nearer to the final triumph over poverty than ever before in the history of any land."

# CHAPTER 37
# THE GREAT DEPRESSION AND THE NEW DEAL, 1929 – 1939

## ESSENTIAL POINTS

1. A combination of the stock market crash, overproduction in manufacturing, underconsumption by households, and a decline in farm income helped cause the Great Depression.

2. The Dust Bowl of the 1930s was centered in Kansas, Oklahoma, and eastern Colorado. John Steinbeck's novel *The Grapes of Wrath* captured the ordeal faced by the "Oakies" as they migrated to California.

3. President Hoover believed that economic recovery depended upon private charity and the business community. Hoover and Roosevelt disagreed most strongly about the desirability of funding a massive program of public works to relieve unemployment.

4. The New Deal included a number of programs designed to address the Great Depression. The Wagner Act recognized labor's right to organize and bargain collectively. The Social Security Act guaranteed retirement payments for enrolled workers beginning at the age of 65.

5. The Supreme Court struck down both the National Industrial Recovery Act and the Agricultural Adjustment Act. FDR proposed a Court Reform Bill to "pack" the Supreme Court so he could appoint justices more sympathetic to the New Deal. Congress rejected the bill as a violation of judicial independence and the separation of powers.

6. Led by John L. Lewis, the Congress of Industrial Organizations (CIO) organized unskilled and semiskilled factory workers on an industry-wide basis.

7. During the New Deal the overwhelming majority of African American voters switched their allegiance from the Republican Party to the Democratic Party. African Americans became an important part of a New Deal coalition that also included labor unions, ethnic minorities, and white southerners.

**TOPIC 178**
# CAUSES OF THE GREAT DEPRESSION

## 8. THE STOCK MARKET CRASH

- In 1929 Wall Street was the financial capital of the world. The heart of Wall Street was an imposing gray building, the New York Stock Exchange. Here soaring stock prices reinforced optimism about America's booming economy. Between January 1921 and September 1929, the New York Times average of stock prices rose from $110 to $455. Many people began to believe that Republican economic policies had ushered in a New Era of rising prosperity.

- Wall Street's speculative bubble burst on Black Thursday, October 29, 1929. Waves of panic selling overwhelmed the New York Stock Exchange. The wild shouting of 1,000 frantic brokers produced what one observer called "a weird roar." The selling reached a crescendo on Tuesday, October 29th. Within less than a week stocks lost 37 percent of their value.

- At first the Wall Street crash appeared to have only hurt the four million investors who owned stock. The United States' vast industrial and agricultural resources were physically unhurt. There seemed to be no reason for prosperity to end. President Hoover tried to reassure the nervous public by confidently predicting, "The crisis will be over in sixty days." But Hoover was wrong. The Wall Street crash dealt a severe blow to investors and to banks. It also revealed and intensified serious economic weaknesses in the U.S. economy.

## 9. OVERPRODUCTION AND UNDERCONSUMPTION

- In 1929, American factories produced nearly half of the world's industrial goods. Rising productivity generated enormous profits. This wealth, however, was unevenly distributed. At the time of the crash the richest 5 percent of the population earned nearly one-third of all personal income. Meanwhile, at the other end of the scale, fully 60 percent of all American families earned less than the $2,000 a year needed to buy basic necessities. Eighty percent of the nation's families had NO savings whatsoever. Thus,

most families were too poor to buy the goods being produced and had no resources to fall back on if they lost their jobs.
- The United States economy was thus simultaneously experiencing overproduction by business and underconsumption by consumers. As a result, store owners reduced their orders and factories began to cut back production and lay off workers. These actions started a downward economic spiral.

## 10.    THE PLIGHT OF THE FARMER
- Many American farmers never shared in the prosperity of the 1920s. Scientific farming methods combined with new trucks and tractors enabled farmers to dramatically increase the yield of crops per acre. At the same time, American farmers faced new competition from grain growers in Australia and Argentina.
- The global surplus of agricultural products drove prices and farm incomes down. Since they were unable to sell their crops at a profit, many farmers could not pay off their loans. These bad debts forced weakened banks to close.

## INSIDER TIP
Many APUSH exams and SAT II tests include multiple-choice questions asking you to identify the factor that contributed the LEAST to the Great Depression. The Great Depression was NOT caused by inflation in workers' wages, excessive government regulation, or declining agricultural production.

## TOPIC 179
# HARD TIMES

## 1. DOWN! DOWN! DOWN!
- Between 1929 and 1932 all the major economic indicators documented the same devastating story of economic collapse. By 1932 investors lost $74 billion as stocks lost 89 percent of their value. During these 3 years 86,000 businesses closed their doors and 9,000 banks declared bankruptcy wiping out 9 million savings accounts.
- The burden of hard times fell most heavily on those least able to afford it. Unemployment rose from just 3.2 percent in 1929 to a staggering 24.9 percent in 1932. Poverty soon became a way of life for one-fourth of the population.

## 2. THE DUST BOWL
- A strong, protective carpet of buffalo grass had once covered the Great Plains. The grass held moisture in the soil and kept the wind from blowing it away. However, as the demand for wheat increased, farmers plowed under

PODCAST 37.1
THE DUST BOWL

INSIDER TIP

APUSH exams and SAT II tests often use pictures and paintings to test your ability to identify the Dust Bowl. For an excellent realist painting of the Dust Bowl see *Drought Stricken Area* by Alexander Hogue.

the buffalo grass exposing the land to wind and sun. During the early 1930s farmers watched apprehensively as a prolonged drought and intense heat dried out the Great Plains.

- Disaster struck without warning or mercy. Great black clouds of dust darkened the sky and covered homes and barns. "The storms were like rolling black smoke," reported one awestruck Texas schoolboy." "We had to keep the lights on all day. We went to school with headlights on and with dust masks on." Large areas of Kansas, the Texas panhandle, Oklahoma and eastern Colorado became known as the Dust Bowl.

- Agriculture virtually ceased in the hardest-hit areas of the Dust Bowl. Over 350,000 desperate people fled the Great Plains during the 1930s. Called "Okies," they loaded their meager belongings into battered cars and headed west along Route 66 to California. John Steinbeck captured the ordeal faced by these proud but impoverished migrants in his powerful novel, *The Grapes of Wrath*.

### 3. HOOVERVILLES

- Prolonged unemployment created an army of homeless people. The jobless stood in breadlines, sold apples on street corners and slept anywhere they could find shelter.
- HOOVERVILLE was the sarcastic term given to shantytowns inhabited by unemployed and homeless people. For Americans used to living in a land of abundance, Hoovervilles were among the most sobering sights of the Great Depression.

## TOPIC 180
# HERBERT HOOVER AND THE GREAT DEPRESSION

### 1. HOOVER'S PHILOSOPHY OF GOVERNMENT

- Like most leaders of business and government, President Hoover did not anticipate the sudden economic downturn that followed the stock market crash on October 29, 1929. He believed that the economy was fundamentally sound and that the real problem was a lack of confidence. Convinced that economic recovery depended primarily on the business community, Hoover summoned industrial leaders to the White House and urged them to maintain wages, jobs, and production. He also implored private charities and local governments to help unemployed workers.

- Hoover rejected calls for federal programs to directly help unemployed workers. He stubbornly opposed a government dole because it ran counter to his belief in "rugged individualism." Hoover argued that a program of direct federal relief to individuals would violate the Constitution and undermine the cherished value of "rugged individualism." Hoover's philosophy of rugged individualism and local voluntarism hardened into a dogma (set of rigid beliefs) that prevented him from supporting federal programs to combat unemployment.

## 2. THE RECONSTRUCTION FINANCE CORPORATION

- While Hoover rejected federal programs to help the poor he did listen to bankers who pleaded for federal aid. In early 1932 Congress created the Reconstruction Finance Corporation (RFC) to make emergency loans to distressed banks and businesses. The RFC loaned $1.78 billion to 7,400 banks, insurance companies, and railroads that needed help.
- The RFC went far beyond anything the federal government had ever done before. Its emergency loans helped limit the number of bankruptcies. However, indignant (outraged) critics accused Hoover of insisting on rugged individualism for people standing in breadlines while at the same time supporting a "billion-dollar soup kitchen" for distressed bankers.

## 3. THE BONUS ARMY

- Hoover's already sinking popularity fell even further because of his mishandling of the Bonus Army. In 1924, Congress promised a bonus of several hundred dollars to World War I veterans. The payment, however, would not be made until 1945.
- Arguing that they needed the bonus money as soon as possible, many unemployed veterans demanded to be paid immediately. In the spring of 1932 a Bonus Army of about 20,000 veterans converged on Washington to

## INSIDER TIP

Don't overlook the Reconstruction Finance Corporation. It marked Hoover's belated attempt to provide emergency loans to distressed banks and businesses. It also set an important precedent for government programs during the New Deal.

lobby Congress to pass a bill providing for the immediate payment of their bonuses. However, Hoover opposed the bill arguing that its $2.5 billion price tag would make it impossible to balance the federal budget. Supported by Hoover, the Senate rejected the bill.

- Although most of the discouraged veterans left Washington, a few thousand remained with their wives and children. Their presence embarrassed the President. In July Hoover ordered about 700 soldiers commanded by General Douglas MacArthur to evict the Bonus Army from downtown Washington. Newsreel cameras captured the jarring spectacle of U.S. Army troops using bayonets and tear gas to drive the veterans and their families from their ramshackle (crumbling, decrepit) shacks. Hoover misjudged outraged public opinion when he proudly boasted, "Thank God we still have a government ... that knows how to deal with a mob."

## 4. THE ELECTION OF 1932

- The deepening depression crippled any chance Hoover had of winning reelection. The ubiquitous (everywhere) breadlines and Hoovervilles seemed to confirm the popular image of Hoover as a leader who was insensitive to the plight of the American people.
- Sensing victory, the Democrats nominated Franklin D. Roosevelt, the popular reform-minded Governor of New York. In a dramatic gesture, Roosevelt broke tradition and flew to Chicago to personally accept his party's nomination. He inspired the convention by promising cheering delegates, "I pledge you, I pledge myself, to a new deal for the American people."
- During the campaign Roosevelt remained deliberately vague about the details of the "new deal." Despite the lack of a real debate on the issues, Hoover and Roosevelt did strongly disagree on the desirability of funding a massive program of public works to relieve unemployment. Unlike Hoover, Roosevelt believed government had a responsibility to take aggressive actions to fight the Depression.
- Americans understood that voting for FDR meant endorsing a change in federal policy. Roosevelt won an overwhelming victory winning 57 percent of the vote while carrying 42 of the nation's 48 states.

## TOPIC 181
# KEY FACTS ABOUT THE NEW DEAL

## 1. RELIEF, RECOVERY, AND REFORM

- When FDR took the oath of office on March 4, 1933 the country had just endured a bleak winter of rising unemployment, failing banks, and closing businesses. The American people called for immediate action to prevent the nation from slipping into economic chaos.

- FDR understood the gravity (seriousness) of the crisis. In his Inaugural Address he announced, "I shall ask the Congress for ...broad executive power to wage a war against the emergency as great as the power that would be given me if we were in fact invaded by a foreign foe."

- FDR and his "brain trust" of advisors were resolved to use government to address the economic crisis. They proposed a pragmatic (practical) series of trial-and-error programs that had three goals: First, adopt measures to restore public confidence and achieve immediate relief. Second, adopt measures to help promote industrial and agricultural recovery. And third, implement long-term measures to reform business practices.

## 2. THE HUNDRED DAYS, MARCH 9 – JUNE 16, 1933

- The Emergency Banking Relief Act: On March 5th, FDR proclaimed a four-day bank holiday. The Emergency Banking Relief Act provided for the reopening of the banks under the supervision of the Secretary of the Treasury. A few days later, FDR addressed the nation by radio in the first of his "fireside chats." He emphasized that most of the banks would reopen in a few days. The next day people making deposits far outnumbered those making withdrawals. As a result, the immediate banking crisis subsided.

- The Civilian Conservation Corp (CCC): Created a jobs program for unemployed young men aged 18 to 25. The men lived in camps and worked on a variety of conservation projects in the nation's parks and recreation areas.

- The Tennessee Valley Authority (TVA): Authorized the construction of a system of dams and hydroelectric plants

## INSIDER TIP

The New Deal included about 25 pieces of landmark legislation. Fortunately, you do not have to memorize each of these "alphabet soup" agencies. Focus on the agencies and key points in this section. It is also important to know that the New Deal did NOT nationalize the banks, restructure the courts, establish the Lend-Lease program, or attempt to replace America's capitalist system.

to provide inexpensive electricity and prevent devastating floods. The TVA provided an important experiment in regional planning and rehabilitation.

- The Agricultural Adjustment Act (AAA): Attempted to increase farm income by paying farmers to leave acres unplanted. New Dealers hoped this action would reduce farm surpluses and thus raise prices. The National Industrial Recovery Act (NIRA): Attempted to combat the Depression by reducing competition. It created a National Recovery Administration to work with business and labor to write codes regulating production, wages, and hours.
- The Glass-Steagall Banking Act: Separated commercial and investment banking to prevent speculative abuses. It also established the Federal Deposit Insurance Corporation (FDIC) to guarantee bank deposits up to $5,000.

### 3. THE SECOND NEW DEAL, 1934 – 1935

- Works Projects Administration (WPA): Funded a massive program of public projects ranging from building bridges to painting murals in post offices.
- Securities and Exchange Commission (SEC): Regulated the stock market.
- Social Security Act: Guaranteed retirement payments for enrolled workers beginning at the age of 65. This act proved to be the most far-reaching New Deal program.
- Wagner Labor Relations Act: Recognized labor's right to bargain collectively. It created the National Labor Relations Board (NLRB) to protect workers from unfair practices and to arbitrate labor-management disputes.

## INSIDER TIP

FDR proposed the Second New Deal because his radical critics were becoming more popular and because the first wave of New Deal measures did not end the Depression.

# TOPIC 182
# THE NEW DEAL UNDER ATTACK

## 1. OPPOSITION TO THE NEW DEAL

- The New Deal helped pull America out of the depths of the Great Depression. Industrial production slowly rose and unemployment fell from about 13 million in 1933 to 9 million in 1936.
- Despite these gains full recovery still seemed elusive (hard to reach). A small but contentious (argumentative) group of critics attacked the New Deal and offered radical plans

to revive the economy. At the same time, the New Deal faced an even greater challenge from the Supreme Court.

## 2. THREE CRITICS

- Father Charles Coughlin was a Michigan-based priest whose popular Sunday radio program reached 40 million listeners. Father Coughlin opposed the New Deal and supported nationalizing the banks and coining more silver dollars.
- Dr. Francis E. Townsend was a California physician who argued that the New Deal did not do enough for older Americans. Townsend wanted every person older than 60 to receive a monthly government check for $200.00. The recipient had to promise to spend all the money each month. The movement led by Townsend contributed to congressional approval for the Social Security Act.
- Huey Long was a Louisiana governor and U.S. Senator. Long wanted to take money from wealthy Americans and distribute $5,000 checks to needy people. His "Share Our Wealth" program attracted widespread support prompting Long to plan a presidential campaign for 1936. Then in September 1935, an assassin shot and killed Long on the steps of the Louisiana capitol in Baton Rouge.

## 3. THE SUPREME COURT PACKING FIGHT

- In the summer of 1935 the Supreme Court began to deliver a series of decisions overturning key New Deal programs. In *Schechter v. United States* the Court unanimously struck down the National Industrial Recovery Act because it gave the federal government powers of economic regulation that could not be justified under the interstate commerce clause. A few months later the Court also invalidated the Agricultural Adjustment Act.
- Roosevelt and the New Dealers feared that the Court would soon strike down both the Wagner Act and the Social Security Act. In 1937, FDR sent Congress the Court Reform Bill. The President surprised Congress by asking for the authority to appoint a new Supreme Court justice for every member older than 70. This would allow Roosevelt to appoint six new justices more receptive to the New Deal.
- Both the public and members of Congress opposed Roosevelt's "court-packing" bill as a violation of judicial

independence and the separation of powers. Although the Democrats enjoyed large majorities in both houses, Congress refused to approve the Court Reform Bill. The rejection marked Roosevelt's first major legislative defeat. Aroused conservatives in both parties made it difficult for Roosevelt to pass additional New Deal reforms.

· Ironically, the Supreme Court proved to be more sympathetic to the New Deal after FDR's court-packing fiasco (disaster). The Court upheld both the Wagner Act and the Social Security Act. In addition, several justices retired and Roosevelt ultimately appointed nine new members of the Court.

## TOPIC 183
# THE IMPACT OF THE NEW DEAL

## 1. THE NEW DEAL AND THE ECONOMY

· As 1937 opened, Roosevelt optimistically pointed to several promising indicators of economic success. Unemployment fell to 14 percent and industrial output returned to pre-Crash levels. Confident that the economic crisis was receding, FDR reduced funding for New Deal programs. These cuts triggered a sudden economic downturn known as the "Roosevelt Recession" of 1937 – 1938. Without the stimulus of federal spending, unemployment jumped to 19 percent.

· The Roosevelt Recession forced many New Dealers to turn to the unorthodox (unconventional) theories of the British economist John Maynard Keynes. Traditional economists had always argued that governments should strive to balance their budgets. Keynes disagreed. He recommended that governments use DEFICIT SPENDING – spending money beyond that which was raised by taxes to stimulate the economy. Although FDR did not fully embrace Keynesian economics he did resume funding the New Deal programs.

· The New Deal did not bring about the full economic recovery FDR had promised. The United States finally emerged from the Great Depression when the federal government sharply increased military spending at the start of World War II.

## 2. THE NEW DEAL AND THE ROLE OF THE FEDERAL GOVERNMENT

- The New Deal accelerated the process first begun during the Progressive Era of expanding the role of the federal government. Under the New Deal the federal government assumed responsibility for the collective welfare of the American people. Social Security payments, farm loans, and relief projects all provided tangible (concrete) examples of how the federal government became a growing part of everyday life in America.
- As the federal government's role expanded so did the size of the federal bureaucracy. The New Deal created a number of federal agencies. By the end of the 1930s, the federal government became the largest single employer in the country.

## 3. THE NEW DEAL AND LABOR

- When the Great Depression began, trade unions represented only about 3 million workers. Most were skilled workers organized by the American Federation of Labor (AFL).
- The Wagner Act (National Labor Relations Act) guaranteed every laborer the right to join a union and use the union to bargain collectively with management. John L. Lewis, the leader of the United Mine Workers, took the lead in forming the Congress of Industrial Organizations (CIO) to unionize workers at all levels within an industry. The AFL and CIO split apart at their national convention in 1935 because the AFL refused to grant charters to new unions organized on an industry-wide basis.
- Undaunted by the split with the AFL, Lewis led a series of strikes in the automobile and steel industries. Workers walked off their jobs or in many cases staged sit-ins inside their plants. Eventually the workers won new contracts guaranteeing better wages, hours, and safety measures. By the end of the decade, unions represented 9 million workers or 28 percent of the nonfarm workforce.

## INSIDER TIP

Be sure you know how the New Deal affected organized labor. The Wagner Act guaranteed laborers the right to organize and bargain collectively. As result, industrial workers gained the most from the New Deal. Needless to say, industrialists were not part of the New Deal coalition.

PODCAST 37.2
THE NEW DEAL
COALITION

## 4. THE NEW DEAL AND AFRICAN AMERICANS

- The New Deal did not directly confront racial injustice. For example, the CCC camps were often segregated. African Americans nonetheless benefitted from New Deal relief programs that attempted to alleviate (relieve) poverty regardless of racial background.

- The New Deal caused a dramatic change in how African Americans viewed the Republican and Democratic parties. In 1932, 75 percent of African American voters supported Herbert Hoover as the candidate of the party of Lincoln. Even though the New Deal did not oppose Jim Crow segregation, it did help African Americans survive the Great Depression. In the 1936 presidential election 95 percent of black voters switched their allegiance to Franklin Roosevelt and the Democratic Party.

- African Americans formed an important part of the New Deal coalition that formed during the 1930s. The coalition also included labor unions, ethnic minorities, and white southerners.

## 5. THE NEW DEAL AND WOMEN

- Many observers noted that women seemed invisible during the Great Depression. The PWA and other New Deal agencies almost exclusively hired men. The CCC excluded women entirely, prompting critics to ask, "Where is the she-she-she?"

- Although the New Deal did not directly challenge gender inequity, First Lady Eleanor Roosevelt did play an important role in promoting equal treatment for women and African Americans. In one highly publicized incident, Eleanor Roosevelt resigned from the Daughters of the American Revolution to protest the organization's decision to bar Marion Anderson, a world-renowned African American singer, from performing at Constitution Hall in Washington, D.C.

**CHAPTER 38**

# THE UNITED STATES AND THE WORLD, 1921 - 1945

## ESSENTIAL POINTS

1. The Good Neighbor Policy opened a new era in relations between the United States and Latin America. The United States renounced armed intervention in the Caribbean and Central America.

2. The Washington Naval Conference restricted the number of battleships and aircraft carriers that the United States, Great Britain, and Japan could build.

3. The isolationists used Washington's Farewell Address to help justify their goal of preventing the United States from becoming entangled in European affairs. The Neutrality Acts of the 1930s were intended to prevent the United States from repeating the mistakes that led it to enter World War I.

4. The Lend-Lease Act committed the United States to aiding Great Britain and the Soviet Union in their effort to defeat Hitler.

5. Following the attack on Pearl Harbor the United States adopted a "get Germany first" military strategy.

6. During World War II large numbers of married women left their homes to work in war industries. Rosie the Riveter became a proud symbol of their patriotism and determination to contribute to the war effort.

7. The internment of Japanese Americans constituted the most serious violation of civil liberties in wartime in American history. In the case of *Korematsu v. United States* the Supreme Court upheld the constitutionality of the Japanese relocation.

# TOPIC 184
# U.S. FOREIGN POLICY, 1921 – 1933

## 1. EUROPE

- America fought World War I as an idealistic crusade to "make the world safe for democracy." However, the war left many Americans bitterly disillusioned. Although the United States emerged from World War I as the world's richest and most powerful nation, it rejected the principle of collective security and never joined the League of Nations.

- Economically, however, the U.S. was not isolated at all. Under the Dawes Plan loans from American banks helped Germany recover from a disastrous 1923 inflation. At the same time, the United States became a major trading partner with countries around the world.

## 2. LATIN AMERICA

- Both TR's Big Stick Diplomacy and Taft's Dollar Diplomacy promoted America's twin goals of achieving political dominance and economic advantage in Latin America. During the 1920s, however, the three Republican administrations began the process of withdrawing American marines from the Caribbean and Central America.

- In 1933, Franklin Roosevelt opened a new chapter in America's relationship with Latin America by proclaiming the beginning of a GOOD NEIGHBOR POLICY. The new policy renounced (disavowed) U.S. armed intervention in Latin America. It is important to note that the United States continued to pursue commercial opportunities in Latin America. During the 1930s the Good Neighbor Policy promoted a common hemispheric front against fascism.

## 3. JAPAN AND CHINA

- Although the United States refused to join the League of Nations it was not completely isolated from global affairs. The U.S. could not ignore Japan's growing threat to American interests in China. In 1921 the Harding administration invited Japan, Great Britain, and other European nations to send representatives to Washington to discuss a range of Asian problems.

- The expensive and growing naval arms race among the U.S., Great Britain, and Japan posed the most pressing problem. After much negotiation the powers agreed to limit battleship and aircraft carrier production in a ratio of 5:5:3 for the United States, Britain, and Japan. The Japanese also signed a treaty agreeing to respect China's independence and America's Open Door policy.

- The Washington Conference appeared to reduce the dangerous escalation of tensions between the United States and Japan. But the pause proved to be temporary. The global depression delivered a devastating blow to the Japanese economy. A group of militarists soon dominated Japan's government. In 1931, Japan broke its treaty promises by invading China's northern province, Manchuria. Secretary of State Henry Stimson responded by declaring a policy of nonrecognition called the Stimson Doctrine. The Japanese ignored the toothless Stimson Doctrine and incorporated Manchuria's rich iron and coal resources into their rapidly expanding empire.

## INSIDER TIP
Don't overlook the Washington Naval Conference. Unlike the Japanese militarists, College Board test writers have paid attention to the naval arms limitations agreed to by the signatory nations.

## TOPIC 185
# ISOLATIONISM, 1934 – 1937

## 1. THE RESURGENCE OF MILITARISM IN ITALY, GERMANY, AND JAPAN

- Mussolini, Hitler, and a group of ironfisted Japanese militarists all emerged from the chaos and economic depression following World War I. Each seized power promising to restore national pride.

- Mussolini dreamed of resurrecting the glories of ancient Rome by building an Italian colonial empire in Africa. In October 1935, Mussolini ordered a massive invasion of Ethiopia. The invasion represented a crucial test of the League of Nation's system of collective security. Although the League condemned the attack, its members did nothing to stop Mussolini.

- The League's failure to deter Mussolini encouraged Hitler to defy the Versailles treaty. In 1936 Hitler sent troops into the Rhineland, German territory that had been demilitarized by the Treaty of Versailles. Although Hitler expected France to resist, its leaders were unwilling to risk a **new war**. Hitler later admitted that, "The forty-eight hours after the march into the Rhineland were the most nerve-wracking in my life. If the French had then marched into the Rhineland, we would have had to withdraw." Emboldened by French inaction, Hitler now planned for additional aggressive actions.

- The Japanese also took advantage of the League's failure to stop aggression. By 1936 the Japanese renounced the Washington Conference treaties and left the League of Nations. In 1937, Japan invaded northern China touching off a full-scale war that marked the beginning of World War II in Asia. Few seemed to notice that the Japanese invasion violated the 1928 Kellogg-Briand Pact condemning recourse to aggressive war.

## 2. THE NYE COMMITTEE

- The horrible cost of World War I created a deep desire for peace. In America ISOLATIONISTS argued that the United States should avoid political commitments to other nations. They urged their fellow countrymen to remember George Washington's Farewell Address admonition (earnest warning) to avoid being involved in European affairs.
- In 1934, Senator Gerald P. Nye, a North Dakota Republican, chaired a special Senate committee that investigated American munitions dealers. After two years, the Nye Committee concluded that America had been duped (tricked) into entering World War I by avaricious (greedy) "merchants of death" who earned enormous profits during the war.

## 3. THE NEUTRALITY ACTS

- The Nye Committee's revelations led isolationists to demand that Congress pass laws to prevent a repeat of the mistakes that pushed the United States into World War I.
- Between 1935 and 1937 Congress passed a series of three Neutrality Acts. These laws banned loans and the sale of arms to nations at war. They also warned Americans not to sail on ships of countries at war. The isolationists were convinced that these laws would keep the United States out of a new foreign war.

## TOPIC 186
# THE ROAD TO WAR, 1938 – 1941

## 1. THE WAR IN EUROPE, 1939 – 1940

- While America tried to remain at peace, Hitler plunged Europe into war. On September 1, 1939 Germany launched a sudden massive blitzkrieg or "lightening war" against Poland. France and Britain responded by immediately declaring war on Germany.
- After a six-month lull in fighting, devastating German blitzkriegs led to the fall of Denmark, Norway, Belgium, and France. Only Great Britain, now led by Winston Churchill, held out against Hitler. Churchill defiantly vowed that Britain would "defend our Island, whatever the cost may be … we shall never surrender."
- The frightening events in Europe persuaded many Americans to support rebuilding the nation's military strength. In 1940 Congress increased the defense budget from $2 billion to $10 billion. Later that year, Congress also approved a Selective Service Act providing for the country's first military draft during peacetime.

## 2. THE LEND-LEASE ACT

- Roosevelt was aware of the continuing strong isolationist sentiment in the United States. He therefore moved cautiously to help Britain resist Nazi Germany. In 1939, Roosevelt persuaded Congress to allow the sale of weapons and other goods to belligerent (fighting) nations by a cash-and-carry policy. Countries at war could buy needed goods as long as they paid for them immediately and took them away on their ships. In September 1940, during the Battle of Britain, Roosevelt went a step further by giving Churchill 50 overage destroyers in return for British air and naval bases in the Western Hemisphere.
- Despite the American aid, the British faced an increasingly dire need for food and war materials. Roosevelt recognized that America's national interests demanded that it help Britain in its fight against Hitler. In a fireside chat on December 29, 1940, FDR explained that America must become an "arsenal of democracy" by providing war supplies to Great Britain. He then asked Congress

PODCAST 38.1
THE LEND-LEASE ACT

## INSIDER TIP

Be sure you can link the phrase "arsenal of democracy" with the Lend-Lease Act. The act initially responded to Britain's need for equipment to fight Hitler. Lend-Lease aid was later extended to the Soviet Union.

to approve a Lend-Lease Act allowing him to send war materials to any country whose defense he considered vital to the United States.

- Congress passed the Lend-Lease Act in March 1941. The new law marked an important turning point. America's mighty industries now roared to life producing weapons to fight Hitler and Mussolini. By the fall of 1941, the U.S. was arming merchant ships and using its navy to protect British ships in the North Atlantic. Although a state of undeclared war existed between the United States and Germany, polls showed that 80 percent of the American people still wanted to stay out of World War II.

## 3. PEARL HARBOR

- The Battle of Britain and the debate over the Lend-Lease Act over-shadowed ominous events taking place in Asia. The long-standing rivalry between the U.S. and Japan for Pacific supremacy further escalated when Japanese forces overran French Indochina in July 1941. President Roosevelt retaliated by ordering a total embargo on all trade with Japan. At that time, Japan imported about 80 percent of its oil and scrap iron from the United States.

- The embargo forced the Japanese leaders to make a fateful decision. They could either give in to the U.S. demand that they withdraw from China and Indochina or they could attack the American fleet at Pearl Harbor and then seize the rich oil fields in the Dutch East Indies. When negotiations with the United States reached an impasse (deadlock), the Japanese decided to launch a surprise attack on Pearl Harbor.

- In late November 1941, a Japanese fleet secretly headed into the vast and empty waters of the North Pacific. The fleet included six aircraft carriers equipped with more than 400 warplanes. At 7:55 AM on December 7, 1941 the first of three waves of planes attacked Pearl Harbor. Within less than two hours the Japanese sank or damaged 18 ships and killed 2,403 men.

- The next day President Roosevelt asked Congress for a declaration of war on Japan. Four days later, Germany and Italy declared war against the United States. An angry and now united American entered World War II determined to crush the Axis powers.

## TOPIC 187
# WARTIME DIPLOMACY

## 1. GET GERMANY FIRST
- America's initial shock and anger were directed at Japan. Outraged Americans demanded a strategy designed to first defeat Japan and then crush Hitler.
- Roosevelt realized that Hitler posed the greatest threat to America's long-term security. If Hitler succeeded in defeating both the Soviet Union and Great Britain he could transform Europe into an unconquerable fortress. The U.S. and Great Britain therefore agreed upon a military strategy to defeat Hitler first.

## 2. THE BIG THREE
- The Big Three referred to Roosevelt, Churchill, and the Soviet leader Joseph Stalin.
- The Big Three first met in November 1943 at Tehran, Iran. The meeting confirmed that the United States and Great Britain would open a second front by invading France. The Big Three also reaffirmed their demand for the unconditional surrender of Germany and Italy.
- The Big Three held their second and final meeting at Yalta in February 1945. Churchill and Roosevelt agreed to a temporary division of Germany. In return Stalin agreed to join the war against Japan three months after the Nazis surrendered. Stalin also agreed that Poland should have a representative government based on free elections.

## TOPIC 188
# THE HOME FRONT

## 1. THE PRODUCTION MIRACLE
- When Stalin met Roosevelt in Tehran, the Soviet dictator offered this admiring toast: "To American production, without which this war would have been lost." Stalin was right. American industry crushed the Axis powers beneath an overwhelming weight of weaponry.
- Prior to World War II, airplanes and ships had been built one at a time. Led by Henry Ford and Henry J. Kaiser,

American companies learned how to use assembly line techniques to mass-produce these and other weapons. By 1944, round-the-clock shifts were turning out a new bomber every hour and a cargo ship every 17 days. Between 1940 and 1945, factories in the United States produced a staggering total of 296,429 warplanes, 5,425 cargo ships, and 102,351 tanks and self-propelled guns.

## 2. ROSIE THE RIVETER

- World War II created new job opportunities for women. As their husbands left to serve in the military about five million additional women joined the nation's workforce.
- The popular song *"Rosie the Riveter"* celebrated the women who worked in factories. Rosie the Riveter soon became more than a nickname for women who performed industrial work. For millions of American women, Rosie was a proud symbol of their patriotism and determination to contribute to the war effort.

## 3. THE AFRICAN AMERICAN EXPERIENCE

- About one million African Americans served in the armed forces during World War II. These black soldiers and sailors continued to serve in segregated units.
- During the war over one million southern blacks moved to industrial cities in the North and West Coast. However, war industries continued to discriminate against black workers. In 1941 A. Philip Randolph, the head of the Brotherhood of Sleeping Car Porters, organized a March on Washington Movement to protest discrimination. Roosevelt wanted to prevent a highly visible and divisive protest march. Supported by Eleanor Roosevelt, the President issued an executive order banning discrimination in defense industries and government agencies. The order established the Fair Employment Practices Commission to monitor and enforce the presidential directive.
- African Americans were keenly aware of the contradiction between fighting for democracy abroad while enduring racial discrimination at home. Blacks enthusiastically supported a "Double V" campaign to win victory over fascism in Europe and victory over discrimination in the United States. This new assertive attitude helped to spark the civil rights movement in the 1950s.

## 4. THE NATIVE AMERICAN EXPERIENCE

- About 44,000 Native Americans served in the armed forces during World War II. This represented over 10 percent of the total Native American population of 350,000.
- About 40,000 Native American women, aged 18 to 50 left their reservations for the first time to find jobs in defense industries.
- During the war about 200 Navajo were recruited into the Marine Corps as code talkers. Their primary duty was to use their native language to transmit important telephone and radio messages. The Navajo language baffled the Japanese who were unable to decipher the "code."

## 5. THE ZOOT SUIT RIOTS

- By the late 1930s about 3 million Mexican Americans lived in the United States. Los Angeles had the highest concentration of Mexicans outside of Mexico. The population influx created rising tension between Mexican Americans and local authorities.
- Young Latinos in Los Angeles enjoyed a youth culture that included a distinctive zoot suit featuring a long coat and baggy trousers fitted snugly at the ankles.
- The armed forces' demand for textiles led to shortages of wool and rayon. The War Production Board then issued ration orders restricting the yardage in clothes. Although the regulations effectively forbade the manufacture of zoot suits, bootleg tailors continued to manufacture the popular garments.
- Sailors and soldiers stationed in Los Angeles resented the baggy zoot suits. They accused Mexican American youth of being unpatriotic by deliberately flouting (showing contempt for) the rationing regulations. In 1943, a series of incidents between young Mexican Americans and off-duty servicemen escalated into riots that lasted a week.

## 6. THE INTERNMENT OF JAPANESE AMERICANS

- In the days and weeks following the attack on Pearl Harbor frightened and angry Americans displaced their rage against Japan to the 110,000 people of Japanese birth and descent who lived on the West Coast. The army insisted that evacuation was a necessary precaution to

## INSIDER TIP

Home front topics have generated far more SAT II and APUSH questions than war front topics. Be sure that you can identify Rosie the Riveter, the Navajo code talkers, the Zoot Suit riot, and the Japanese internment. The 2009 APUSH exam included an essay question on the home front experiences of Japanese Americans, African Americans, Mexican Americans, and Jewish Americans. See Question 5 for an excellent Fact Sheet on the experiences of these groups.

PODCAST 38.2
**THE JAPANESE INTERNMENT**

prevent Japanese Americans from posing a threat to national security.

- On February 19, 1942 President Roosevelt issued Executive Order 9066 authorizing the military to evacuate all people of Japanese ancestry from the West Coast. About 110,000 Japanese Americans were interred, or kept confined, in ten detention camps located on desolate lands owned by the federal government.
- No specific charges were ever filed against the Japanese Americans and no evidence of subversion was ever found. The internment constituted the most serious violation of civil liberties in wartime in American history.
- Fred Korematsu was a Japanese American who knowingly violated the internment order. In *Korematsu v. United States* he argued that Executive Order 9066 deprived Japanese Americans of life, liberty, and property without due process of law. In a controversial decision the Supreme Court upheld the constitutionality of the government's evacuation policy citing the existence of "the gravest imminent danger to the public safety."

## TOPIC 189
# THE MANHATTAN PROJECT AND THE ATOMIC BOMB

### 1. THE MANHATTAN PROJECT
- On October 11, 1939 President Roosevelt received a letter from the world famous physicist Albert Einstein explaining the destructive potential of nuclear fusion. Einstein warned that if the United States did not act quickly, the Germans might develop an atomic bomb first. FDR responded by approving the $2 billion top secret Manhattan Project.
- Nuclear scientists constructed three atomic bombs in a laboratory at Los Alamos, New Mexico. The scientists tested the first bomb on July 16, 1945 at a desolate stretch of desert called Alamogordo. The blast created a fireball with a core temperature three times hotter than the sun.

## 2. THE DECISION TO USE THE ATOMIC BOMB

- Franklin Roosevelt died on April 12, 1945. Two weeks later Secretary of War Henry L. Stimson informed President Truman about the new atomic bomb.

- Truman learned about the Manhattan Project as American forces closed in on the Japanese home islands. His generals warned that an invasion of Japan would be a desperate struggle that would inflict heavy casualties on both the American forces and Japanese civilians. On July 26, 1945 Truman, Churchill, and Stalin issued the Potsdam Declaration calling upon Japan to surrender unconditionally or suffer "the utter devastation of the Japanese homeland." The Japanese government ignored the warning as "unworthy of public notice."

- President Truman authorized the use of the atomic bomb on the cities of Hiroshima and Nagasaki. At least four factors seemed to influence Truman's decision: First and foremost, he wanted to avoid a costly invasion of Japan. Second, he wanted to shock the Japanese government into an immediate surrender. Third, he wanted to end the war before the Soviet Union could gain any influence over the postwar settlement with Japan. And finally, he wanted to convince Stalin to be more cooperative in formulating postwar plans. Since the atomic bomb was a secret, public opinion played no role in Truman's decision.

- The atomic bombs destroyed both Hiroshima and Nagasaki. Aghast at the horrible loss of life, Emperor Hirohito told his war council, "I cannot bear to see my innocent people suffer any longer." The formal surrender ceremony took place on September 2, 1945 on the deck of the American battleship *Missouri* in Tokyo Bay. World War II was now over, but the atomic age and the Cold War were about to begin.

# CHAPTER 39
# TRUMAN AND THE COLD WAR, 1945 – 1952

## ESSENTIAL POINTS

1. George Kennan urged the United States to develop a foreign policy designed to contain the spread of Soviet Communism. The Truman Doctrine committed the United States to use its military and economic strength to block the expansion of Soviet influence in strategic areas such as Greece, Turkey, and Western Europe.
2. The Marshall Plan provided massive economic assistance to help European nations recover from World War II.
3. The Berlin blockade represented the first great Cold War test of containment. The Berlin Airlift thwarted the Soviet attempt to cut off supplies to West Berlin.
4. The North Korean surprise invasion of South Korea precipitated the Korean War. President Truman did not want to be accused of "losing" South Korea. Truman did not ask Congress for a declaration of war. Instead, American troops fought under UN auspices.
5. Senator McCarthy skillfully exploited the climate of political paranoia following the fall of China and the revelations that Soviet spies infiltrated government agencies.
6. The Taft-Hartley Act curbed the power of labor unions.
7. President Truman issued an executive order ending racial segregation in the armed forces. As a result, African Americans served in integrated units in the Korean War.

## TOPIC 190
# KEY QUOTE – TRUMAN PLEDGES THE UNITED STATES "TO SUPPORT FREE PEOPLES."

## 1. THE SETTING

- As World War II ended, the United States hoped for a new period of cooperation with the Soviet Union. "We really believed," recalled one presidential advisor, "that this was the dawn of the new day we had all been praying for." Yet within a short time this optimism vanished as the two former allies became bitter rivals.

- The Soviet Union steadily tightened its grip on Eastern Europe. While the United States demobilized its forces, the Red Army supported new Communist governments. Communist officials imprisoned opponents, censored newspapers, and established state-controlled radio stations. Guards patrolled the borders to prevent people from escaping.

- In a speech in Fulton, Missouri, Winston Churchill warned that, "an Iron Curtain has descended across the continent." The nations of Eastern Europe were now satellites controlled by the Soviet Union.

- With each report about the loss of freedom in Eastern Europe, tensions increased between the United States and the Soviet Union. The two nations soon entered a prolonged era of economic and political conflict called the COLD WAR. The Cold War, however, did not involve direct military conflict between the two rival powers.

- George Kennan, a leading expert on Soviet affairs, believed that Cold War hostility would remain a constant factor for years to come. In an influential 1947 article Kennan recommended that the United States should adopt a policy of "long-term, patient but firm and vigilant containment." By CONTAINMENT he meant adopting a strategic policy of blocking the expansion of Soviet influence.

- The threat of Communist expansion was not limited to Eastern Europe. In early 1947, Communist pressure threatened the independence of Greece and Turkey.

## INSIDER TIP
George Kennan is often called "the father of containment." His offspring include a large number of multiple-choice questions that regularly appear on APUSH exams and SAT II tests.

President Truman accepted America's responsibility to become the leader of the Free World. On March 12, 1947 he asked Congress for $400 million for military and economic aid to help Greece and Turkey.

## 2. THE QUOTE

- "It must be the policy of the United States to support free peoples who are resisting attempted subjugation by armed minorities or by outside pressures. I believe that we must assist free peoples to work out their own destinies in their own way."

## 3. IMPORTANCE

- Congress overwhelmingly approved Truman's request. The aid played a vital role in helping Greece and Turkey successfully confront the Communist threat.
- The Truman Doctrine marked the first use of containment. As the leader of the Free World, America pledged to use its strength to limit the spread of communism throughout the world. This global commitment dominated American foreign policy from 1947 to the collapse of the Soviet Union in 1991.

PODCAST 39.1
THE TRUMAN
DOCTRINE

# TOPIC 191
# CONTAINMENT IN EUROPE

## 1. THE MARSHALL PLAN

- Greece and Turkey were not the only countries that needed aid. World War II left Western Europe in ruins. Homeless families struggled to survive in shattered cities. Devastated factories could not provide employment or produce badly needed goods. In France and Italy many frustrated workers cast their votes for the Communist Party.
- Secretary of State George Marshall argued that the United States had to act quickly. Speaking at Harvard University in June 1947, he proposed a bold plan to offer massive economic aid to help reconstruct Europe. "Our policy," he said, "is directed not against any country or doctrine, but against hunger, poverty, desperation, and chaos."
- The Marshall Plan helped revive European hopes and spark a dramatic economic recovery. During the next four years,

sixteen Western European countries received $13 billion. American dollars helped to rebuild apartments and retool factories. Within four years, industrial production in the countries receiving Marshall Plan aid was 41 percent higher than it had been on the eve of World War II. The Marshall Plan thus accomplished its twin goals of reconstructing Europe and containing Communism.

## 2. THE NATO ALLIANCE

- The Truman Doctrine and the Marshall Plan represented the first two phases of America's new containment policy. The third phase came in 1949 when the United States, Canada, and ten Western European nations formed the North Atlantic Treaty Organization (NATO).

- The NATO members pledged military support to one another in case any member was attacked. America's decision to join an alliance based upon collective security marked a decisive break from its prewar policy of isolationism.

- The NATO alliance escalated the Cold War. The Russians retaliated by forming a military alliance with its Eastern European satellites called the Warsaw Pact. Two hostile alliances now confronted each other across a divided Europe.

## 3. THE BERLIN AIRLIFT

- At the end of World War II, the Allies divided Germany into four separate zones. The city of Berlin, lying 110 miles inside the Soviet zone, was also divided among the Allies.

- In June 1948, the United States, Great Britain, and France agreed to merge their three occupation zones into a new German republic. Stalin reacted quickly to thwart this plan. On June 24, 1948, the Soviets suddenly cut off all highway and railroad traffic into West Berlin. The 2.2 million people living in West Berlin had coal supplies for 45 days and enough food for just 36 days.

- The Berlin blockade represented the first great Cold War test of wills between the United States and the Soviet Union. If Truman withdrew from West Berlin he would lose the city and the confidence of all Western Europe.

- Truman refused to give in to Stalin. He ordered a massive airlift to supply the 4,500 tons of food and fuel which Berliners needed each day. As the Berlin airlift succeeded, tensions slowly eased. The constant roar of plans over Berlin provided a vivid demonstration of American power and will. On May 12, 1949, Stalin reopened road and rail traffic into West Berlin.

# TOPIC 192
# CONTAINMENT IN ASIA

## 1. A NEW JAPAN
- President Truman placed General Douglas MacArthur in charge of the Japanese occupation. Under MacArthur's direction, Japan adopted a new constitution that created a democratic government. At the same time, American aid helped Japan rebuild factories, launch new electronic industries, and implement a program of land reform. By 1953, the Japanese economy was performing at prewar levels.
- MacArthur's display of firm but fair leadership won the respect of the Japanese people. The United States and Japan gradually came to view each other as allies.

## 2. THE FALL OF CHINA
- While the Japanese recovered, a civil war divided China. As World War II ended, conflict between the Nationalists led by Chiang Kai-shek and the Communists led by Mao Zedong spread across the country.
- Despite massive American aid, Chiang's forces steadily lost ground. An American military advisor reported that the Nationalist losses were due to "the world's worst leadership" and "a complete loss of will to fight."
- On October 1, 1949, Mao triumphantly announced the birth of the People's Republic of China. Meanwhile, Chiang and the remnants of his defeated army fled to Formosa (renamed Taiwan), an island 100 miles from the Chinese mainland.
- In early 1950, Mao signed a treaty of friendship with the Soviet Union. Alarmed Americans viewed the Chinese Revolution as part of a menacing Communist monolith (a single unified force). The fall of China represented a bitter defeat for American Cold War diplomacy. The U.S. refused to establish diplomatic relations with Mao's new

government. Instead, Truman recognized the government in Taiwan as the representative of all China.

## 3. THE OUTBREAK OF THE KOREAN WAR

- Korea occupies a strategic peninsula which borders China and Russia and extends to within 100 miles of Japan. After World War II, the United States and the Soviet Union agreed to divide Korea at the 38th parallel. The Soviets quickly established a Communist government in North Korea and the United States supported a noncommunist government in South Korea.

- On June 25, 1950 the North Korean army suddenly attacked South Korea. Supported by artillery and heavy tanks, about 90,000 North Korean soldiers smashed through the South Korean defenses and rolled south.

- The North Korean surprise attack stunned the United States. Truman saw the invasion as a test of containment and an opportunity to prove that the Democrats were not "soft" on Communism. He immediately called for an emergency meeting of the UN Security Council. Normally the Soviets would have vetoed any plan of action. However, the Soviet representative was boycotting the Security Council because it would not seat Communist China in place of the Nationalist government in Taiwan. The Security Council promptly condemned the North Korean aggression and called upon member nations to aid South Korea.

- Within days, American troops commanded by General MacArthur rushed into South Korea. The American forces formed the core of a UN army that included units from fourteen other nations. It is important to note that Truman decided to fight the war under the auspices of the UN. As a result, he did not ask Congress for a declaration of war.

## 4. TRUMAN FIRES MACARTHUR

- By the end of September 1950, MacArthur's reinforced army recaptured all of South Korea. The next month, MacArthur confidently crossed the 38th parallel in a bid to reunite the entire Korean peninsula.

- The Chinese warned that they would not "stand idly by" and allow a North Korean defeat. On November 25th China launched a devastating counterattack that caught MacArthur by surprise and drove the UN forces back into South Korea.

- Truman now decided to give up the attempt to unify Korea and instead adopted a policy of fighting a limited war to save South Korea. MacArthur publicly questioned Truman's decision saying, "We must win. There is no substitute for victory." This open act of insubordination forced Truman to remove MacArthur from all his commands. Truman's action ignited a firestorm of public outrage. However, the American public gradually came to accept MacArthur's recall as a necessary decision to protect the principle of civilian control of the military.

## 5. THE KOREAN ARMISTICE

- The Korean War continued for another two years. The prolonged stalemate was a source of mounting frustration that influenced both the rise of Senator McCarthy and the election of Dwight Eisenhower in 1952.
- The North Koreans finally signed an armistice agreement on July 27, 1953. The armistice provided for a cease-fire that left the border between the two Koreas along the 38th parallel.

## INSIDER TIP

The 2004 APUSH exam included a free-response question asking students to evaluate the successes and failures of containment in Asia, Europe, Latin America, and Middle East. See Essay 5C for an excellent analysis of containment in Asia and Europe.

# TOPIC 193
# THE COLD WAR AT HOME

## 1. A SECOND RED SCARE

- The Communist victory in China followed by the outbreak of the Korean War shocked America. Public apprehension deepened when the Soviet Union exploded its first atomic bomb thus ending America's nuclear monopoly.
- These stunning reversals heightened the public's fear that Communist agents had infiltrated the State Department and other sensitive government agencies. This apprehension did not seem unjustified. Prodded by the relentless investigation of Richard Nixon, the House Un-American Activities Committee (HUAC) discovered that a prominent State Department official named Alger Hiss had been a Soviet spy in the 1930s. Even more disquieting (unsettling), news surfaced when the government discovered that a British-American spy network had transmitted secret information about the development of the atomic bomb to the Soviet Union. This discovery led

INSIDER TIP
McCarthyism has generated a significant cluster of multiple-choice questions on both the APUSH exam and the SAT II test. Be sure you can identify the Hollywood blacklists as an example of McCarthyism. It is also interesting to note that John F. Kennedy launched his political career as a strong anticommunist.

PODCAST 39.2
McCARTHYISM

to the arrest and ultimate execution of Julius and Ethel Rosenberg for espionage.
- The Red Scare even extended to Hollywood. Motion picture executives drew up a "blacklist" of about 500 writers, directors, and actors who were suspended from work for their supposed political beliefs and associations. The popularity of movies about alien invasions from outer space also reflected the anxieties caused by the Red Scare.

## 2. THE RISE OF MCCARTHYISM

- The Hiss and Rosenberg cases touched a sensitive public nerve. The American people believed that they were locked in a life-or-death struggle with world Communism. Angry and bewildered citizens wanted to know why America appeared to be losing the Cold War.
- Joseph McCarthy, a previously obscure Senator from Wisconsin, skillfully exploited the political climate of paranoia. On February 9, 1950, McCarthy told an audience in Wheeling, West Virginia that America's foreign policy failures could be traced to Communist infiltration of the State Department. He menacingly declared, "I have in my hand a list of 205 – a list of names known to the Secretary of State as being members of the Communist Party and who nevertheless are still working and shaping policy in the State Department." In speeches given the next two days, McCarthy repeated his charges but dropped the number of names on his list to 57.
- McCarthy failed to uncover a single Communist. His practice of making unsubstantiated accusations of disloyalty without evidence became known as McCARTHYISM. Nonetheless his campaign of innuendo (indirect hints) and half-truths made him one of the most powerful and feared politicians in America.

## 3. THE FALL OF MCCARTHY

- Many of President Eisenhower's advisors urged him to use his own great prestige to confront McCarthy. But Ike refused saying, "I will not get in the gutter with that guy."
- McCarthy finally caused his own downfall in the spring of 1954 when he launched a televised investigation of the U.S. Army. A national audience of more than 20 million people watched as McCarthy bullied witnesses, twisted people's testimony, and used phony evidence. The Army-

McCarthy hearings swiftly turned public sentiment against McCarthy. In December 1954 the full Senate formally censured McCarthy for his dishonorable conduct. Flashing his famous grin, Ike asked his cabinet, "Have you heard the latest? McCarthyism is McCarthywasm."

## TOPIC 194
# LABOR RELATIONS AND RACIAL RELATIONS

### 1. THE TAFT–HARTLEY ACT

- Many economists predicted that a new depression would follow the end of World War II. Instead the economy began a new boom. During the war, Americans saved about $140 billion. Consumers were now eager to spend their savings on new homes, cars, and household appliances.
- Unfortunately, frustrated consumers soon found that the demand for goods exceeded the supply. When Congress removed the wartime wage and price controls the price of food, clothing, and fuel jumped 50 percent between 1946 and 1948.
- As prices rose labor leaders demanded higher wages. When management refused, the unions went out on strike. In 1946 there were a record 5,000 strikes, involving 4.7 million workers. For a time walkouts by coal miners and railroad workers threatened to paralyze the economy.
- Conservative Democrats and Republicans argued that the wave of strikes demonstrated that unions were abusing their power and endangering national security. In June 1947, Congress enacted the Taft-Hartley Act over President Truman's veto. The act contained a number of provisions designed to curb the power of labor unions. It authorized the federal government to issue an 80-day injunction against a strike that would endanger the "national health or safety." It also prohibited direct union contributions to political campaigns and required union leaders to file affidavits that they were not Communists. An especially controversial provision permitted states to enact right-to-work laws that made it possible for a worker to hold a job without being required to join a union.

INSIDER TIP

Don't overlook the Taft-Hartley Act. Remember that the **Wagner Act** placed restrictions on management, while the Taft-Hartley Act placed restrictions on labor unions.

## 2. CIVIL RIGHTS

- In the months before the 1946 congressional election, black leaders attempted to start a voter registration drive in the South. Ku Klux Klan members and their supporters responded by threatening and even killing African Americans who tried to exercise their rights.

- The violence outraged the black community. President Truman responded to their complaints by appointing a presidential commission to study mob violence and civil rights. In the Fall of 1947 the committee issued a report calling for a federal anti-lynching law, a civil rights division within the Justice Department, and a permanent Fair Employment Practices Committee. However, southern opposition blocked any action by Congress.

- The battle over civil rights continued at the Democratic national convention. Minneapolis mayor Hubert H. Humphrey called upon the delegates to support a civil rights plank in the party platform. He passionately declared: "The time has arrived for the Democratic Party to get out of shadow of states' rights and walk forthrightly into the bright sunshine of human rights."

- Segregationist delegates from the Deep South promptly walked out of the convention. Two weeks later they met in Birmingham, Alabama and nominated South Carolina governor Strom Thurman to head a new States' Rights or "Dixiecrat" Party. Although Truman eventually won the 1948 presidential election, the Dixiecrats carried four southern states. The election showed that lifelong southern Democrats would desert their party over the issue of segregation.

- Southern resistance continued to block civil rights action in Congress. Truman was nonetheless able to use the power of the presidency to issue an executive order ending racial segregation in the armed forces. As a result, African Americans served in integrated units in the Korean War.

# CHAPTER 40
# THE EISENHOWER YEARS, 1953 – 1960

## ESSENTIAL POINTS

1. Unprecedented prosperity, rapid suburbanization, a population explosion known as the baby boom, and the return of the cult of domesticity all characterized the 1950s.

2. The Federal Highway Act of 1956 appropriated $25 billion to construct a 40,000-mile system of interstate highways. The new interstates played a key role in promoting the growth of suburbs outside large cities.

3. Social commentators, **BEAT GENERATION** writers, Abstract Expressionist artists, and even rock and roll singers all protested the excessive materialism and conformity in American life.

4. The Supreme Court case of *Brown v. Board of Education of Topeka* used the Equal Protection Clause of the Fourteenth Amendment to reverse the "separate but equal" doctrine established in *Plessy v. Ferguson*.

5. Dr. King advocated the use of nonviolent civil disobedience to achieve his goal of opposing unjust segregation laws. The lunch counter sit-ins were a grass-roots student protest that put Dr. King's ideas into concrete practice.

6. The fear of nuclear war combined with the Eisenhower administration's policies of massive retaliation and brinksmanship created a widespread sense of public unease.

7. Sputnik challenged America's long-standing sense of scientific and technological superiority. Congress responded to the Sputnik challenge by creating NASA and by funding science and math programs in the nation's public schools and colleges.

# TOPIC 195
# KEY ECONOMIC AND SOCIAL TRENDS

## 1. UNPRECEDENTED PROSPERITY

- During the 1950s Americans enjoyed a period of unprecedented prosperity. The gross national product soared from $200 billion in 1945 to $500 billion in 1960. With just 6 percent of the world's population, Americans drove 75 percent of the world's automobiles, consumed half of its energy, and produced almost half of its manufactured products.
- Several factors combined to produce this remarkable economic boom. Cold War defense spending represented the single most important catalyst. America's commitment to contain Communism in Europe and fight the Korean War in Asia pushed the defense budget from 13 billion in 1949 to over 50 billion in 1953. At the same time, World War II rationing created a pent-up consumer demand for cars, appliances, and most of all new homes in the suburbs.

## 2. SUBURBANIZATION

- Robust economic growth sparked a strong demand for new homes. William Levitt successfully applied assembly-line production techniques learned in the automobile and shipping industries to building homes. Levitt's affordable mass-produced homes provided a model for builders across the country.
- Of the 13 million new homes constructed in the 1950s, 11 million sprung up in the suburbs. The G.I. Bill enabled veterans to buy new homes with little or no down payments and then make modest monthly payments for 20 to 30 years.
- A system of new highways also promoted suburban growth. The Federal Highway Act of 1956 appropriated $25 billion for a ten-year project to construct a 40,000-mile system of four lane interstate highways. The new interstates accelerated suburbanization by enabling people to work in the cities and commute to their homes in the suburbs.

## 3. THE BABY BOOM

- The nation's thriving economy provided jobs and incomes that renewed people's faith in the future. More and more Americans married at an ever younger age. By 1956 the average age of marriage for men dropped to 22 and just 20 for women.
- The marriage boom triggered a postwar baby boom. The 1950s witnessed 40 million births. They were part of a huge baby boom generation that included 76 million people born from 1946 to 1964.

## 4. THE NEW CULT OF DOMESTICITY

- By 1960 nearly three-fourths of all women between the ages of 20 and 24 were married. The soaring marriage and birth rates encouraged a return to traditional gender roles in which men were breadwinners and women were housewives.
- The mass media reinforced and idealized the new cult of domesticity. In the popular TV show *Leave It to Beaver*, June Cleaver is a middle-class housewife who is dedicated to her family. When her two boys arrive home from school, June is usually preparing dinner in her immaculate (spotless) kitchen. A special issue of *Life* magazine featured "ideal" suburban housewives who, like June Cleaver, were dedicated to their husbands and children and yet still found time to attend PTA meetings.

## 5. CONSUMERISM

- The spreading affluence (prosperity) promoted a zeal for consumerism. Shopping became a major recreational activity as suburban families drove to the new shopping centers mushrooming across the country.
- Nothing seemed to occupy more leisure time than television. In 1946 there were just 7,000 TV sets and 6 TV stations in the entire country. By 1953 half of all homes had a TV set. Many people rescheduled social engagements so they could be home to watch such favorite shows as *The Honeymooners*, *Father Knows Best*, and *I Love Lucy*. On January 19, 1953, a record audience turned on over 70 percent of America's television sets to watch an episode featuring the birth of Lucy's baby.

INSIDER TIP

Test writers expect you to know what characterized the Eisenhower years and also what did not characterize this period. For example, Eisenhower did not dismantle New Deal welfare programs, students did not protest the nuclear arms race, and women did not complete college before getting married.

**TOPIC 196**
# SOCIAL CRITICS AND NONCONFORMISTS

## 1. SOCIAL CRITICS
- The new suburban lifestyle did not enjoy unanimous approval. Social critics decried (denounced) mass-produced Levittowns filled with endless rows of identical box houses. To these critics the suburbs created a superficial (shallow) lifestyle and a generation of spoiled children.
- Influential social commentators extended their criticism to the large corporations where many suburbanites worked. In 1960, 38 percent of the nation's workforce was employed by organizations with more than 500 employees. In his book *The Organization Man*, William H. Whyte described how the corporate emphasis upon "the Team" created stifling conformity that squelched personal identity. Harvard sociologist Daniel Riesman also studied alienation and conformity in large corporations. In his bestselling book *The Lonely Crowd*, Riesman argued that the corporate culture produced other-directed employees who prized getting along above taking individual risks.
- Criticism of the suburban lifestyle was not limited to sociologists. Novelists also joined the chorus of critics who found cracks in the suburban picture windows. For example, Sloan Wilson's novel *The Man in the Gray Flannel Suit* tells the story of a young couple, Tom and Betsy Rath, who struggle against the pervasive (spread everywhere) pressures of middle-class conformity. The book's title comes from Tom's sudden realization that "all I could see was a lot of bright young men in gray flannel suits rushing around New York in a frantic parade to nowhere." Tom then looks at himself and is aghast (horrified) to discover that he too is wearing a gray flannel suit.

## 2. THE BEAT GENERATION
- A small but culturally influential group of self-described "beats" also rejected middle America's carefree consumption and mindless conformity. The beats congregated in San Francisco and New York's Greenwich

Village. These urban enclaves enabled them to avoid the "square" world. Beats often met in small bookshops where they listened to jazz, discussed Buddhist philosophy, and read works by popular Beat Generation poets.

- Jack Kerouac was the best-known Beat Generation author. His autobiographical novel *On the Road* describes the eclectic (varied) mix of people he met on spontaneous road trips across America.

### 3. ARTISTIC REBELS

- Edward Hopper continued to paint in the realistic tradition. His paintings capture the loneliness and alienation of American life. For an excellent example see *Office in a Small City*.
- Jackson Pollock refused to portray specific subject matter. Instead he created Abstract Expressionist paintings by spontaneously dripping oil on a canvas spread across the floor. For an excellent example see *Autumn Rhythm*.

### 4. ROCK AND ROLL

- Relatively few Americans read Beat Generation poems or visited trendy art galleries to see Abstract Expressionist paintings. However, most Americans did listen to music on their radios. The pop sound that dominated the early 1950s was typically emotionless, cute, and bland. For example, in one hit song a perky Patti Page hopefully asked, "How much is that doggy in the window?"
- While white Americans listened to pop music, black musicians combined gospel, blues, and jazz into a new sound called rhythm and blues. Within a short time an increasing number of young white music fans began to buy rhythm and blues records and attend concerts by black performers. A Cleveland disc jockey named Alan Freed renamed the new sound "rock and roll."
- In the Spring of 1953 a poor truck driver dropped into Sun Records in Memphis and politely introduced himself: "My name is Elvis Presley and I want to make a record." The head of the studio, Sam Philips, soon realized that Elvis was "a white man who had the Negro sound and the Negro feel." Elvis soon became the best-selling recording artist in America. His songs and sexually suggestive onstage gyrations thrilled teenagers and horrified their parents.

## INSIDER TIP

The 2006 APUSH exam included a free-response question asking students to discuss how intellectuals and youth protested the consensus and conformity of the 1950s. Be sure that you can identify David Riesman and William H. Whyte. In addition, do not neglect Sloan Wilson's novel *The Man in the Gray Flannel Suit* and Jack Kerouac's novel *On the Road*.

- In the beginning, rock and roll was the music of teenagers who bought 70 percent of all released albums. Rock and roll proved to be more than just a passing fad. Like Beat Generation writers, rock and roll singers challenged accepted beliefs about sex, race, and work. Rock and roll soon became the sound that helped shape and define the new teenage culture.

## TOPIC 197
# *BROWN v. BOARD OF EDUCATION OF TOPEKA*

### 1. WHAT HAPPENED?
- When the 1953 – 54 school year opened, 2.5 million African American children attended all-black schools in 17 Southern states and the District of Columbia. The black schools were separate from the schools white students attended, but their facilities were far from being equal. In 1954 the South spend an average of $165.00 for its white students and $115.00 for its black students.
- Since its founding in 1909 the National Association for the Advancement of Colored People (NAACP) had adopted the strategy of filing legal cases to gain justice and civil rights for African Americans. Led by Thurgood Marshall, the NAACP legal team chose five test cases to challenge state laws mandating segregation in the public schools. The famous *Brown* case took its name from the first name on the list – Oliver Brown of Topeka, Kansas.  Brown wanted his eight-year-old daughter, Linda, to attend a nearby all-white elementary school instead of traveling 25 blocks to a black elementary school.
- Thurgood Marshall argued that the segregated schools in Topeka were unconstitutional because they denied black children the "equal protection of the laws" guaranteed by the Fourteenth Amendment. Led by Chief Justice Earl Warren the Supreme Court agreed with Marshall. In a unanimous decision, the Court reversed the long-standing "separate but equal" doctrine of *Plessey v. Ferguson*.

## 2. WHY DID THE SUPREME COURT REVERSE *PLESSY V. FERGUSON*?

- Thurgood Marshall argued that separate schools were inherently unconstitutional because they unjustly stigmatized (branded) all black children. He insisted that the system of racially segregated schools perpetuated inferior treatment for black Americans.

- Chief Justice Earl Warren agreed with Marshall's contention that the doctrine of "separate but equal" should be struck down. He also believed that the Equal Protection Clause of the Fourteenth Amendment gave the Court the necessary authority to reverse *Plessy v. Ferguson*.

- Speaking for a unanimous Court, Warren declared that, "We conclude that in the field of public education, the doctrine of separate but equal has no place. Separate educational facilities are inherently unequal."

## 3. WHY SHOULD YOU REMEMBER *BROWN v. BOARD OF EDUCATION OF TOPEKA*?

- The *Brown* decision opened a new era in the African American struggle for equal rights. The Court's landmark ruling awakened the nation's more than 15 million black citizens to begin demanding "Freedom Now!"

- One year after issuing the *Brown* decision, the Supreme Court unanimously directed the states to desegregate their public schools "with all deliberate speed." Outraged Southern leaders responded by calling for "massive resistance" to the Court's decision. In Congress, 82 representatives and 19 senators signed a Southern Manifesto that accused the Supreme Court of "a clear abuse of judicial power."

- President Eisenhower did not use his enormous personal prestige to morally support the civil rights movement. Ike privately believed that, "You cannot change people's hearts merely by laws."

- Massive resistance became a reality in Little Rock, Arkansas. The local school board adopted a desegregation plan that called for nine black students to integrate Little Rock's Central High School when classes began on September 3, 1957. The crisis began when over 1,000 whites attacked blacks and sympathetic whites outside the school. The 150 city policemen failed to protect the nine black students

PODCAST 40.1
*BROWN v. BOARD OF EDUCATION OF TOPEKA*

INSIDER TIP
The *Brown* decision has generated a very large cluster of multiple-choice questions. While almost all APUSH students are familiar with this landmark case many overlook Eisenhower's role in enforcing the Court's decision. It is important to note that Ike was not a strong supporter of the civil rights movement. Nonetheless he did take vigorous action by sending federal troops to Little Rock.

from the howling mob. This display of resistance forced President Eisenhower to act. The next day he sent 1,100 paratroopers to Little Rock to protect the black students and enforce the desegregation order. Ike explained his action by stating that, "The very basis of our individual rights and freedoms rests upon the certainty that the President and the Executive Branch of Government will support and insure the carrying out of the decisions of the federal courts, even, when necessary, with all the measures at the President's command."

## TOPIC 198:
# DR. KING AND THE BEGINNING OF THE CIVIL RIGHTS MOVEMENT

## 1. THE MONTGOMERY BUS BOYCOTT
- On December 1, 1955 a white Montgomery City Lines bus driver ordered Rosa Parks to give up her seat to a white passenger. Rosa Parks was a 42-year-old black seamstress who was a respected member of the local black community. Even though she was tired from a long day at work, Parks was also tired of enduring the injustices of racial segregation. As the driver impatiently waited for an answer, Rosa Parks did the unexpected. She refused the driver's order by saying just one word, "No." The bus driver promptly called the police who arrested Parks and fined her $10.00.
- Rosa Parks' refusal to give up her seat sparked the Montgomery Bus Boycott. Led by her young minister, the 26-year-old Dr. Martin Luther King, Jr., the black community supported Parks by boycotting the Montgomery buses. The boycott worked. Fifteen months later the U.S. Supreme Court upheld a lower court ruling that bus segregation was unconstitutional.

## 2. DR. KING AND NONVIOLENT CIVIL DISOBEDIENCE
- The Montgomery Bus Boycott catapulted Dr. King into America's most recognized and influential African American leader. Dr. King inspired his followers with a message of nonviolent civil disobedience derived from

the writings of Henry David Thoreau and the actions of Mahatma Gandhi in India. Dr. King energized the Montgomery boycotters by reminding them that they stood for truth and righteousness. "The strong man," Dr. King insisted, "is the man who can stand up for his rights and not hit back."

- Following the success of the Montgomery Bus Boycott, Dr. King founded the Southern Christian Leadership Conference (SCLC). Under his leadership, the SCLC sought to apply the principles of nonviolent civil disobedience to other Southern cities.

## 3. THE SIT–IN MOVEMENT

- In 1960, lunch counters throughout the South remained segregated. Dr. King's philosophy of nonviolent civil disobedience inspired four black college students in Greensboro, North Carolina to take action. Calling segregation, "evil pure and simple," the Greensboro Four sat down at a "whites-only" Woolworth lunch counter and ordered coffee and apple pie. Although the waitress refused to serve them, the students did not vacillate (waver). They returned the next day with more black student protesters. Within six months the Greensboro Woolworth desegregated its lunch counter.

- The sit-in movement begun by the Greensboro Four galvanized (energized) activists throughout the South. Later that year, black and white students formed the Student Nonviolent Coordinating Committee (SNCC) to work with Dr. King's SCLC. Soon a wave of student protesters held "read-ins" at libraries, "watch-ins" at movie theaters, and "swim-ins" at pools and beaches. Although they were taunted by segregationists, the black and white activists demonstrated courage and conviction as they remained true to Dr. King's principles of nonviolent protest.

## INSIDER TIP

Test writers recognize that students can identify Rosa Parks and Dr. King. As a result, many tests now include a question on the lesser known but still very important sit-in movement.

## PODCAST 40.2

DR. KING AND NONVIOLENT CIVIL DISOBEDIENCE

## TOPIC 199
# THE COLD WAR AND SPUTNIK

### 1. "A MULTIPLICITY OF FEARS"

- On the surface a majority of Americans seemed to enjoy a good life in the mid-1950s. The country liked Ike because his administration brought a material prosperity unequalled in memory. And of course everyone loved Lucy because the TV star's zany antics brought a weekly dose of comic relief.

- The surface appearance of calm belied (misrepresented) the reality of an underlying sense of anxiety and even fear. In a press conference in 1954 President Eisenhower noted that Americans were "suffering from a multiplicity of fears." The President was right. The fear of international Communism, the fear of domestic subversion, and most of all the fear of nuclear annihilation all produced a deep sense of anxiety.

### 2. "THE BALANCE OF TERROR" AND MASSIVE RETALIATION

- The fear of nuclear war was not imaginary. By 1954 both the United States and the Soviet Union had exploded hydrogen bombs. What Winston Churchill called a "balance of terror" seemed real. Popular magazines warned that in the new missile age Americans would have at most 35 minutes warning before a Soviet missile attack hit the United States. Millions of public school students hid under their desks as part of Duck and Cover drills. Adults could dash into newly built fallout shelters located in many public buildings. Worried homeowners added an extra layer of security by building bomb shelters in their basements.

- President Eisenhower and his Secretary of State John Foster Dulles added to public anxiety by announcing a "New Look" defense policy. The United States would no longer become involved in expensive limited wars. Instead, Dulles announced a new strategy called MASSIVE RETALIATION. This meant that the United States would consider using its nuclear weapons to halt Communist aggression. To threaten the use of using nuclear weapons would require nerves of steel. "If you are scared to go to the brink," Dulles warned, "you are lost." Journalists soon called this policy of going to the brink of nuclear war without going over the edge BRINKSMANSHIP.

## 3. BEEP, BEEP, BEEP

- While anxious Americans prepared for the worst, the Soviets appeared surprisingly confident. In Moscow, Soviet Premier Nikita Khrushchev told visiting British and French officials that, "Whether or not you like it, history is on our side."

- Khrushchev's boast seemed to come true on October 4, 1957. That night millions of Americans turned on their television sets and heard a newscaster tell them, "Listen now for the sound which forever separates the old from the new." The beeping sound they heard came from a 184 pound satellite called Sputnik which the Russians shot into orbit earlier that day.

## 4. THE IMPACT OF SPUTNIK

- Sputnik jolted America's self-confidence. A stunned public concluded that the Russians had overcome America's scientific and technological lead. *Time* magazine grimly warned that Sputnik" posed the United States with the most dramatic military threat it has ever faced."

- Congress took vigorous actions to respond to the Sputnik crisis. In July 1958 Congress created the National Aeronautics and Space Administration (NASA) to compete with the Soviet space program. Within a year, NASA named seven men America's first astronauts. Congress also passed the National Defense Education Act to fund enriched science and math programs in the nation's public schools and colleges.

## INSIDER TIP

Many APUSH prep books contain lengthy discussions on **unrest in Iran**, the **Hungarian revolt**, and the **Eisenhower Doctrine**. We don't! You can safely **skip** these topics and focus on **Cold War domestic fears** and the **Sputnik crisis.**

NAFTA

Cuban Missle
 Blockade w/ Naval & Air

**CHAPTER 41**

# THE NEW FRONTIER, GREAT SOCIETY, AND VIETNAM WAR, 1961 – 1968

## ESSENTIAL POINTS

1. The Bay of Pigs invasion was an unsuccessful attempt to overthrow Fidel Castro. Its failure damaged Kennedy's international credibility and led the Soviet Union to send nuclear missiles to Cuba.

2. The Birmingham demonstrations prompted President Kennedy to call Congress to pass a sweeping civil rights bill. The March on Washington was organized to mobilize public support for the bill.

3. Both the Great Society and the New Deal used the federal government to promote social welfare and solve social problems. Both programs led to an increase in federal spending for social services.

4. Unlike the New Deal, the Great Society included landmark legislation to protect the civil liberties and voting rights of African Americans.

5. America's involvement in Vietnam grew out of the Cold War policy of containment and the **DOMINO THEORY**'s assumption that the fall of one country to Communism would inevitably topple nearby countries.

6. Congress approved the Gulf of Tonkin Resolution based upon an alleged attack on U.S. warships by North Vietnamese gunboats. The Gulf of Tonkin Resolution gave President Johnson a blank check to escalate the U.S. war effort in Vietnam.

7. The Vietnam War raised social tensions by dividing America into **HAWKS** that supported the war and **DOVES** who opposed it. The **COUNTERCULTURE** contributed to culture wars that have played a role in U.S. politics for nearly four decades.

8. The Tet Offensive marked a significant turning point in the Vietnam War. It undermined public support for the war and played a key role in President Johnson's decision not to seek re-election.

# TOPIC 200
# JFK AND THE COLD WAR

## ☆ 1. THE 1960 ELECTION

- As expected, the Republicans nominated Vice-President Richard Nixon. The veteran politician quickly became the front-runner as he promised to continue Ike's popular policies.

- The Democrats countered by nominating Senator John F. Kennedy of Massachusetts. Kennedy was young, handsome, and a Roman Catholic. At age 43, his youth suggested inexperience. If Kennedy won, he would become the youngest person ever elected President. In addition, many worried that voters would reject him because of his religion.

- Kennedy forcefully dealt with the religious issue in a speech to a group of Protestant ministers in Houston. He firmly rejected the belief that a Catholic President would have divided loyalties between America and Rome. "I am not the Catholic candidate for President," Kennedy reminded his audience. "I am the Democratic Party's candidate for President who happens also to be a Catholic."

- Kennedy dispelled lingering doubts about his age during a first-ever series of nationally televised presidential debates. While Nixon appeared tense and tired, Kennedy radiated confidence and poise. He impressed viewers with his crisp fact-filled answers and inspiring pledge to lead America into a "New Frontier."

- Kennedy narrowly defeated Nixon by a razor-thin popular margin of 116,000 votes. "The margin is narrow," Kennedy admitted, "but the responsibility is clear."

*[handwritten: Kennedy wins "New Frontier" views]*

## 2. CAMELOT

- Kennedy became President on an inauguration day filled with high excitement and drama. Millions of television viewers watched as Dwight Eisenhower, then the oldest man ever to serve as President, sat beside the first President born in the twentieth century. As a brilliant January sun sparkled on a layer of newly fallen snow, the new President proudly announced that "the torch has passed to a new generation of Americans."

- The vigorous President and his glamorous wife and young children fascinated the American public. The First Family's youthful charm seemed like a fairy tale come to life. A popular musical at that time portrayed the romance and adventure of King Arthur's court at Camelot. Kennedy and his dedicated band of advisors reminded many of a modern day Camelot. The nation waited with high expectations as Kennedy began the difficult task of transforming his campaign promises into concrete realities.

## 3. THE PEACE CORPS AND THE ALLIANCE FOR PROGRESS

- In March 1961, Kennedy announced two new programs to help the developing nations in Africa, Asia, and Latin America. In a special message to Congress, he recommended the creation of a Peace Corps to train volunteers to live and work for two to three years in a developing nation. Thousands of Americans volunteered to help battle hunger, disease, and illiteracy by working as agricultural agents, nurses, and teachers. Their good will and hard work made the Peace Corps a symbol of American idealism and generosity.
- President Kennedy also expressed particular concern for Latin America. Widespread poverty, a soaring birth rate, and high illiteracy threatened the stability of this region. Kennedy called upon the nations of Latin America to join the United States in an Alliance for Progress. The U.S. pledged to contribute $10 billion over ten years to help construct new houses and hospitals and increase agricultural productivity. Like the Marshall Plan, the Alliance for Progress used America's economic strength to build prosperity and thus thwart Communist expansion.

## 4. THE BAY OF PIGS INVASION

- In the late 1950s, Fidel Castro led a popular revolution that overthrew Cuba's corrupt dictator Fulgencio Batista. The United States at first welcomed Castro's victory and believed his promise to turn Cuba into a democratic nation. But these hopes quickly faded when Castro seized dictatorial powers and established close ties with the Soviet Union.
- Many Cubans who had supported Castro felt betrayed. Thousands became exiles and fled to the United States.

When he became President, Kennedy learned that the CIA had been secretly training a small army of Cuban exiles. The plan called for them to invade Cuba at the Bay of Pigs on the island's southern coast. The armed exiles would then set off a popular uprising that would lead to the overthrow of the Cuban government. Despite having serious doubts, Kennedy allowed the invasion to take place on April 17, 1961.

- The dream of overthrowing Castro turned into a nightmare. A Cuban army of 20,000 men supported by tanks attacked and surrounded the exiles. Despite heroic resistance, the outnumbered exiles were forced into surrender.

- The Bay of Pigs fiasco (disaster) handed Kennedy an embarrassing defeat that damaged his international credibility. Nonetheless, the President took full responsibility for the failure. Although Kennedy warned that he would resist any further Communist expansion in the Western Hemisphere, Castro defiantly welcomed additional Soviet aid.

## 5. THE CUBAN MISSILE CRISIS

- Khrushchev ignored Kennedy's warning to temper his aid to Castro. In a daring gamble, the Soviet leader secretly allowed Russian technicians to build 42 missile sites in Cuba. Each missile carried a nuclear warhead 20 to 30 times more powerful than the bomb that destroyed Hiroshima. Furthermore, the missiles could reach American cities up to 2,000 miles away in less than five minutes.

- High-flying U-2 spy planes discovered the missile sites on October 14, 1962. After careful deliberation, Kennedy announced a "quarantine" or blockade of Cuba to prevent the arrival of new missiles. If the Soviets refused to remove the missiles already in Cuba, the United States would launch a massive invasion force to destroy them.

- For the next week the world faced the terrifying possibility of a nuclear war. After tense negotiations, Khrushchev agreed to remove the missiles in return for an American pledge not to invade Cuba.

## INSIDER TIP

Both the Bay of Pigs invasion and the Cuban Missile Crisis have generated a significant number of multiple-choice questions. It is interesting to note that the Bay of Pigs invasion is regularly featured on SAT II tests while the Cuban Missile Crisis is regularly featured on APUSH exams.

# TOPIC 201
# "WE SHALL OVERCOME"

## ⭐1. THE FREEDOM RIDERS

- Young black and white activists continued to press for a faster pace of desegregation. In May 1961, the Congress of Racial Equality (CORE) sent an integrated group of thirteen "freedom riders" on a bus trip scheduled to begin in Washington, D.C. and end in New Orleans. They hoped to find out if a 1960 Supreme Court decision outlawing segregation in bus stations was being obeyed. They quickly learned that it wasn't. A mob of angry whites attacked the freedom riders in Anniston, Montgomery, and Birmingham, Alabama.

- Violence did not stop the freedom riders. By the end of 1961, Attorney General Robert Kennedy convinced the Interstate Commerce Commission to issue an order banning segregation in interstate bus terminals. The freedom riders thus proved that direct action would work. Across the country, more and more blacks marched against segregation as they sang the civil rights anthem, "We shall overcome."

*CORE*
*Congress of Racial Equality*

## 2. BIRMINGHAM

- The focus of the civil rights struggle now shifted to Birmingham, Alabama where Dr. King planned to lead a massive demonstration to protest segregation. At that time, Birmingham was the largest segregated city in the United States. "If we could break through the barriers in Birmingham," Dr. King predicted, "all the South would go the same way."

- The Birmingham demonstrations began in April 1963. The city Commissioner of Public Safety Eugene "Bull" Connor promptly arrested over 3,000 demonstrators including Dr. King. While in jail, Dr. King wrote his famous "Letter from Birmingham City Jail" in which he defended civil disobedience as a justified response to unjust segregation laws. Dr. King insisted that African Americans would no longer endure "the stinging darts of segregation." He called upon white clergymen to join him in being "extremists for the cause of justice."

- Bull Connor did not read Dr. King's letter. On May 3rd his men used clubs, snarling police attack dogs, and high-pressure fire hoses to disperse a peaceful demonstration. Although the fire hoses knocked demonstrators to the ground, they did not wash away their dignity. Connor's strategy backfired when outraged Americans watched news broadcasts of what one journalist called, "a visual demonstration of sin, vivid enough to rouse the conscience of the entire nation."

## 3. PRESIDENT KENNEDY CALLS FOR A STRONG CIVIL RIGHTS BILL

- The public outrage forced President Kennedy to act. In a televised address on June 11, 1963, he forcefully argued for racial justice: "We are confronted primarily with a moral issue … The heart of the question is whether all Americans are to be afforded equal rights and equal opportunities, whether we are going to treat our fellow Americans as we want to be treated."
- Kennedy's speech marked a major turning point in the civil rights movement. Eight days later, the President called upon Congress to pass a sweeping civil rights bill that would prohibit segregation in public places, speed up school integration, and ban discrimination in hiring practices.

## 4. THE MARCH ON WASHINGTON

- Dr. King recognized the importance of building a nationwide alliance or "coalition of conscience" to support President Kennedy's civil rights bill. Dr. King and other black leaders called for a massive March on Washington to demonstrate public support for the bill.
- The public responded to the call in record numbers. As the nation watched on television, over 200,000 black and white marchers staged what was the largest civil rights demonstration in American history. The unified marchers sang "We shall overcome" and repeatedly chanted "Pass the bill!"
- The climax of the day came when Dr. King addressed the crowd. His famous "I Have a Dream" speech left an indelible (can't be erased) memory on everyone who heard it. Dr. King articulated the hopes and dreams of both black and white Americans. The speech increased

public support for Kennedy's civil rights bill. It did not, however, guarantee that Congress would quickly pass the bill. Strong opposition from Southern conservatives insured a long and difficult struggle.

## 5. FOUR DAYS IN NOVEMBER

- In the fall of 1963, President Kennedy appeared to be fulfilling his promise as a leader. He met the Soviet challenge in Cuba and launched a moral and legislative attack on segregation. About 60 percent of the public approved his performance. But history can sometimes be unpredictable. No one foresaw the terrible national tragedy that lay just ahead.
- An assassin shot and killed President Kennedy on November 22, 1963 in Dallas, Texas. The tragic news flashed instantly across the nation and then around the world. Television became what one reporter called "the window on the world." Shocked viewers saw a somber Vice-President Lyndon Johnson take the oath of office on the Presidential plane as a grief-stricken Jacqueline Kennedy stood by his side.
- On Monday November 25th all work stopped as America mourned its fallen President. Mrs. Kennedy ended the ceremony by lighting an eternal flame over the President's grave.

## INSIDER TIP

It is important to remember that Dr. King's nonviolent philosophy was inspired by Thoreau's essay "On Civil Disobedience" and Gandhi's campaign of demonstrations in India.

# TOPIC 202
# THE GREAT SOCIETY

## 1. THE 1964 CIVIL RIGHTS ACT

- President Johnson plunged into his presidential duties in the dark days following the tragedy in Dallas. Johnson understood that civil rights was the nation's most urgent social problem.
- President Johnson proudly signed the 1964 Civil Rights Act into law on July 2, 1964. The new act was the most important civil rights law since Reconstruction. It barred discrimination in public facilities such as hotels, restaurants, and theatres. It authorized the attorney general to bring suits to speed school desegregation. In addition, the act outlawed discrimination in employment on the basis of

*stopped discrimination*

race, religion, national origin, or sex. It is important to note that women's groups would use the clause barring discrimination based on sex to secure government support for greater equality in education and employment.

- President Johnson and civil rights leaders now turned to the issue of voting rights. The Fifteenth Amendment gave black males the right to vote. However, a combination of literacy tests and poll taxes effectively nullified the amendment. The Voting Rights Act of 1965 made the Fifteenth Amendment an operative part of the Constitution. The law ended literacy tests and other devices used to prevent blacks from voting. At the same time, the Twenty-fourth Amendment outlawed the poll tax in federal elections. Taken together, the Voting Rights Act and the Twenty-fourth Amendment allowed millions of blacks to register and vote for the first time.

## 2. THE WAR ON POVERTY

*Education*

- The passage of the Voting Rights Act marked a climatic moment in the civil rights movement. President Johnson believed that his landslide victory in the 1964 election gave him a mandate to pursue his dream of creating a Great Society that would end poverty and create educational opportunities for all Americans.

- America's great affluence (prosperity) masked the continuing existence of poverty. In a widely read book entitled *The Other America*, the social critic Michael Harrington argued that about one-fifth of the nation's families were mired (stuck) in a "culture of poverty." Shocked by this jarring fact, LBJ declared an "unconditional War on Poverty."

*Programs for poverty to get educated and a job*

- Congress passed a host of new federal programs to help the poor. High school dropouts learned new skills in over 50 Job Corps camps. Half-a-million pre-school children attended special Head Start programs to help prepare them for school. In Appalachian communities stretching from Pennsylvania to northern Georgia unemployed workers built highways and new health centers. Although many criticized the War on Poverty for waste, it gave hope to millions and helped reduce the number of poor by nearly 10 million people from 1964 to 1967.

## 3. LANDMARK LEGISLATION

- The Great Society included significant legislation designed to improve the quality of American education. The Elementary and Secondary Education Act of 1965 provided over one billion dollars in federal aid to help school systems purchase textbooks and new library materials. The National Endowment for the Arts and Humanities provided federal funding and support for artists and scholars.
- The Great Society included far-reaching health care legislation. The Social Security Amendments of 1965 created Medicare and Medicaid. These programs established government health insurance coverage for elderly and poor Americans.
- The Immigration Act of 1965 abolished the system of national quotas instituted in the National Origins Act of 1924. Although it was not recognized at the time, the new law had the unintended consequence of permitting a new wave of immigration from Latin America and Asia.

## INSIDER TIP

A number of multiple-choice questions ask students to identify a program that was NOT part of the Great Society. The Great Society did NOT establish the Peace Corps, create Social Security, guarantee employment, or place new restrictions on immigration.

## 4. A COMPARISON OF THE GREAT SOCIETY AND THE NEW DEAL

- Both the Great Society and the New Deal used the federal government to promote social welfare, fight poverty, and solve social problems. Both programs led to an increase in federal spending for social services. And finally, both the Great Society and the New Deal supported the arts, encouraged housing construction, helped the elderly, and instituted government-sponsored employment programs.
- Unlike the New Deal, the Great Society created a program to provide preschool education for disadvantaged children. It is very important to note that unlike the New Deal, the Great Society included significant legislation to protect the civil liberties and voting rights of African Americans.

## 5. THE SUPREME COURT AND REFORM

- Led by Chief Justice Earl Warren, the Supreme Court continued to issue landmark decisions that promoted significant political and legal changes.
- As America became more urbanized the population shifted from rural areas to cities. However, rural counties

## PODCAST 41.1
**THE GREAT SOCIETY**

continued to be over-represented in state legislatures while urban counties were greatly under-represented. As a result, in all but six states, less than forty percent of the population could elect a majority of the state legislature. In *Baker v. Carr* the Court ordered state legislatures to create legislative districts with roughly equal populations. The Court later extended this "one man, one vote" rule to congressional districts.

- The Supreme Court also handed down a series of controversial decisions that defined the rights of accused criminals. In *Gideon v. Wainwright* the Court ruled that states are constitutionally required to provide counsel for indigent defendants. In *Miranda v. Arizona*, the Court ruled that persons apprehended by the police must be advised of their constitutional rights to remain silent and to have legal counsel at public expense. If the police do not read these "Miranda rights" to an accused person, his or her testimony would be inadmissible in state or federal courts.

## TOPIC 203
# THE VIETNAM WAR, 1954 – 1968

## 1. FRANCE AND VIETNAM

- In 1954 most Americans knew very little about Vietnam. Yet, events were taking place in this remote Asian country that would transform both it and America.

- During the late 1800s, France conquered first Vietnam and then all of Indochina. By the 1930s, Vietnam produced all of France's raw rubber and much of its imported rice.

- The Nazi occupation of France in 1940 enabled the Japanese to seize control of French Indochina. Following the Japanese defeat in World War II, Communist forces led by Ho Chi Minh declared Vietnam an independent country. The French, however, refused to accept the loss of their valuable colony. They soon become entangled in a costly war with Ho's guerrilla forces.

- In 1954, the French suffered a disastrous defeat at the Battle of Dien Bien Phu. The exhausted French and the victorious Vietnamese reached an agreement known as the Geneva Accords. Both sides agreed to divide Vietnam

*Geneva Accords split Vietnam

at the 17th parallel. Ho Chi Minh and his Communist government would rule north of the parallel, while a French-backed government would rule south of it. A final agreement specified that free elections would be held in 1956 to unify Vietnam under one government.

## 2. EISENHOWER AND THE DOMINO THEORY

- The French defeat forced President Eisenhower to make a fateful decision. Eisenhower refused to abandon Vietnam to the Communists. At a news conference he explained that, "When you have a row of dominoes set up, you knock over the first one, and what will happen to the last one is the certainty that it will go over very quickly." Ike's message was clear. The United States could not allow Ho Chi Minh to take over South Vietnam. The fall of South Vietnam would inevitably lead to Communist expansion throughout the rest of Southeast Asia. This belief was soon called the DOMINO THEORY.

- The election called for in the Geneva Accords never took place. Instead, the United States sponsored a new government in South Vietnam headed by Ngo Dinh Diem. Within a short time, South Vietnamese Communists called Viet Cong began to fight a guerrilla war to overthrow Diem.

## 3. KENNEDY AND VIETNAM

- During his Inaugural Address, President Kennedy pledged that the United States would "pay any price, bear any burden, meet any hardship ... to assure the survival and the success of liberty." At the time that he made this pledge there were about 900 American military advisors in South Vietnam. No advisor had yet died in combat.

- The Vietnam War presented Kennedy with a difficult problem. The Viet Cong continued to spread terror across much of South Vietnam thus threatening the stability of the Diem government. Afraid of either negotiating a settlement or committing American combat troops, Kennedy cautiously chose to follow a middle path. In late 1961 he ordered a substantial increase in economic and military aid to Diem. At the time of Kennedy's death, over 16,000 American advisors helped train the South Vietnamese army.

## INSIDER TIP

The Gulf of Tonkin Resolution has generated a significant number of multiple-choice questions. Be sure you know that President Johnson used an alleged report of North Vietnamese aggression to gain sweeping congressional authority for military action.

## PODCAST 41.2
THE GULF OF TONKIN RESOLUTION

## 4. JOHNSON AND THE GULF OF TONKIN RESOLUTION

- President Johnson inherited a dangerous situation in South Vietnam. In late 1963 a group of generals overthrew and killed Diem. At the same time, bombings by Viet Cong terrorists became an almost daily occurrence. Sensing that South Vietnam was on the verge of collapse, the North Vietnamese sent more aid to reinforce the Viet Cong.
- President Johnson was determined to meet the Communist challenge. On August 4, 1964 he received unsubstantiated reports that North Vietnamese gunboats fired on two American destroyers patrolling the Gulf of Tonkin. The next day, Johnson asked Congress to pass a resolution authorizing him to take "all necessary measures to repel any armed attack against the forces of the United States and to prevent further aggression." The House unanimously supported the resolution while only two Senators opposed it. The Gulf of Tonkin Resolution gave President Johnson a blank check to escalate the American war effort in Vietnam.

## 5. JOHNSON AND ESCALATION

- The situation in South Vietnam continued to worsen. In March 1965, President Johnson took the fateful step of ordering a massive escalation of U.S. forces in Vietnam.
- When he realized that North Vietnam could not be quickly defeated, Johnson poured additional men and money into the war effort. The air war soon became more destructive than anyone had expected. Huge B-52 bombers dropped more tons of bombs on North and South Vietnam than had been used in all of World War II.
- As the air war escalated, the ground war became even more violent. By the end of 1967, almost 500,000 American soldiers guarded South Vietnam's cities and patrolled its rice paddies. Search-and-destroy missions killed over 200,000 enemy soldiers and left one-fourth of the people in South Vietnam homeless. Almost 16,000 American soldiers lost their lives between 1965 and 1967.

## TOPIC 204
# A DIVIDED NATION – FLOWER POWER AND BLACK POWER

## 1. HAWKS VERSUS DOVES

- When President Johnson escalated the war about two-thirds of the public approved his decision. "I don't like being over here," wrote one marine, "but I am doing a job that must be done." Supporters of the war agreed. Known as HAWKS, they argued that America was fighting a just cause to defend the freedom of South Vietnam. Without American help, South Vietnam would fall and the Communists would eventually control all of Southeast Asia.

- When the war did not end quickly, a growing number of people began to question America's involvement in Vietnam. Citizens who opposed the war were called DOVES. They argued that the U.S. could not win a guerrilla war in Asia. The tragic loss of life was too great. Instead of saving South Vietnam, American bombers were destroying it. The doves pointed out that the billions spent in Vietnam would be better spent at home rebuilding America's cities and helping the poor. By 1967, America was almost evenly divided between those who approved the war and those who opposed it.

## 2. THE COUNTERCULTURE

- A number of young people called hippies believed that love not war was the solution to America's problems. Hippies were usually young people between the ages of 17 and 25. Hippies wanted to replace violence and injustice with peace and love. They argued that this could only be done by creating a new alternate way of life or COUNTERCULTURE.

- As children of middle class families, hippies had been taught to value a neat appearance, hard work, and economic success. The new counterculture emphasized the importance of being "groovy" by "doing your own thing." Being groovy meant wearing jeans, love beads, and long hair instead of business suits and dresses. It also meant living with large groups of friends on rural commune instead of owning a home in the suburbs. Hippies had a particular penchant (liking) for huge outdoor music concerts such as the Woodstock Music Festival.

## 3. THE LONG HOT SUMMERS

- While the hippies preached love and peace, inner cities across America burst into flames. During the long hot summers of 1966 and 1967, racial riots struck over 100 cities and towns. The most serious violence occurred in Detroit where the worst racial riot in American history left 43 dead and 5,000 homeless.
- The problems in Detroit and other inner cities were not unique. During the years since Pearl Harbor, almost 3 million blacks left the South and moved to cities in the North and West Coast. Unskilled and unprepared for urban life, many were forced to live in poverty-stricken inner city neighborhoods.
- The civil rights movement and the war on poverty raised high hopes which could not be quickly fulfilled. Freedom marches could win laws against segregation but they could not build new homes or create jobs.

## 4. BLACK POWER

- The riots shook the civil rights movement's confidence in peaceful reform. Dr. King still preached nonviolence and insisted that "we can't win violently." However, in the tumultuous atmosphere of the late 1960s some blacks questioned King's nonviolent tactics and his dream of a fully integrated society. New leaders such as Malcolm X and Stokely Carmichael called for a more militant approach.
- Malcolm X first came to public attention as a minister for the Nation of Islam, a religious group known as the Black Muslims. Malcolm X underscored his differences with Dr. King when he told his followers, "When I say fight for independence right here, I don't mean any nonviolent fight, or turn the other cheek fight. Those days are gone, those days are over." Assassins representing a rival faction of Black Muslims shot and killed Malcolm X in Harlem in 1965 thus silencing the most articulate spokesman for black militancy since Marcus Garvey.
- With Malcolm X gone, Stokely Carmichael became the most militant black leader. Carmichael was impatient with

King's nonviolent marches. In a speech in Mississippi, he excited his followers by boldly calling for "black power." As explained by Carmichael, BLACK POWER meant that blacks should control their own communities by developing black-owned businesses and electing black representatives. As the head of SNCC he implemented his separatist philosophy by ousting (expelling) whites from the previously integrated organization.

- As the war in Vietnam escalated, the black power movement became angrier and more militant. Carmichael moved to Oakland, California where he joined Huey Newton and Eldridge Cleaver's Black Panther Party. As the antithesis (opposite) of King's nonviolent marchers, the Black Panthers captured the imagination of inner city black youths while alarming the general public.

## INSIDER TIP

Be sure that you know the difference between the SCLC and SNCC. The SCLC was founded and led by Dr. King. SNCC originally included both black and white students who were committed to nonviolence. However, Stokely Carmichael ousted whites and committed SNCC to the principles of black power.

# TOPIC 205
## 1968

### 1. THE TET OFFENSIVE

- As 1968 began, President Johnson faced a swirling maelstrom (whirlpool) of pressing problems. Angry blacks demanded new programs to help the inner cities. Frustrated students protested the seemingly endless war in Vietnam. Exasperated middle Americans demanded law and order at home and peace with honor in Vietnam.
- Of all these problems, the Vietnam War concerned President Johnson the most. On January 31, 1968, the first day of the Vietnamese New Year (Tet), Viet Cong and North Vietnamese forces attacked over one hundred cities, villages, and military bases across Vietnam.
- The Tet Offensive marked a turning point in the Vietnam War. Although U.S. forces regained the initiative and won a military victory, the heavy fighting undermined Johnson's confident prediction that "victory was just around the corner." As Americans questioned the President's credibility, public support for the war dropped.
- As Johnson' popularity sank, two Democratic senators launched campaigns to challenge him for the Democratic presidential nomination. The campaigns by Eugene McCarthy and Robert Kennedy inspired antiwar activists

and placed enormous additional pressure on the beleaguered (beset with problems) President.

## 2. JOHNSON'S SURPRISE ANNOUNCEMENT

- As the situation in Vietnam worsened and his popularity plummeted, President Johnson felt increasingly bitter and isolated. The cost of the Vietnam War was undermining his Great Society programs. In 1968 the United States spent $322,000 to kill each Communist soldier while Great Society programs received just $53.00 for each person being helped.

- On March 31, 1968, President Johnson announced a series of shocking decisions. He rejected General Westmoreland's request for 206,000 more troops and instead ordered a halt to most of the bombing in North Vietnam. He also called upon the leaders of North Vietnam to begin peace talks. Johnson then paused and told a nationally televised audience a final decision: "I have decided that I shall not seek, and will not accept the nomination of my party for another term as your President." LBJ hoped that these decisions would restore a sense of national unity. But before the healing process could begin, shocking new blows stunned and divided the nation.

## 3. TWO ASSASSINATIONS

- Three days after President Johnson's speech, Dr. King travelled to Memphis to support the demands of striking sanitation workers. Tragedy struck the next day. A man later identified as James Earl Ray shot and killed Dr. King as the civil rights leader stood on a balcony near his motel room. Ray's motives for the crime are still unknown.

- The news of Dr. King's death touched off a wave of violent riots. After Dr. King's funeral, many blacks looked to Robert Kennedy as the only national leader who could bring about peaceful change. Hispanics and many working-class whites also looked to Kennedy for leadership. Backed by these groups Kennedy defeated McCarthy in the crucial California primary. On June 5, 1968, an already shaken nation watched in stunned disbelief as Kennedy was shot and killed after he thanked his triumphant supporters for their help. The assassin was an Arab nationalist named Sirhan Sirhan who opposed Kennedy's support for Israel.

- The sudden violent deaths of Dr. King and Robert Kennedy deeply disturbed an already troubled nation. While these tragedies occurred, little progress took place in the peace talks that had begun with the North Vietnamese. The great hopes for peace in Vietnam that followed LBJ's speech now faded.

## 4. THE DIVIDED DEMOCRATS

- The deeply divided Democratic Party met in Chicago where they nominated Vice-President Hubert Humphrey for President. However, violent antiwar demonstrations marred Humphrey's nomination. The spectacle of police firing tear gas at demonstrators badly tarnished the Humphrey campaign.
- The Democrats also faced another divisive problem when Alabama Governor George C. Wallace ran as a third-party candidate. Wallace began his career as a determined opponent of civil rights whose motto was "segregation now … segregation tomorrow … segregation forever." Wallace threatened to take away many traditional Democratic votes by appealing to working-class Americans who were upset by the urban riots and antiwar demonstrations.

## 5. AND THEN THERE WAS NIXON

- The war in Vietnam, the deaths of Dr. King and Robert Kennedy, and the violence at the Chicago Democratic convention dominated the news during most of 1968. While these events captured the headlines, Richard Nixon staged a remarkable political comeback. Nixon believed that most Americans were tired of hippies, antiwar demonstrators, and urban rioters. He carefully avoided controversy while promising that he had a plan to find an honorable end to the Vietnam War.
- Republican primary voters strongly supported Nixon. As a result he easily won the party's presidential nomination. The dissension within the Democratic Party gave Nixon an early lead. However, the Democrats finally rallied behind Humphrey when he announced that if elected he would stop all bombing of North Vietnam. On election day Nixon won a solid majority of the electoral votes while winning a narrow margin of the popular votes. Richard Nixon now assumed the burden of ending the Vietnam War and reuniting a badly divided country.

## INSIDER TIP

Be sure that you can identify George Wallace. He was a well-known opponent of integration who also opposed the counterculture and antiwar movement.

**CHAPTER 42**

# KEY EVENTS AND MASS MOVEMENTS DURING THE NIXON AND CARTER PRESIDENCIES, 1969 – 1980

## ESSENTIAL POINTS

1. Nixon believed that his policy of **VIETNAMIZATION** would bring a "peace with honor" that would allow him to end American participation in the Vietnam War.
2. The "silent majority" supported Nixon and became a key part of the emerging Republican coalition of voters.
3. Nixon achieved a number of important diplomatic successes. He was the first President to visit China and Moscow. His daring diplomacy opened a new era of **DÉTENTE** with the Soviet Union.
4. The Arab oil embargo ended the post-World War II economic boom and began a new period of inflation that plagued the U.S. economy during the 1970s.
5. Betty Friedan wrote *The Feminist Mystique* and helped found the National Organization for Women (NOW). Friedan challenged traditional gender roles and worked to eliminate sex discrimination in the workplace.
6. Congress passed the Equal Rights Amendment. However, a campaign led by Phyllis Schlafly successfully blocked passage of the ERA in several state legislatures. As a result, the ERA was NOT ratified.
7. Rachel Carson's book *Silent Spring* alerted Americans to the high risks of overusing pesticides. *Silent Spring* helped launch the national environmental movement.
8. The Camp David summit marked the high point of the Carter presidency. His administration was severely weakened by stagflation at home and the hostage crisis in Iran.

# TOPIC 206
# THE VIETNAM WAR, 1969 – 1975

## 1. VIETNAMIZATION

- Nixon inherited a difficult situation in Vietnam. At the time of his inauguration, 540,000 American soldiers were still in Vietnam. A growing number of Americans wanted to end a war that had already claimed the lives of 31,000 of their countrymen. The North Vietnamese, however, remained determined to control South Vietnam. Thus, no real progress had been made at the Paris peace talks.
- Nixon found himself squeezed between an impatient public at home and an intransigent (unyielding) enemy abroad. The President and his National Security Advisor, Dr. Henry Kissinger, developed a "two-track" strategy to end American involvement and prevent a Communist take-over of South Vietnam. First, they would continue to negotiate for a peace settlement. Second, the United States began a gradual withdrawal of American forces and their replacement by South Vietnamese soldiers. This new policy of training the South Vietnamese to take over the fighting was called VIETNAMIZATION.
- Nixon appealed to "the great silent majority" of Americans to support his policies. The SILENT MAJORITY included hard-working "nonshouters and nondemonstrators" who were typically white Americans living in fast-growing states in the South and West. This conservative group formed the core of a new Republican coalition of voters.

## 2. CAMBODIA AND KENT STATE

- Nixon's strategy of Vietnamization appeared to be working. Then, on April 30, 1970, Nixon surprised the nation by announcing that he was sending American ground troops into Cambodia. Nixon explained that the Viet Cong and North Vietnamese used bases inside Cambodia to launch attacks on South Vietnam. The bases had to be destroyed before American forces could leave Vietnam.
- Nixon's announcement stunned the nation. Outraged doves questioned Nixon's strategy of shortening the war by escalating it. Skepticism (doubt) turned to anger as indignant (outraged) college students protested the

## INSIDER TIP
The 2002B APUSH exam included a free-response question asking students to analyze how the "silent majority" helped shape American politics during the 1970s. For an excellent discussion of the silent majority see Question 5, Essay A.

invasion of Cambodia. Police and even National Guard soldiers had to be called upon to maintain order on some campuses. Then on May 4, 1970, tragedy struck at Kent State University in Ohio. Frightened National Guard soldiers opened fire on demonstrators, killing four student bystanders.

- News of the shootings at Kent State ignited a tidal wave of student protest. Over 400 colleges closed as thousands of protesting students boycotted classes. Almost 100,000 antiwar demonstrators staged a huge protest march in Washington. The demonstrators' chant, "All we are saying is give peace a chance," could be heard throughout the nation's capital. Nixon later wrote that "Those few days after Kent State were among the darkest of my presidency."

## 3. THE PARIS ACCORDS

- After nearly three years of bloody fighting and intense U.S. bombing raids, the peace negotiations between Henry Kissinger and the North Vietnamese finally reached a conclusion. Dr. Kissinger later wrote that the talks were filled with "peaks and valleys of extraordinary intensity."
- On January 23, 1973, President Nixon announced that an agreement had been reached "to end the war and bring peace with honor to Vietnam and Southeast Asia. " For days later, American and North Vietnamese officials signed an 18 page treaty called the Paris Accords.
- The agreement called for the United States to withdraw its remaining troops within 60 days. In return, the North Vietnamese would release almost 600 American prisoners of war. The Paris Accords left the South Vietnamese government in power. However, they also permitted almost 150,000 North Vietnamese troops to remain in South Vietnam. Both sides agreed "to maintain the cease-fire and to ensure a lasting and stable peace."

## 4. THE FALL OF SAIGON

- The North Vietnamese chose to ignore their promise "to maintain the cease-fire." In March 1975 they launched a full-scale armored invasion of South Vietnam. As the North Vietnamese advanced upon Saigon, helicopters rescued Americans from the roof of the U.S embassy to the safety of nearby warships. The South Vietnamese government surrendered on April 30, 1975.

- Nixon had promised the South Vietnamese government that he would support them if the North Vietnamese launched a major attack. However, Nixon was unable to keep his promise. Congress repealed the Gulf of Tonkin Resolution and in November 1973 passed the War Powers Act. This legislation required the President to report any use of military force within 48 hours. It also directed that without a declaration of war by Congress hostilities must cease within 60 days. In addition, serious charges of misconduct in the Watergate scandal weakened Nixon and led to his resignation on August 9, 1974.

## 5. THE LEGACY OF VIETNAM

- The Vietnam War has had a number of important and long-lasting consequences. More than 58,000 U.S. troops died and another 300,000 were wounded. The war took funds away from Great Society programs and ultimately forced President Johnson to resign.
- The bitter public debate over the war divided families, friends, and eventually the entire nation. It shattered the liberal consensus that supported the New Deal and the Great Society and helped spark the conservative resurgence (revival) that began with the rise of Nixon's silent majority.
- The Vietnam War also created skepticism about international involvements called the "Vietnam Syndrome." Many Americans questioned foreign entanglements that might become "another Vietnam."

## INSIDER TIP

The Vietnam War has generated two recent essay questions. See the 2010B exam for a free-response question and the 2008 exam for a DBQ.

# TOPIC 207
# KEY EVENTS DURING THE NIXON PRESIDENCY, 1972 – 1974

### 1. NIXON'S VISIT TO CHINA

- During the years after World War II, American leaders divided the world into two rival blocs of nations – the Communist World and the Free World. As the leader of the Free World, the United States attempted to contain the Soviet expansion and isolate the People's Republic of China. Nixon and Kissinger believed that the time had come to pursue bold foreign policy initiatives that would reshape global politics.

- In February 1972, Nixon took a historic trip to the People's Republic of China. The President met with Mao Zedong, exchanged toasts with Chinese leaders, and visited the Great Wall. Nixon's dramatic visit opened a new era of cultural exchanges and trade between the two countries. The United States and the People's Republic of China established formal diplomatic relations in 1979.

## 2. DÉTENTE WITH THE SOVIET UNION

- Three months after returning from China, Nixon stunned the world again by becoming the first American president to visit Moscow. During the seven-day summit, Nixon and Soviet Premier Leonid Brezhnev agreed upon a joint space mission and signed a Strategic Arms Limitation Treaty. The SALT I agreement did not end the nuclear arms race, but it did place limitations on both the number of intercontinental ballistic missiles and the construction of anti-ballistic missile systems.

- The SALT I treaty signaled the beginning of a new period of relaxed tensions between the two rival superpowers that Kissinger called DÉTENTE.

## 3. THE YOM KIPPUR WAR

- In October 1973, Egypt and Syria attacked Israel on Yom Kippur, the holiest day of the Jewish year. The attack caught the Israelis by surprise and forced them to send President Nixon an urgent request for emergency equipment.

- President Nixon now faced a momentous (very important) decision. He understood that American military aid would anger the entire Arab world. However, Nixon also recognized that he could not permit Soviet-backed countries to defeat an American ally. Within days, huge American transport planes airlifted 20,000 tons of weapons to Israel. This massive aid enabled the Israeli army to push back the Arab forces. After over two weeks of intense fighting, both sides agreed to a United Nations cease-fire.

## 4. THE ARAB OIL EMBARGO AND INFLATION

- Although the fighting had ended, the consequences of the Yom Kippur War had only just begun. Nixon's decision to help Israel angered many oil-rich Arab nations. As the most important members of the Organization of Petroleum Countries (OPEC), they had the power to reduce the supply of oil and raise prices. On October 20, 1973 they chose to do both.
- The Arab oil embargo stunned America. Frustrated Americans waited in long gas lines only to discover that the price of a gallon had soared from 35 cents to over $1.00. The Arabs finally agreed to lift the embargo in April 1974.
- The energy crisis did not end with the lifting of the embargo. The oil crisis marked the end of the post-World War II economic boom and the beginning of a period of inflation that plagued the U.S. economy during the rest of the 1970s. The Arab oil embargo also forced the United States to confront an unsettling new economic reality. For the first time in its history, the United States could not rely upon a endless supply of its own inexpensive natural resources. The Arab oil embargo compelled Americans to realize that their economic future was linked to an often unpredictable global economy.

## 5. THE WATERGATE SCANDAL

- On June 17, 1972, police arrested five burglars who had broken into the headquarters of the Democratic National Committee at the Watergate apartment and office complex in Washington. Painstaking (very thorough) investigation later revealed that the break-in was part of a much larger campaign of "dirty tricks" financed and directed by the Committee to Reelect the President (CREEP).
- Nixon was never directly implicated in the Watergate break-in. However, instead of firing the corrupt officials responsible for the crime, he chose to "play it tough" and attempt to cover-up the scandal. The House Judiciary Committee ultimately voted to recommend the impeachment of Nixon for obstruction of justice.

## INSIDER TIP

The Watergate scandal is a complex event that unfolded over a period of two years. Fortunately, APUSH exams and SAT II tests do not expect students to remember the names of investigators and White House officials. Just remember that Nixon helped orchestrate the cover-up and that the Constitution's system of checks and balances worked.

- On August 9, 1974, Richard Nixon became the first President to resign from office. Vice-President Gerald Ford thus became the nation's 38th President. "My fellow Americans," Ford declared, "our long national nightmare is over. Our Constitution works."

## TOPIC 208
# THE WOMEN'S MOVEMENT

### 1. BETTY FRIEDAN AND *THE FEMININE MYSTIQUE*

- Women played an active role in the civil rights movement. This experience sharpened their awareness that women also suffered from unfair discrimination. For example, women with college degrees earned only half as much as similarly educated men.
- Betty Friedan was the first to express the sense of injustice felt by many women. Her book, *The Feminine Mystique* (1963), challenged the cult of domesticity that prevailed since the 1950s. Friedan exposed the previously unspoken frustration felt by suburban housewives as they performed a seemingly endless routine of buying groceries, cooking meals, and chauffeuring their children. Friedan ultimately asked a "silent question" that suburban women had all been afraid to ask – "Is this all?"

### 2. THE NATIONAL ORGANIZATION FOR WOMEN (NOW)

- In 1966, Friedan and other women activists formed the National Organization for Women (NOW) to work for equal rights and challenge sex discrimination in the workplace. Supported by NOW, women filed suit for equal wages and also demanded that companies provide day care for their infant children. Congress responded to the call for reform by requiring colleges to institute "affirmative action" programs to ensure equal opportunity for women.
- NOW also supported two controversial Supreme Court decisions. In *Griswold v. Connecticut* the Court ruled that a Connecticut law criminalizing the use of contraceptives violated the right to marital privacy. The Court further

## INSIDER TIP
Betty Friedan has generated a significant cluster of multiple-choice questions on both the APUSH exam and the SAT II test. Be sure that you know that Friedan criticized traditional gender roles. Test writers often include her question "Is this all?" in quote identification questions. It comes from the opening paragraph of *The Feminist Mystique*.

## PODCAST 42.1
BETTY FRIEDAN AND NOW

## INSIDER TIP
The phrase "Sisterhood is powerful" was the title of an anthology first published by Robin Morgan in 1970. The phrase became a popular rally cry during the 1970s.

argued that the right to privacy was implied by the rights stated in the Bill of Rights. In *Roe v. Wade*, the Supreme Court ruled that abortion is protected by the right to privacy implied by the Bill of Rights.

### 3. THE EQUAL RIGHTS AMENDMENT
- In 1972, Congress passed the Equal Rights Amendment and then sent it on to the states for ratification. The amendment stated that, "Equality of rights under the law shall not be denied or abridged by the United States or by any State on account of sex."
- The ERA quickly passed 35 of the 38 state legislatures needed for ratification. However, opponents led by Phyllis Schlafly mounted a successful campaign to block the ERA. The time limit for ratifying the ERA expired and the amendment went down to defeat.

## TOPIC 209:
# KEY QUOTE – RACHEL CARSON WARNS ABOUT "MAN'S ASSAULTS UPON THE ENVIRONMENT"

### 1. THE SETTING
- During the 1950s, most biologists accepted the prevailing scientific paradigm (framework of thought) that DDT and other chemical pesticides were useful tools to eradicate (eliminate) mosquitoes and other harmful insect pests. However, an American marine biologist named Rachel Carson refused to accept this viewpoint. Her research studies indicated that DDT and other chemicals were in fact having an inimical (very harmful) effect upon the environment.
- Carson published her findings in a groundbreaking book titled, *Silent Spring*. She forcefully warned that the unrestricted use of chemical pesticides was destroying much of America's wildlife. Readers were shocked to learn that the California condor, the whooping crane, and even the bald eagle were all threatened with extinction.

## 2. THE QUOTE

- "The history of life on earth has been a history of interaction between living things and their surroundings. To a large extent, the physical form and habits of the earth's vegetation and its animal life have been molded by the environment … The most alarming of all man's assaults upon the environment is the contamination of air, earth, rivers, and sea with dangerous and even lethal materials."

## 3. SIGNIFICANCE

- *Silent Spring* helped launch the national environmental movement. By the early 1970s, 70 percent of Americans ranked the environment as the nation's most pressing problem. Congress responded by passing 35 environmental laws that set clean air and water standards and protected wildlife. Beginning in 1970, millions of Americans participated in Earth Day activities to help clean up the environment.
- The environmental movement also expressed concerns about the waste produced by nuclear power plants. An accident at the Three Mile Island nuclear plant intensified these concerns. On March 28, 1979, some 800,000 gallons of radioactive water leaked from a reactor threatening a meltdown of the reactor core. About 100,000 people were forced to evacuate their homes. The crisis at Three Mile Island increased public support for a movement opposed to nuclear power.

# TOPIC 210
# KEY EVENTS DURING THE CARTER PRESIDENCY, 1977 – 1980

## 1. STAGFLATION ✸

- Carter began his presidency with high hopes. However, he soon faced a seemingly intractable (very hard to manage) economic problem. The American economy was simultaneously experiencing a combination of both rising unemployment and double-digit inflation. Economists called this unusual phenomenon STAGFLATION.

- Stagflation had at least two deep-rooted causes. First, President Johnson attempted to pay for both the Vietnam War and the Great Society without raising taxes. This created strong inflationary pressures. Second, the United States economy had become dangerously dependent upon inexpensive imported oil. The OPEC price increases played a significant role in driving up the cost of everything from gasoline to groceries.

## 2. THE CAMP DAVID ACCORDS

- President Carter's idealistic foreign policy resembled that of Woodrow Wilson. Carter pledged that human rights would be "the soul of our foreign policy." He vowed that his actions would be guided by "fairness, not force."
- Carter's commitment to patient negotiating achieved a dramatic breakthrough in Middle East diplomacy. The Arab-Israeli conflict had exploded into war in 1948, 1956, 1967, and the Yom Kippur War of 1973. World leaders feared that the cease-fire which ended the Yom Kippur War would soon collapse.
- In September 1978, Carter boldly invited Egyptian President Anwar Sadat and Israeli Prime Minister Manachem Begin to meet with him at Camp David, the presidential retreat in Maryland. At times, both Sadat and Begin threatened to leave without an agreement. But Carter skillfully persuaded them to continue the talks. After 13 difficult days, a beaming Carter announced that the two sides had reached a historic peace agreement.
- The Camp David Accords included two key provisions. First, Israel and Egypt agreed to sign a peace treaty ending thirty years of hostility. And second, Israel agreed to return the Sinai Peninsula to Egypt.

## 3. THE IRAN HOSTAGE CRISIS

- The Camp David Accords marked Carter's greatest triumph. Within months, events in Iran plunged the Carter presidency into a crisis it was unable to successfully resolve.
- In early 1979 a fundamentalist Islamic revolution led by Ayatollah Khomeini overthrew Iran's pro-American Shah. The Shah's fall hurt America's economy. Iran normally produced 10 percent of the world's supply of oil. During the revolution, the Iranians suddenly reduced their

production. The global demand for oil now exceeded the supply. OPEC used this opportunity to once again raise oil prices. The rising cost of oil pushed inflation in the United States to over 11 percent.

- The bad news from Iran soon became much worse. In October 1979, President Carter allowed the Shah to enter the United States for medical treatment. Carter's action infuriated the Iranians. On November 4, 1979, a mob stormed the American embassy in Tehran and took over 50 Americans hostage. The Iranians demanded that Carter return the Shah to stand trial.
- Carter refused to surrender the Shah. The Iranians then paraded the blindfolded hostages before enormous crowds and repeatedly threatened to execute them. Carter authorized a secret rescue mission which ended in an ignominious (humiliating) failure when rescue helicopters malfunctioned in the desert south of Tehran.

## 4. THE ELECTION OF 1980

- The hostage crisis and the soaring rate of inflation damaged Carter's popularity. Opinion polls reported that less than 25 percent of the public approved his leadership.
- Sensing victory, the Republicans nominated Ronald Reagan for President. During the campaign Reagan repeatedly asked the American people to answer one question: "Are you better off now than you were four years ago?" On election day, the voters overwhelmingly answered no. Reagan and his running mate, George Bush, won a landslide victory.

## INSIDER TIP

President Carter's biggest success (the Camp David Accords) and his biggest failure (the Iran hostage crisis) both occurred in the Middle East.

**CHAPTER 43**
# KEY EVENTS AND DEMOGRAPHIC TRENDS, 1981 – 2000

## ESSENTIAL POINTS

1. **REAGANOMICS** advocated cutting federal tax rates and deregulating businesses and financial institutions. Also called supply-side economics, Reaganomics attempted to encourage private investment.
2. The **REAGAN DOCTRINE** called for an aggressive policy to confront and contain Soviet influence.
3. President Bush organized an international coalition to liberate Kuwait.
4. President Clinton supported both the North American Free Trade Agreement (NAFTA) and the World Trade Organization (WTO).
5. Three key demographic trends shaped American society during the last decades of the twentieth century. First, the aging or "graying" population threatened the viability of social security. Second, SUNBELT states in the South and West became the nation's fastest growing region. And third a massive new wave of immigration included a significant number of people from Latin America and Asia.

## TOPIC 211
# THE REAGAN PRESIDENCY, 1981 – 1989

### 1. A NEW BEGINNING

- At noon on January 20, 1981, Ronald Reagan placed his left hand on a family Bible and solemnly swore to "preserve, protect, and defend the Constitution of the United States." As howitzers sounded a 21-gun salute, the new President turned to face the huge crowd gathered at the West Front of the Capitol. Reagan acknowledged that the nation faced serious economic problems. But, he also rejected the idea that America faced "an inevitable decline." Instead, the new President confidently called upon America to "begin an era of national renewal."
- While the President delivered his Inaugural Address, a bus 6,300 miles away carried 52 American hostages onto an airport runway outside Tehran, Iran. A beaming President Reagan now told the nation the news it has waited 444 days to hear: "Some 30 minutes ago, the planes bearing our prisoners left Iranian airspace and are now free of Iran." The President's dramatic announcement triggered a wave of national joy and relief.
- Reagan's inauguration marked a new beginning for America. The long hostage crisis had finally ended and a new presidency had begun.

### 2. REAGANOMICS

- President Reagan wasted little time in announcing his plans to revive the economy. Less than three weeks after taking office, the President told the nation, "We're in the worst economic mess since the Great Depression." He then identified inflation, high interest rates, too much government spending, high taxes, and unemployment as five key problems that had to be solved.
- Reagan opposed the use of a New Deal-type program to revive the economy. "Government is not the solution to our problem," Reagan declared. "Government is the problem." Reagan boldly championed a series of new solutions to deal with stagflation. He called upon Congress to sharply reduce government funding of social and

PODCAST 43.1
REAGANOMICS

welfare programs. Reagan argued that these cuts would help curb (control) federal spending and fight inflation. He also asked Congress to enact a 3-year 30 percent cut in personal income taxes. The President believed that these cuts would stimulate the economy. With more money to spend, consumers would buy more goods. At the same time, Reagan also called upon Congress to ease government regulations of business. He believed that free-market capitalism would create jobs and promote economic growth.

- Reporters promptly labeled the President's supply-side economic program REAGANOMICS. Critics argued that Reaganomics would hurt the needy and fail to stimulate the economy. But, Reagan skillfully used television speeches to generate support for his program. The President's success soon earned him the nickname the "Great Communicator." Within a few months, Congress passed Reagan's budget and tax cuts.

- Reaganomics failed to produce immediate results. Instead of reviving, the economy sank into a steep recession. Unemployment climbed to over 10 percent – the highest since the Great Depression. Despite the difficult beginning, Reagan urged the public "to stay the course."

- Reagan's confidence proved to be justified. America enjoyed a sustained period of economic growth from late 1982 to 1988. During that time the economy added more than 17 million jobs, inflation dropped to single digits, and the gross national product showed the biggest percentage increase in 33 years.

- However, Reaganomics also produced troubling long-term problems. Despite deep cuts in social programs, federal spending continued to escalate as the defense budget soared to counter the perceived Soviet threat. Because of Reagan's massive tax cuts, the government took in less money and had to borrow heavily to pay its bills. From George Washington to Jimmy Carter the United States had accumulated $1.1 trillion in national debt. Under Reagan the United States added $1.8 trillion in debt. Once the world's biggest lender, the United States had become its largest debtor.

## INSIDER TIP
Most APUSH and SAT II multiple-choice questions on the Reagan presidency focus on Reaganomics. It is important to remember that Reaganomics encouraged private investment by cutting taxes for business and the wealthy. Reaganomics did NOT eliminate taxes for the poor.

## 3. U.S. – SOVIET RELATIONS

- While economic problems received Reagan's highest priority, relations with the Soviet Union played a dominant role in his foreign policy. Reagan believed that the Soviet Union caused much of the world's troubles. In a speech given on March 8, 1983, Reagan charged the Soviet Union with being "the focus of evil in the modern world." Reagan's "Evil Empire" speech electrified dissidents behind the Iron Curtain.

- Soviet actions seemed to support Reagan's accusations. In late 1979 the Red Army invaded Afghanistan. Events in Poland further strained U.S. – Soviet relations. In 1980, Polish workers formed an independent labor union called Solidarity. Under the leadership of Lech Walesa, Solidarity demanded greater freedom for the Polish people. The Soviet leader refused to permit a more open Polish government. In December 1981, Communist authorities in Poland arrested Walesa and abolished Solidarity.

- The Soviet actions in Afghanistan and Poland helped convince many Americans that the United States needed a much more aggressive approach toward the Soviet Union. President Reagan agreed. The REAGAN DOCTRINE is the name given to the Reagan administration's strategy to confront and oppose the global influence of the Soviet Union.

- The Reagan Doctrine led to a massive military buildup. Between 1980 and 1985, U.S. defense budgets increased from $144 billion to $295 billion. In 1983, President Reagan proposed a Strategic Defense Initiative as an additional check on Soviet nuclear capability. Reagan envisioned creating a space-based missile defense system capable of striking down nuclear missiles before they reached the United States. The press promptly called Reagan's plan "Star Wars."

## 4. THE 1984 ELECTION

- President Reagan's popularity rose as the 1984 election approached. Americans liked Reagan's can-do personality and admired his ability to lead the nation. The President proudly pointed to the nation's strong economic recovery and to his tough new foreign policy. Declaring that he wanted to "make America great again," the President told voters, "You ain't seen nothin' yet."

- While the Republicans unanimously renominated Reagan and Bush, the Democrats selected former Vice-President Walter Mondale. In a bold break with tradition, Mondale chose a female running mate, Congresswoman Geraldine Ferraro of New York.
- The Mondale-Ferraro team ran a spirited race. However, they proved to be no match for Reagan and Bush. Millions of voters agreed with Republican ads proclaiming that "America is back, standing tall." On election day, Reagan won a landslide victory carrying 49 states.
- Reagan enjoyed strong support from a conservative movement called the NEW RIGHT. The New Right's emphasis upon patriotism and family values attracted strong support from the South, the middle class, and from working class "Reagan Democrats."

## 5. THE IRAN–CONTRA AFFAIR
- Colonel Oliver North and other senior administration officials devised an "arms for hostages plan." Their plan called on the United States to sell arms to Iran. The Iranians would then use their influence to help free American hostages held in Lebanon. The clandestine (secret) plan ignored the fact that America had an official trade embargo with Iran.
- The money derived from the sale of arms to Iran would then be used to fund anticommunist fighters in Nicaragua called "Contras." The plan therefore attempted to circumvent (bypass) Congressional legislation regulating how much funds could go to the Contras.
- The Iran-Contra Affair forced nearly a dozen Reagan administration officials to resign.

## TOPIC 212
# THE BUSH AND CLINTON PRESIDENCIES, 1989 – 2001

### 1. THE BUSH PRESIDENCY, 1989 – 1993

- The Bush presidency witnessed both the fall of the Berlin Wall (1989) and the collapse of the Soviet Union (1991).
- On August 2, 1990 Saddam Hussein ordered Iraqi forced to invade Kuwait. Hussein's decision to conquer Kuwait was part of his plan to become the Arab world's most powerful leader. Kuwait owned about 10 percent of the world's proven oil reserves. Since Iraq also had 10 percent, taking Kuwait would double Iraq's oil reserves. Hussein would then be in a position to intimidate Saudi Arabia and dominate the global oil market.
- President Bush argued that Iraq had to be confronted. The United States could not allow any nation to dominate the Persian Gulf and thus control the world's oil supply. Bush skillfully forged an international coalition of 28 nations to force Hussein to withdraw from Kuwait. Led by the United States, Operation Desert Storm successfully crushed Hussein's army and liberated Kuwait.

### 2. THE CLINTON PRESIDENCY, 1993 – 2001

- The North American Free Trade Agreement (NAFTA) created a free-trade zone with Canada and Mexico.
- The World Trade Organization (WTO) was established in 1984 to oversee trade agreements and enforce trade rules.
- The House of Representatives impeached President Clinton for perjury and obstruction of justice. However, the Senate did not uphold the charges.
- It is important to note that both presidents Andrew Johnson and Bill Clinton were impeached by the House but not convicted by the Senate.

**TOPIC 213**
# THREE KEY DEMOGRAPHIC TRENDS, 1981 – 2000

PODCAST 43.2
**KEY DEMOGRAPHIC TRENDS, 1981 – 2000s**

## 1. THE "GRAYING" OF AMERICA

- After reaching a peak of 4.3 million births in 1957, the baby boom began to decline. Between 1970 and 1988, an average of less than 3.5 million births occurred each year. The declining birth rate caused a significant drop in the percentage of Americans under the age of 17.
- While the number of young Americans declined, the number of older Americans increased. In 1900, just 4.1 percent of the population was over 65. By 2000, the percentage climbed to about 12 percent. This "graying" of the population poses a threat to the long-term viability (workability) of social security.

## 2. THE RISE OF THE SUNBELT

- Many older citizens chose to retire in the South and West. Known as the SUNBELT, the band of states that stretches from the Carolinas to Southern California also attracted millions of other Americans. Fast growing electronics and computer industries offered job opportunities to go along with the Sunbelt's mild climate.
- By 2000, a majority of Americans lived in the Sunbelt states. In 1994 Texas passed New York as the nation's second most populous state.

## 3. A NEW WAVE OF IMMIGRANTS

- Immigration has played an important role in shaping American culture. The Immigration Act of 1965 triggered a major new wave of immigration. Between 1990 and 2000 over 10 million immigrants entered the United States, more than in any previous decade in the nation's history.
- The largest number of immigrants came from Latin American and Asia. By 2000, over half the foreign-born population of the United States came from Latin America and about one-quarter came from Asia.

# CHAPTER 44
# MAKING KEY COMPARISONS, 1920 – 2000

## ESSENTIAL POINTS

1. Recent APUSH exams have included a significant number of free-response questions asking students to make comparisons between events, peoples, colonies, geographic regions, and social movements. These comparison essays require substantial relevant information and an effective analysis of similarities and differences. This chapter is the fourth of four chapters designed to provide you with a clear and succinct comparison of frequently tested topics.

**TOPIC 214**

# COMPARING HOW ANDREW JACKSON AND DWIGHT EISENHOWER RESPONDED TO SUPREME COURT DECISIONS THEY DISAGREED WITH

## 1. ANDREW JACKSON AND *WORCESTER v. GEORGIA*

- In the late 1820s, Georgia demanded that the federal government eliminate the substantial Indian enclaves within their borders.
- The Cherokee nation posed the greatest obstacle to voluntary relocation. The Cherokee had achieved literacy in their own language, instituted a republican form of government, and made progress toward adopting a settled agrarian way of life.
- Georgia ignored this progress and extended its state laws over the Cherokee. This legislation defied provisions of the Constitution giving the federal government jurisdiction over Indian affairs.
- In *Worcester v. Georgia*, Chief Justice John Marshall denied the right of a state to extend its jurisdiction over tribal lands.
- President Jackson refused to enforce the court order, defiantly declaring, "John Marshall has made his decision; not let him enforce it." Jackson asserted the primacy of states' rights over Indian rights and called for the prompt removal of all eastern Indians to designated areas beyond the Mississippi.
- In 1838, the U.S. Army forcibly removed about 17,000 Cherokees from their ancestral lands and marched them on an 800-mile journey to Indian Territory. About one-fourth of the Cherokee died from disease and exhaustion on what came to be known as the Trail of Tears.

## 2. DWIGHT EISENHOWER AND *BROWN v. BOARD OF EDUCATION*

- In 1954, the Supreme Court unanimously ruled in *Brown v. Board of Education* that the doctrine of "separate but equal" violated the Equal Protection Clause of the Fourteenth Amendment.

- One year later, the Supreme Court directed the states to desegregate their public schools "with all deliberate speed." Outraged Southern leaders responded by calling for "massive resistance" to the Court's decision.
- President Eisenhower did not use his enormous personal prestige to morally support the civil rights movement. Ike privately believed that, "You cannot change people's hearts merely by laws."
- The school board in Little Rock, Arkansas adopted a desegregation plan that called for nine black students to integrate Central High School when classes opened on September 3, 1957. A crisis began when a mob of over 1,000 whites blocked the entrance to the school.
- This display of resistance forced President Eisenhower to make a decision. Unlike President Jackson, Ike chose to enforce the Supreme Court's decision. On September 4, 1957, President Eisenhower sent 1,100 paratroopers to Little Rock to protect the nine black students. He explained his action by stating that, "The very basis of our individual rights and freedoms rest upon the certainty that the President and the Executive Branch of Government would support and insure the carrying out of the decisions of the federal courts, even, when necessary, with all the measures at the President's command."

# TOPIC 215
# COMPARING MARCUS GARVEY AND DR. MARTIN LUTHER KING, JR.

## 1. MARCUS GARVEY
- Marcus Garvey was one of the earliest and most influential black nationalist leaders in the twentieth century.
- Garvey organized the Universal Negro Improvement Association to increase racial pride and promote black nationalism. Unlike Dr. King, Garvey championed black separatism and Pan-Africanism.
- Garvey stressed black solidarity. He believed that integration and civil rights legislation would not achieve black equality. Instead, he focused on transforming black heritage from a mark of inferiority into the basis of a program of pride. "The world has made being black a

crime. Instead of making it a crime," Garvey proclaimed, "I want to make it a virtue."

- Garvey's message of black nationalism and racial solidarity captured the imagination of black people in America, the Caribbean, and Africa. Within a short time, Garvey was one of the most famous black spokesmen in the world.
- Garvey's fame and influence did not last long. Irregularities in fund-raising for the Black Star Line led to his arrest and conviction for mail fraud. President Coolidge commuted Garvey's sentence and he was deported to his native Jamaica.

## 2. DR. MARTIN LUTHER KING, JR.

- Dr. King was the most influential black civil rights leader of the twentieth century. Dr. King's goal was the peaceful integration of all races in all areas of American society.
- Dr. King inspired his followers with a message of nonviolent civil disobedience derived from the writings of Henry David Thoreau and the actions of Mahatma Gandhi in India.
- Following the success of the Montgomery Bus Boycott, Dr. King founded the Southern Christian Leadership Conference (SCLC). Under his leadership, the SCLC sought to apply the principles of nonviolent civil disobedience to other Southern cities.
- Dr. King recognized the importance of building a nationwide alliance or "coalition of conscience" to lobby Congress to pass the landmark Civil Rights Act of 1964.
- Dr. King's dream of racial harmony and equality continues to inspire people in American and around the world. Today, Dr. King's birthday is a national holiday and he is the first African American to be honored with a statue in the National Mall in Washington, D.C.

## TOPIC 216
# COMPARING THE NEW DEAL AND THE GREAT SOCIETY

## 1. THE NEW DEAL

- The New Deal was a response to the economic crisis caused by the Stock Market Crash and the Great Depression.
- New Deal relief programs provided direct federal assistance to unemployed Americans.

- New Deal recovery programs used deficit spending for public works projects to revive the economy.
- New Deal reform programs attempted to address instability in the stock market and banking system.
- The Social Security Act of 1935 created a federal pension system funded by taxes on a worker's wages and by an equivalent contribution by employers. The aging of the U.S. population is now widely seen as a threat to the long-term viability of the Social Security system.
- New Deal programs helped African Americans survive some of the worst hardships of the Great Depression. The New Deal did not directly confront racial segregation. As a result, there was no major civil rights legislation.
- New Deal programs were partially successful in reducing unemployment and reviving the economy. The United States did not fully emerge from the Great Depression until the massive military expenditures prompted by World War II.
- The New Deal did NOT integrate the armed forces, sponsor the Equal Rights Amendment, nationalize basic industries or provide recognition for migrant workers.

## 2. THE GREAT SOCIETY
- The Great Society was conceived and enacted during a period of economic prosperity. Like the New Deal, the Great Society used the power of the federal government to promote the social welfare.
- The Great Society launched a War of Poverty. Great Society programs attempted to provide a safety net for the poorest members of American society. Education and job training programs helped disadvantaged people overcome the cycle of poverty limiting their opportunities.
- Medicaid and Medicare programs extended Social Security. These programs established government health insurance coverage for elderly and poor Americans.
- The Great Society included preschool education for disadvantaged children. These programs were NOT an extension of the New Deal.
- The Great Society included landmark civil rights legislation. The Civil Rights Act of 1964 and the Voting Rights Act of 1965 protected the civil liberties and voting rights of African Americans.

- The Great Society was undermined by government spending during the Vietnam War.
- The Great Society did NOT establish the Peace Corps, create Social Security, guarantee employment or place new restrictions on immigration.

## TOPIC 217
# COMPARING LITERARY DEVELOPMENTS IN THE 1950S AND 1960S

## 1. LITERARY DEVELOPMENTS IN THE 1920S
- The 1920s were a period of prosperity as mass produced consumer goods, radio, and advertising reshaped American culture.
- A group of writers known as the Lost Generation became disillusioned with America's mass culture. Lost Generation writers such as Sinclair Lewis and F. Scott Fitzgerald criticized middle-class materialism and conformity. Several Lost Generation writers moved to Paris.
- A second group of writers known as the Harlem Renaissance expressed pride in their African American culture. The Harlem Renaissance was an outpouring of black literary and artistic creativity. Key figures in the Harlem Renaissance included Zora Neale Hurston, Langston Hughes, James Weldon Johnson, Claude McKay, and Jean Toomer.

## 2. LITERARY DEVELOPMENTS IN THE 1950S
- The 1950s witnessed a period of sustained prosperity, rapid suburbanization, and a return of the cult of domesticity.
- A group of writers and poets known as the Beat Generation rejected middle-class culture and conformity. Led by Jack Kerouac, Beat writers expressed their alienation and disillusionment with America's carefree consumption and mindless conformity. Beat writers congregated in bohemian enclaves in New York City and San Francisco.
- A second group of social commentators also criticized the conformity of postwar American life. Writers such as Sloan Wilson decried mass-produced Levittowns filled with endless rows of identical box houses. While Wilson

criticized the superficial suburban lifestyle, William H. Whyte and David Riesman described how corporations created a culture of stifling conformity that emphasized getting along above taking risks.

## TOPIC 218
# COMPARING THE KOREAN WAR AND THE VIETNAM WAR

### 1. THE KOREAN WAR
- The Korean War began when North Korea invaded South Korea on June 25, 1950. President Truman saw the invasion as a test of containment and an opportunity to prove that the Democrats were not "soft" on Communism.
- Truman took advantage of a temporary Soviet absence from the United Nations Security Council to obtain a unanimous resolution condemning North Korea as an aggressor. The Korean War thus marked the first use of collective military action by the United Nations.
- The Korean War was a limited conflict that extended America's containment policy to Asia. The war quickly became a prolonged  stalemate that frustrated the American people and led to the rise of Senator McCarthy and the election of Dwight Eisenhower in 1952.
- The combatants finally signed an armistice in 1953 that set the boundary between North Korea and South Korea near the 38th parallel.
- The Korean War marked the first time that American forces fought in integrated units.

### 2. THE VIETNAM WAR
- The first phase of the Vietnam War involved a conflict between France and forces loyal to Ho Chi Minh that lasted from 1946 to 1954. The war ended in a disastrous French defeat that left Vietnam divided at the 17th parallel. Ho Chi Minh and his Communist government ruled north of the parallel while a French-backed government ruled south of the parallel.
- The French defeat forced President Eisenhower to support South Vietnam. Ike believed that the fall of South Vietnam would inevitably lead to Communist expansion throughout

the rest of Southeast Asia. This belief was soon called the domino theory. The domino theory grew out the policy commitments and assumptions of containment.

- President Kennedy continued Ike's policy of supporting South Vietnam. At the time of Kennedy's death in 1963, over 16,000 American advisors helped train the South Vietnam army.

- President Johnson was determined to meet the Communist challenge. Like Truman, LBJ wanted to prove that he was not "soft" on Communism.

- In August 1964, Congress responded to unsubstantiated reports that North Vietnamese vessels attacked U.S. destroyers by overwhelmingly passing the Tonkin Gulf Resolution. The resolution gave President Johnson a "blank check" to escalate the War in Vietnam.

- President Johnson used the Tonkin Gulf Resolution to begin a dramatic escalation of the Vietnam War. Unlike the Korean War, the Vietnam War was not fought under the auspices of the United Nations.

- The seemingly endless Vietnam War polarized America into hawks who supported the war effort and doves who demanded that America end the conflict. The cost of the war undermined Johnson's Great Society programs and eroded his popularity.

- The Tet Offensive in 1968 undermined Johnson's prediction that "victory was just around the corner." Public discontent forced LBJ to reject calls for troop increases and to announce his decision not to seek re-election.

- President Nixon won election in 1968 on a promise to achieve "peace with honor" in Vietnam. Nixon announced a policy called Vietnamization that called for training South Vietnamese soldiers while beginning the gradual withdrawal of American forces.

- The Vietnam War finally ended in 1975 when the North Vietnamese captured Saigon and unified Vietnam. Unlike the armistice that ended the Korean War, the fall of Saigon resulted in a defeat for the U.S. policy of containment.

# CHAPTER 45
# THE ESSENTIAL GUIDE TO THE DBQ

## ESSENTIAL POINTS

1. The DBQ consists of 8-to-10 documents. Your DBQ essay will be scored on a 1-to-9 scale. Each point on this scale is worth 4.5 points.
2. High-scoring essays have a sophisticated thesis that is supported by a majority of the documents and substantial relevant outside information.
3. The College Board maintains an official website called AP Central. It is a treasure trove of valuable information for the DBQ.
4. A well-developed thesis is a key part of a successful DBQ. The thesis should be a clear statement of your position on the DBQ question. It should also identify the topics you are going to analyze.
5. Outside information is also an essential component of a high-scoring DBQ essay. An essay that lacks outside information will NOT receive a score above a 4.
6. The documents are designed to be cues that can trigger outside information that you can weave into your narrative.
7. The annotated DBQ essay at the end of this chapter is designed to illustrate the components of a high-scoring essay.

## TOPIC 219
# KEY FACTS AND TIPS

## 1. KEY FACTS ABOUT THE DBQ

- The DBQ follows the multiple-choice section. It begins with a mandatory 15-minute reading and planning period. You will then have 45 minutes to write your essay.
- The DBQ consists of 8 – 10 documents. The documents include letters, newspaper editorials, personal letters, speeches, charts, political cartoons, photographs, and maps.
- The DBQ is scored on a 1-to-9 scale. Each point is worth 4.5 points. A perfect score of 9 is thus worth 40.5 points (9 x 4.5), a 6 is worth 27 points (4 x 4.5), and a 4 is worth 18 points (4 x 4.5).

## 2. SCORING GUIDE FOR THE DBQ

- The 8 – 9 essay begins with a sophisticated, well-constructed thesis. The thesis is supported by information from a majority of the documents. The thesis is also supported by relevant and substantial outside information. The essay may contain minor errors.
- The 5 – 7 essay begins with a clear thesis. The thesis is supported by information from some documents. The thesis is also supported by some relevant outside information. The essay may contain errors that do not detract from the overall quality of the thesis.
- The 2 – 4 essay begins with a limited or underdeveloped thesis. The thesis is minimally supported by the documents. The thesis is not supported by outside information. The essay contains major errors.
- The 0 – 1 essay either lacks a thesis or begins with a confused thesis. It shows a poor understanding of the questions and documents. The essay contains numerous factual errors.

## 3. DBQ DO'S

- Read the question carefully. Make sure that you understand your assignment. Carefully identify each part of the question.

- Quickly jot down a few major events and people you associate with the DBQ topic. This will help jog your mind and guide your response.
- Carefully read each document. Pay attention to the date, author, and historic context. Note the documents that support or oppose a possible viewpoint. This viewpoint will become your thesis.
- Write a preliminary thesis. Then write an outline of your major points. Refer to this outline as you write your essay.
- Integrate the documents into your essay. Always focus on using the documents to support your thesis.
- Include relevant outside information. Remember, you cannot score above a 4 unless your essay includes outside information.
- Keep an eye on the clock. You should aim to write your DBQ essay in 45 minutes. Don't panic if you need an extra 5 minutes to complete your DBQ essay. The DBQ is not like the SAT or ACT. Your proctor will not call time. The proctor will simply inform you that you now have 70 minutes to work on the free-response essays. So remain calm and businesslike. Finish your DBQ and then move on to the free-response essays.
- Write a concise conclusion that restates your thesis and major major supporting arguments.

## 4. DBQ DON'TS
- Don't digress from the topic.
- Don't use "I" statements.
- Don't use long quotes from the documents.
- Don't summarize the documents. Instead, always strive to analyze and evaluate the documents.
- Don't try to impress the reader with "big" SAT-type vocabulary words. Strive to be clear not wordy.
- Don't begin your essay until you have a clear sense of your thesis and an outline of the topics you will use to support it.

**TOPIC 220**
# FINDING AND USING AP CENTRAL

## 1. THE IMPORTANCE OF AP CENTRAL

- The College Board maintains an official website called AP Central.
- AP Central is an essential tool for preparing for the APUSH exam. It contains a treasure trove of valuable information on the DBQ and Free-Response questions.

## 2. FINDING AP CENTRAL

- First go to Google and enter AP Central.
- Second, click on the heading AP Central – AP Courses and Exams. Now click on the green button "AP Courses and Exams." This will bring up a menu of choices. Click on the button, "Course Home Pages."
- Third, you will now see a chart with all 34 AP courses. Click on US History.
- Fourth, go to the 3rd heading entitled, "Exam Information and Resources." Then go to the 3rd sub-heading entitled "AP US History Exam Information." Click on this sub-heading.
- Fifth, you will now see a bar with Free-Response questions from 1999 to the most recent test. NOTE THAT THE BUTTON FOR THE 1999 – 2002 TESTS IS ON THE FAR RIGHT.

## 3. A GUIDED TOUR OF WHAT'S AVAILABLE FOR THE DBQ

### ALL QUESTIONS

The All Questions button on the far left provides you with the DBQ for the year you are searching. The DBQ is always Question 1 and it always comes first. Note that beginning with the 2002 exam, the College Board administered two separate APUSH exams each year. They administered the B exam to international students.

### SCORING GUIDE

The Scoring Guide is an extremely valuable resource for the DBQ. It provides you with a summary of key points and key inferences for each document in the DBQ.

## SCORING COMMENTARY

The Scoring Commentary section provides evaluations and scores for three sample DBQ essays.

## SAMPLE RESPONSES

The DBQ is always Essay 1. Click on Essay 1 and you will find a high, medium, and low sample essay. Remember, you have to go to the Scoring Commentary section to find out the score and code for each essay.

# 4. THE LEVEL 9 DBQ ESSAYS

- The level 9 DBQ essays are VERY VALUABLE to read. They are excellent tools that provide you with concrete examples of what the APUSH Readers are looking for.
- The level 9 essays are VERY IMPRESSIVE. Don't let them intimidate you. Remember, they represent the best essays from a group of over 350,000 APUSH students. It is extremely important to remember that you don't need to score an 8 or a 9 to achieve a 5. Your pragmatic (practical) goal is to earn 120 points or 66 percent of the 180 available points. So, if you score a 6 on your DBQ you are on your way to a 5. Your motto should be, a 6 equals a 5!

# 5. THE TOP TEN LEVEL 9 DBQ ESSAYS

- Essay I on the 2000 exam (Organized labor, 1875 – 1900)
- Essay IC on the 2002B exam (The Era of Good Feelings)
- Essay I on the 2003B exam (Progressive Era reformers)
- Essay 1I on the 2003 exam (New Deal and Great Depression)
- Essay 1A on the 2004B exam (US foreign policy, 1920 – 1941)
- Essay 1C on the 2004 exam (Consequences of the French and Indian War)
- Essay 1A on the 2005 exam (Impact of the Revolutionary War)
- Essay 1A on the 2007B exam (LBJ's response to political, economic, and social problems)
- Essay 1A on the 2008 exam (Vietnam War)
- Essay 1A on the 2010 exam (Influence of Puritans on New England colonies, 1630 – 1670)

**TOPIC 221**
# HOW TO WRITE A SOPHISTICATED THESIS FOR A DBQ ESSAY

## 1. WHAT IS A THESIS AND WHY IS IT SO IMPORTANT?

- Everyone agrees that a clear well-constructed thesis is essential for a high DBQ score. Don't be intimidated by the word "thesis." A thesis is the position you are taking to answer the DBQ question.
- A thesis is important because it tells your APUSH reader two key things. First, it spells out your position on the question. Second, it identifies the categories you will use in your analysis. The categories are simply the topics you will discuss and evaluate. For example, if the question asks you to analyze the successes and limitations of the New Deal, successes and limitations would be your two key categories.

## 2. CHARACTERISTICS OF A SOPHISTICATED THESIS

- The level 8 and 9 DBQ essays always have what the AP Central scoring commentary calls "a sophisticated thesis."
- A sophisticated thesis is clear and well-constructed. But, it is also nuanced. A nuance is a shade of difference. For example, the 2001 DBQ asked students to evaluate how successfully President Eisenhower addressed Cold War fears. A one-dimensional thesis would simply state that Eisenhower's policies successfully addressed Cold War fears. A nuanced thesis would be more sophisticated. It would state that some of Eisenhower's policies were successful and some were less successful.

## 3. A CASE EXAMPLE OF A SOPHISTICATED THESIS

- Let's say that your DBQ question asked you to evaluate how successfully reform movements expanded democratic ideals during the Age of Jackson, 1828 – 1840.
- Here is a sophisticated thesis for this question: The Age of Jackson witnessed a number of far-reaching political and social reforms. Jackson's election signaled the beginning

of a new era in American political history. As the hero of the "common man" Jackson endorsed expanding the suffrage to include virtually all white men. The Jacksonians also created a more open political system by replacing legislative caucuses with a party nominating convention. At the same time, reformers addressed the evils of slavery and the need for special hospitals for the mentally ill. However, the impulse for reform did not extend to the rights of American women.

- Note that this thesis provides a clear well-constructed answer to the DBQ question. But is also goes one step further by acknowledging that reform movements during this period did not address the rights of American women. This qualification is the hallmark of a sophisticated thesis.

# TOPIC 222
# HOW TO USE DBQ DOCUMENTS AS CUES FOR OUTSIDE INFORMATION

## 1. WHAT IS OUTSIDE INFORMATION AND WHY IS IT SO IMPORTANT?

- Everyone agrees that outside information is an essential component of high-scoring DBQ essays. According to the College Board's official scoring guide A DBQ ESSAY THAT LACKS OUTSIDE INFORMATION WILL NOT RECEIVE A SCORE ABOVE A 4.
- Outside information includes pertinent facts, events, people, and historic generalizations that go beyond the information provided in the DBQ documents. Outside information adds depth and insight to your essay.

## 2. VIEW EACH DOCUMENT AS A HISTORIC CUE

- The 8-to-10 documents represent different points of view on a given topic.
- It is helpful to view each document as a cue designed to elicit a variety of historic responses. For example, what comes to your mind when you see a 1955 picture of a family inside a bomb shelter? The shelter is clearly a response to the fear of a Soviet nuclear attack. You might also recall

the Duck and Cover drills conducted in public and private schools. The fear of a Soviet nuclear attack and Duck and Cover drills are both examples of outside information.

- You should strive to weave relevant outside information into your essay. However, don't panic if you can't think of outside information for each document. High-scoring level 8 and 9 essays include outside information from a majority of the documents.

### 3. A CASE EXAMPLE OF HOW TO USE A DOCUMENT AS A CUE

- Learning how to use documents as cues to trigger outside information requires practice. Here is an example that will help give you practice developing this skill.
- Roger Williams, "A Plea for Religious Liberty," 1644

"God requireth not a uniformity of religion to be enacted and enforced in any civil state; which enforced uniformity sooner or lateris the greatest occasion of civil war, ravishing of conscience, persecution of Christ Jesus in his servants, and of the hypocrisy and destruction of millions of souls." Roger Williams is an important historic cue. What comes to your mind when you think of him? First and foremost, he was a religious dissenter who challenged the authority of the Puritan leaders. Williams advocated religious toleration and the complete separation of church and state. Can you think of another Puritan dissenter? Anne Hutchinson also challenged Puritan authorities by questioning the subordinate role of women. The Puritans expelled both Williams and Hutchinson. Williams fled to Rhode Island, which became a haven for religious dissenters.

## TOPIC 223
# AN ANNOTATED DBQ SAMPLE ESSAY

1. The 2003B APUSH exam contained a DBQ on the Progressive Era. The DBQ asked students to "evaluate the effectiveness of Progressive Era reformers and the federal government in bringing about reforms at the national level." Students were asked to analyze both the "successes

and limitations" of reform efforts. The question limited the discussion to the period from 1900 to 1920.

2. The 2003B DBQ included 10 documents. You can read the full text of these documents at AP Central. Go to the 2003B exam bar and then click on "All questions." The DBQ documents are on pages 2 – 6.

3. For purposes of easy reference here is a brief description of each of the ten documents:

- Document A – A well-known political cartoon depicting Theodore Roosevelt as a big-game hunter who shot a bear labeled "bad trusts" and restrained a bear labeled "good trusts."
- Document B – An excerpt from the Neill-Reynolds Report documenting unsanitary conditions in the meat-packing industry.
- Document C – A passage by Jane Addams decrying the lack of child labor laws.
- Document D – A speech by Theodore Roosevelt calling for direct presidential primaries and the direct election of US senators.
- Document E – An excerpt from the Clayton Antitrust Act declaring that price discrimination is unlawful. At the same time the act specifically states that antitrust laws do not apply to labor organizations.
- Document F – An excerpt from an essay by Herbert Croly questioning the success and scope of Wilson's legislative achievements.
- Document G – An excerpt from the Supreme Court decision in *Hammer v. Dagenhart* striking down federal child labor laws.
- Document H – A photograph showing a suffragette holding a sign reminding President Wilson that American women still did not have the right to vote.
- Document I – An excerpt from an editorial by W.E.B. Du Bois pointing out the contradiction experienced by black soldiers who fought for freedom in France and then experienced racial discrimination in America.
- Document J – A bar graph depicting a sharp decline in the percentage of eligible voters in presidential elections from 1900 to 1920. The graph implies that many women did not exercise their right to vote in the 1920 presidential election.

4. Here is a sample essay that uses these documents to address the 2003B question. Carefully read the essay and the annotations that follow most of the paragraphs.

The Gilded Age witnessed the rise of political machines led by corrupt city bosses and monopolistic trusts led by powerful robber barons. The urban-industrial revolution of the late nineteenth century left a legacy of complex economic, social, and political problems. Progressive reformers shared an optimistic belief that the federal government should and could become an instrument for addressing social problems and improving the quality of American life. Between 1900 and 1920 Progressive reformers and the federal government achieved a number of impressive successes. At the same time, they failed to address the rising tide of racism. The Progressive Era thus left a mixed legacy of impressive accomplishments and disappointing limitations.

*Our sample DBQ essay opens with a sophisticated thesis. Note that the essay acknowledges Progressive Era accomplishments while also noting that reformers failed to address racism. This nuanced approach is the hallmark of a sophisticated thesis.*

By 1900, decades of laissez-faire economic policies enabled powerful trusts to monopolize business, restrain trade, and fix prices. This unprecedented concentration of economic power posed a problem for all three Progressive Era presidents. President Roosevelt began the process of regulating trusts by making a distinction between "good trusts" and "bad trusts" (Doc. A). Posing as a big game hunter, TR busted bad trusts like the Northern Securities Company while regulating good trusts that behaved responsibly. Although not known as a trust-buster, President Taft actually dissolved more trusts than Roosevelt. Like TR and Taft, Wilson opposed concentrated economic power. He signed the Clayton Antitrust Act (Doc. E). This landmark legislation strengthened the Sherman Antitrust Act and specifically stated that the law was not to be used to break up labor unions.

*This paragraph incorporates two documents (A and E) into the narrative. Note how the essay uses these documents as cues to bring in outside information. Document A serves as a cue to identify the Northern Securities Company as a "bad trust." Document E serves as a cue to note that the Clayton Antitrust Act strengthened the Sherman Antitrust Act.*

Wilson was proud of his legislative achievements. But, Herbert Croly wondered if Wilson's legislation had in fact "made the future clear and bright with the promise of best things." (Doc. F) We now know that during the 1920s the regulatory agencies created during the Progressive Era often came under the influence of the very businesses they were intended to regulate.

*This paragraph uses Document F as a cue to address a limitation of antitrust laws. Also note that the essay uses a brief quote from Document F. It is acceptable to weave a brief quote into your narrative. However, you should avoid using long quotes that detract from your analysis.*

Rampant urbanization and industrialization created a number of pressing social problems. Muckrakers like Upton Sinclair vividly described the deplorable conditions in America's meatpacking plants. After reading *The Jungle*, a disgusted President Roosevelt created a special commission to investigate Sinclair's accusations. The Neill-Reynolds Report further outraged an already nauseated public (Doc. B). Congress responded by passing the Meat Inspection Act requiring strict sanitary regulations and the Pure Food and Drug Act requiring labels to list all ingredients.

*This paragraph provides an excellent example of how to use a document as a cue. The Neill-Reynolds Report serves as a springboard to introduce Upton Sinclair and his famous novel The Jungle. This nicely illustrates the relationship between muckraking and reform legislation.*

While Upton Sinclair focused the nation's anger on the meatpacking industry, Jane Addams attempted to arouse moral outrage at the plight of children working long hours in unsafe factories (Doc. C). Addams' passionate appeals helped mobilize public support for the Keating-Owen Act of 1916. This legislation banned goods produced by children from interstate commerce. However, just two years later, the Supreme Court struck down the act.

> This paragraph takes advantage of how Documents C and G "talk" to each other. In Document C, Jane Addams points out that state laws on child labor were inadequate. However, the conservative Supreme Court did not support Progressive reforms.

Progressive reformers believed that dishonest city bosses and venal national politicians had corrupted America's democratic system. Progressives proposed a number of reforms designed to democratize local, state, and national governments. Progressives focused particular attention on the US Senate. At that time, senators were still chosen by their state legislatures. In a scathing series of muckraking articles David Phillips charged that senators were merely puppets of powerful trusts. Theodore Roosevelt agreed and threw his support behind a constitutional amendment providing for the direct election of senators (Doc D). After much debate and delay, the Senate finally passed the Seventeenth Amendment.

> This paragraph uses Roosevelt's speech in Document D as a cue to discuss Phillips' muckraking attack on the Senate and the passage of the Seventeenth Amendment.

While the Seventeenth Amendment marked an important victory for the democratic process, increasingly impatient women pointed out that they were still denied the right to vote (Doc. H). Led by Carrie Catt, a new generation of women successfully fought for the passage of the Nineteenth Amendment giving women the right to vote. The amendment culminated a long struggle that began with the Seneca Falls Convention in 1848.

*This paragraph provides another example of how to use a document as a cue. The essay uses Document H to weave both Carrie Chapman and the Seneca Falls Convention into the narrative. It is interesting to note that the essay does not refer to Document J. Remember, you do not have to use all the documents to hear a high score.*

Progressive reformers waged long and determined campaigns for the passage of the Seventeenth and Nineteenth Amendments. However, they ignored the plight of African Americans (Doc. I). The failure of the Progressives and the federal government to address Jim Crow segregation and the disfranchisement of African American voters is more than a limitation; it is a glaring injustice. It is a tragic fact that the Progressive Era witnessed the resurgence of the Ku Klux Klan. The Wilson administration ignored W.E.B. Du Bois' outraged plea for justice.

*This paragraph makes a key point – the Progressives ignored the plight of African Americans. Note that the author is very assertive in making this point. Graders will reward essays that make specific and forceful points.*

During the Progressive Era, reformers worked to make America a better place. Progressives broke up and regulated trusts, ensured safe foods and drugs, and won the right to vote for women. However, their successes were not complete. Corporations eluded many of the regulations, children still worked in factories, and African Americans still endured the indignities of Jim Crow segregation.

*This paragraph provides an excellent model of how to write a conclusion. Note that the paragraph restates the thesis and concisely summarizes the major supporting points.*

# CHAPTER 46
# THE ESSENTIAL GUIDE TO THE FREE-RESPONSE ESSAY

## ESSENTIAL POINTS

1. You must write two free-response essays. Each essay will be scored on a 1-to-9 scale. Each point on the scale is worth 2.75 points.

2. High-scoring free-response essays have a sophisticated thesis that is supported by relevant evidence.

3. The College Board maintains an official website called AP Central. It contains a particularly rich collection of resources that will help you understand how to write a high-level essay.

4. The annotated essay at the end of this chapter is designed to illustrate the components of a high-scoring free-response essay.

# TOPIC 224
# KEY FACTS AND TIPS

## 1. KEY FACTS ABOUT THE FREE-RESPONSE QUESTIONS

- The free-response section follows the DBQ. It consists of two questions that cover topics before the Civil War and two questions that cover topics after the Civil War. You must select one question from each pair of topics.
- You are allotted 70 minutes to write the two free-response essays. The College Board recommends that you devote 5 minutes to plan each essay and 30 minutes to write each essay.
- Each free-response essay is scored on a 1-to-9 scale. Each point is worth 2.75 points. A perfect score of 9 is worth 24.75 points (9 x 2.75), a 6 is worth 16.50 points (6 x 2.75), and a 4 is worth 11 points (4 x 2.75). Taken together, the two free-response essays are worth a combined total of 49.50 points.

## 2. THE SCORING GUIDE FOR THE FREE-RESPONSE ESSAY

- The 8 – 9 essay begins with a clear, well-developed thesis that addresses each part of the question. The thesis is supported by substantial relevant information. The essay is well-organized and may contain minor errors.
- The 5 – 7 essay begins with a partially developed thesis that does not fully address all parts of the question. The thesis is supported by some relevant information. The essay has an acceptable organization and may contain errors that do not seriously detract from its overall quality.
- The 2 – 4 essay begins with a poorly developed thesis. The essay provides few relevant facts to support its thesis. The essay is poorly organized and may contain major errors that detract from its quality.
- The 0 – 1 essay has no thesis and demonstrates no understanding of the topic. It may contain numerous errors.

## 3. FREE-RESPONSE DO'S

- Read each pair of questions very carefully. Choose the question that you know the most about. Remember, your goal is to earn the most points that you can!
- Write a preliminary thesis. Then write a brief outline of the major topics you will discuss in your essay.

- Keep an eye on the clock. You should allocate 30 minutes to write each essay. Remember, your proctor will not let you know how much time is left. It is up to you to keep up with the time.
- Write well-developed paragraphs that support your thesis.
- Write a concise conclusion that restates your thesis and your major supporting arguments.

## 4. FREE-RESPONSE DON'TS
- Don't digress from the topic.
- Don't use "I" statements.
- Don't try to impress the reader with "big" SAT-type vocabulary words. Strive to be clear not wordy.
- Don't begin your essay until you have a clear sense of your thesis and an outline of your supporting evidence.

# TOPIC 225
# AP CENTRAL AND THE FREE-RESPONSE ESSAYS

## 1. FINDING AP CENTRAL
- AP Central contains a particularly rich collection of resources that will help you understand how to write a high-level free-response essay.
- Topic 220 in Chapter 45 provides a detailed description of how to find AP Central and then navigate the site.

## 2. SAMPLE FREE-RESPONSE ESSAYS AND INFORMATION SHEETS
- AP Central provides three sample free-response essays for each question on each test. One essay is usually an 8 or 9, one is a 5, 6, or 7 and one is a 3 or 4.
- In addition to providing sample free-response essays, AP Central often provides Information Sheets that explain the key points associated with each essay topic. It is important to note that the Information Sheets vary in quality. Some are just lists of key facts and people. Others provide very useful summaries that include insights into the topic. Chapters 1 – 43 contain boxes that identify many of the most useful Information Sheets.

## 3. THE LEVEL 9 FREE-RESPONSE ESSAY

- The level 9 free-response essays are VERY VALUABLE to read. They are excellent instructional tools that provide you with concrete examples of what the APUSH readers are looking for.
- The level 9 essays are VERY IMPRESSIVE. Don't let them intimidate you. Remember, they represent the best essays from a group of over 350,000 APUSH students. It is extremely important to remember that you don't need to score an 8 or 9 to achieve a 5. Your pragmatic (practical) goal is to earn 120 points or 67 percent of the 180 available points. So, if you score a 6 on each of your free-response essays you are on your way to a 5. Your motto should be, a 6 equals a 5!

## 4. THE TOP TEN FREE-RESPONSE ESSAYS

- Essay J, Question 5 on the 2000 exam (cultural change in the 1960s)
- Essay VA, Question 5 on the 2002 exam (the civil rights movement in the 1950s and 1960s)
- Essay I, Question 2 on the 2003 exam (the Articles of Confederation)
- Essay I, Question 3 on the 2003 exam (transportation developments before the Civil War)
- Essay 2A, Question 2 on the 2004B exam (the Revolution of 1800)
- Essay 5A, Question 5 on the 2005 exam (civil rights, antiwar, and women's movements in the 1960s and 1970s)
- Essay 5A, Question 5 on the 2006B exam (cultural trends in the 1920s)
- Essay 2A, Question 2 on the 2007 exam (Shays' Rebellion and the Whiskey Rebellion)
- Essay 3A, Question 3 on the 2008 exam (the market revolution before the Civil War)
- Essay 3A, Question 3 on the 2009 exam (the emergence of the Republican Party)

## TOPIC 226
# HOW TO WRITE A SOPHISTICATED THESIS FOR A FREE-RESPONSE ESSAY

## 1. WHAT IS A THESIS AND WHY IS IT IMPORTANT?

- Everyone agrees that a clear well-constructed thesis is essential for a high free-response essay score. Don't be intimidated by the word "thesis." A thesis is the position you are taking to answer the free-response question.

- A thesis is important because it tells your APUSH reader two key things. First, it spells out your position on the question. Second, it identifies the categories you will use in your analysis. The categories are simply the topics you will discuss and evaluate. For example, if the question asks you to identify and analyze the factors that promoted urbanization between 1860 and 1900 industrialization, transportation, and immigration would be your key categories.

## 2. CHARACTERISTICS OF A SOPHISTICATED THESIS

- The level 8 and 9 free-response essays always have what the AP Central scoring commentary calls, "a sophisticated thesis."

- A sophisticated thesis is clear and well-constructed. But, it is also nuanced. A nuance is a shade of difference. For example, the 2003 APUSH exam asked students to compare and contrast consumerism and race relations in the 1920s and 1950s. A one-dimensional thesis would simply state that both decades were characterized by excessive materialism and racial segregation in the South. A nuanced thesis would be more sophisticated. It would state that race relations in the early 1950s did resemble the 1920s. However, Supreme Court decisions and a growing civil rights movement led by Dr. King began to challenge Jim Crow segregation in the second half of the decade.

### 3. A CASE EXAMPLE OF A SOPHISTICATED THESIS

- The 2004 APUSH exam included a free-response question asking students to evaluate the effectiveness of the Cold War policy of containment in Europe and Asia between 1945 and 1975.

- Here is a sophisticated thesis for this question:

The Cold War policy of containment was originally intended to block the spread of Communist influence in Europe. The Marshall Plan and the NATO alliance successfully used American's vast economic and military resources to revive and defend Western Europe. However, containment did not enjoy the same success in Asia. The United States did transform Japan into a thriving ally. At the same time, China "fell" to Communism, Korea became a divided peninsula, and Communist North Vietnam conquered South Vietnam.

- Note that this thesis provides a clear well-organized answer to the 2004 free-response question. But it also goes one step further by acknowledging that while containment was a success in Western Europe, it enjoyed mixed results in Asia. This qualification is the hallmark of a sophisticated thesis.

## TOPIC 227
# AN ANNOTATED FREE-RESPONSE SAMPLE ESSAY

### 1. A SAMPLE QUESTION:

- Evaluate the role that geographic, economic, and social factors played in the growth of slavery in the Southern colonies between 1607 and 1775.

### 2. AN ANNOTATED SAMPLE ESSAY:

Geographic, economic, and social factors all played key roles in the growth of slavery in the Southern colonies between 1607 and 1775. Textbook authors emphasize the dominant role played by geographic and economic factors. Indeed, these two factors are often portrayed as making slavery all but inevitable. At the same time, social factors are typically relegated to a position of secondary importance. In fact, social factors played a pivotal role in creating a stable slave society in the South. Without widespread social support the slave system would not have endured.

> *Our sample free-response essay opens with a sophisticated thesis. The essay acknowledges the role that geographic and economic factors played in the growth of slavery in the south. However, the essay states that social factors have been underestimated. This nuanced approach is the hallmark of a sophisticated thesis with a very strong point of view.*

Geography influenced the growth of slavery in the South. The region's fertile land, warm climate, abundant rainfall, and long growing season all enabled planters to grow tobacco, rice, and indigo as cash crops. Numerous navigable rivers provided convenient routes for transporting goods to ports such as Norfolk, Charleston, and Savannah. Taken together, these geographic conditions made farming a potentially lucrative business.

> *This paragraph provides a concise summary of the role that geography played in the Southern commitment to cash crops.*

Tobacco and other cash crops required a large supply of inexpensive labor. The spread of tobacco cultivation beyond the Chesapeake colonies created additional demand for inexpensive labor. At first, the planters relied upon indentured servants imported from England. Between 1607 and 1676 indentured servants comprised the chief source of agricultural labor in the Chesapeake colonies of Virginia and Maryland.

> *This paragraph begins the essay's treatment of the role played by economic factors.*

At first, the system of indentured labor benefited both the workers and the planters. It gave unemployed English workers an opportunity to improve their lives in America. The planters benefited by using the headright system to attract more settlers to Virginia. Under this system, planters received 50 acres for each person (or head) they brought to the colony.

> *This paragraph continues the discussion of the system of indentured labor. The paragraph explains that both*

*workers and planters benefited from this system.*
*Note the clear explanation of the headright system.*

The use of indentured servitude proved to be unreliable and unstable. As the English Civil War ended and economic conditions improved, the number of people willing to become indentured servants sharply declined. In 1676 former indentured servants led by Nathaniel Bacon rebelled against both Governor Berkeley and the planter aristocracy that had exploited their labor. Bacon's sudden death enabled Berkeley to crush the now leaderless rebels.

*This paragraph explains why the system of indentured servants proved to be unsustainable.*

Bacon's Rebellion exposed tensions between poor former indentured servants and the wealthy tidewater gentry. The rebellion persuaded planters to replace the troublesome indentured servants with slaves imported from Africa. This commitment to slave labor led to the growth of the South's "peculiar institution." By the mid-1700s, slaves comprised about 40 percent of the South's population.

*This paragraph explains the significance of Bacon's Rebellion. It exposed tensions in southern society that forced the planters to find an alternative system of labor. Bacon's Rebellion is thus a key link in the chain of events that led to the beginnings of slavery in the Southern colonies.*

Slave ownership was not evenly distributed across Southern society. A small but powerful group of wealthy planters dominated Southern society. Since the majority of white families in the South did not own slaves why did slavery become entrenched in Southern society? The answer to this all-important question can be found in three key social factors. First, few white colonists in the South questioned human bondage as morally unacceptable. Second, although the majority of white families in the South did not own slaves, they did aspire to become slave owners. And finally, poor whites felt superior to black slaves thus providing a subtle but vital level of psychological support for the slave system.

*This paragraph plays a key role in supporting the essay's thesis that social factors played a pivotal role in the growth of slavey in the Southern colonies.*

Geographic, economic, and social factors all played a role in the growth of the slave system in the South. A favorable climate to grow cash crops did not make slavery inevitable. Planters turned to slave labor when the system of indentured servants proved to be no longer viable in the aftermath of Bacon's Rebellion. The slave system grew and matured because nonslaveholding whites did not question the South's "peculiar system." Instead, they aspired to become slave owners and felt superior to black slaves.

*This paragraph provides an excellent model of how to write a conclusion. Note that the paragraph restates the thesis and concisely summarizes the essay's major supporting points.*

# REVIEW · TOP 10'S
# THE DRIVE FOR FIVE

## PART 1
## TOP 10 LISTS: A CHRONOLOGICAL REVIEW

## I. TOP 10 EVENTS FROM THE SPANISH YEARS, 1492 – 1606

### 1. THE FIRST SPANISH EXPEDITIONS
Columbus hoped to find a new sea route to Asia. He adopted a highly ethnocentric attitude toward the Native Americans he encountered. It is important to note that the Portuguese were actually the first Europeans to conduct regular maritime expeditions into the South Atlantic.

### 2. THE COLUMBIAN EXCHANGE
Name given to the exchange of plants, animals, and diseases between Europe and the New World following Columbus' discovery of the New World in 1492. The Spanish introduced Europe to such New World crops as potatoes, tomatoes, and corn.

### 3. THE FALL OF THE AZTECS AND THE INCAS
Both the Aztecs and the Incas had centralized governments. Cortes defeated the Aztecs and Pizarro defeated the Incas.

### 4. THE ENCOMIENDA SYSTEM
Spanish rulers rewarded local officials by granting them villages and control over native labor. Known as the encomienda system, this practice cruelly exploited Indian labor.

### 5. THE FOUNDING OF FLORIDA
Florida was the first part of what is now the continental United States to be visited by Europeans. The Spanish began construction of a fortress at St. Augustine in 1565, thus founding the oldest continuously inhabited European settlement in what is now the United States.

### 6. THE RISE OF NEW SPAIN
By the mid-16th century, New Spain included hundreds of flourishing towns. Mexico City boasted an impressive cathedral and a new university.

## 7. THE SPANISH SOUTHWEST

By 1630, 3,000 Spaniards lived in New Mexico. The Spanish had the most contact with the Pueblo, Hopi, and Zuni.

## 8. THE IMPACT OF DISEASE

Demographers estimate that over 50 million people inhabited the New World in 1492. European diseases such as small pox decimated the Native American population.

## 9. THE DEFEAT OF THE SPANISH ARMADA, 1588

In 1588, Philip II sent the Spanish Armada to invade and conquer England. However, the English defeated the Armada thus beginning a new era of English exploration and colonization.

## 10. THE IROQUOIS CONFEDERACY

The Iroquois formed the most important and powerful North American political alliance. The Iroquois lived in settled villages.

# II.    TOP 10 EVENTS FROM THE COLONIAL YEARS, 1607 – 1763

## 1. THE FOUNDING OF JAMESTOWN, 1607

Jamestown was founded by a joint-stock company to earn a profit. Tobacco quickly became the colony's key cash crop.

## 2. JOHN WINTHROP'S "CITY UPON A HILL" SERMON, 1630

The Puritans have a special mission to build a model Christian community. Winthrop's speech marked the first expression of American Exceptionalism.

## 3. THE PURITANS BANISH ROGER WILLIAMS AND ANNE HUTCHINSON, 1638

Puritan authorities banished both Roger Williams (1636) and Anne Hutchinson (1638) for their unorthodox religious views. Williams founded a colony in Rhode Island based upon freedom of religion and the separation of church and state.

## 4. BACON'S REBELLION, 1676

Bacon's Rebellion exposed tensions between poor former indentured servants and the wealthy tidewater gentry. The rebellion persuaded planters to turn to imported slave labor from Africa.

## 5. THE PUEBLO REVOLT, 1680

Led by Popé, the Pueblo successfully drove the Spanish out of their territory. However, the Spanish returned a dozen years later and reestablished control.

## 6. WILLIAM PENN FOUNDS PENNSYLVANIA, 1682

William Penn founded Pennsylvania as a refuge for Quakers. The Quakers practiced religious toleration, opposed slavery and refused to bear arms. Pennsylvania quickly became noted for its prosperous economy and heterogeneous population.

## 7. STONO REBELLION, 1739

Slaves living south of Charleston seized guns and killed nearby planters. The slaves hoped to reach Florida where they would gain their freedom. However, the local militia put down the rebellion killing dozens of slaves.

## 8. THE FIRST GREAT AWAKENING, 1730S AND 1740S

The First Great Awakening was a wave of religious enthusiasm that began in New England and then swept across the rest of the colonies. Jonathan Edwards and George Whitefield were the leading preachers. The First Great Awakening split the Congregational and Presbyterian churches and encouraged missionary work to African slaves and Native Americans.

## 9. THE ALBANY PLAN OF UNION, 1754

Proposed by Benjamin Franklin, the Albany Plan of Union called for a unified response to the threat posed by the Indians and the French. Franklin supported the plan with his famous "Join, or Die" cartoon. Both the colonies and the British rejected the Albany Plan.

## 10. THE FRENCH AND INDIAN WAR, 1754 – 1763

The colonies and Great Britain successfully ended French power in North America. However, the war left Great Britain with a huge war debt.

# III. TOP 10 EVENTS FROM THE REVOLUTIONARY YEARS, 1764 – 1789

## 1. THE STAMP ACT, 1765

Parliament passed the Stamp Act to raise revenue to support British troops stationed in the colonies. The Stamp Act provoked a debate over Parliament's right to tax the colonies.

## 2. THE COERCIVE ACTS, 1774

The Coercive Acts were designed to punish Boston for the Tea Party. The British strategy of isolating Boston failed.

## 3. THE FIRST CONTINENTAL CONGRESS, 1774

Elected representatives met in Philadelphia to reach a unified response to the Coercive Acts. The First Continental Congress called for a complete boycott of British goods and also urged the colonists to organize a militia for defensive purposes.

## 4. *COMMON SENSE*, 1776

Thomas Paine rejected monarchy as a form of government and urged Americans to create an independent government based upon republican principles.

## 5. THE DECLARATION OF INDEPENDENC, 1776

Jefferson used Locke's philosophy of natural rights to justify the colonies right to rebel against the British king.

## 6. THE BATTLE OF SARATOGA, 1777

The American victory revived the colonial cause and helped convince France to declare war on Great Britain and openly support the American cause.

## 7. THE TREATY OF PARIS, 1783

Ended the Revolutionary War on favorable terms to the United States. Under the terms of the treaty, America's boundaries stretched west to the Mississippi, north to the Great Lakes, and south to Florida.

## 8. THE NORTHWEST ORDINANCE OF 1787

Enacted under the Articles of Confederation. The Northwest Ordinance established an orderly procedure for territories to become states equal to the original thirteen states. It banned slavery from the Northwest Territory thus becoming the first national law to prohibit the extension of slavery.

## 9. SHAYS' REBELLION, 1787

Shays' Rebellion was sparked by frustrated Massachusetts farmers who were losing their land because they could not repay their debts to eastern creditors in hard currency. Shays' Rebellion helped convince Washington, Madison, and Hamilton that the Articles of Confederation were too weak and that the United States needed a stronger federal government.

## 10. RATIFICATION OF THE CONSTITUTION, 1789

The Constitution created a federal system of government that divided power between a national government and state government. The Constitution divided power into legislative, executive, and judicial branches. The Great Compromise created a bicameral Congress. The Three-Fifths Compromise provided that slaves be counted as three-fifths of a person for purposes of representation and taxation.

# IV. TOP 10 EVENTS FROM THE EARLY REPUBLIC YEARS, 1790 – 1824

## 1. HAMILTON'S FINANCIAL PLAN, 1790

Hamilton's plan called for the federal government to assume the debts, adopt an excise tax on liquor, impose high tariffs on imported manufactured goods, and charter a national bank. Hamilton argued that the necessary and proper clause gave Congress the power to charter a national bank. Jefferson countered by arguing that what the Constitution does not permit it forbids.

## 2. WASHINGTON'S FAREWELL ADDRESS, 1796

Washington urged future leaders to avoid forming permanent alliances with foreign nations. During the 1930s, isolationists used Washington's Farewell Address to justify the Neutrality Acts.

## 3. THE ALIEN AND SEDITION ACTS, 1798

The Alien and Sedition Acts were a response to the contentious debate over the Quasi-War with France. The acts were intended to intimidate the Democratic-Republicans. Jefferson and Madison denounced the acts in the Virginia and Kentucky Resolutions. Their arguments inspired the doctrine of states' rights.

## 4. THE REVOLUTION OF 1800

The election of 1800 marked a peaceful transition of power from the Federalists to the Democratic-Republicans.

## 5. THE LOUISIANA PURCHASE, 1803

The purchase doubled the size of the United States. Jefferson agreed to the purchase even though it contradicted his belief in a strict interpretation of the Constitution. He believed that that the new territory would fulfill his vision of enabling America to become an agrarian republic.

## 6. *MARBURY v. MADISON*, 1803

The Marshall Court established the principle of judicial review.

## 7. THE CONSEQUENCES OF THE WAR OF 1812

The War of 1812 led to a new spirit of nationalism. It also promoted domestic industries and dealt a fatal blow to the Federalist Party.

## 8. THE AMERICAN SYSTEM, 1816 – 1824

Henry Clay's grand plan to use tariffs to promote domestic industries and fund a network of roads and canals (internal improvements). Clay also supported the national bank.

## 9. THE MISSOURI COMPROMISE, 1820

The Missouri Compromise admitted Maine as a free state and Missouri as a slave state. It forbade slavery in the Louisiana Territory north of 36°30'. The Missouri Compromise temporarily defused the controversy over slavery.

## 10. THE MONROE DOCTRINE, 1823

The Monroe Doctrine was a unilateral declaration of principles that asserted American independence from Europe in foreign policy. It warned the European nations against further colonial ventures in the Western Hemisphere.

# V.   TOP 10 EVENTS FROM THE ANTEBELLUM YEARS, 1825 - 1860

## 1. THE OPENING OF THE ERIE CANAL, 1825

The Erie Canal connected Albany on the Hudson River with Buffalo on Lake Erie. The canal transformed New York City into America's greatest commercial center. It created commercial ties between the Northeast and the Midwest.

## 2. THE SECOND GREAT AWAKENING, 1820 - 1840

The Second Great Awakening was a wave of religious enthusiasm led by itinerant preachers such as Charles Finney. It played a key role in making Americans aware of the moral issues posed by slavery.

## 3. WILLIAM LLOYD GARRISON, 1831

Garrison published the first issue of *The Liberator* on January 1, 1831. He called for the "immediate and uncompensated emancipation of the slaves."

## 4. *WORCESTER v. GEORGIA*, 1832

The Marshall Court upheld the Cherokee Nation's legal right to their ancestral lands. However, President Jackson refused to enforce the ruling. Jackson's policy led to the removal of the Cherokee from their homeland to lands across the Mississippi River. About one-quarter of the Cherokee people died on what came to be called the Trail of Tears.

## 5. THE SENECA FALLS CONVENTION, 1848

The Seneca Falls Convention was organized and led by Elizabeth Cady Stanton and Lucretia Mott. The "Declaration of Sentiments and Resolutions" called for greater rights for women including the right to vote. The meeting marked the beginning of the women's rights movement in America.

### 6. IRISH IMMIGRATION, 1840 – 1860

Most Irish settled in cities along the east coast. Irish immigrants played a key role in the rise of big city political machines. The wave if Irish immigrants aroused intense anti-Catholic prejudice that expressed itself in the rise of the Know-Nothing political party.

### 7. THE WILMOT PROVISO, 1846

The Wilmot Proviso called for the prohibition of slavery in lands acquired in the Mexican War. The Wilmot Proviso never became federal law. However, it reopened the sectional debate about extending slavery into the western territories.

### 8. THE KANSAS–NEBRASKA ACT, 1854

The Kansas-Nebraska Act stated that popular sovereignty would be used to determine the status of slavery in the Kansas and Nebraska territories. The act led to the demise of the Whig Party and the rise of the Republican Party.

### 9. SLAVERY IN THE OLD SOUTH, 1825 – 1860

By 1860 there were 4 million slaves in the South. The majority of white families did not own slaves. Nonetheless, the majority of white Southerners defined slavery as a "positive good."

### 10. THE DRED SCOTT CASE, 1857

The Supreme Court ruled that Dred Scott was a slave and thus could not sue in federal court. The Court further ruled that slaves were private property and could be taken to any state or territory. The Dred Scott ruling thus invalidated the Northwest Ordinance of 1787 and the Missouri Compromise of 1820.

# VI. TOP 10 EVENTS FROM THE INDUSTRIAL YEARS, 1861 – 1896

### 1. THE BATTLE OF ANTIETAM, 1863

The Union victory at Antietam persuaded England and France to remain neutral. The victory also enabled Lincoln to issue the Emancipation Proclamation.

### 2. BLACK CODES, 1865

Southern state legislatures passed Black Codes to limit the civil rights and economic opportunities of African Americans.

### 3. THE FOURTEENTH AMENDMENT, 1868

Overturned the Dred Scott decision by making the former slaves citizens. The amendment prohibited states from depriving "any person of life, liberty, or property, without due process of law; nor deny any person within its jurisdiction equal protection of the laws."

## 4. THE CHINESE EXCLUSION ACT, 1882

The act prohibited the immigration of Chinese to America. The Chinese Exclusion Act was the first law in American history to exclude a group because of its ethnic background.

## 5. THE NEW IMMIGRANTS, 1880 – 1896

Term used to describe a new wave of immigrants from small towns and villages in Southern and Eastern Europe. The New Immigrants primarily settled in large cities in the Northeast and Midwest.

## 6. THE DAWES ACT, 1887

The Dawes Act was partially inspired by public pressure following the publication of Helen Hunt Jackson's *Century of Dishonor*. The legislation's goal was to turn Native Americans into self-supporting farmers by dividing tribal lands into individual homesteads. The Dawes Act ignored the reliance of traditional Indian culture on tribally owned land.

## 7. SOCIAL DARWINISM, 1880S

Social Darwinism was the belief that the "laws" of biological evolution also apply to human society. Social Darwinists promoted competition and rugged individualism and opposed government intervention in the free market.

## 8. THE POPULIST REVOLT, 1890 – 1896

Agrarian discontent was sparked by falling farm prices and discriminatory railroad rates. The Populist platform called for government control of the railroads, free coinage of silver, and the direct election of U.S. senators.

## 9. *PLESSY v. FERGUSON*, 1896

Plessy v. Ferguson was a landmark Supreme Court case that sanctioned "separate but equal" facilities for African Americans. The decision allowed Jim Crow segregation laws to spread across the South.

## 10. THE ELECTION OF 1896

The Election of 1896 featured a presidential contest between William Jennings Bryan and William McKinley. Bryan endorsed free silver and was supported by a coalition of Democrats and Populists. McKinley endorsed tariffs and the gold standard and was supported by the Republicans. McKinley's victory led to the collapse of the Populist Party and a generation of almost unbroken Republican dominance.

# VII. TOP 10 EVENTS FROM THE PROGRESSIVE YEARS, 1897 – 1920

## 1. THE SPANISH–AMERICAN WAR, 1898

The Spanish-American War marked the end of Spain's New World empire and the emergence of the United States as a world power. The Treaty of Paris ceded Puerto Rico and Guam to the United States. Spain recognized Cuban independence and agreed to cede the Philippine Islands to the United States for $20 million.

## 2. THE OPEN DOOR POLICY, 1899

The Open Door policy was designed to protect American commercial interests in China.

## 3. THE FOUNDING OF THE NAACP, 1909

The NAACP was founded by W.E.B. Du Bois and other civil rights leaders. The organization rejected Booker T. Washington's policy of gradualism and instead focused on using the courts to strike down Jim Crow segregation laws.

## 4. THE MUCKRAKERS, 1900 – 1920

The Muckrakers were investigative reporters who expressed the new spirit of Progressive reform by uncovering social and economic wrongs. Ida Tarbell, Lincoln Steffens, and Upton Sinclair were the leading muckrakers. Sinclair's novel *The Jungle* prompted Congress to pass the Meat Inspection Act and the Pure Food and Drug Act.

## 5. THE ELECTION OF 1912

The election of 1912 featured a presidential contest among William Howard Taft, Theodore Roosevelt, and Woodrow Wilson. TR's Bull Moose Party split the Republican vote thus enabling Wilson and the Democrats to win the White House.

## 6. THE OPENING OF THE PANAMA CANAL, 1914

The Panama Canal gave the United States a commanding position in the Western Hemisphere. The canal made the security of the Caribbean a vital American interest. The Roosevelt Corollary justified American's unrestricted right to regulate Caribbean affairs.

## 7. THE GREAT MIGRATION, 1914 – 1919

The wartime demand for industrial workers encouraged over 400,000 southern blacks to move to northern and Midwestern cities.

## 8. THE FOURTEEN POINTS, 1918

The Fourteen Points were Woodrow Wilson's blueprint for post-World War peace. Wilson's fourteenth and most famous point called for a League of Nations.

## 9. THE SENATE REJECTS THE VERSAILLES TREATY, 1919

Led by Senator Lodge, the Senate rejected the Treaty of Versailles and thus the League of Nations. Lodge argued that the League would force American to abandon its long-standing policy of avoiding foreign entanglements.

## 10. THE NINETEENTH AMENDMENT, 1920

The Nineteenth Amendment guaranteed women the right to vote. The amendment culminated the long fight for women's suffrage that began at the Seneca Falls Convention in 1848.

# VIII. TOP 10 EVENTS FROM THE BOOM AND BUST YEARS, 1921 - 1945

## 1. THE MASS PRODUCTION OF CARS, 1921 - 1929

Henry Ford applied the principles of assembly line production to the manufacture of cars. Automobile sales stimulated demand for steel, rubber tires, glass, gasoline, and highways.

## 2. MASS CULTURE, 1921 - 1929

Radio and motion pictures contributed to the rise of American mass culture during the 1920s. Movies were the decades most popular form of mass entertainment.

## 3. FLAPPERS, 1921 - 1929

Flappers provided the most visible and shocking manifestation of the new American woman. Flappers challenged conventional norms of feminine appearance by wearing short skirts, heavy makeup, and short bobbed hair.

## 4. THE HARLEM RENAISSANCE, 1921 - 1929

The Harlem Renaissance was an outpouring of African American literary and artistic creativity. Harlem Renaissance writers such as Langston Hughes and Zora Neale Hurston celebrated the African American experience while also calling for equal civil rights.

## 5. THE HUNDRED DAYS, 1933

The name given to the period from March 9 to June 16, 1933 in which Congress passed New Deal laws to relieve unemployment, reform banking system, and promote industrial and agricultural recovery.

## 6. THE DUST BOWL, 1930 - 1936

Name given to parts of Oklahoma, Kansas, eastern Colorado and the Texas panhandle that suffered from a prolonged heat wave and drought. Desperate people called "Okies" moved to California to seek jobs. John Steinbeck described the plight of the Okies in The Grapes of Wrath.

## 7. THE NYE COMMITTEE, 1934

The Nye Committee concluded that greedy munitions dealers played a key role in America's entry into World War I. The Nye Committee encouraged isolationists to demand that Congress pass Neutrality Acts designed to keep the United States out of a new foreign war.

## 8. ROSIE THE RIVETER, 1941 – 1945

Rosie the Riveter was the name given to women who performed industrial work during World War II. For millions of American women, Rosie was a proud symbol of their patriotism and determination to contribute to the war effort.

## 9. THE JAPANESE INTERNMENT, 1942 – 1945

On February 19, 1942 President Roosevelt issued Executive Order 9066 authorizing the military to evacuate all people of Japanese ancestry from the West Coast. About 110,000 Japanese Americans were interred, or confined, in ten detention centers located on desolate lands owned by the federal government. The Supreme Court ruling in *Korematsu v. United States* upheld the constitutionality of the internment as a wartime necessity.

## 10. THE MANHATTAN PROJECT, 1939 – 1945

Name given to the secret project to develop and test an atomic bomb. President Truman authorized the military to drop atomic bombs on Hiroshima and Nagasaki. The atomic bomb's awesome power forced the Japanese to surrender.

# IX.  TOP 10 EVENTS FROM THE COLD WAR YEARS, 1946 – 1974

## 1. THE TRUMAN DOCTRINE, 1947

The Truman Doctrine committed the United States to a policy designed to contain Soviet aggression.

## 2. THE MARSHALL PLAN, 1947

The Marshall Plan was a program of economic aid that helped revive Europe and prevent the spread of communist influence.

## 3. THE RISE AND FALL OF SENATOR McCARTHY, 1950 – 1954

Senator McCarthy skillfully exploited the climate of political paranoia following the fall of China and the revelations that Soviet spies infiltrated government agencies. McCarthy finally caused his own downfall in the Spring of 1954 when he launched a televised investigation of the U.S. Army. The Army-McCarthy hearings turned public sentiment against McCarthy.

## 4. SPUTNIK, 1957

Launched by the Soviet Union, Sputnik was the first human-made satellite to orbit the Earth. Sputnik challenged America's long- standing sense of scientific and technological superiority. Congress responded to the Sputnik challenge by creating NASA and by funding science and math programs in the nation's public schools and colleges.

## 5. THE CIVIL RIGHTS ACT OF 1964

The Civil Rights Act of 1964 was the most important civil rights law since Reconstruction. It barred discrimination in public facilities such as hotels, restaurants, and theatres. The act further outlawed discrimination in employment on the basis of race, religion, national origins, and sex.

## 6. THE COUNTERCULTURE, 1967 – 1969

The name given to the alternate lifestyle advocated by hippies. The counterculture promoted communal living and "doing your own thing." Hippies attended outdoor music concerts such as the Woodstock Music Festival.

## 7. NIXON'S VISIT TO CHINA, 1972

In February 1972, President Nixon took a historic trip to the People's Republic of China. Nixon's dramatic visit opened a new era of cultural exchanges and trade that led to the establishment of formal diplomatic relations between the two countries in 1979.

## 8. NIXON'S DÉTENTE WITH THE SOVIET UNION, 1972

President Nixon stunned the world by becoming the first American president to visit Moscow. Nixon's visit ushered in a new era of détente with the Soviet Union that relaxed Cold War tensions between the two superpowers.

## 9. THE ARAB OIL BOYCOTT, 1973 – 1974

The Arab oil embargo ended the post-World War II economic boom and began a new period of inflation that plagued the U.S. economy during the rest of the 1970s.

## 10. THE WATERGATE SCANDAL, 1972 – 1974

The Watergate Scandal began with a burglary of the Democratic National Committee headquarters in the Watergate office complex in Washington, D.C. Although President Nixon has never been implicated in the burglary, he was involved in the ensuing cover-up. President Nixon resigned on August 9, 1974.

# X. TOP 10 EVENTS FROM RECENT HISTORY, 1975 - PRESENT

## 1. STAGFLATION, 1975 - 1982
The combination of rising unemployment and double-digit inflation that plagued the U.S. economy during the late 1970s and early 1980s.

## 2. THE CAMP DAVID SUMMIT, 1978
The Camp David summit marked the high point of the Carter presidency. Under the terms of the Camp David Accords, Israel and Egypt agreed to sign a peace treaty ending thirty years of hostility.

## 3. THE IRAN HOSTAGE CRISIS, 1979
In early 1979, a fundamentalist Islamic revolution led by Ayatollah Khomeini overthrew Iran's pro-American Shah. On November 4, 1979, a mob stormed the American embassy in Tehran and took over 50 Americans hostage. The hostage crisis and stagflation damaged Carter's popularity and led to his defeat in the 1980 presidential election.

## 4. REAGANOMICS, 1981 - 1988
Name given to President Reagan's economic program to promote growth by cutting taxes and deregulating business. Reagan's program is also called supply-side economics.

## 5. THE REAGAN DOCTRINE, 1983
The Reagan Doctrine is the name given to the Reagan administration's strategy to confront and oppose the global influence of the Soviet Union. The Reagan Doctrine led to a massive military buildup.

## 6. THE PERSIAN GULF WAR, 1991
Operation Desert Storm successfully crushed Saddam Hussein's Iraqi forces and liberated Kuwait.

## 7. NORTH AMERICAN FREE TRADE ASSOCIATION, 1994
NAFTA created a free-trade zone with Canada and Mexico. It was enacted during the Clinton presidency.

## 8. THE GRAYING OF AMERICA, 1990S TO THE PRESENT
America's population is becoming older as the Baby Boom generation ages and retires. This "graying" of the population poses a threat to the long-term viability of the social security system.

## 9. THE GROWTH OF THE SUNBELT, 1990S TO THE PRESENT
Many older Americans are choosing to retire to the South and West. These Sunbelt states now include a majority of the U.S. population.

## 10. A NEW WAVE OF IMMIGRATION, 1990S TO THE PRESENT
The 1965 Immigration Act triggered a major new wave of immigration. The largest number of immigrants are now coming from Latin America and Asia.

# PART II
# TOP 10 LISTS: A THEMATIC REVIEW

# XI.  TOP 10 AFRICAN AMERICAN LEADERS

## 1. FREDERICK DOUGLASS (1818 – 1895)
America's best-known black abolitionist. His famous autobiography exposed Americans to the horrors of slavery.

## 2. IDA B. WELLS (1862 – 1931)
Early African American civil rights advocate. Best-known for her opposition to lynching.

## 3. BOOKER T. WASHINGTON (1856 – 1915)
Urged African Americans to practice economic self-help rather than seek political rights.

## 4. W.E. B. DU BOIS (1868 – 1962)
Most prominent black critic of Booker T. Washington. Called for full political, economic, and social equality for all African Americans. Du Bois urged a "talented tenth" of educated blacks to spearhead the fight for equal rights.

## 5. MARCUS GARVEY (1887 – 1940)
Organized the Universal Negro Improvement Association to increase racial pride and promote black nationalism. Unlike Du Bois, Garvey championed black separatism.

## 6. DR. MARTIN LUTHER KING, JR. (1929 – 1968)
Most famous and influential African American leader during the civil rights movement. Dr. King inspired his followers with a message of nonviolent civil disobedience. He founded and led the Southern Christian Leadership Conference (SCLC).

## 7. GREENSBORO FOUR, 1960
Four black college students who led the first sit-in demonstration at a Woolworth lunch counter in downtown Greensboro, North Carolina.

## 8. MALCOLM X (1925 – 1965)
Black Muslim minister best-known for his advocacy of black power.

### 9. STOKELY CARMICHAEL (1941 – 1998)

Leader of the Student Nonviolent Coordinating Committee (SNCC) who ousted white members and advocated a separatist philosophy based upon black power.

### 10. HUEY NEWTON (1942 – 1989)

Founder and leader of the Black Panther Party.

# XII. TOP 10 WOMEN REFORMERS

### 1. ABIGAIL ADAMS (1774 – 1818)

Early proponent of women's rights who urged her husband to "remember the ladies."

### 2. ELIZABETH CADY STANTON (1815 – 1902)

Leading figure in the early women's movement. She was one of the organizers of the Seneca Falls Convention and the author of the Declaration of Sentiments.

### 3. SARAH MOORE GRIMKÉ (1792 – 1873)

One of the first women to publicly support abolition and women's suffrage.

### 4. DOROTHEA DIX (1802 – 1887)

Best-known for her work on behalf of the mentally ill.

### 5. HARRIET BEECHER STOWE (1811 – 1896)

Author of *Uncle Tom's Cabin*. Only the Bible sold more copies. Her novel intensified Northern opposition to slavery.

### 6. JANE ADDAMS (1860 – 1935)

Founder of Hull House. Best-known for her work as a leader of the settlement house movement.

### 7. MARGARET SANGER (1879 – 1966)

Outspoken reformer who openly championed birth control for women.

### 8. ELEANOR ROOSEVELT (1884 – 1962)

First Lady of the United States from 1933 – 1945. She was a strong and outspoken advocate of women's rights and African American civil rights.

### 9. RACHEL CARSON (1907 – 1964)

Wrote *Silent Spring* to warn the public about the effects of pesticides on human and animal life. *Silent Spring* helped launch the environmental movement in the United States.

### 10. BETTY FRIEDAN (1921 – 2006)

Wrote the *Feminist Mystique* to challenge the existing role of women as housewives. She was one of the founders of the National Organization of Women (NOW).

# XIII. TOP 10 SUPREME COURT CASES AND FAMOUS TRIALS

## 1. *MADISON v. MARBURY*, 1803
Established the principle of judicial review.

## 2. *DARTMOUTH COLLEGE v. WOODWARD*, 1819
Upheld the sanctity of contracts.

## 3. *WORCHESTER v. GEORGIA*, 1831
Upheld the rights of the Cherokee tribe. However, President Jackson refused to enforce the Court's decision.

## 4. *DRED SCOTT v. SANFORD*, 1857
Ruled that African Americans were not citizens and therefore could not petition the Court. Invalidated both the Northwest Ordinance and the Missouri Compromise line.

## 5. *PLESSY v. FERGUSON*, 1896
Sanctioned "separate but equal" public facilities for African Americans.

## 6. SACCO AND VANZETTI TRIAL, 1920S
Illustrated the widespread fear of radicals and recent immigrants.

## 7. THE JOHN T. SCOPES TRIAL, 1925
Illustrated the cultural conflict between fundamentalism and modernism.

## 8. *KOREMATSU v. UNITED STATES*, 1944
Upheld the constitutionality of the Japanese internment as a wartime necessity.

## 9. *BROWN v. BOARD OF EDUCATION TOPEKA*, 1954
Reversed the principle of "separate but equal" established in *Plessy v. Ferguson*. Ruled that racially segregated public schools are inherently unequal.

## 10. *MIRANDA v. ARIZONA*, 1966
Rules that persons apprehended by the police must be advised of their constitutional rights to remain silent and to have legal counsel at public expense.

# XIV. TOP 10 EVENTS IN US RELATIONS WITH LATIN AMERICA

## 1. MONROE DOCTRINE, 1823
Unilateral declaration warning European nations against further colonial ventures in the Western Hemisphere.

## 2. MEXICAN WAR, 1846 – 1848
Transformed the United States into a continental nation that spanned from the Atlantic to the Pacific.

## 3. TREATY OF GUADALUPE HIDALGO, 1848
Mexico ceded New Mexico and California to the United States and accepted the Rio Grande as the Texas border.

## 4. SPANISH–AMERICAN WAR, 1898
Spain relinquished control of Puerto Rico, Cuba, and the Philippines.

## 5. ROOSEVELT COROLLARY, 1904
Claimed the right of the United States to intervene in Latin American affairs. First applied in the Dominican Republic.

## 6. DOLLAR DIPLOMACY, 1909
Taft's policy of using American money to influence Caribbean nations.

## 7. GOOD NEIGHBOR POLICY, 1933
Renounced United States armed intervention in Latin America.

## 8. ALLIANCE FOR PROGRESS, 1961
Offered joint economic projects. Part of an overall effort to contain Communism.

## 9. BAY OF PIGS INVASION, 1961
Failed attempt to overthrow Castro. Prompted Khrushchev to send nuclear missiles to Cuba.

## 10. THE CUBAN MISSILE CRISIS, 1962
Soviets withdraw their missiles from Cuba in exchange for a U.S. promise not to attack Castro.

# XV. TOP 10 EVENTS IN THE VIETNAM WAR

## 1. FRANCE WITHDRAWS FROM VIETNAM, 1954
France agrees to the Geneva Accords and withdraws from Vietnam.

## 2. EISENHOWER ADVANCES THE DOMINO THEORY, 1954
President Eisenhower refused to abandon Vietnam to the Communists saying that the fall of South Vietnam would inevitably lead to Communist expansion throughout the rest of Southeast Asia.

## 3. THE GULF OF TONKIN RESOLUTION, 1964
Congressional resolution giving President Johnson a blank check to escalate the Vietnam War.

## 4. THE TET OFFENSIVE, 1968
Surprise attack by the Viet Cong and North Vietnamese across all of South Vietnam. Undermined public support for the war.

## 5. OPPOSITION TO THE VIETNAM WAR, 1967
Led by antiwar college students. Later supported by Senator Eugene McCarthy and Senator Robert F. Kennedy.

## 6. INVASION OF CAMBODIA, 1970
Surprise attack to destroy Viet Cong and North Vietnamese bases or "sanctuaries" in Cambodia.

## 7. KENT STATE SHOOTINGS, 1970
Frightened National Guard soldiers killed four student bystanders. Ignited a tidal wave of student protests.

## 8. VIETNAMIZATION, 1969 – 1973
President Nixon's policy to train South Vietnamese soldiers to take over the fighting.

## 9. THE PARIS ACCORDS, 1973
Agreement between the United States and North Vietnam to end the Vietnam War.

## 10. VIETNAM SYNDROME, 1973 – 2000
Widespread public skepticism about becoming involved in foreign entanglements that might become "another Vietnam."

# XVI. TOP 10 ARTISTS, ARTISTIC MOVEMENTS, PHOTOGRAPHERS

## 1. THE HUDSON RIVER SCHOOL, MID–1800S
America's first native school of art. Members painted idealized landscapes that emphasized America's grandeur and immensity.

## 2. THOMAS COLE (1801 – 1848)
Founder and leader of the Hudson River School.

## 3. THE ASHCAN SCHOOL, 1908 – 1913
Realistic paintings of urban life in New York City.

## 4. THE ARMORY SHOW, 1913
Art show in New York City that exposed Americans to the Cubist paintings of Picasso and other modern masters.

## 5. DOROTHEA LANGE (1895 – 1965)
Famous for documentary photos that captured the plight of migrant workers during the Great Depression.

## 6. EDWARD HOPPER (1882 – 1967)
Paintings captured the loneliness and alienation of life in America.

## 7. ABSTRACT EXPRESSIONISM, 1950S
Style of art based on the free application of paint with no references to visual reality.

## 8. JACKSON POLLOCK (1912 – 1956)
Best known Abstract Expressionist artist. Famous for his "drip" paintings.

## 9. POP ART, 1960S
Used recognizable images drawn from popular ("pop") culture.

## 10. ANDY WARHOL (1895 – 1930)
Best-known Pop artist. Famous for his pop portraits of Marilyn Monroe and Campbell soup cans.

# XVII.  TOP 10 LITERARY AUTHORS

## 1. ANNE BRADSTREET (1612 – 1672)
The first published American poet and the first woman to be published in America.

## 2. PHILLIS WHEATLY (1753 – 1784)
Colonial woman who was the America's first notable African American poet.

## 3. NATHANIEL HAWTHORNE (1804 – 1864)
Author of *The Scarlet Letter*. Hawthorne criticized the Puritan legacy of conformity and rigid orthodoxy.

## 4. WILLIAM HOLMES MCGUFFEY (1800 – 1873)
Compiler and editor of the *McGuffey Readers*, also known as the *Eclectic Reader*. The *McGuffey Readers* featured stories supporting patriotic and moral values.

## 5. RALPH WALDO EMERSON (1803 – 1882)
Leading Transcendental author. Emerson believed that human intuition transcended or rose above the limits of reason. Intuitionnenabled him to discover and understand spiritual truths.

## 6. WALT WHITMAN (1819 – 1892)
America's leading Romantic poet. In *Leaves of Grass*, Whitman rejected reason and celebrated his own feelings and emotions.

## 7. HORATIO ALGER (1832 – 1899)
Wrote popular novels that described how impoverished young boys succeeded through hard work, honesty, perseverance, and luck.

## 8. L. FRANK BAUM (1856 – 1919)
Wrote *The Wonderful Wizard of Oz* as a political allegory of free silver and the plight of American farmers.

## 9. JOHN STEINBECK (1902 – 1968)
His famous novel *The Grapes of Wrath* captured the ordeal faced by the Oakies as they fled the Dust Bowl and migrated to California.

## 10. JACK KEROUAC (1922 – 1969)
The best known Beat Generation author. His autobiographical novel *On the Road* describes the eclectic mix of people he met on spontaneous road trips across America.

# XVIII.    TOP 10 ACTS IN AMERICAN HISTORY

## 1. STAMP ACT, 1765
Intended to raise revenue. Provoked a heated debate over Parliament's right to tax its American colonies.

## 2. KANSAS–NEBRASKA ACT, 1854
Broke the uneasy truce between the North and the South. Repealed the Missouri Compromise. Led to the demise of the Whigs and the sudden emergence of the Republican Party.

## 3. HOMESTEAD ACT, 1862
Passed during the Civil War. Opened the Great Plains to settlers.

## 4. DAWES ACT, 1887
Divided tribal lands into individual homesteads. Tried to "civilize" Native Americans by turning then into self-supporting farmers.

## 5. NATIONAL ORIGINS ACT OF 1924
Established quotas to limit the flow of New Immigrants from Southern and Eastern Europe.

## 6. SOCIAL SECURITY ACT, 1935
Guaranteed retirement payments for enrolled workers beginning at age 65. Proved to be the most far-reaching New Deal program. Its long-term viability is now threatened by the "graying of America."

## 7. LEND–LEASE ACT, 1941
Ended American neutrality. Allowed FDR to send war material to Great Britain.

## 8. FEDERAL HIGHWAY ACT OF 1956
Created the Interstate Highway System and played a key role in promoting suburban growth.

## 9. THE VOTING RIGHTS ACT OF 1965
Made the Fifteenth Amendment an operative part of the Constitution. The law abolished literacy tests and other devices used to prevent blacks from voting.

## 10. THE IMMIGRATION ACT OF 1965
Abolished the system of national quotas instituted in the National Origins Act of 1924. The law had the unintended consequence of permitting a new wave of immigration from Latin America and Asia.

# XIX. TOP 10 EVENTS IN LABOR HISTORY

## 1. FORMATION OF THE KNIGHTS OF LABOR, 1869
The Knights attempted to unite all working men and women into a national trade union. The Knights began to lose strength when the public unjustly blamed them for causing the Haymarket Square riot.

## 2. THE AMERICAN FEDERATION OF LABOR, 1886
The AFL was an alliance of skilled workers in craft unions. Under the leadership of Samuel Gompers, the AFL focused on "bread and butter" issues such as higher wages and shorter hours.

## 3. THE GREAT RAILROAD STRIKE OF 1877
The first major interstate strike in American history. Signaled the beginning of a period of strikes and violent conflicts between labor and management.

## 4. THE SHERMAN ANTTRUST ACT, 1890
The act had little impact on the regulation of large trusts. However, it was used to curb labor unions.

## 5. THE PULLMAN STRIKE, 1894
Began when the Pullman Palace Car Company cut the wages of its workers but did not reduce the rent or prices it charged workers in company-run stores at the "model" town of Pullman outside Chicago. The Pullman Strike forced railroad traffic to a halt. The strike ended when President Cleveland ordered federal troops to intervene on the grounds that the strike obstructed delivery of the U.S. mail.

## 6. THE WAGNER ACT OF 1935
Also known as the National Labor Relations Act. The act guaranteed every laborer the right to join a Union and use the union to bargain collectively with management.

## 7. THE CONGRESS OF INDUSTRIAL ORGANIZATIONS, 1935
Founded and led by John L. Lewis. The CIO unionized workers at all levels within an industry.

## 8. THE SPLIT BETWEEN THE AFL AND THE CIO, 1935
The AFL and the CIO split apart at their national convention in 1935 because the AFL refused to grant charters to new unions organized on an industry-wide basis.

## 9. THE TAFT–HARTLY ACT, 1947
Intended to curb the power of labor unions.

## 10. FORMATION OF THE UNITED FARM WORKERS, 1962
Founded and led by César Chávez.

# XX. TOP 10 MOST INFLUENTIAL POLITICAL AND SOCIAL WORKS

## 1. *COMMON SENSE*, 1776
Written by Thomas Paine. Rejected monarchy as a form of government and urged Americans to create an independent nation based upon republican principles.

## 2. *DECLARATION OF INDEPENDENCE*, 1776
Written by Thomas Jefferson. Inspired by John Locke's philosophy of natural rights. Jefferson insisted that governments derive "their just powers from the consent of the governed."

## 3. *THE FEDERALIST PAPERS*, 1787
Written by James Madison, Alexander Hamilton, and John Jay. Intended to support ratification of the Constitution. In Federalist No. 10, Madison argued that political factions are undesirable but inevitable.

## 4. *THE LIBERATOR*, 1831
Published by William Lloyd Garrison. Called for the "immediate and uncompensated emancipation of the slaves."

## 5. "ON THE DUTY OF CIVIL DISOBEDIENCE," 1849
Written by Henry David Thoreau. Denounced the Mexican War as an unjust conflict designed to extend slavery into the territories. Thoreau argued that individuals have a moral responsibility to oppose unjust laws. Thoreau influenced Dr. King's philosophy of nonviolent disobedience.

## 6. *A CENTURY OF DISHONOR*, 1881
Written by Helen Hunt Jackson. Documented the misdeeds of corrupt Indian agents and duplicitous government officials. Aroused public support for a new Indian policy leading to the passage of the Dawes Act.

## 7. *HOW THE OTHER HALF LIVES*, 1890
Written and photographed by Jacob Riis. Used poignant pictures to document the poverty and despair of immigrants living in New York City's Lower East Side.

## 8. *THE JUNGLE*, 1906
Written by Upton Sinclair. Muckraking novel that exposed the filthy conditions in the Chicago meatpacking industry. Prompted Congress to pass the Meat Inspection Act.

### 9. *THE OTHER AMERICA*, 1962

Written by Michael Harrington. Compelling description of impoverished areas of America. Played a role in persuading President Johnson to make the war on poverty the centerpiece of his Great Society.

### 10. "*LETTER FROM BIRMINGHAM CITY JAIL*," 1963

Written by Dr. Martin Luther King, Jr. Defense of civil disobedience as a justified response to unjust segregation laws.

# PART III
# A PERSONAL HISTORY

# XXI. HISTORY AND MY BIOGRAPHY: A PERSONAL REVIEW, 1948 – 1970

I have always taught my students that events are real and that you never know when history will reach out and touch your personal biography. I'd like to conclude the Drive For Five section with a personal review of APUSH events from 1948 to 1970 that intersected my life.

## MY EARLY YEARS, 1948 – 1960

1.  I was born in 1948. So that makes me part of the Baby Boom generation, the huge demographic group of 76 million Americans born between 1946 and 1964. We're about to start retiring. According to an APUSH question on the 2006 exam were are threatening the viability of the Social Security, the most far-reaching New Deal program.

2.  The year I was born President Truman issued an executive order integrating the armed forces. That same year the Dixiecrats walked out of the Democratic Convention (and onto free-response Question 4 of the 2009B APUSH exam) to protest Truman's liberal civil rights policies. But I was just one year old and unaware of any of this.

3.  My first APUSH memory occurred when I was in the 2nd grade. Polio was then a feared illness that paralyzed young children. One day my whole class formed a line, held hands, and marched to the gym. A nurse rolled up my right sleeve and gave me a shot – the Salk Vaccine. I was saved from polio! I distinctly remember thinking, "The Salk Vaccine could be on a future APUSH exam."

4.  1956 was a great year. We liked Ike and loved Lucy. Congress passed the Federal Highway Act creating the Interstate Highway System. Two interstates would soon

intersect a few miles from my home. Little did I realize that the beautiful fields would one day be paved over and transformed into a shopping center with a huge Walmart. But that was all literally down the road.

5.  "Leave it to Beaver" was my favorite TV show. I do remember thinking that June Cleaver illustrated the revival of the cult of domesticity. Rosie the Riveter left her job in the defense industries and returned home to raise virtuous kids like me.

6.  Many things were going on that I didn't know about. The Supreme Court ordered schools to desegregate in *Brown v. Board of Education*. Then Rosa Parks refused to give up her seat and Dr. King led the Montgomery Bus Boycott. But I lived in a small town in western North Carolina and Alabama was like a foreign country to me.

7.  In 1957 I was very much aware of Sputnik, the first satellite to orbit the Earth. I was very upset because it meant that the Soviets were ahead in what would soon be called the Space Race. Congress created NASA and funded math and science education. One day my 5th grade teacher divided us into "advanced" and "regular" math groups. I was in the advanced group. Yea! Now I could do my part to help us win the Cold War.

8.  The Cold War dominated the news. My teacher taught us all about the US policy of containment. We even learned about a great man named George Kennan who was responsible for the policy.

9.  Thanks to the Cold War our school had "duck and cover" drills. An alarm sounded and we ducked under our desks. This was supposed to protect us from a nuclear attack. I took the practice very seriously and even developed a plan to turn the basement in my home into a fallout shelter.

10. As 1960 began I was very curious about a young and dynamic Democratic presidential candidate named John F. Kennedy. I remember watching the Kennedy-Nixon debates on television. I hoped JFK would win. He did and the torch of leadership passed to a new generation. The amazing 1960s were about to begin.

## MY TEENAGE YEARS, 1961 – 1966

11. JFK's inauguration sparked a wave of idealism. The Sixties were beginning and I was now a teenager. JFK called upon America's youth to join him in exploring what he called "The New Frontier." Many idealistic college students joined the Peace Corps. Most people supported the Alliance for Progress with Latin America. Anything and everything seemed possible.

12. The Cold War continued to dominate the news. The Soviets scored a first by sending Yuri Gagarin into space. Now we were behind in the Space Race. For my Civics class I drew a poster of Soviet Premier Khrushchev belligerently pointing his finger at the US while a mushroom-shaped nuclear bomb exploded behind him. I only got a B. What? I still think I should have received an A.

13. Remember my plan for a home fallout shelter? Well, it didn't seem so far-fetched in October 1962. I have a vivid memory of turning on the television and watching President Kennedy announce that the Soviets were building nuclear missile sites in Cuba. The Cuban Missile Crisis scared everyone. Fortunately, the Soviets agreed to withdraw their missiles from Cuba. In exchange, JFK agreed not to invade Cuba. Now I had to empty the sandbags from our basement.

14. Meanwhile, the sit-in movement spread from nearby Greensboro to my hometown, Statesville, North Carolina. My father owned a shoe store where I worked on weekends. Like other stores, ours was segregated with whites in the front and blacks in the back. My father was one of the first merchants to integrate his store. I saved a chair from the store. I always sit in it as I write the first draft of my books.

15. In May 1961, my family visited Rock Hill, South Carolina. Unknown to us, a few days before a biracial group of students boarded a bus in Washington, D.C. and headed south. As they passed through Rock Hill I witnessed an angry crowd shouting and throwing rocks at the bus. I have a vivid memory of hearing the Freedom Riders singing, "Freedom's coming and it won't be long."

16. My teachers ignored the Civil Rights Movement. I believe it must have been too controversial. Even so, I read about it in news magazines in the school library. I read Dr. King's famous "Letter From Birmingham Jail." He wrote that civil disobedience was a justified response to unjust laws. I have a framed *Time* Magazine cover of Dr. King on my office wall.

17. I entered high school in the Fall of 1963. On November 22, 1963 I walked into my US History class and saw tears streaming down our teacher's face. She told our stunned class that President Kennedy has just been assassinated in Dallas. Like everyone else I watched TV the next four days. Everything was about to change in ways I could not possibly have foreseen.

18. If someone had come up to me in 1964 and said, "Tell me everything you know about Vietnam" I would have said: "We learned in a current events class that Vietnam is in Southeast Asia. We have men there because the French lost and we have to contain Communism." I would also have known that Murray Moseley, the former captain of our football team, would be serving in Vietnam.

19. On August 7, 1964 Congress passed the Gulf of Tonkin Resolution. Today, it is recognized as a pivotal event that gave President Johnson a blank check to escalate the Vietnam War. It now generates a significant number of APUSH questions. At the time, Vietnam was still barely a tiny cloud on my horizon. I was going to be a junior and that meant preparing for the SAT and thinking about colleges.

20. My favorite teacher was Mr. Williams. To this day I remember his American literature classes. He brought everything to life from colonial poets like Anne Bradstreet to "modern" writers like Ernest Hemingway (Mr. William's favorite) and John Steinbeck. Mr. Williams you did a great job preparing me for college and my future as an author.

You also scored hits on future APUSH exams with Bradstreet's poems and Steinbeck's *Grapes of Wrath*. And Hemingway's "economy of style" has been a frequent example on SAT sentence completion questions.

21. US History was not as much fun. We took lots of notes and had to memorize them for our tests. I remember giving an oral report on Henry Clay that focused on the American System and his role as a "Great Compromiser." I later bought a biography of Clay that became the first book in my library. It is on the shelf behind my desk.

22. Civil rights continued to be the biggest historical event in the small Southern town where I lived. The 1964 Civil Rights Act barred discrimination in public facilities such as hotels and restaurants. That ended over 75 years of Jim Crow segregation. So now the local blacks no longer had to climb up the fire escape stairs to enter the Playhouse Theater. They could enter the front door like everyone else. As Bob Dylan sang, "The times they were a changin."

23. Remember how I said that the Vietnam War was a tiny cloud? Well that cloud suddenly turned into a thunderstorm. LBJ used the Tonkin Gulf Resolution to rapidly escalate the number of soldiers fighting in Vietnam. The number of troops suddenly jumped from 24,000 advisors in 1964 to 385,000 soldiers in 1966. Our school was shocked when Murray Moseley died serving our country in Vietnam. Years later I saw his name on the Vietnam Memorial Wall and cried.

24. I graduated from high school in June 1966. I couldn't wait to leave my small town and go to UNC – Chapel Hill! I do remember our class valedictorian's speech. It was entitled, "Do I Dare Disturb the Universe?" Little did Margaret and the Class of 66 know what awaited us. Yes, we would disturb the universe.

## MY COLLEGE YEARS, 1966 – 1970

25. I was so excited to be a freshman at UNC – Chapel Hill. It is interesting to look back on what life was like in the Fall of 1966 on a big southern university. Believe it or not, we had separate dorms for men and women. We also had a curfew. If a guy brought his date back to her dorm after the curfew then she would be penalized and not the guy. The Resident Advisor on my dorm hall was black and everyone else was white. I do not remember any Asian students in my dorm.

26. Colleges provide a great opportunity to meet different people and hear all kinds of invited speakers. In the fall of 1967, UNC invited Stokely Carmichael to speak at Carmichael Auditorium the home of our beloved UNC Tar Heels. The arena was full. Stokely Carmichael was the head of the Student Nonviolent Coordinating Committee (SNCC) and a militant black leader who coined the phrase "black power." I remember Stokely saying that America's racist past could be seen in our historic names. For example, we built a Great White Fleet, celebrated a White Christmas, and of course constructed the White House for our presidents. According to Stokely, black power meant that black was beautiful. Stokely and his followers had huge Afros. When Stokely

made a key point, his followers would raise their right arms in a black power salute and exclaim, "Right on Brother Stokely!" To this day, my APUSH students love saying "Right on Brother Stokely" when we review Stokely's role in the civil rights movement.

27. President Johnson continued to escalate the Vietnam War. That meant that there was less money for his Great Society programs that we studied in my Sociology class. It also meant that more and more guys were being drafted into the army. We had a morbid joke that if your grades fell you would soon be sent to UNC – Saigon. So I studied hard, watched the news, and worried more and more about the Vietnam War.

28. During the Spring of 1968 I decided to stop watching the news and become a part of history. So I volunteered to work for Senator Eugene McCarthy's presidential campaign. Senator McCarthy had been the first Democrat to challenge President Johnson. No one gave him a chance. But then idealistic students across America rallied to support McCarthy. We admired his courage and agreed with his convictions. I passed out flyers, wrote letters, and even manned a booth in front of the post office. Remember, we had to do things the old fashioned way because Facebook and Twitter didn't exist.

29. A thunderstorm of events now rained down upon our once peaceful campus. On March 31, 1968, President Johnson announced that he would not seek reelection. Just three days later, an assassin killed Dr. King in Memphis. LBJ's announcement touched off a celebration since we hoped it would mean an end to the Vietnam War. Dr. King's assassination touched off riots across America and demonstrations in Chapel Hill. When I was in high school, history was something we studied in books. Now history was something we were all a part of.

30. During the summer of 1968 I continued working for Senator McCarthy. I went door to door passing out campaign literature. To be honest, most of the people I met were for George C. Wallace, the segregationist governor of Alabama who was running as a third party candidate. I remember a blue collar worker telling me that Wallace had been a boxer who was now fighting for "the little guy."

31. I worked hard for the McCarthy campaign and was rewarded with an opportunity to work for him at the 1968 Democratic Convention in Chicago. I was so excited to be a part of history. I met McCarthy and Humphrey volunteers from all over America. I even met a number of hippies. The hippies were part of a new counterculture. They wore lots of beads, talked about living in communes, and listened to the Grateful Dead. But my mind was on working for Senator McCarthy.

32. The Democratic Party was bitterly divided. The party machine supported Vice-President Hubert H. Humphrey. They controlled the convention and easily nominated HHH. However, violent antiwar demonstrations marred Humphrey's nomination. I was in the Conrad Hilton hotel as the police and demonstrators battled on Michigan Avenue and in Grant Park. I remember the acrid smell of tear gas and hearing the

embattled demonstrators chant, "The whole world is watching." I remember wanting to go outside. Fortunately, I stayed inside the hotel where I was safe. I still remember my days in Chicago when I look at the McCarthy campaign buttons I saved.

33. I was 20 years old on election day. So even though I had participated in the campaign, I was too young to vote. Remember, the voting age would not be lowered to 18 until the 26th Amendment was adopted in 1971. I felt helpless on election day. Richard Nixon won a very close victory and promised to "bring us together." Of course, as usual the future would be filled with surprises.

34. I was a senior in the Fall of 1969. The Vietnam War was now my biggest personal worry. What would happen? Would I be a soldier fighting in Vietnam in a year? President Nixon began a new policy called Vietnamization that meant replacing American soldiers with Vietnamese soldiers. Needless to say, I strongly supported Vietnamization.

35. President Nixon then announced a new plan. There would be a lottery to determine the order in which young men would be drafted. I remember the lottery as if it were yesterday. I sat in a large room surrounded by other equally worried guys. We watched on TV as a beauty queen (I think it was Miss America) reached into a large jar and pulled out a capsule. Each capsule contained a specific date. If your birthday was in the first 120 dates called you should start planning on joining the army. If your birthday was in the next 120 dates you might or might not be drafted. And finally, if your birthday was called in the last 120 dates you were safe from the draft. I later learned that my mother was so nervous that she had to take a tranquilizer. My draft number finally came up – I was Number 274! I was safe and so were many of my friends. A number of students were so happy they jumped in the chilly university pool.

36. Of course, the Vietnam War did not go away. On April 30, 1970 President Nixon shocked the nation and the UNC campus by announcing that he was sending American ground troops into Cambodia. Indignant students protested the invasion of Cambodia believing that Nixon was in fact escalating the war. A few days later, tragedy struck when National Guard troops killed four students at Kent State in Ohio. Campuses all across America erupted with student protests. The demonstrations turned out to be the last big student antiwar protests. Today, students are frequently asked to identify Kent State on APUSH multiple-choice questions.

37. I graduated in June 1970 and promptly began a Masters in the Arts of Teaching (MAT) program at Chapel Hill. We were all very idealistic and eagerly looking forward to teaching and making a difference. Little did I realize what lay ahead. I would meet my future wife, Susan, and begin my teaching career at Olympic High School in Charlotte, North Carolina. Lots of history awaited me. However, APUSH exams typically have very few questions after 1970.

Good luck on your APUSH exam. Remember, history is very exciting. You never know when historic events will reach out and tap YOU on the shoulder!

**PRACTICE QUESTIONS**
# 100 PRACTICE MULTIPLE-CHOICE QUESTIONS

## ESSENTIAL POINTS

The APUSH exam begins with 80 multiple-choice questions that are worth 90 points or half of your total possible score of 180. According to the guidelines in the College Board's AP US History Course Description booklet the multiple-choice questions are distributed as follows:

### 1. PRE-COLUMBIAN TO 1789
20 PERCENT OR 16 QUESTIONS

### 2. 1790 TO 1914
45 PERCENT OR 36 QUESTIONS

### 3. 1915 TO THE PRESENT
35 PERCENT OR 28 QUESTIONS

This section is designed to give you an opportunity to apply your knowledge to 100 realistic practice APUSH questions. The first 20 questions are devoted to the Colonial Period. The second set of 45 questions cover key topics between 1790 and 1914. The final set of 35 questions cover key topics from 1915 to the present. A list of answers follows each of the three sets of questions.

# PART ONE
## PRE-COLUMBIAN TO 1789

1. **The governmental system created by the US Constitution in 1787 included all of the following EXCEPT**
   A. a provision for ratifying the Constitution
   B. a provision for creating an Electoral College
   C. a provision for impeaching the President
   D. a provision for requiring an annual presidential State of the Union message
   E. a provision for a two-term limit for presidents
   *↳ this was the result of washington*

2. **The decline of religious zeal led Puritan authorities to**
   A. invite Roger Williams to return to Massachusetts
   B. support Bacon's Rebellion
   C. institute the Halfway Covenant  *1662*
   D. protect British mercantile policies
   E. grant married women more property rights

3. **Anne Bradstreet and Phillis Wheatly were**
   A. notable Hudson River School artists
   B. notable New Light preachers
   C. notable Quaker abolitionist leaders
   D. notable colonial American poets
   E. notable Seneca Falls Convention organizers

4. **Which of the following was a key tenet of eighteenth century republicanism?**
   A. the virtues of agrarian life  *- 1700's agriculture*
   B. survival of the fittest
   C. the necessity of having a favorable balance of trade
   D. government dominated by the rich, well-born, and able
   E. belief that people can create utopian communities based upon the principles of cooperation and mutual respect

5. **Shays' Rebellion exposed tensions between**
   A. slaves and planters
   B. loyalists and patriots
   C. debtors and creditors
   D. federalists and anti-federalists
   E. former indentured servants and the Tidewater gentry

6. **The Battle of Saratoga was important because it**
   A. convinced Great Britain to revoke the Coercive Acts
   B. convinced France to openly support the American cause
   C. convinced Jackson to defend New Orleans
   D. convinced Great Britain to end the War of 1812
   E. convinced Lee to invade Pennsylvania

7. **Which of the following was NOT true of the Great Awakening?**
   A. It spread a renewed missionary spirit that led to the conversion of many African slaves.
   B. It was energized by itinerant preachers such as George Whitefield.
   C. It led to an increase in the number of women in church congregations.
   D. It created divisions within both the Congregational and the Presbyterian churches.
   E. It primarily impacted merchants and townspeople in port cities such as Philadelphia and Boston.

8. **Which of the following was the most important consequence of the French and Indian War?**
   A. The Iroquois Confederacy emerged as the strongest Native American alliance in the southern colonies.
   B. The colonies forged a strong political alliance
   C. Great Britain gained control over American lands east of the Mississippi but also inherited a large war debt.
   D. Great Britain gained control over American lands east of the Mississippi.
   E. Great Britain adopted new mercantile laws to encourage the colonies to develop their own munitions industry.

9. **Bacon's Rebellion in 1676 illustrates the tension between**
   A. Federalists and Anti-Federalists
   B. New England and the Chesapeake colonies
   C. Puritans and religious dissidents
   D. Former indentured servants and the Tidewater gentry
   E. Massachusetts farmers and their creditors

10. **"In an expanding Republic, so many different groups and viewpoints would be included in the Congress that tyranny by the majority would be impossible."**
The statement above expresses the views of

   A. John Winthrop in this "city on a hill" sermon
   B. Roger Williams in a sermon supporting the Halfway Covenant
   C. James Madison in the Federalist Papers
   D. Patrick Henry in a speech opposing ratification of the Constitution
   E. Daniel Shays in a letter explaining why Massachusetts farmers favored increased circulation of paper currency

11. **Which of the following is a correct statement about English indentured servants?**

   A. They helped suppress Bacon's Rebellion.
   B. They instigated the Stono Rebellion.
   C. They were the primary source of agricultural labor in Virginia and Maryland before 1675.
   D. They greatly outnumbered African slaves in every southern colony by 1776.
   E. They supported Roger Williams and other Massachusetts dissidents.

12. **Anne Hutchinson is most noted for her**

   A. poems about frontier life
   B. unorthodox religious views
   C. outspoken support for women's suffrage
   D. emotional First Great Awakening sermons
   E. opposition to slavery

13. **Which of the following was the most important cash crop in the Chesapeake colonies during the seventeenth century?**

   A. cotton
   B. tobacco
   C. rice
   D. indigo
   E. sugar

14. **The primary purpose of the Stamp Act was to**

   A. support New Light colleges in New England
   B. reform the Navigation Acts
   C. protect the infant industries in New England
   D. raise revenue for the British government
   E. increase colonial representation in Parliament

15. **"Remember the Ladies, and be more generous and favorable to them than your ancestors. Do not put such unlimited power into the hands of the Husbands. Remember all Men would be tyrants if they could. If particular care is not paid to the Ladies we are determined to foment a revolution."**

*The statement above was made by*

A. Anne Hutchinson urging Jonathan Edwards to give women a greater role in the Great Awakening.

B. Anne Bradstreet urging Patrick Henry to support the formation of a Daughters of Liberty.

C. Abigal Adams urging her husband John Adams to become an advocate for greater rights for women.

D. Andrew Jackson urging delegates to the 1832 Democratic convention to extend the suffrage to white women.

E. W.E.B. Du Bois urging delegates to the first meeting of the NAACP to fight for equal rights for all citizens.

16. **The Northwest Ordinance of 1787**

A. provided free land for settlers in the Northwest Territory

B. called for a convention to revise the Articles of Confederation

C. influenced Jefferson's theory of natural rights

D. banned slavery from the Northwest Territory

E. granted Great Britain temporary control over a number of frontier forts

17. **All of the following statements about British mercantilist polices are true EXCEPT:**

A. They impeded the growth of colonial manufacturing.

B. They were implemented by the Navigation Acts.

C. They were not rigorously enforced prior to 1763.

D. They reduced colonial consumption of French and Dutch goods.

E. They encouraged other European powers to establish colonies in North America.

18. **Conservative leaders such as George Washington and Alexander Hamilton believed that Shays' Rebellion demonstrated the need for**

A. a convention to revise the Articles of Confederation

B. more just slave codes

C. more paper currency to ease the problems of debtors

D. a strong alliance with France

E. greater tolerance of unorthodox religious views

## 19. The Great Compromise
A. created a bicameral Congress
B. created the Electoral College
C. resolved a dispute between the free states and the slave states
D. established the Supreme Court
E. allowed the President to negotiate treaties that had to be ratified by the Senate

## 20. "For we must consider that we shall be as a city upon a hill, the eyes of all people are upon us. So that if we shall deal falsely with our God in this work we shall have undertaken, and so cause Him to withdraw His present help from us, we shall be made a story and a by-word through the world."

*The statement above was made by*
A. George Whitefield preaching to a mass gathering during the Great Awakening.
B. John Winthrop expressing his belief that the Puritan colonists had a special pact with God to build a model Christian society.
C. Lord Baltimore defining the purpose of the Maryland colony.
D. Roger Williams defending the excessive religiosity of the Puritans.
E. Thomas Paine urging Americans to reject British sovereignty and create an independent nation.

## ANSWERS
## PART 1
## PRE-COLUMBIAN TO 1789

| | | | |
|---|---|---|---|
| 1. E  pg 50 | 7. E  pg 149 | 13. B  pg 8 | 19. A  pg 48 |
| 2. C  pg 350 | 8. C  pg 29 | 14. D  pg 30 | 20. B  pg 14 |
| 3. D  pg 26 | 9. D  pg 60 | 15. C  pg 51 | |
| 4. A  pg 36 | 10. C  pg 48 | 16. D  pg 45 | |
| 5. C  pg 46 | 11. C  pg 363 | 17. E  pg 25 | |
| 6. B  pg 38 | 12. B  pg 16 | 18. A  pg 46 | |

# PART TWO
## 1790 – 1914

**21. William Lloyd Garrison's newspaper, *The Liberator*, was dedicated to**

A. promoting utopian communities
B. supporting women's temperance
C. opposing temperance
D. defending labor unions
E. advocating abolitionism

**22. The Supreme Court's ruling in *Marbury v. Madison* established the principle of**

A. federalism
B. gerrymandering
C. judicial review
D. states' rights
E. strict scrutiny

**23. The Black Codes passed by southern states in the years immediately following the Civil War were intended to**

A. implement President Johnson's executive order to redistribute land to the former slaves
B. implement the Supreme Court's decision in Plessy v. Ferguson
C. limit the power of the former planter aristocracy
D. limit the civil rights of former slaves
E. extend voting rights to former slaves

**24. Muckrakers were writers who**

A. exposed corruption and social injustice during the Progressive Era
B. urged President McKinley to annex the Philippines
C. opposed passage of the Nineteenth Amendment
D. exposed racial injustice in the South
E. criticized consumerism and rampant materialism during the 1920s

**25. The Populist Party platform included a call for all of the following EXCEPT**

A. an end to discriminatory freight rates
B. direct election of United States senators
C. legislation to raise tariffs
D. free coinage of silver
E. legislation to increase the market power of farmers

## 26. Frederick Jackson Turner was the first historian to

A. analyze the effects of an open frontier on American national development

B. analyze the impact of immigration on nativist political movements

C. analyze the contributions of third party movements

D. compare and contrast the goals of the Populist and Progressive movements

E. compare and contrast the New Deal and Great Society programs

## 27. Members of the Ashcan school of art are best known for their paintings of

A. religious themes

B. landscapes

C. battle scenes and military commanders

D. skyscrapers and bridges

E. urban barrooms and tenements

## 28. Which of the following best exemplifies "big stick" diplomacy?

A. The construction of the Panama Canal

B. The use of American banks to refinance the foreign debt of Nicaragua

C. The agreements reached at the Washington Naval Conference

D. The US decision to sign the Kellogg-Briand Pact

E. The proclamation of the Stimson Doctrine

## 29. Which of the following is true of the Missouri Compromise?

A. It opened most of the Louisiana Territory to slavery.

B. It accepted the principle of popular sovereignty.

C. It inflamed the political crisis over slavery.

D. It failed to maintain the balance between free and slave states in the US Senate

E. It provided for the admission of Missouri as a slave state and Maine as a free state.

## 30. Which of the following was NOT a consequence of the Kansas-Nebraska Act?

A. The demise of the Whig Party

B. The emergence of the Republican Party

C. The migration of Exodusters to Kansas

D. The outbreak of fighting in Kansas

E. The heightening of sectional tensions

**31. Theodore Roosevelt's views on the importance of naval power were most strongly influenced by the writings of**

A. Frederick Jackson Turner

B. Ida B. Wells

C. Jacob Riis

D. Alfred Thayer Mahan

E. Upton Sinclair

**32. The "Trail of Tears" refers to**

A. The forced relocation of slaves from Virginia and Maryland to the Deep South

B. The forced internment of Japanese Americans during World War II

C. The New Immigrants who were forced to return to Europe

D. The relocation of Native Americans to the Indian Territory

E. The route Lee's army followed after the Battle of Gettysburg

**33. Which of the following Presidents is most closely associated with the expansion of white male suffrage?**

A. George Washington

B. John Adams

C. James Madison

D. John Quincy Adams

E. Andrew Jackson

**34. During the Progressive Era, women reformers were involved in all of the following EXCEPT**

A. Campaigns to promote civil rights legislation to abolish segregation

B. Campaigns to support anti-lynching laws

C. Campaigns to support women's suffrage

D. Campaigns to limit the working hours of women

E. Campaigns to sponsor child labor legislation

**35. Unlike Democratic-Republicans such as Thomas Jefferson, Alexander Hamilton and his followers supported**

A. a reduction in the scope and activities of the federal government

B. a pro-France foreign policy

C. a protective tariff and a national bank

D. an agrarian way of life

E. a strong states' rights policy

36. "This treaty must of course be laid before both Houses, because both have important functions to exercise respecting it. They, I presume, will see their duty to their country in ratifying and paying for it, so as to secure a goal which would otherwise probably be never again in their power. But I suppose they must then appeal to the nation for an additional article to the Constitution, approving and confirming an act which the nation had not previously authorized."

*This statement was made by*
A. Thomas Jefferson about the purchase of the Louisiana Territory
B. James Polk about the Wilmot Proviso
C. Franklin Pierce about the Ostend Manifesto
D. William McKinley about the annexation of the Philippines
E. Theodore Roosevelt about the acquisition of the Panama Canal Zone

37. **Jane Addams is most closely associated with the**
A. abolitionist movement
B. settlement house movement
C. temperance movement
D. Transcendentalist movement
E. Hudson River School movement

38. **Marcus Garvey is remembered as an African American leader who**
A. promoted the talented tenth
B. promoted black pride and black nationalism
C. advocated accommodation to white society
D. advocated nonviolent civil disobedience
E. organized the March on Washington

39. **Contraband was a term used to describe**
A. a technique used to disfranchise black voters during Reconstruction
B. colonists who remained loyal to Great Britain
C. runaway slaves who fled to the Union lines
D. Irish immigrants who moved to Boston in the 1840s
E. Whigs who supported popular sovereignty

**40. The House of Representatives impeached Andrew Johnson because he**

A. obstructed Radical Reconstruction
B. worked to repeal the Black Codes
C. opposed the Homestead Act
D. opposed the Thirteenth Amendment
E. proposed the Compromise of 1877

**41. The case of *Dartmouth College v. Woodward* established the principle**

A. that the Supreme Court had the authority to declare acts of Congress unconstitutional
B. that a state cannot tax an agency of the federal government
C. that a state cannot encroach on a contract
D. that state legislatures must be reapportioned to represent the Principle of "one man, one vote."
E. that the Bill of Rights implies a right to privacy

**42. The founders of the American Colonization Society worked to**

A. promote settlements in the Louisiana Territory
B. concentrate Native Americans on reservations west of the Appalachian Mountains
C. improve the condition of Irish immigrants in America
D. encourage immigrants to settle in the South
E. return freed slaves to west coast of Africa

**43. *McGuffey Readers* (or *Eclectic Readers*) featured stories that**

A. taught the basic principles of Transcendentalism
B. taught young readers how to understand Hudson River School paintings
C. intensified opposition to slavery
D. promoted patriotism and moral values
E. encouraged young readers to oppose unjust laws

**44. The World's Columbian Exposition of 1893**

A. celebrated American technological progress
B. revived the Ghost Dance
C. featured the debut of the film The Birth of a Nation
D. rallied public support for the labor movement
E. endorsed the goals of the Populist Party

45. "Upon these considerations, it is the opinion of the court that the act of Congress which prohibited a citizen from holding and owning  property of this kind in the territory of the United States north of the line therein mentioned, is not warranted by the Constitution, and is therefore void; and that neither the plaintiff himself, nor any of his family, were made free by being carried into this territory; even if they had been carried there by the owner, who intended to become a permanent resident."

*The act of Congress referred to in the passage was the*
A. Land Ordinance of 1785
B. Missouri Compromise
C. Wilmot Proviso
D. Treaty of Guadalupe Hidalgo
E. Fugitive Slave Act

46. All of the following statements about the Monroe Doctrine are true EXCEPT:
A. It asserted American independence in foreign policy.
B. It warned European nations that the American continents were no longer open to colonization.
C. It expressed the belief that European monarchies are antithetical to American republican institutions.
D. It was a unilateral declaration of principles.
E. It expressed a desire for a closer alliance with Great Britain.

47. Henry Clay's American System called for
A. the gradual abolition of slavery
B. a strict policy of neutrality in international affairs
C. a federal system of government based upon a division of power between state and national governments
D. internal improvements that would promote increased trade among America's different regions
E. state banks to replace the Second Bank of the United States

48. Between 1880 and 1920, the United States drew the most immigrants from
A. Ireland and Germany
B. England and France
C. Canada and Mexico
D. Italy and Russia
E. China and Japan

**49. Henry David Thoreau's essay "Civil Disobedience"**

A. was a response to the Indian Wars that later influenced passage of the Dawes Act

B. was a response to the Mexican War that later influenced Dr. King's Strategy of nonviolent marches

C. was a response to the War of 1812 that later influenced the Monroe Doctrine

D. was a response to the Know-Nothings that later influenced the Immigration Act of 1965

E. was a response to the Spanish-American War that later influenced the Cuban Missile Crisis.

**50. "The great principle is the right of every community to judge and decide for itself whether a thing is right or wrong ... It is no answer to this argument to say that slavery is an evil, and hence should not be tolerated. You must allow the people to decide for themselves whether it is good or evil."**

*In this passage from his debates with Abraham Lincoln, Stephen A. Douglas explained the doctrine of*

A. states' rights that was embodied in the South Carolina Ordinance of Secession

B. segregation that was later embodied in the Supreme Court's decision in Plessy v. Ferguson

C. popular sovereignty that was embodied in the Kansas-Nebraska Act

D. nullification that was used by John C. Calhoun to oppose the Tariff of Abominations

E. imperialism that was later used by McKinley to justify the annexation of the Philippines

**51. The religious spirit of the Second Great Awakening led many reformers to**

A. oppose the annexation of the Philippines

B. oppose Manifest Destiny

C. oppose Margaret Sanger's campaign for birth control

D. regard slavery with renewed hostility

E. support the Populist program to regulate the railroads

**52. The purpose of the Dawes Act of 1887 was to**

A. force Native Americans to give up tribal lands and become self-sufficient farmers

B. concentrate Native Americans on compact reservations

C. exclude all Chinese immigrants from coming to the United States

D. curb the power of labor unions

E. set up a Civil Service Commission

## 53. Texas remained an independent republic for nine years because

A. Daniel Webster threatened to invoke the doctrine of nullification to prevent the admission of another slave state

B. Southern politicians were more interested in annexing Cuba

C. the residents of Texas preferred to remain an independent "Lone Star Republic"

D. President Jackson wanted to avoid a war with Mexico

E. President Jackson feared the debate over the admission of Texas would spark renewed sectional controversy over the expansion of slavery

## 54. Henry Grady and other leaders of the "New South" movement in the late nineteenth century advocated

A. gradually relaxing Jim Crow segregation laws

B. building a more diversified economy in the South

C. encouraging immigrants from southern and eastern Europe to settle in the South

D. forming strong labor unions to represent textile workers

E. reviving a tobacco-based economy

## 55. The Cult of Domesticity

A. idealized women in their roles as nurturing mothers and faithful wives

B. supported the Lowell experiment in New England factories

C. supported the Declaration of Sentiments issued by the Seneca Falls Convention

D. encouraged women to join utopian communities

E. encouraged women to support the Homestead Act

## 56. "This, then, is held to be the duty of the man of wealth: to consider all surplus revenues which come to him simply as trust funds, which he is called upon to administer and strictly bound as a matter of duty to administer in the manner which, in his judgment, is best calculated to produce the most beneficial results for the community – the man of wealth thus becoming the mere agent and trustee for his poorer brethren."

*These sentiments reflect*

A. John D. Rockefeller's theory of horizontal integration

B. Frederick W. Taylor's theory of scientific management

C. Robert Owen's principles of how to form a utopian community

D. Andrew Carnegie's belief in the Gospel of Wealth

E. Samuel Gomper's criticism of the robber barons

57. **Which state would have been most likely to cast its electoral votes for William Jennings Bryan in the 1896 presidential election?**
    A. Kansas
    B. Ohio
    C. New York
    D. California
    E. Pennsylvania

58. **D.W. Griffith's film *The Birth of a Nation* used innovative production techniques to**
    A. produce Hollywood's first "talkie"
    B. dramatize the firing on Fort Sumter
    C. portray the Ghost Dance
    D. glamorize the rise of the Ku Klux Klan
    E. reenact the signing of the Declaration of Independence

59. **Frederick Douglass was America's foremost**
    A. black abolitionist
    B. supporter of manifest destiny
    C. advocate of naval power
    D. educational reformer
    E. Progressive Era reformer

60. **The Open Door was intended to support American trading opportunities in**
    A. Latin America
    B. China
    C. Japan
    D. West Africa
    E. the Philippines

61. **Emilio Aguinaldo was**
    A. a Mexican rebel leader who "invaded" New Mexico
    B. the leader of the Viet Minh who defeated the French
    C. the leader of the Filipino resistance fighters
    D. the co-founder of the National Farm Workers Association
    E. the Cuban leader who was overthrown by Castro

62. "In all things that are purely social we can be as separate as the fingers, yet one as the hand in all things essential to material progress ... The wisest among my race understand that the agitation of questions of racial equality is the extremist folly, and that progress in the enjoyment of all the privileges that will come to use must be the result of severe and constant struggle rather than of artificial forcing."

*This quote reflects the views of*
A. W.E.B. Du Bois
B. Booker T. Washington
C. Ida B. Wells
D. Marcus Garvey
E. William Lloyd Garrison

63. All of the following people are correctly matched with the reform movement they led EXCEPT
A. Dorothea Dix .. mentally ill
B. Horace Mann .. education
C. Jane Addams .. urban poor
D. Ida B. Wells .. anti-lynching
E. Margaret Sanger .. temperance

64. Which of the following is NOT an accurate statement about the antebellum South?
A. The presence of slaves discouraged immigrants from moving to the South.
B. The majority of white families in the antebellum South were independent yeoman farmers who owned few, if any, slaves.
C. The South lagged behind the North in industrial development and trade.
D. The South's commitment to growing cotton slowed urban growth.
E. By the 1830s thoughtful Southerners recognized that slavery was a "necessary evil" that would have to be gradually abolished.

65. The Fourteenth Amendment
A. abolished slavery
B. provided for equal protection of the laws for all citizens
C. extended the suffrage to black males
D. gave Congress the right to tax income
E. provided for the direct election of United States Senatorss

# ANSWERS
## PART II
## PART II: 1790 – 1914

| | | | | | | | |
|---|---|---|---|---|---|---|---|
| 21.E | pg 103 | 33.E | pg 88 | 45.B | pg 79 | 57.A | pg 200 |
| 22.C | pg 74 | 34.A | pg 205 | 46.E | pg 80 | 58.D | pg 192 |
| 23.D | pg 155 | 35.C | pg 68 | 47.D | pg 78 | 59.A | pg 104 |
| 24.A | pg 205 | 36.A | pg 73 | 48.D | pg 187 | 60.B | pg 221 |
| 25.C | pg 197 | 37.B | pg 190 | 49.B | pg 126 | 61.C | pg 220 |
| 26.A | pg 173 | 38.B | pg 248 | 50.C | pg 132 | 62.B | pg 234 |
| 27.E | pg 193 | 39.C | pg 144 | 51.D | pg 114 | 63.E | pg 115 |
| 28.A | pg 224 | 40.A | pg 157 | 52.A | pg 172 | 64.E | pg 97 |
| 29.E | pg 79 | 41.C | pg 79 | 53.E | pg 124 | 65.B | pg 156 |
| 30.C | pg 133 | 42.E | pg 102 | 54.B | pg 162 | | |
| 31.D | pg 219 | 43.D | pg 115 | 55.A | pg 289 | | |
| 32.D | pg 87 | 44.A | pg 177 | 56.D | pg 178 | | |

# PART THREE
## 1915 – PRESENT

66. The Truman Doctrine, Marshall Plan, and NATO were all influenced by
   A. Turner's frontier thesis
   B. Kennan's essay on containment
   C. Mahan's book on sea power
   D. Eisenhower's military-industrial speech
   E. Washington's Farewell Address

67. The primary domestic issue during the Carter administration was
   A. stagflation
   B. welfare reform
   C. tariff policy
   D. human rights
   E. education reform

68. All of the following foreign policies are correctly matched with a President EXCEPT
   A. Taft .. Dollar Diplomacy
   B. Truman .. Containment
   C. Eisenhower .. Massive retaliation
   D. Nixon .. Détente
   E. Carter .. Brinksmanship

69. What triggered the shift of African American voters to the Democratic Party?
   A. Coolidge's New Era prosperity
   B. Hoover's decision to create the Reconstruction Finance Corporation
   C. Roosevelt's New Deal programs
   D. Truman's executive order to integrate the armed forces
   E. Eisenhower's decision to send federal troops to Little Rock

70. Which of the following was a key problem in the American economy just prior to 1929?
   A. low tariffs
   B. rising prices for agricultural goods
   C. rising unemployment
   D. overproduction and underconsumption
   E. crippling railroad strikes

71. "The history of life on earth has been a history of interaction between living things and their surroundings. To a large extent, the physical form and the habits of the earth's vegetation and its animal life have been molded by the environment...The most alarming of all man's assaults upon the environment is the contamination of air, earth, rivers, and sea with dangerous and even lethal materials."

    *The passage above is from*
    A. *The Other America* by Michael Harrington
    B. *On the Road* by Jack Kerouac
    C. *The Organization Man* by William H. Whyte
    D. *How the Other Half Lives* by Jacob Riis
    E. *Silent Spring* by Rachel Carson

72. **All of the following contributed to the climate of McCarthyism in the 1950s EXCEPT**
    A. The execution of Julius and Ethel Rosenberg for giving atomic secrets to the Soviet Union.
    B. The House Un-American Activities Committee's investigation of Alger Hiss.
    C. The Soviet Union's successful test of a hydrogen bomb.
    D. The "fall of China" to Communists led by Mao Zedong.
    E. The "fall of Turkey" to Soviet influence

73. **"The very basis of our individual rights and freedoms rests upon the certainty that the President and the Executive Branch of Government will support and insure the carrying out of the decisions of the federal courts, even, when necessary, with all the means at the President's command."**

    *Which of the following Presidents made this statement?*
    A. President Jackson explaining his decision to enforce the Supreme Court's ruling in Worcester v. Georgia.
    B. President Theodore Roosevelt explaining his decision to send federal troops to end the Anthracite Coal Strike of 1902.
    C. President Eisenhower explaining his decision to send federal troops to Little Rock to enforce desegregation orders.
    D. President Nixon explaining his decision to use federal troops to restore order at Kent State University.
    E. President Truman explaining his decision to integrate the armed forces.

**74. The primary purpose of the National Origins Act of 1924 was to restrict the flow of immigration from**

A. Asia and Latin America

B. Mexico and the Caribbean

C. Mexico and Canada

D. Northern and Western Europe

E. Southern and Eastern Europe

**75. The "zoot-suit" riot was the name given to**

A. disturbances caused by hippies at the Woodstock Music Festival

B. attacks by sailors on Mexican American youth in Los Angeles in 1943

C. protests by members of the Anti-Imperialist League opposed to the annexation of the Philippines

D. attacks by police on antiwar demonstrators at the 1968 Chicago Democratic convention

E. conflict between the police and antiwar demonstrators in Washington, D.C. following the Kent State shooting in 1970

**76. The Gulf of Tonkin Resolution marked an important turning point in the Vietnam War because**

A. Congress rejected the Geneva Accords and the United States replaced France as the dominant Western power in South Vietnam

B. Congress granted President Johnson sweeping authority to escalate military action in Vietnam

C. Congress approved the domino theory as the official U.S. foreign policy in Indochina.

D. Congress endorsed President Nixon's policy of Vietnamization

E. Congress placed restrictions on a President's ability to wage wars

**77. Which of the following is best described as an outpouring of black cultural achievements during the 1920s?**

A. The Talented Tenth Movement

B. The Niagara Movement

C. The Lost Generation

D. The Beat Generation

E. The Harlem Renaissance

## 78. The Immigration Act of 1965 was significant because it

A. led to a new wave of immigration from Latin America and Asia

B. led to a renewed wave of immigration from Southern and Eastern Europe

C. strengthened the quotas in the National Origins Act of 1924

D. continued to enforce the Chinese Exclusion Act of 1882

E. introduced a new Open Door policy of immigration

## 79. A painting of a can of Campbell's Soup by Andy Warhol would be most closely associated with which of the following artistic schools?

A. The Hudson River School

B. The Romantic movement

C. The Ashcan artists

D. Abstract Expressionism

E. Pop Art

## 80. President Reagan's primary foreign policy objective was to

A. overthrow Castro

B. repudiate the treaties giving Panama control over the Panama Canal

C. promote human rights in Africa

D. confront and contain the Soviet Union

E. continue the Good Neighbor Policy in Latin America

## 81. Which of the following events did NOT happen in 1968?

A. The assassination of Dr. King

B. President Johnson's announcement that he would not run for reelection

C. The shooting of four students at Kent State

D. The Tet Offensive

E. The assassination of Robert F. Kennedy

## 82. Which of the following books influenced President Johnson's decision to declare a war on poverty?

A. *Century of Dishonor* by Helen Hunt Jackson

B. *How the Other Half Lives* by Jacob Riis

C. *The Jungle* by Upton Sinclair

D. *The Grapes of Wrath* by John Steinbeck

E. *The Other America* by Michael Harrington

**83. President Wilson's Fourteen Points included a call for**

A. an International Monetary Fund
B. recognition of the Soviet Union
C. self-determination of peoples
D. secret agreements with Great Britain
E. a global currency

**84. The policies of Lyndon Johnson differed most consistently from those of Franklin D. Roosevelt in which area?**

A. support for the arts
B. help for the elderly
C. increased federal spending for social services
D. government-sponsored employment programs
E. civil rights legislation

**85. The racial integration of the armed forces of the United States first occurred during which war?**

A. World War I
B. World War II
C. the Korean War
D. the Vietnam War
E. the Iraq War

**86. All of the following home front developments occurred during World War II EXCEPT**

A. The forced relocation of Japanese Americans on the West Coast
B. The hiring of millions of women in defense industries
C. The migration of African Americans from the South to cities in the North and West
D. The zoot-suit riot in Los Angeles
E. Franklin Roosevelt's decision to not seek a fourth term

**87. Which of the following was associated with the increased radicalization of some African Americans during the 1960s?**

A. The sit-in movement
B. The Freedom Riders
C. The demonstrations in Birmingham, Alabama
D. The March on Washington
E. The selection of Stokely Carmichael to lead the Student Nonviolent Coordinating Committee (SNCC)

## 88. Supporters of the Social Gospel believed that

A. In human society, as in nature, only the fittest will survive

B. America's churches have a moral responsibility to take the lead in actively confronting social problems

C. truth and self-knowledge can be found in nature

D. the wealthy have a responsibility to regard their surplus fortunes as a trust to be administered for the benefit of the community

E. labor unions should unify all working men and women into one national union

## 89. Members of the Beat Generation are best characterized as

A. teenagers who listened to the music of Elvis Presley and other early rock and roll singers

B. hippies who joined counterculture communes

C. Dixicrats who walked out of the 1948 Democratic convention

D. writers who rejected America's mindless conformity during the 1950s

E. writers who exposed elements of society needing reform

## 90. Which of the following was a demographic phenomenon in the United States between 1980 and 2000?

A. A large-scale movement of people to cities in the Northeast

B. A decrease in the number of service workers

C. A new wave of immigrants from Latin America and Asia

D. An increase in the farm population

E. A decrease in the proportion of the population over sixty-five

## 91. Under Earl Warren's leadership, the United States Supreme Court did which of the following?

A. Upheld the supremacy of state legislation over federal legislation

B. Issued landmark decisions that defined the rights of accused criminals

C. Issued landmark decisions that strengthened the position of big business

D. Upheld the constitutionality of the Japanese internment as a wartime necessity

E. Narrowed the meaning and effectiveness of the Fourteenth Amendment

## 92. The Camp David Accords

A. announced Nixon's policy of Vietnamization

B. ended the Vietnam War

C. established a new era of détente with the Soviet Union

D. formally established diplomatic relations with the People's Republic of China

E. ended 30 years of intermittent hostility between Egypt and Israel

**93. Eleanor Roosevelt is best remembered as a champion of**

A. women's rights and civil rights during the New Deal era
B. the League of Nations during the Senate ratification debate
C. the Great Society's War on Poverty
D. the election of United States Senators by popular vote
E. the use of Reaganomics to revive the U.S. economy

**94. President Kennedy's objective in the Bay of Pigs invasion in 1961 was to**

A. overthrow the Khrushchev government in the Soviet Union
B. overthrow the Castro government in Cuba
C. overthrow the Ho Chi Minh government in North Vietnam
D. defend American rights in South Korea
E. defend American rights in West Berlin

**95. All of the following statements about the federal government in the 1920s are true EXCEPT**

A. antipoverty programs were expanded
B. scandals tarnished the Harding administration
C. tax rates for the wealthy were reduced
D. tariffs were raised
E. antitrust regulations were ignored

**96. John Steinbeck's *The Grapes of Wrath***

A. was originally written as a political commentary on free silver and the plight of American farmers
B. was originally written as a social satire on the excessive materialism of American life in the 1920s
C. was originally written as a political commentary on labor Strife in the 1930s
D. captured the ordeal of the Plains Indians as they lost their land to the settlers
E. captured the ordeal faced by Oakies as they fled the Dust Bowl

**97. The primary purpose of the Congress of Industrial Organizations (CIO) under the leadership of John L. Lewis was to organize**

A. unskilled and semiskilled factory workers in basic manufacturing Industries such as steel and automobiles
B. skilled workers in craft unions for economic gains
C. all industrial and agricultural workers into "one big union"
D. students and workers into a Social-Democratic labor party
E. migrant farm workers into a union of agricultural laborers

## 98. Which of the following did NOT happen during the 1920s?

A. Making "dollar down, dollar a week" down payments
B. Buying a Model T automobile
C. Listening to a radio account of Lindbergh's flight across the Atlantic
D. Watching an episode of *I Love Lucy* on TV
E. Watching a new "talkie" movie

## 99. Following the attack on Pearl Harbor, America adopted an overall strategy of

A. defeating Japan first
B. defeating Germany first
C. devoting equal resources to both the European and Japanese fronts
D. turning North America into an impregnable military fortress
E. trying to reach a negotiated settlement with Hitler

## 100.  Betty Friedan is best known as the

A. author of The *Feminist Mystique* and a founder of the National Organization for Women (NOW)
B. most outspoken opponent of the Equal Rights Amendment
C. most outspoken opponent of nuclear power
D. Supreme Court justice who wrote the majority opinion in Roe v. Wade
E. Secretary of State who accompanied Nixon on his visit to China

## ANSWERS:
## PART III
## 1915 – PRESENT

| | | | | | | | |
|---|---|---|---|---|---|---|---|
| 66.B | pg 276 | 76.B | pg 308 | 86.E | pg 269 | 96.E | pg 254 |
| 67.A | pg 323 | 77.E | pg 248 | 87.E | pg 394 | 97.A | pg 261 |
| 68.E | pg 294 | 78.A | pg 333 | 88.B | pg 190 | 98.D | pg 243 |
| 69.C | pg 256 | 79.E | pg 385 | 89.D | pg 288 | 99.B | pg 269 |
| 70.D | pg 252 | 80.D | pg 330 | 90.C | pg 333 | 100.A | pg 321 |
| 71.E | pg 322 | 81.C | pg 311 | 91.B | pg 306 | | |
| 72.E | pg 282 | 82.E | pg 303 | 92.E | pg 324 | | |
| 73.C | pg 292 | 83.C | pg 230 | 93.A | pg 262 | | |
| 74.E | pg 247 | 84.E | pg 303 | 94.B | pg 299 | | |
| 75. B | pg 271 | 85.C | pg 284 | 95.A | pg 249 | | |

# GLOSSARY OF KEY TERMS

# I.  COLONIAL AMERICA, 1607 - 1776

## 1. COLUMBIAN EXCHANGE

The exchange of plants and animals between Europe and the New World. For example, corn, potatoes, and tomatoes are all New World crops that revolutionized the European diet. Horses, cows, and pigs revolutionized life in the New World.

## 2. ENCOMIENDA

Exploitative labor system designed to reward Spaniards with large land grants that included local villages and control over native labor.

## 3. JOINT–STOCK COMPANY

A financial arrangement in which investors share the risks and profits in proportion to their part in the total investment. Virginia was financed by a joint-stock company for the express purpose of making a profit.

## 4. HEADRIGHT SYSTEM

Virginia planters received 50 acres for each person (or head) they brought to the colony.

## 5. AMERICAN EXCEPTIONALISM

Belief that America has a mission to be a beacon of hope and democracy for the rest of the world.

## 6. PREDESTINATION

Puritan belief that God has chosen certain people for salvation even before they were born. These chosen people are called the "elect."

## 7. HALFWAY COVENANT

Puritan policy to ease the requirements for church membership by allowing the baptism of the children of parents who could not provide testimony of their own "election."

## 8. FIRST GREAT AWAKENING

A wave of religious revivals that began in New England in the mid-1730s and swept across all the colonies during the 1740s.

## 9. MERCANTILISM

British economic policy designed to achieve a favorable balance of trade by purchasing raw materials from the American colonies and then selling them manufactured goods. Mercantilism was intended to increase British wealth by making the colonial economy dependent upon the mother country.

## 10. REPUBLICANISM

The belief that government should be based on the consent of the people. This belief inspired Americans to declare their independence from Great Britain.

## 11. DEISM

Part of the Enlightenment. Deists believed that natural laws regulate both the universe and human society. These natural laws could be discovered by human reason. The discovery of natural laws of economics and government would improve society and make progress inevitable.

# II. THE NEW REPUBLIC, 1776 – 1865

## 12. CONFEDERATION

A type of government based upon a loose union among sovereign states.

## 13. STATES' RIGHTS

Doctrine asserting that the Constitution arose as a compact among sovereign states. The states therefore retained the power to challenge and if necessary nullify federal laws. First formulated in the Virginia and Kentucky Resolutions.

## 14. JUDICIAL REVIEW

Established by John Marshall in the case of Marbury v. Madison. Gave the Supreme Court the authority to determine the constitutionality of congressional acts.

## 15. INTERNAL IMPROVEMENT

Refers to transportation projects in antebellum America. Internal improvements were a key part of Clay's American System.

## 16. DOCTRINE OF NULLIFICATION

The supposed right of any state to declare a federal law inoperative within its borders. John C. Calhoun based this concept on the states' rights arguments first formulated in the Virginia and Kentucky Resolutions.

## 17. MARKET REVOLUTION

The process by which new methods of transportation created a national economy during the antebellum period.

## 18. REPUBLICAN MOTHERHOOD

The new American republic offered women the important role of raising children to be virtuous citizens.

## 19. CULT OF DOMESTICITY

Idealized women in their roles as wives and mothers.

## 20. SECOND GREAT AWAKENING

A wave of religious enthusiasm that spread across America during the early nineteenth century. It inspired reform movements to abolish slavery, promote women's rights, and restrict the sale of alcoholic beverages.

## 21. PERFECTIONISM

Faith in the human capacity to achieve a better life on earth through conscious acts of will. Utopian communities such as Brook Farm and New Harmony provide examples of attempts to implement perfectionist principles.

## 22. TEMPERANCE MOVEMENT

A widespread campaign to convince Americans to drink less alcohol or none at all.

## 23. TRANSCENDENTALISM

A small but influential group of writers and thinkers who stressed the importance of human intuition, nonconformity, and the belief that truth could be found in nature. Ralph Waldo Emerson, Henry David Thoreau, and Margaret Fuller were the leading transcendentalists.

## 24. NATIVISM

An anti-foreign reaction among native-born Protestants. It was originally sparked by the great wave of Irish and German immigrants in the 1840s and 1850s. The Know-Nothings were America's first nativist political party.

## 25. MANIFEST DESTINY

Belief that American was foreordained to extend its civilization across the North American continent.

## 26. POPULAR SOVEREIGNTY

Concept introduced by Stephen A. Douglas that the settlers in a given territory have the right to decide whether or not to accept slavery. Popular sovereignty led to a civil war in Kansas during the 1850s.

## 27. CONTRABAND

Official term given to fugitive slaves who sought protection behind Union lines during the Civil War.

# III. INDUSTRIAL AMERICA, 1865 – 1917

## 28. SHARECROPPING

Following the Civil War, Southern states adopted a sharecropping system in which newly freed slaves exchanged their labor for the use of land, tools, and seed. The sharecropper typically gave the landowner half of his crop.

## 29. CARPETBAGGERS

Northerners who supposedly packed their belongings into a carpet Suitcase and headed south to seek power and profit.

## 30. SCALAWAGS

Southerners who "betrayed" the South by supporting and then benefitting from Republican Reconstruction policies.

## 31. EXODUSTERS

African Americans who migrated from the South in 1879 and 1880 to begin a new life in Kansas.

## 32. TURNER'S FRONTIER THESIS

Frederick Jackson Turner's argument that the frontier experience played a key role in making American society more democratic. Turner emphasized the importance of America's vast supply of cheap, sparsely settled land.

## 33. HORIZONTAL INTEGRATION

The process by which a company gains control over other firms that produce the same product.

## 34. VERTICAL INTEGRATION

The process by which a single company owns and controls the entire production process from the unearthing of raw materials to the manufacture and sale of finished products.

## 35. SOCIAL DARWINISM

Belief that Darwin's theory of survival of the fittest can be applied to individuals, corporation, and nations. According to Social Darwinists, individuals and corporations are engaged in a ruthless struggle for profit in which only the fit prosper and survive.

## 36. GOSPEL OF WEALTH

Andrew Carnegie's belief that the rich have a responsibility to serve society by using their wealth to support worthy causes.

### 37. SOCIAL GOSPEL

Belief that America's churches have a moral responsibility to take the lead in actively confronting social problems and helping the poor.

### 38. PROGRESSIVISM

A widespread, multifaceted reform movement to build a more democratic and just society. The Progressive movement was at its peak between 1900 and 1917.

### 39. TAYLORISM

System of scientific management developed by Frederick W. Taylor. He used time-and-motion studies to eliminate wasted movements, reduce costs, and promote greater efficiency in factories and assembly lines.

### 40. MUCKRAKERS

Journalists who exposed corruption and social problems through investigative reporting. Ida Tarbell, Upton Sinclair, and Jacob Riis were three of the best-known muckrakers.

### 41. TRUST

A large business combination formed by merging several smaller companies under the control of a single governing board.

# IV. BOOM, BUST, AND WAR, 1917 – 1945

### 42. LOST GENERATION

Writers during the 1920s who criticized middle-class conformity and materialism. F. Scott Fitzgerald and Sinclair Lewis were two of the best-known Lost Generation authors.

### 43. HARLEM RENAISSANCE

An African American literary and artistic movement that flourished during the 1920s. Harlem Renaissance writers such as Langston Hughes and Zora Neale Hurston expressed pride in their African American culture.

### 44. HOOVERVILLE

A sarcastic term given to shantytowns inhabited by unemployed and homeless people during the Great Depression.

### 45. DEFICIT SPENDING

When the federal government spends more money than it receives in taxes. First advocated by the British economist John Maynard Keynes. The purpose of deficit spending is to stimulate the economy during a recession or depression.

### 46. GOOD NEIGHBOR POLICY

Franklin Roosevelt formally renounced American armed intervention in the affairs of Latin America.

### 47. ISOLATIONISM

During the 1930s, isolationists argued that the United States should avoid making political commitments to other nations. The isolationists drew upon principles first expressed in Washington's Farewell Address.

# V. MODERN AMERICA, 1900 - 2000

### 48. COLD WAR

A prolonged period of economic and political conflict between the United Sates and the Soviet Union. The Cold War began with the announcement of the Truman Doctrine in 1947 and ended with the fall of the Berlin Wall in 1989 and the collapse of the Soviet Union in 1991.

### 49. CONTAINMENT

Cold War strategy of blocking the expansion of Soviet influence. First proposed by George Kennan and then implemented in the Truman Doctrine.

### 50. MCCARTHYISM

Refers to the making of unsubstantiated public accusations of disloyalty. Associated with Senator McCarthy's anti-communist campaign during the early 1950s.

### 51. BEAT GENERATION

A small but influential group of writers in the 1950s who rejected middle America's carefree consumption and mindless conformity. Jack Kerouac was the best-known Beat Generation writer.

### 52. MASSIVE RETALIATION

The Eisenhower administration's threat to use nuclear weapons to respond to acts of Soviet aggression.

### 53. BRINKSMANSHIP

Secretary of State John Foster Dulles' strategy of going to the brink of nuclear war without actually going over the edge.

### 54. DOMINO THEORY

Belief that the fall of one country to Communism would inevitably lead to the fall of other nearby countries. The domino theory played a key role in President Johnson's decision to escalate the Vietnam War.

## 55. HAWKS AND DOVES

Hawks supported America's involvement in the Vietnam War. In contrast, Doves opposed American's involvement in the Vietnam War.

## 56. COUNTERCULTURE

An alternate lifestyle advocated by hippies during the 1960s. The Woodstock Musical Festival is a particularly well-known example of a countercultural gathering.

## 57. BLACK POWER

Belief that African Americans should control their own communities by developing black-owned businesses and electing black public officials. Malcolm X and Stokely Carmichael were the two best-known advocates of Black Power.

## 58. VIETNAMIZATION

President Nixon's policy of training the South Vietnamese to take over military responsibilities from American troops.

## 59. SILENT MAJORITY

President Nixon used the term to describe hard-working Americans who supported his policies in Vietnam. The Silent Majority typically included white middle-class Americans who often lived in fast-growing states in the South and West.

## 60. DÉTENTE

Name given to Nixon's policy of relaxing tensions with the Soviet Union. Examples of détente include the SALT I treaty and Nixon's trip to Moscow.

## 61. STAGFLATION

The combination of high inflation and high unemployment that affected the American economy during most of the 1970s.

## 62. REAGANOMICS

Refers to President Reagan's economic policies. Also called supply-side economics. Reagan attempted to promote growth and investment by cutting taxes and deregulating business.

## 63. REAGAN DOCTRINE

Name given to the Reagan administration's strategy to confront and oppose the global influence of the Soviet Union.

## 64. NEW RIGHT

A conservative movement that supported President Reagan, emphasized patriotism, and stressed family values.

## 65. SUNBELT

The band of fast-growing states that stretch from the Carolinas to Southern California.

# PREMIUM PODCASTS
## FOR AP US HISTORY: THE ESSENTIAL CONTENT

## THANK YOU FOR USING
# INSIDER TEST PREP
## TO HELP YOU PREPARE AND TEST WITH CONFIDENCE.

### Find more help at
## insidertestprep.com